THE TRUE WAY OF

The Pacific Story of the Melai

1925-2000

Brian Macdonald-Milne TSSF
Chaplain and Tutor of the Melanesian Brotherhood
1968-1973

with

Reflections on the Missionary Calling of the Brotherhood

by

Brother Richard Carter MBH
Chaplain of the Brotherhood

CHRISTIANS AWARE
and
THE MELANESIAN BROTHERHOOD
2003

To
my Brothers and Companions of
the Melanesian Brotherhood
who waited patiently for
this book to be researched
and written

and

to
my mother and
all whose patience
has been rewarded at last,
however inadequately,
by the publication of
this history

and
in memory of
Brother Nathaniel Sado, MBH
Sir Frederick Soaki,
and others recently killed
while they sought to bring peace
to Solomon Islands

TO GOD BE THE GLORY

GREAT THINGS HE HAS DONE

Daily Prayer of the Brotherhood

God's Loving Plan

The Lord called to him those he wanted,
And they came to him.

He chose seventy others also, and sent them out before him,
two by two, into every town and place.
Where he himself was going to come.

Almighty God,
your Son, our Lord, Jesus Christ,
by obeying you and offering himself,
has shown us **the true way of service**:
may we and all our Brothers serve you in the way that he did,
showing faithful love and being true to you alone;
so that, by your power,
the work we are called to do may bear good fruit
and make your loving plan for all people come true,
to the glory of your name;
through Jesus Christ our Lord,
who lives and rules with you and the Holy Spirit,
one God, now and for ever. **Amen.**

Contents

Foreword

I imagine one would only contemplate writing a history of a Religious Order if that Order had had a glorious history or was currently enjoying a meaningful present. In the case of the Melanesian Brotherhood, both are true.

Founded in 1925 by Ini Kopuria, a Guadalcanal policeman who had been educated by the fledgling Anglican Mission, the Brotherhood was 'tailor made' for Melanesians. It provided a purposeful 'employment' of young men without requiring a life commitment, thus enabling those men later to fulfil cultural commitments by marrying and 'continuing the line'. It provided a strong community base, not dissimilar to the community of their own village. It provided a status and opportunity for the Brothers to show their commitment of faith in Jesus Christ. It provided a strong network of Companions which Brothers joined, once released from their promises, thus enabling them to continue their contacts and to express their commitment beyond their membership of the Brotherhood.

Their work in primary evangelism in the Solomon Islands and the New Hebrides (now Vanuatu) has been one of the great success stories of the Anglican Church in those islands.

Today, they are to be found not only in those two countries, but also in Papua New Guinea and Philippines. In the recent past they have had Households in Fiji and Cape York Peninsula, Australia. Invitations have been received from Central Africa, South America and New Zealand to start new work there. But their work of evangelism has also taken them to New Zealand and England, especially Chester Diocese. Their mission (of 30 Brothers and Novices) to the northern part of New Zealand in February 2000 was a resounding success, showing that their influence is not confined to their own culture.

Why is it that these Brothers and Novices are able to exercise such a dynamic witness? I believe it is because of their uncomplicated faith in God, their strong base of prayer, their love for the commitment to one another as Brotherhood, their youthful zeal and their unbounded joy.

Recently, a New Zealand bishop who had just witnessed their dramatic presentation of *From Creation to Salvation*, summed then up by saying, "It was as if they were living the parts, not acting them."

One of the 'hats' I wear is that of Father to the Brotherhood. It is a role which I cherish and one which sustains me no matter what hat I am wearing. The Brothers nurture and sustain people, young and old, wherever they go and

I never cease to thank God for them.

I thank Fr Brian Macdonald-Milne also. As a former Chaplain of the Brotherhood he has some rare insights into the life and witness of the Brotherhood. His research has been exhaustive. We are indeed fortunate that he has produced for us this valuable record of a precious jewel.

+ Ellison L Pogo

The Most Reverend Sir Ellison L Pogo
Archbishop of Melanesia
Father of the Brotherhood

Brother Harry Gereniu
in Chester House, Honiara, Solomon Islands.

Photo: Barbara Molyneux, Companion

Introduction

I first heard of the Melanesian Brotherhood during my childhood. Ever since, I have always wanted to be one of its adherents, to be a full member and active participant in its daily routine and ministry.

Through close attachment one can say that the Melanesian Brotherhood has a life of joy and nearness to God. Being in it, that is partly true. Nevertheless, one can only fully enjoy and experience the depths of God's divine grace in this community and what it means, if one becomes an active and dedicated participant in this life. For those who become members pursuing self-interest and having wrong agenda in mind, it is no more than another institution with a strict legalistic lifestyle and hard discipline.

However, those who have humbly and openly immersed themselves in the abounding grace of God along this narrow path can tell that it is God's signpost. It is God's signpost that appeals and challenges. It offers an avenue in Christ whereby the great majestic God respects mere sinful earthly creatures and they become friends with him and one another. It offers an opportunity for those who have one common desire and love for God to offer service for all of God's creation. It informs one of the spiritual depth, width and height that a fully dedicated and consecrated being can experience under God's divine grace. It gives a fair concept of the love and reverence God deserves.

These are some of the aspects that, as a dedicated Brother, one can experience and so produce a God-centred, fruitful and worthwhile ministry. This is possible where there is humility, willing obedience, self-denial, complete dedication and selfless love for God in prayer and self-discipline.

This sums up the life of those dedicated to service in this Brotherhood, to whom this book pays respect. I pay them my humble respect likewise.

Harry Gereniu MBH
Head Brother
2000-2003

Preface

When I took over from Fr Ernest Ball SSM as Chaplain and Tutor of the Melanesian Brotherhood in 1968, there was one thing he asked me to do – write a history of the Brotherhood. He had already begun to collect information and reminiscences from ex-Brothers with the help of the Reverend Dr Charles Elliot Fox, then an ex-Brother and the only 'white man' to have been a member of the Brotherhood. He later rejoined when back in his 'home' country, New Zealand; he would have preferred to have had Solomon Islands citizenship, but he died before the country became independent in 1978. I continued to collect information and encourage research, making the 50th anniversary of the foundation of the Brotherhood by Ini Kopuria the focus of plans to publish a history. Even when I ceased to be Chaplain, the research continued, being conducted in the Solomon Islands by Brother Edward Das from Fiji and others, in the New Hebrides by Brother Shadrack Vulum from Papua New Guinea and others, in cooperation with the Pacific Churches Research Centre, of which I was by then Coordinator. This Centre was based in Port Vila, now the capital of the Republic of Vanuatu, as the New Hebrides gained its independence and adopted that name in 1980. The Centre subsequently closed, but research was taken up later by other Brothers and ex-Brothers in the 1990s with the encouragement of Fr Richard Carter, who became Chaplain of the Brotherhood before himself joining as a professed Brother. Parochial and other work prevented the writing of the book after I returned to the United Kingdom at the end of 1980, so it has taken many years for this work to be completed. It now appears at a suitable time to celebrate 75 years since the foundation of the Brotherhood, an event which was marked by great celebrations at the Mother House on Guadalcanal, Solomon Islands in 2001. The book also covers events in that period in Melanesia and other parts of the Western Pacific in the life of the Anglican Church, some of which had not been covered by Dr Fox in *Lord of the Southern Isles: Being the Story of the Anglican Mission in Melanesia, 1849-1949*, or by Dr David Hilliard in *God's Gentlemen: A History of the Melanesian Mission, 1849-1942*. Both of these books have been very valuable in providing information about the periods they cover. The 150th anniversary of the founding of the Melanesian Mission was celebrated in 1999, and I wrote a shorter account of the Brotherhood for the occasion, entitled *The Melanesian Brotherhood and the Tradition of Indigenous Evangelism in the Anglican Church in the Pacific Islands.*

The last few years have seen the publication of the histories of a number of Anglican religious orders, among them *This Poor Sort: A History of the European Province of the Society of St Francis* by Petà Dunstan in 1997, *Sisters of the Raj: The Clewer Sisters in India* by Valerie Bonham in 1997, and *Whether we be Many or Few: A History of the Cambridge/Delhi Brotherhood* by C M Millington, published in India in 1999. Many religious orders, both Anglican and Roman Catholic, have been returning to their roots to understand their founders' intentions, but have also been revising their rules and constitutions to make them more attuned to modern conditions. A notable example has come from the Society of St John the Evangelist, commonly known as the 'Cowley Fathers', as their Mother House was originally at Cowley, Oxford, in England. The Society's North American Congregation published in 1997 *Living in Hope: A Rule of Life for Today.* This is significant as the SSJE was the first order for men under vows to be founded in the Anglican Communion after the Reformation, in the year 1865.

The Melanesian Brotherhood drew on a long tradition in 'Western' Christianity of the Religious Life under the traditional threefold vows, but from the beginning lived it in a Melanesian way, gradually developing its own constitution and special ethos. Thousands of men have passed through it; some have died in it. It has also encouraged the formation of a parallel Sisterhood, the Community of the Sisters of Melanesia. In the Western Pacific there are now also other Anglican religious orders, all of which are growing and youthful, including the First and Third Orders of the Society of St Francis, the Community of the Sisters of the Church, and the Community of the Visitation, founded in Papua New Guinea. The area is indeed now the main centre for growth in religious orders in the whole Anglican Communion. This gives the story of the Brotherhood a special significance, particularly as the Brothers have begun work in England and have been invited at different times to minister in Australia, New Zealand and the Philippines.

Throughout the book the term 'heathen' has been used to describe those who follow Melanesian or Polynesian animistic or other beliefs and worship. This word is commonly used throughout the Pacific and does not imply a lack of appreciation of some of the positive spiritual aspects of traditional religion, or the insights gained from a study of such religion by anthropologists and others. The Anglican Church of Melanesia itself produced three outstanding anthropologists, who were also well versed in Pacific linguistics – the Reverend Dr C H Codrington MA, Hon DD, viewed by many as the 'Father' of Melanesian anthropology and linguistics because of his books *The Melanesians* and *Melanesian Languages*; the Reverend Dr Walter G Ivens MA, LittD, FRGS, author of *The Island Builders of the Pacific* (about Mala, Solomon Islands); and the Reverend Dr C E Fox MA, LTh, LittD, author of both *Threshold of the Pacific* (about Arosi District, Makira, Solomon Islands) and dictionaries of three Solomon Island languages.

The use of the title 'Father' for Anglican clergy is universal throughout the Pacific Islands, and is even appended to other titles; so people might address a Bishop as 'Father Bishop'. Correspondence between converts to the Christian faith and early missionaries sometimes indicates that the latter were seen as spiritual fathers and mothers, whatever their denomination, and addressed as such. Today, younger people in particular would still sometimes see the clergy and their wives as spiritual fathers and mothers and refer to themselves in correspondence as 'sons' and 'daughters'. In Melanesia, people have in 'custom' more than one 'father', as the brothers of the natural father are also called by the same name. The mother's brother, however, who is the closest male relative, is called by a different relationship term. Informal adoption is also practised, so there is a wider concept of fatherhood and motherhood than is common in 'white' cultures today. Wives of the clergy in Solomon Islands are sometimes called *Mami* (from the English 'Mummy'), while their husbands may be called 'Father'or its equivalent in the local language. However, the title *Mama* (Mota for 'Father') is still widely used, as at one time the language of Mota in the Banks Islands of the northern New Hebrides (Vanuatu) was used as the common language of the Anglicans throughout that country and the Solomon Islands. In Vanuatu, wives of the clergy and members of the Mothers' Union are given the title of respect *Veve* (Mother). The exception, so far as the clergy are concerned, is the clergy in the Melanesian Brotherhood and in the First Order of the Society of St Francis, who are addressed as 'Brother', following the example of St Francis himself, who wanted all his Brothers, whether ordained or lay, to be known by that simple and humble 'title'. For Melanesians and Polynesians and others from very diverse linguistic, cultural and social backgrounds, 'Brother' has a very deep spiritual meaning, and is often used when addressing another Brother instead of the Christian name. The use of the title 'Father' in the Anglican Communion was traditionally restricted to Bishops, when addressed as 'Father-in-God'. With the reestablishment of religious orders, it was used for priest members of some Orders, then its use spread more widely to some members of the clergy in different countries.

Information about life in some of the Households of the Brotherhood at different periods has been difficult to obtain and much information has had to be sought from the *Southern Cross Log* and reports to Brothers' and Companions' Conferences. Great assistance in this was provided by Mrs Pauline Cameron, who was secretary in the office of the Melanesian Mission in Auckland, New Zealand, for many years, and who responded to my request for extracts from that mission publication which referred to the Brothers. She typed out all the relevant portions for the period 1926 to 1968, using the New Zealand edition. (A separate edition was produced for supporters of the Mission in England.) For 21 years she assisted Mr Harry Bullen, during part of the long time that he was General Secretary of the Mission and of the Diocese of Melanesia, when its office was based in New Zealand. Because of her help, references in the book to the *Southern Cross Log* are normally to the New Zealand edition, which ceased publication in the early 1970s.

In some parts of the world 'missionary work' has been seen as an aspect of 'white' colonialism. In the Western Pacific, the Melanesian Mission was at work long before the British and the Germans established colonial rule over different parts of the Solomon Islands archipelago, or the British and French decided to establish joint rule in the New Hebrides as a 'Condominium'. From the earliest days of missionary work and evangelism in the Pacific Islands, starting in the late 18th century, many of the 'missionaries' have been Pacific Islanders. Their names are now recorded, as far as they can be ascertained, in a book in the chapel of the ecumenical Pacific Theological College in Fiji. A significant number of the early white and indigenous missionaries were martyred, many of them in Melanesia, particularly in the New Hebrides. More were martyred in the Second World War. This has been a potent influence in the life of the Pacific Churches, whose members know that their spiritual forebears were willing to witness to their faith with their lives. Among the Anglicans, the martyrdom of the first Bishop of Melanesia and his companions – one from New Zealand, one from the Solomon Islands – is still an inspiration and challenge to Christians today, not least to those Melanesian Brothers who work in non-Christian areas. Because of the special character of the island world of Oceania and its largely Christian ethos, many Pacific people see themselves as the 'Fourth World' rather than the 'Third World', and prefer their region to be seen as a separate area, rather than as just a part of the 'Asia-Pacific' region.

I am indebted to many people for their assistance, particularly those who have worked as researchers or contributed their memories or other information to this book. I received encouragement from Queen's College, Birmingham, the ecumenical theological college in England, when I was Research Fellow there from 1982 to 1983, and in particular from the Reverend Gordon Wakefield, the Methodist Principal. He had a special regard for Bishop George Augustus Selwyn and went to live in retirement in Lichfield, where Bishop Selwyn became Diocesan Bishop in 1868 on his return from New Zealand. I am also grateful to the Reverend David Hutt, who provided accomodation at weekends and outside term while I assisted him during that period at the Church of St Alban and St Patrick in central Birmingham, and who is now Canon and Sub-Dean of Westminster Abbey, London.

Bishop Geoffrey Rowell, Bishop of the Anglican Diocese of Gibraltar in Europe, was also insistent that this history ought to be written. I was working as Acting Chaplain at Trinity College and then St Peter's College in Oxford in the early 1980s when he was Chaplain of Keble College and Chairman of the Board of the Faculty of Divinity in the University of Oxford.

Photographs have come from various sources, including the Brotherhood itself, the Melanesian Mission UK, and Mrs C.Luxton of Papua New Guinea Church Partnership. Some taken by Mr Harry Bullen have been provided by his niece, Mrs Anne Friswell, and her husband. A number of these have been processed by their son David, a member of the staff of USPG, the United Society for the Propagation of the Gospel, which long ago provided assistance to Bishop G A Selwyn in various ways when he was Bishop of New Zealand. Other photographs have been taken recently by Miss Barbara Molyneux when she went to Melanesia in 2001 with three other women Companions of the Brotherhood from the Diocese of Chester, England, and visited various Brotherhood Households in Vanuatu and the Solomons, as well as attending the 75th anniversary celebrations at Tabalia, the Mother House. Chester Diocese has established a strong link with the Province of Melanesia in recent years and provided the funding for the building of the Brotherhood's 'rest house' in Honiara, Solomon Islands. This is therefore called 'Chester House' and provides accomodation not only for Brothers, but also for many visitors to Solomon Islands and to its capital, Honiara.

I am grateful for the encouragement over the years of the Archbishops of Melanesia, especially Sir Ellison Pogo, the present Father of the Brotherhood, and of the present Head Brother, Brother Harry Gereniu, and of many of the Brothers and Companions throughout the world. The help of Mrs Barbara Butler of Christians Aware has been most appreciated, and the last stage of work on this book has been greatly assisted by the wise and generous help of Bishop Derek Rawcliffe, at one time Bishop of the New Hebrides, who has not only typed the manuscript and assisted in its preparation for publication, but who has also checked it for accuracy. I am also grateful to Dr Brian Stanley, Director of the Henry Martyn Mission Studies Centre, part of the Cambridge Theological Federation (which enables the theological colleges and institutes there of most of the main Christian denominations to work cooperatively), for his comments before publication.

May God grant that the endeavours of many recorded in this history will bear fruit to his honour and glory.

Brian Macdonald-Milne
Waterbeach, Cambridge, England
2002

Mota (Hat Island) from Vanua Lava, Banks Islands
– first Christian island established by the Anglicans in Melanesia.

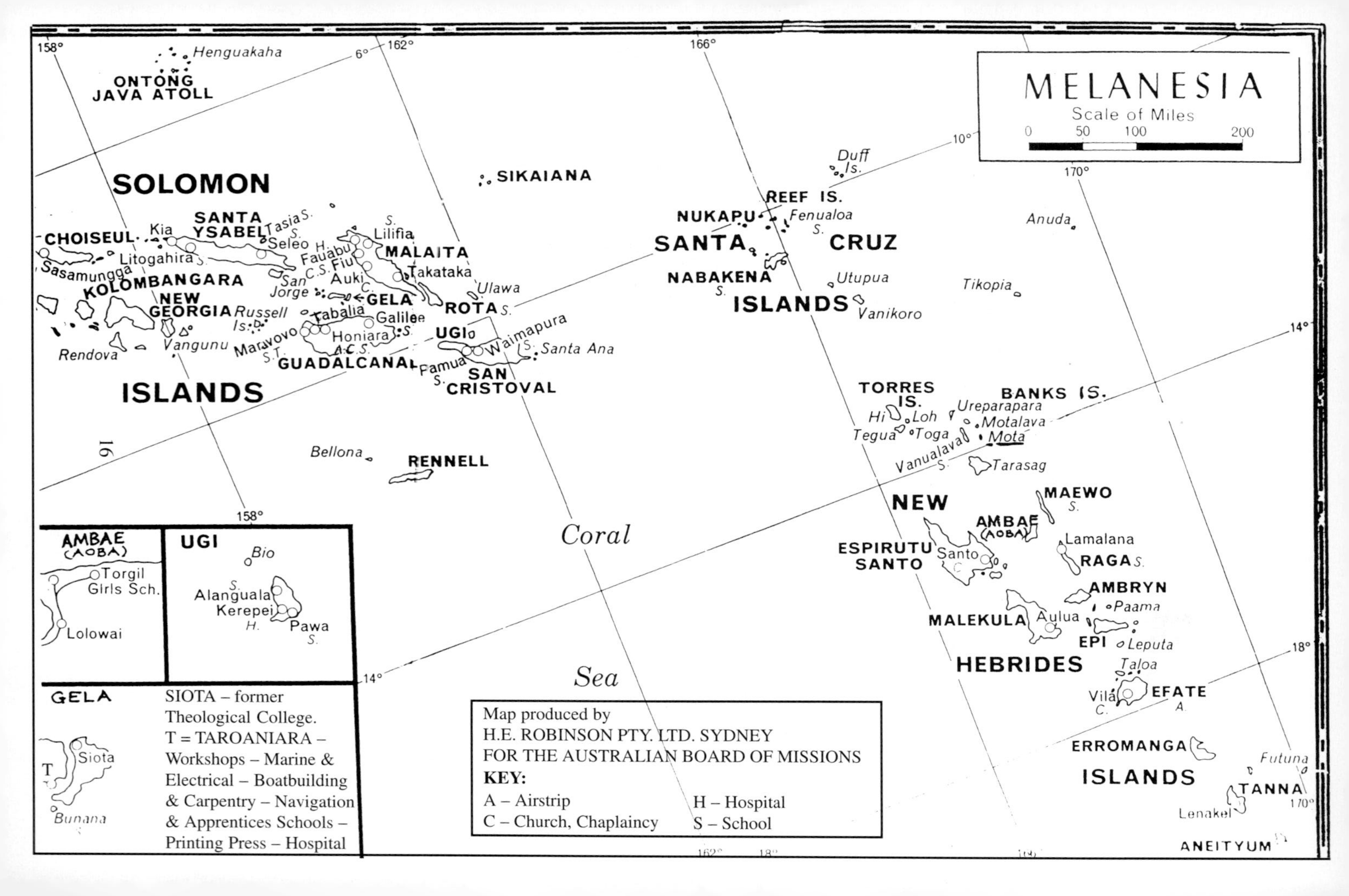
MELANESIA
Scale of Miles
0 50 100 200
SOLOMON
ISLANDS
ONTONG JAVA ATOLL
Henguakaha
SIKAIANA
CHOISEUL
Kia
SANTA YSABEL
Tasia S.
Seleo S.
Litogahira S.
Sasamungga
KOLOMBANGARA
NEW GEORGIA
Russell Is.
Rendova
Vangunu
San Jorge
Fauabu H.
Fiu C.S.
Auki C.
Lilifia S.
MALAITA
Takataka
GELA
Tabalia
Galilee S.
Honiara A.C.S.
Maravovo S.T.
GUADALCANAL
Ulawa
ROTA S.
UGI
Waimapura S.
Santa Ana
Pamua S.
SAN CRISTOVAL
Bellona
RENNELL
Coral
Sea
Duff Is.
REEF IS.
NUKAPU
Fenualoa S.
SANTA
CRUZ
NABAKENA S.
ISLANDS
Utupua
Vanikoro
Tikopia
Anuda
TORRES IS.
Hi
Loh
Tegua
Toga
BANKS IS.
Ureparapara
Motalava
Mota
Vanualava S.
Tarasag
NEW
HEBRIDES
ISLANDS
ESPIRUTU SANTO
Santo
MAEWO S.
AMBAE (AOBA)
Lamalana
RAGA S.
AMBRYN
Paama
MALEKULA
Aulua
EPI
Leputa
Taloa
Vila C.
EFATE A.
ERROMANGA
Futuna
TANNA
Lenakel
ANEITYUM
AMBAE (AOBA)
Torgil Girls Sch.
Lolowai
UGI
Bio
Alanguala S.
Kerepei H.
Pawa S.
GELA
Siota
T
Bunana
SIOTA – former Theological College.
T = TAROANIARA – Workshops – Marine & Electrical – Boatbuilding & Carpentry – Navigation & Apprentices Schools – Printing Press – Hospital
Map produced by
H.E. ROBINSON PTY. LTD. SYDNEY
FOR THE AUSTRALIAN BOARD OF MISSIONS
KEY:
A – Airstrip
C – Church, Chaplaincy
H – Hospital
S – School
158°
162°
166°
170°
6°
10°
14°
18°

Anglican Missionary influence came with the consecration of George Augustus Selwyn as Bishop of New Zealand in 1841, and his first Missionary journey into Melanesia in 1849.

Bishop George Augustus Selwyn

Selwyn, a remarkable man, was followed by John Coleridge Patteson, the first Bishop of Melanesia, who shared Selwyn's insights and sensitivity to the indigenous peoples, whose vision from the very beginning was to establish a Church which was truly Melanesian. Patteson was to be one of Melanesia's many martyrs.

Bishop John Coleridge Patteson

CHAPTER ONE

Bishop Patteson with Melanesians at Norfolk Island Left: George Sarawia (first Melanesian priest).

Melanesian pupils at the Norfolk Island School.

Melanesians at Norfolk Island in "custom dress" with native artefacts.

The Reverend Martin Marau outside the Church at Madoa, Ulawa, Solomon Islands, with altar servers. (Ordained priest in 1924, he had full charge of the Church there).

CHAPTER ONE

BACKGROUND TO THE FORMATION OF THE BROTHERHOOD

Melanesia was a part of the world that others knew little about until the nineteenth century. The arrival of the first European settlers in Australia with the 'First Fleet' of 1788 meant that regular contact was developed by European ships with the islands of the South Pacific. Samuel Marsden, the second Anglican chaplain to arrive in the Colony of New South Wales, had contact with missionaries of the London Missionary Society (LMS) in the Society Islands, especially Tahiti in Eastern Polynesia, and welcomed some of them to the colony when they had to leave for a while. He also had contact with Maori people from New Zealand who sometimes travelled across the Tasman Sea on European ships. In 1814 he started the Anglican mission to New Zealand ('Aotearoa' to the Maori) with the aid of the Church Missionary Society. This eventually led to the establishment of the Diocese of New Zealand in 1841, and George Augustus Selwyn was chosen in England to be the first Bishop. He did not arrive until 1842, after a long sea voyage on which he had learned navigation and Maori language. One of his first acts was to found a school and training college which he called the College of St John the Evangelist. This was for both the Pakeha (Europeans) and Maori. In 1849 he made a voyage to the islands north of New Zealand in his ship the *Undine* to get Melanesian people to his school, and this was the beginning of the Melanesian Mission. On an exploratory voyage in 1848 he had consulted LMS and Methodist missionaries in Polynesia. He visited first the islands in Southern Melanesia – New Caledonia, the Loyalty Islands and the New Hebrides (now called Vanuatu) – before going on to the Solomon Islands on later voyages. He saw the work extending eventually to New Guinea and even beyond. Missionaries from the LMS and some Presbyterians from Canada had begun work in the New Hebrides, but a number were killed, including Polynesian missionaries from the Cook Islands. Roman Catholic missionaries from the Society of Mary (the Marist Fathers) had also begun work in the New Hebrides and the Solomon Islands, but their Bishop had been killed in the Solomons and they withdrew for a while.

Bishop Selwyn became convinced that the emphasis in the Anglican mission should be on preparing Melanesian missionaries to go to their own people. The European missionaries should be there primarily to train and support the Melanesians: 'a black net with white corks'. The Melanesian school he started near Auckland in New Zealand was therefore to be the key to doing a new kind of missionary work in Melanesia. His plans, however, depended on two main things: people and ships. Bishop Selwyn visited England in 1854 and raised money for a ship, which he called the *Southern Cross*, and he found a helper in John Coleridge Patteson, a young priest, who was the son of an old friend of his, Sir John Patteson, a judge. Patteson returned with him to New Zealand on the *Southern Cross* and gradually took over responsibility for the Melanesian school and the work in the islands. In 1861 he became the first Bishop of Melanesia and in 1866 he moved the Melanesian school to Norfolk Island. The only inhabitants then were Pitcairners. They were descendants of the crew of the *Bounty* and of the Tahitian men and women whom they had taken to Pitcairn Island after they had mutinied against the captain, William Bligh, and cast him and others adrift in the ship's boat. They had been moved to Norfolk Island in 1856 and with them had come their Anglican pastor, the Reverend George Hunn Nobbs, who had settled on Pitcairn and later been ordained. He eventually offered his son Edwin to Bishop Patteson to be trained with Fisher Young, descendant of a mutineer, as Pacific Island missionaries. They were the first Anglican missionaries to be martyred, as they were killed on Santa Cruz to the east of the Solomon Islands in 1864. In 1871 Bishop Patteson himself was killed on the island of Nukapu[1] in the Reef Islands, not far from Santa Cruz. Others killed at the same time were Joseph Atkin, a missionary priest from New Zealand, and Stephen Taroaniara from the island of Makira, or San Cristobal, as the 16th century Spanish explorers had named it. It is also known as San Cristoval. Stephen was being prepared for ordination as the first priest from Solomon Islands. Patteson had already ordained George Sarawia as a deacon in 1868, but he was from the Banks Islands, north of the New Hebrides. For a while, it looked as if Selwyn and Patteson's plan for the conversion to the Christian faith of the people of the Northern New Hebrides and Solomon Islands by 'native agents' would fail, because of the death of these people. However, the Reverend Dr Robert Henry Codrington maintained the work of the Mission, running the school at Norfolk Island and superintending the work until a second bishop was appointed – John Richardson Selwyn, son of Bishop G.A. Selwyn. He had joined the Mission in 1873 and was elected Bishop by the staff soon after his arrival, but not consecrated until 1877. He remained as Bishop until 1891.

One of the great difficulties at the beginning was the fact that chiefs in the islands usually sent to the school young men or boys who had little authority or influence when they returned home, and eventually it was decided that the white missionaries should work alongside the black missionaries and support them. At first, the white people spent only part of the year in the islands, then some took up more permanent residence, living all the year round and superintending the work in large areas. Bishop Cecil Wilson, the third Bishop of Melanesia, was consecrated in Auckland in 1894 and recruited more white staff. Among them were Charles Elliot Fox and John Manwaring Steward, who both arrived in the diocese in 1902. Through their work and cooperation there were many new developments in the diocese.

Charles Fox was a priest from New Zealand who had studied geology at university, but who was also interested in anthropology, the study of different peoples and their customs, and in languages. There was another priest on the staff who was an anthropologist, Walter George Ivens, a New Zealander who worked in the islands of Ulawa and South Malaita in the Solomons. Both of them looked back to the earlier work of the Reverend Dr Codrington, who worked at Norfolk Island from 1867 to 1887 and from 1892 to 1893. He published the first books on the culture and languages of the Melanesians. Fox taught at St Barnabas College, Norfolk Island, from 1903 to 1905 and from 1907 to 1911; then he went to Makira (San Cristobal) where he ran the school at Pamua. He was the District Missionary from 1915 to 1924, when he went to Pawa School on the nearby island of Ugi to be headmaster till 1932. His father was a priest who had come out from England when Fox was a small child to work in New Zealand. John Steward's father was a priest who worked in England, but died while John was a student at university. Steward had been a teacher before ordination and was an assistant curate in England for two years before coming to Melanesia. He was keen on rowing, just as Fox was keen on cricket, and both had a strong sense of humour and good self-discipline. Like Fox, Steward learnt a number of Melanesian languages, and both of them used the Mota language, which had been adopted by the Mission as a common language. This was largely because it was the language of George Sarawia, the first Melanesian priest, and some other early converts, and not too difficult to learn or speak. Steward took an interest in anthropology, but criticised most anthropologists for not understanding the people they studied well enough, as they did not live with them all the time and over a long period. He believed they could be easily misled and come to wrong conclusions. He and Fox believed that missionary priests should, as far as possible, live among the people they served, observe their culture and customs carefully and try to live in a Melanesian way. Fox even went to work for a time as a labourer on a plantation, to share the life of the men there, and exchanged his name with a young man from Makira, thus becoming a member of his clan.

The next Bishop of Melanesia, Cecil John Wood, left after disagreements with his staff. The same staff then proceeded, for the first time, to choose one of their own number, whom they knew well, as candidate for the bishopric, and recommended him to the New Zealand Bishops. The one they wanted was John Steward, who had been a district priest, also later running a small theological training college at Maravovo[2] on Guadalcanal, which had been the first in the Solomons. He became Bishop in September 1919 and almost immediately closed St Barnabas College on Norfolk Island and moved the headquarters of the Mission to Siota on Gela in the Central Solomons, where an impressive Cathedral in leaf materials was erected. Teachers (catechists) were trained at Siota in the Solomons and at Lolowai on Aoba (Ambae) in the New Hebrides, while a senior boys' school was established at Pawa on Ugi (Uki ni Masi) in the Eastern Solomons. It was called All Hallows after a church in England which supported the Mission at that time.[3] All Hallows means All Saints. Siota had originally been the site of St Luke's School, a junior school to Norfolk Island, built on land purchased in 1893, and the first permanent station for white Anglican missionaries in the Solomons. After the Second World War, St Peter's Theological College was established there to train clergy from both countries.

Steward started 'Sacred Synods' of his clergy and insisted that decision making should be shared by Europeans and Melanesians equally. He even began to envisage a Pacific Province of the Anglican Church, with its own Archbishop – a vision which helped to inspire the establishment of the Province of Melanesia in 1975.

NOTES

1 According to ex-Brother Titus Tenu, in an interview with the author, his great-grandfather had a brother who was one of the five men stolen by a recruiting ship and taken to Fiji as labourers, the event which led to the death of Bishop Patteson. Some of those stolen were from the same tribe, and they had paddled out to the ship and had been shown over it. Others were taken from the village, together with some pigs. Two of those stolen later paddled back from Fiji via the New Hebrides (Vanuatu). People from Pileni paddled to

Nukapu when they saw the *Southern Cross* in the bay, but Bishop Patteson had already been killed. Later the people of Nukapu became Christians and took the Gospel by *te puke* (large sea-going canoe) to the main Reef Islands, one of which, called Fenualoa in their language – meaning 'long island' – they converted. They also went to the Duff Islands (Taumako) and Santa Cruz. Fr Willie Au of Ngwalade, Malaita, interviewed old people on Nukapu, Pileni and Fenualoa to trace the story of their coming to Christian faith.

2 According to Fox, *Lord of the Southern Isles*, p 232: Bishop Wilson bought land at Veranaaso (as it was at first called) for a coconut plantation. Bishop Wood decided to establish a Theological College there in 1913 and this became operational in 1916. It moved to Siota on Gela in 1920. Bishop Steward then started a Technical College under George Warren, but this did not develop as hoped and became St Mary's School, Maravovo in 1922. It developed into the Junior School of the Mission after the closure of Buñana and Pamua (both of which later were restarted as schools for girls). Steward, according to Hilliard, *God's Gentlemen*, p 301, was at Maravovo and the Theological College 1911-1919. Women missionaries arrived at Maravovo in 1913 (p 151). Maravovo School was the fifth and largest of the boys' schools (Fox, p 232).

3 All Hallows, Hampstead Heath, London, visited by the Revd R Hodgson, the first headmaster, while on furlough from Melanesia.

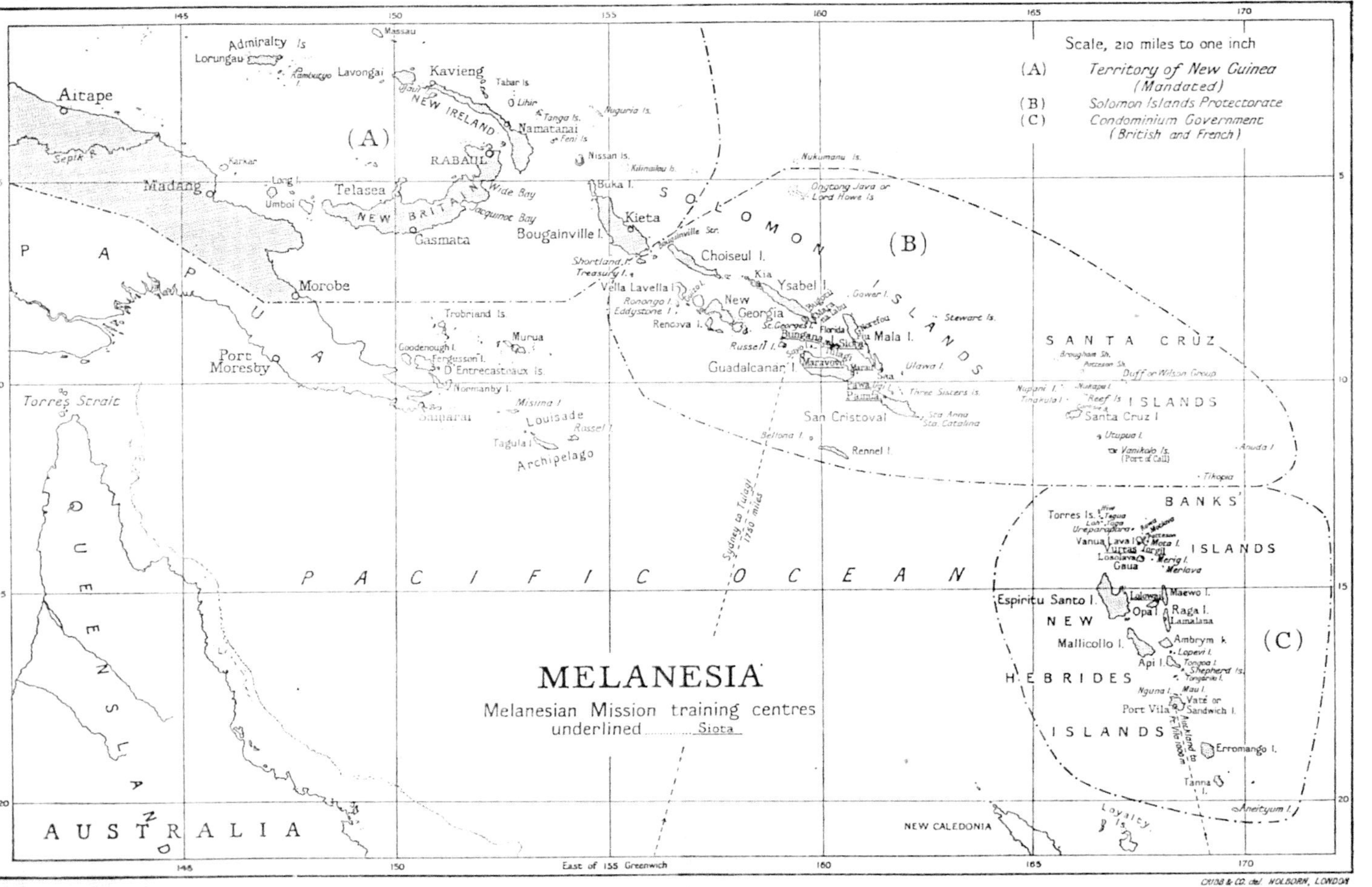

FROM "MELANESIA TODAY" S.P.C.K. LONDON FOR THE MELANESIAN MISSION, ENGLAND 1927

Guadalcanal
GUADALCANAL
SOLOMON
SEA
HONIARA
TABALIA
Lungga Pt
Lungga
Lungga Plateau
Mt Popori
Mt Gallego
Cone Peak
Bomb Lode
Empty Tin
Mt Vatunjae
Mt Tambunanggu
Mt Popomanaseu
Mt Tanareirei
Mt Namolava
Mt Tavisana
Mt Vatupochau
Mt Kaichui
Mt Pinau
Mt Nasuha
Lee's Lake
Gold Ridge
Old Case
Nughu I
Nudha I
Papari I
Rua Sura I
Surakiki I
Vulelua (Neal) I
Aola (Tenaghau)
Round I
Komukomutou
Arona (North)
Kesao Pt
Visale
Tambea
Kohimarama
Veranaaso
Ndoma Beach Resort
Ruaniu
Tenaru
Nazareth
Mbetikama
Nguvia
Tetere
Ruavatu
Simiu Bank
Vata Eo Pt
Maosambagha Pt(Cape Austin)
Nggoinggoi (Cape Beaufort)
Vaghato Pt (Cape Hunter)
Keona Ngali Pt (Cape Henslow)
Mbelatania Pt
Lauvi Pt
Korasahulu Reef
Avu Avu (Kolotambu)
Haimarao
Komunimbaimbai
Manikara-ku
Tavani
Marulapa
Valesule
Chikora
Valearanisi
Marasa
Veravaolu
Mbambanakira
Chaukandora
Kologhona
Tasi
Tulambirua
Taombo
Komate
Chocho
Hachogha
Makaruka
Chuma
Alundava
Veralava
Hanjohapeulu
Homba
Mbuasavia
Makanakolopao
Na Poli
Na Hau
Na Kuma
Na Vura
0
10
20
30
40
50
KILOMETRES
160° E
10° S
© SOUTH PACIFIC MAPS PTY. LTD. 1993

CHAPTER TWO

Brother Ini Kopuria, the founder.

St. Luke's Cathedral, Siota, Gela
Largest leaf building in the Solomon Islands,
destroyed by the Japanese in the Second World War.

Bishop John Manwaring Steward
(from the Melanesian Mission English Committee "Annual Report" 1924).

CHAPTER TWO

INI KOPURIA AND HIS VOW

Maravovo became the first Christian village on Guadalcanal (or Guadalcanar), the main island of the Solomon Islands. However, before that happened, two young men had been captured at Jarupehe near there by raiders from the nearby island of Savo and sold at different times to Soga the First, the great headhunting paramount chief of Bugotu in the island of Santa Ysabel.[1] The two young men were Gorovaka and his elder brother Basilei. Soga was baptised in 1889 and the two men from Guadalcanal also became Christians. They went to train at Norfolk Island before returning to Santa Ysabel to marry, having been found on Santa Ysabel by Bishop John Richardson Selwyn, then Bishop of Melanesia. Hugo Gorovaka started a school at Sepi, Soga's village. George Basilei eventually returned to Guadalcanal and worked in the bush there for three years with no response. Then he persuaded his brother to join him.

When Hugo arrived, he and George and their families went and stayed with their relatives, who asked them to come to Vatutoturuka. However, only the small children there became Christians. Later they moved to Tatuvu and then to Tapure, where George died. George's widow went with Hugo and his family down to Maravovo to get a ship, but when the *Southern Cross* arrived, the Reverend Percy Williams was on board with some teachers and he persuaded them to stay at Maravovo and form the nucleus of a Christian community there in 1900.[2] Meanwhile Soga went to Savo continually to ask for Hugo and George, as there was an understanding that one day they would go back to Santa Ysabel, but they never did.

The Reverend Percy Temple Williams was grandson of Henry Williams, a pioneer missionary priest of the Church Missionary Society in New Zealand. Henry Williams and his brother William, also a priest, served among the Maori people for about fifty years. The priest and teachers at Maravovo were concerned about two developments which challenged the growing Anglican work on the island. There was, firstly, the threat from Sulukavo, a powerful warrior leader who was hostile to all missions. However, the mission was accepted by the new colonial government, which had established a British Protectorate over part of the Solomon Islands in 1893. Partly because of this, Sulukavo eventually ceased his threats of violence and sorcery, and catechist-teachers from the island of Gela began to take the Christian message out from Maravovo to other villages in West

Guadalcanal.

Secondly, the Protectorate Government also welcomed other missions, so that soon there were Roman Catholic, Methodist, and later South Sea Evangelical and Seventh Day Adventist missions at work in the country, as well as the Anglicans. The Melanesian Mission therefore had to come to terms with this new development. The Roman Catholics and the South Sea Evangelicals (originally the Queensland Kanaka Mission) began to work in areas where the Anglicans had expected to be the only mission, but the Methodists agreed to work in the Western Solomons only, so the Anglicans did not establish themselves there. French priests of the Society of Mary had arrived on Guadalcanal in 1898 and were based first on the small island of Rua Sura off the north coast, but then they moved into the main island, arriving at Visale near Maravovo in 1904. This was a challenge to the Anglicans, who had done little on Guadalcanal except in the west of the island and almost nothing in the bush villages. Only one white Anglican priest, David Ruddock, attempted to work in the bush and he was not accepted there.

Ini Kopuria was born about the year 1900 at Simbo near the coastal light, not far from Maravovo.[3] His father was Solowai from Visale and his mother, Helen Koimbo, from Metapono.[4] He was baptised by a young European priest, Frank Bollen, who also baptised Ini's parents and brothers, and they were the 'first-fruits' of the Church in that district. Ini was not a Melanesian name, but the name of a king of Wessex, a Christian kingdom in the south of England in the days before England became one kingdom in the year 829. There is a stone in the Maravovo river where Frank Bollen used to lie down and read his book – it was known as his 'bed'.[5] Sadly, he died of overwork in 1909, but he had made notes on the pagan religion of Guadalcanal and wrote that the missionary "is dealing with men who had been feeling after God and had not found him, but had satisfied the religious instincts God had given them with these [pagan] gods. Far better that they should believe these than nothing at all."[6]

John Steward arrived on Guadalcanal in 1903 and stayed till 1906, when he moved to Gela to be priest-in-charge there. He returned to Guadalcanal in 1911 and established himself at Maravovo. He started a small theological college, which transferred to Siota on Gela in 1920. In 1910 he had attended the Edinburgh Missionary Conference, the third such international conference to be held, as one of three delegates from the Melanesian Mission. There had been previous conferences in 1888 and 1900. There he learned of the increasing number of indigenous (native) clergy in other parts of the world and had decided that Melanesia should also try to increase their number as swiftly as possible. He also believed in the value of religious orders, as he knew they were working effectively in India and Africa. He realised the value of cooperation with other denominations and established good relationships with the Roman Catholic clergy at Visale.

At Kodovele, some miles east of Maravovo and Visale, Ben Musu had started a school on the edge of his traditional land as the people were frightened of *vele*, the form of sorcery practised by the *vele* men on the island. People there had been dying, including four brothers of Daniel Sade of Maravovo. Ini was taken into this school when he was very young. He then continued his schooling at Maravovo under Hugo Gorovaka. The Maravovo school was superintended by John Steward and it had about 25 boys in it in 1912. Ini was among those taught by John Steward, and he sent him on to Pamua School on Makira (San Cristoval), in 1913, where he was taught by Frederick H.Drew, who died in 1915. St Michael's School, Pamua, in the Eastern Solomons, was started by Charles Fox in 1911 at the Bishop of Melanesia's request, and he was headmaster there from 1911 to 1914. So it was during Ini's childhood that he first came in touch with the two men with whom he was later to work so closely, John Steward and Charles Fox.

While Fox was at Pamua as headmaster, he had the idea of forming a brotherhood to work in the bush villages of the island of Makira. In about 1912 he got together a group of boys who had been to school at Norfolk Island, and also some local boys and young men who had been at village schools, and formed the Brotherhood of St Stephen.[7] There were about twelve of them, and a young man from the Maravovo area of Guadalcanal called Ellison Kokoe[8] was chosen by Fox to be the Head Brother. This would have impressed the dark little boy from the same area of Guadalcanal who had come to study at Pamua School, Ini Kopuria. Fox wanted to serve in the new Brotherhood himself, but he was asked by the Bishop of Melanesia, Cecil Wood, to become the priest in charge of San Cristoval District instead. One result of Fox's being stopped from joining it was that the Brotherhood did not last long. However, Fox was able to encourage the Brothers in their work, as they used to come down from the bush to rest at his District Headquarters at Raubero.[9] Although the Bishop was interested in the Brothers' work, he did not know how they operated. He asked Brother Ellison: "When you go to the heathen, what do you preach first, God the Creator or Jesus the Saviour?" Ellison replied: "First, we teach ABC!" Fox later wrote to Fr Ernest Ball, then chaplain and tutor of the Melanesian Brotherhood: "And that is what I always saw. 'Will you have a school?' 'Yes' – and then more. No use standing up and preaching. No knowledge of language, and they would not listen. So ABC, gradual teaching, gradual conversion. Some deeply attached to the Brothers, love for *them* first. That was the way of it. The lives of the Brothers won *some* of the people. Conversion followed later. In Melanesia they could preach."[10] After the Brotherhood of St Stephen was disbanded, Ellison Kokoe returned to Guadalcanal and died there soon afterwards. Charles Fox studied the culture of the Arosi people of the island of Makira and submitted a thesis to the University of New Zealand, which rewarded him with a Doctorate of Letters (Litt.D) in 1922.

Fox was not the only one interested in the idea of Brotherhoods in Melanesia. John Steward on Guadalcanal had also thought of forming one, but it was to be a group of priests living among non-Christian people in the middle of the bush on Malaita Island. He had indeed approached Fox in 1907 with an invitation to join, but it had come to nothing. However, a similar idea had been tried out on the island of Santa Cruz. There a group of priests and laymen, with the support of Bishop Wilson, had started the Santa Cruz Brotherhood in 1910, but it had lasted only for 18 months. Bishop Wilson left Melanesia in 1911 and it was not revived. Nevertheless, these experiments prepared the ground for what was to follow in the 1920s.

Ini Kopuria was confirmed by Bishop Cecil Wood and went on from Pamua to St Barnabas' College on Norfolk Island. There Charles Fox saw him again when he was temporarily headmaster in 1914, before going on leave to England. Ini was smaller than the other boys in his class, and at first staff thought that he was also not very bright. However, he soon became leader of nearly everything. One of his teachers was Miss Florence Edith Coombe, who taught there from 1905 to 1911 and from 1915 to 1919. She wrote that he was "rather a chatterbox, sharp as a needle, painstaking, fond of music and interested in everything." She found him "very strong-willed and independent, but happily at the same time a genuinely good little lad; he was so keen to learn it was a pleasure to teach him." He had some original ideas, one of which was his own way of keeping Lent. Appearing on Miss Coombe's verandah very early on Ash Wednesday – which was against the College rules – he handed her a letter written in the Mota language and then fled away. The letter read: "Mother! Lent begins today. I have made my resolution for the season not to speak at all. Wherefore I beseech you to excuse me my repetition for the next six weeks and to ask me no questions in school, lest you tempt me to break my vow." Neither his teacher nor the Warden of the College could persuade him to speak, and it was only on the third day, after the Bishop himself had promised to release him from his vow, that he relented and spoke again. Charles Fox later called him a 'ball of indiarubber', always on the move, always joyful and only occasionally sad. Coming home once on the *Southern Cross*, a cyclone hit the ship in the Banks group of Islands. A missionary priest, Robert Wilson, went below and saw that Ini was playing the fool in a group of boys and laughing. He cried out, "Ini! Ini! Stop laughing! Don't you know that we are all going to die?" It made no difference. He went on playing, oblivious to death. He was quite fearless and full of fun.

In 1919 Ini was sent for a time to St John's College, Auckland. It was expected that he would become a catechist-teacher, probably on his own island. However, wanting something more challenging, he decided to join the British Solomon Islands Protectorate Native Armed Constabulary, which he did in 1921 or 1922. Although he found the discipline rather difficult, he rose to the rank of Lance-Corporal and would probably have gone on to become a Sergeant if he had remained a policeman.[11] At that time there were few other occupations open to Solomon Islanders in which they could rise in the service of the colonial government. He was indeed highly regarded by Captain Hill, the District Officer on Guadalcanal, under whom he worked. However, after two years he had an accident while visiting one of the bush villages, where it was his duty to go and get prisoners if there had been a report of any trouble. He injured a leg and, for the first time in his life, found himself in the Government Hospital, where he had to stay for some months. His injury left him permanently but only slightly lame. This lameness made it unlikely that he would be able to continue in the Constabulary and, as he gradually got better, he began to think deeply about his past and his possible future.

He had till then taken for granted all the opportunities he had had at school – for many of his fellows had had no chance of going to school at all. Then he realised that all he had received had been free and he had never questioned who had paid for it all. He began to feel that it had been a gift from God and that he had done nothing to show his gratitude. He promised in his heart that, if he recovered, he would do his utmost to repay in some way. He later told Dr Fox that he had also had a vision or dream in which Jesus had appeared to him and told him he was not doing the work that he wanted him to do. More than a year before, he had read a letter from John Steward, who had become Bishop of Melanesia in 1919. This was published in the newspaper of the mission (written in the Mota language), which was distributed by the *Southern Cross* in each of her voyages to the islands. The Bishop had written about 'service' and suggested that some of its readers might hear a call to complete self-dedication to the service of God. Ini remembered what the Bishop had written and determined that on coming out of hospital he would go and see the Bishop and ask his advice and help, which he did in 1925. He told Bishop Steward in a letter that he wanted to make the offer of himself and all that he possessed to God. Bishop Steward was delighted and, after a long talk with Ini, he suggested that they travel on the *Southern Cross* to various islands to see if there were any among his friends there who were of the same mind. He found five others and they returned to the Bishop's home at Siota to discuss the project. Ini had also had time discussing things with Arthur Innes Hopkins, who had been at Maravovo from 1919 to 1921 and had moved to Siota to be in charge of the Theological College from 1921 to 1925. Ini had probably learnt about religious orders in Europe from history lessons at Norfolk Island, and he had known Ellison Kokoe and what he had attempted with the Brotherhood on Makira. But it was through Hopkins that he learnt more of the earlier Brotherhoods, and it may well have been St Francis who inspired him most, as the Brotherhood he founded with Bishop Steward's help was very Franciscan, as well as Melanesian, in its character.[12]

The discussions at Siota were very important, as they led to the foundation of the Brotherhood. The Bishop wrote: "We determined to found a Brotherhood of young men, all of whom should promise to remain unmarried, to receive no payment and to go wherever the head of the Brotherhood, who was always to be the Bishop, should decide to send them." The earlier Brotherhood of St Stephen had been established on similar lines, but the Bishop then had not been so directly involved. It was agreed that the Brothers would live in Households of six to eight Brothers and choose an Elder Brother to lead them, and each Household would have an area which they would tour in pairs, going out 'two by two' as Jesus had first sent out his apostles in the land of Palestine. They would leave their evangelistic work among the 'heathen' when a catechist-teacher could be found to take over. The Elder Brothers were to report their progress or failure to the Bishop, as Father of the Brotherhood, four times a year, and they would all meet with him in Chapter once a year. Brothers were to bring all complaints against each other to the Chapter and what they could not settle among themselves was to be referred to the Bishop. The way seemed clear for the Brotherhood to begin!

In 1925 Frederick Merivale Molyneux came out from England to be Assistant Bishop with special responsibility for the New Hebrides. In the same year, Anglican work in New Britain came under the care of Bishop Steward, and an Assistant Bishop from Australia was appointed to be responsible for 'Northern Melanesia', living on New Britain in the Mandated Territory of New Guinea, formerly German New Guinea.

A centre for the Brotherhood was found at Tambiriu[13] on Guadalcanal, on the north coast, east of Maravovo and Visale, land which Ini claimed was his own. Ini cleared the bush and planned where the Brotherhood buildings would be erected. By October it was possible to take the first step in the actual establishment of the Brotherhood. The *Southern Cross* carried the Bishop and Assistant Bishop, together with A.I.Hopkins and Ini, to Guadalcanal and they arrived on the Feast of St Simon and St Jude, October 28, 1925, which from then on was considered the date of the Founding of the Brotherhood. The annual chapter of the Brothers was usually held as near to that date as possible.

Bishop Molyneux wrote: "On our way to Maravovo occurred an event which will long live in my memory. At Tabulivu we put ashore Ini Kopuria, a teacher from the College at Siota who has been developing a scheme for forming a Brotherhood for evangelising the bush villages of Guadalcanar. From the shore we were led by Ini inland till we came to a place in the bush which he told me was his property. Then in the presence of the Bishop, Hopkins and myself, he made a confession and vowed all his property to God, and himself to a life of celibacy and service to Our Lord; he then asked us to bless and pray for him. He is so obviously sincere and whole-hearted that we hope for great things .... Ini has hopes of six or seven others joining him shortly: will all who read this pray especially for him and for right guidance of this new and very promising development."

Bishop Steward wrote that a 'few natives' were also there and all "went to see the site of the Brotherhood buildings, and here Ini made his promise of self-dedication, kneeling under the shade of a large tree, close to the spot where he hoped to build the Brotherhood House. Afterwards they went back to the ship, the Bishop and Ini following the others."

The form of vow or promise which Ini made was written by himself in Mota. Translated, it reads:

"Trinity All Holy, from today until the day of death I promise in the Name of the Father and of the Son and of the Holy Ghost, and before Angels and Archangels, Spirits and Saints, and before the Bishop, John Manwaring Steward, Bishop Frederick Merivale Molyneux and the Reverend Arthur Innes Hopkins, representing the Church here in Melanesia. I promise three things:–

"I give myself and my land, together with all that is mine, to Thee. I will take no payment from the Mission for the work to which Thou sendest me. I will remain Thy celibate always till my death.

"Strengthen me that I may remain firm, remain peaceable, remain faithful therein all my days till death; who livest and reignest, Three in One God, world without end. Amen."[14]

This was a great moment in the lives of both Ini and his Bishop. A close friend of John Steward, the Reverend M.R.Newbolt, who knew of his love of food and drink and comfort, recognised in him also "the gaiety and the stern self-mastery of the genuine Franciscan." He also wrote: "He is never at his best in speaking of his greatest moments; when he writes of the Brothers, a subject closer than any other to his heart, he is tongue-tied."[15] Fox considered Steward to be the cofounder of the Brotherhood; he believed that without his interest, encouragement and backing, it would not have happened. He wrote: "One thing is certain, no Bishop of Melanesia has ever been so loved by the Melanesians."

Bishop Steward himself wrote in the *Southern Cross Log* of October 1, 1926 that he saw the work of the Brothers as being threefold. Firstly, to go to places in the bush where it would be difficult for European missionaries to go, and which require the energy of young men to face the difficult conditions they would find. Secondly, to prepare the way for others – teacher-catechists and priests – to come and build on their initial work. Thirdly, to provide an opportunity for young Melanesian men to do some special work for God before 'settling down' in their villages, probably as 'village teachers', in this way providing them with an incentive to continue to dedicate their lives to God's service.

He wrote: "Ini and I sought for a good name; we could not find a really good and suitable one – but they were a band of Brothers; why not call them 'the Brothers' and have done with it? And, on consideration, there seemed no answer to this. They were Brothers, just plain Brothers, and nothing else. So 'Brothers' they were and are called. Some day, we dream of Households all through Melanesia, wherever heathen still are to be found. We dream of a Brotherhood Centre, a house for each Household. A Church complete in the beauty of holiness. Great gatherings for devotions, discussion, refreshment and renewal of vows. Somewhere in our dream we seem to see white Brothers too, we seem to see the little flowers of St Francis blossoming in the desert places of the islands. No longer do we hear the cry, 'Send us more men.' For a greater Voice than ours has called and been obeyed. Is it only a dream? Well, old men dream dreams ..... May God grant that the young men may see the Vision, hear the call and respond to it, till the earth is full of the knowledge of the Lord. John, Bishop of Melanesia."[16]

His dream – eventually – came true, and the men and women of the Islands increasingly caught the Vision.

On his retirement, the Brothers wanted him to continue as their Father. He declined, writing to Ini Kopuria on March 5, 1928: "I find that my body is not strong, and I do not want to begin a work I cannot complete .... But if my body is far away, remember always that my heart will be near you always."[17]

In a review of *John Steward's Memories*, which was published in Chester, England, in 1939 and edited by his friend, M.R.Newbolt, the reviewer wrote: "The dream of the first Selwyn became fact through the inspiration of John Manwaring Steward and the instrumentality of Ini Kopuria."[18]

By 1940 the number of Brothers had reached over 150 and the Reverend A.I.Hopkins had written a book about his experiences in Melanesia whose publication in England had been delayed "until conditions in the Homeland are more settled." He confirmed his part in the training of Ini, writing: "In some of my Church History lessons I dwelt upon the topic of those early monks, to whom Germany, for example, owes the founding of Christianity, especially those who came from England to the wild tribes in the bush in Germany. I explained the threefold vows of poverty, chastity and obedience under which they worked. One boy, a remarkably able one, sensitive to any new thing and keen to try it, listened eagerly." He went on to describe the founding of the Brotherhood by Ini, with Bishop Steward's help. He summed up all that had been achieved as follows: "The work is living, and being congenial to the Melanesian temperament, gives scope for individual enterprise and independence. It has, of course, its dangers. One is the opening up of more than can be occupied and the appeal to novelty rather than the steady routine work. But there is room and place for its energies. The follow up is the problem."[19]

NOTES

1 Both Guadalcanal and Santa Ysabel, or Isabel, have Spanish names; it appears also that it was the Spanish explorers who named the whole group after King Solomon, as they hoped to find gold there and encourage European settlement.

2 Information supplied by Dr C.E.Fox concerning details of what happened after Hugo Gorovaka's arrival.

3 This was according to Fr Daniel Sade, but Tabulivu is given as the name of the place in the *Southern Cross Log* of July 1, 1937.

4 Information supplied to the author by Ini's widow, Laisa Loe.

5 Information supplied by Dr C.E.Fox.

6 *Southern Cross Log*, October 1909, quoted in *God's Gentlemen*, p.192.

7 Hilliard in *God's Gentlemen* calls it the Brotherhood of St Aidan and says it lasted for four years and that it was established in 1916, but Fox says it did not last so long – see article by Fox on the Brotherhood in the *Southern Cross Log* of March 1962. Stephen Taroaniara of Makira was martyred with Bishop Patteson, which suggests why 'St Stephen' is probably correct, as used by Fox in an obituary of Ini Kopuria in *Southern Cross Log*, January 1946.

8 Sometimes referred to as Kokou.

9 *Southern Cross Log*, June 1, 1946.

10 Letter of Dr Fox to Fr E.Ball SSM, dated July 17, 1964.

11 The opinion of Dr Fox, who probably by mistake referred to him as 'Police Sergeant' in an obituary in the *Southern Cross Log* of January 1946; he was also called sergeant in a short biography in *Southern Cross Log*, April 1, 1934.

12 See the leaflet *The Response of Melanesia to the Holy Spirit*, published by the Melanesian Mission, London, in the 1930s, where the writer states (p.3): "The story of the life of St Francis took such hold on the mind of one young native Christian in the Solomon Islands that he approached his Bishop with a request that he might 'wed holy poverty' and take the 'three canonical vows'." A review of *John Steward's Memories* in *Southern Cross Log*, July 1, 1939, refers to them as "modern imitators of St Francis, whose immediate forebears were head-hunting cannibals."

13 The headquarters of the Brotherhood was subsequently referred to as Tabalia.

14 See *The Brothers*, Auckland, New Zealand, 1928 (including contributions by Bishop J.M.Steward and Brother Ini Kopuria, who wrote short biographies of each of the first group of his Brothers, which were translated from Mota, in which language he wrote them).

15 *John Steward's Memories*, ed. M.R.Newbolt, Chester: Phillipson and Golder, 1939.

16 Margaret Lycett, *Brothers: the Story of the Native Brotherhood of Melanesia*, London: SPCK, 1935, p.23.

17 *Southern Cross Log*, April 1, 1935.

18 *Southern Cross Log*, October 1, 1939.

19 *Southern Cross Log*, July 1, 1940.

CHAPTER THREE

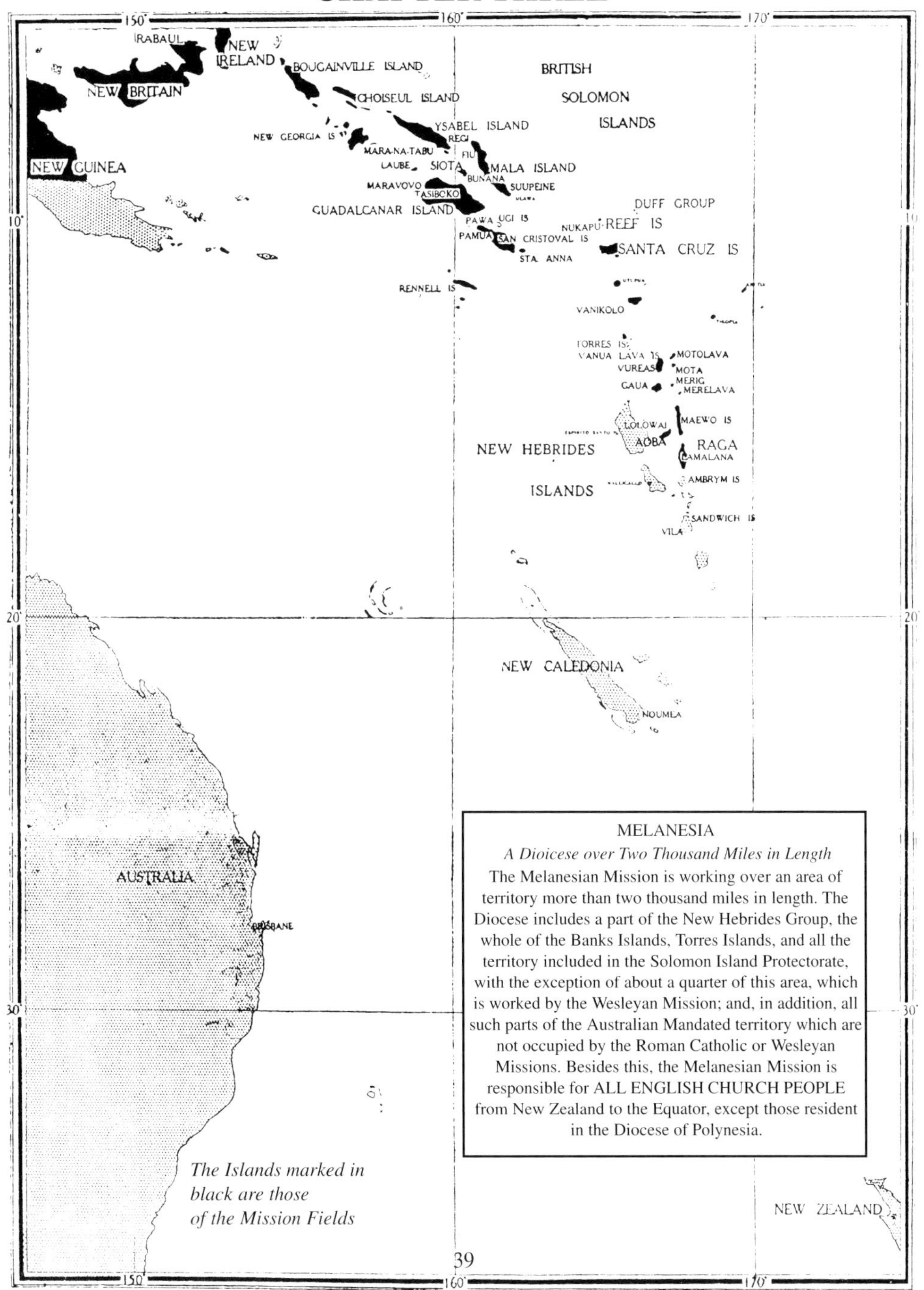

Map published in "The Brothers" by Margaret Lycett 1935

The first Brothers,
with Brother Ini standing second from the left in the back row.

Bishop Steward with a larger group of Brothers with Brother Ini sitting beside him, second from the left in the front row.

The interior of Pawa School Chapel before the Second World War, with altar inlaid with mother-of-pearl.

At Pawa on Ugi Island in the south east Solomons.

CHAPTER THREE

GOING OUT TO GUADALCANAL

Ini Kopuria spent the months after taking his life vow writing an article for the Mission's internal magazine, *O Sala Ususur* (which means *The Messenger* in the Mota language), about his plan to take the Gospel to the remaining non-Christian villages on Guadalcanal. He also toured the islands and visited Pawa School in the mission ship, *Southern Cross.* He was seeking for any who might decide to join him, or who were interested in learning more about his plans for a Brotherhood and its future work. He also wrote letters[1] to people in the Russell Islands (Laumbe)[2], Santa Ysabel and Guadalcanal. After his visit to All Hallows School, Pawa (then situated near the shore, but later moved to higher ground on the island of Ugi) four young men from the school went home to Ysabel to discuss with their relatives the idea of them working among the 'heathen'. As a result of his efforts, six men offered themselves to become Brothers: Dudley Bale, Moffat Ohigita, Cecil Lujagathaga and Maurice Maneae from Bugotu District, Santa Ysabel; Hugo Holun from the Russell Islands, who had responded to the letter Ini sent there; and Benjamin Bokoe from Gaimali, Guadalcanal, whom Ini knew personally. At this stage he received a response only from Solomon Islanders.

In the middle of May 1926, the volunteers gathered with the Bishop, John Steward, at Siota on Gela to discuss the rules of the new community. He asked them how they felt about it all and they answered (according to Dudley Bale), "Yes, father, we will try it." So on Whitsunday, May 23, after Evensong in the College chapel at Siota, the Brotherhood was formally constituted. They agreed to call it, in Mota language, *Ira Retatasiu*, or in English, *The Brothers.* The Bishop received the vows of dedication from the six new members and, laying his hands on the head of each one in turn, admitted them into the new Brotherhood. They made their vows of poverty, celibacy and obedience for one year only, promising to receive no payment, to remain unmarried and to obey 'those set in authority over them'. The vows could be renewed each year, for those who wished to continue as Brothers.

They set out with the Bishop the next day and landed at Tabulivu. Ini had already prepared a house up in the bush, with the help of a few others, near the spot where he had made his own life vow, and this came to be known as Tabalia. Two of those who had helped him build it had not been able to go to school, so as well as working with them clearing the site, he had also taught them to read. According to Bishop Molyneux, the house had 'eight cells'.[3] After examining what had already been done, the Bishop and the Brothers discussed where to put further buildings. At the service of Preparation for Holy Communion, held that evening, the Bishop addressed them about the challenges ahead of them. The next morning they gathered for Holy Communion and then for the first Chapter of the Brothers, at which the Bishop presided. Ini explained his ideas about how to start the evangelistic work among the 3,000 to 4,000 people in about 30 villages whom he reckoned had not heard the Gospel, out of a total population then on Guadalcanal of about 12,000 in 90 villages. So about a third of the population of the large island, especially those in isolated bush villages, had not by then become Christians of any denomination. They planned an itinerary, based on this information. Ini was chosen by the others as the first Elder Brother (*Moemera* in Mota) and this was approved by the Bishop. It was agreed to hold the Annual Chapter on St Simon and St Jude's Day, October 28, when Ini had made his vow, and the Bishop said this would be kept as 'Brotherhood Day' in the Diocese. The same day the *Southern Cross* took them down the Guadalcanal coast to Point Cruz, near to a path leading into the hills, arriving about 6 p.m.[4] The Bishop accompanied them ashore and people from the nearest village, Mataniko, met them and invited them to sleep there before going up into the hills. By the light of the moon, the seven of them knelt on the beach for the Bishop's blessing,[5] and he commended them to God, whom they wished to serve, before returning to the ship. He left them to start their mission by going into Bagomea District. Their aim was already clear in their Rule: to evangelize those people whom the white missionaries found it difficult to reach, to preach the Gospel, and to prepare the way for 'teachers' to follow and build up the Church.

The first Brothers (who all wore beards) were accompanied by another man called Ambrose, who was there for one of the Brothers who might 'need attention', but he had made no vow or promise.[6] Daniel Sade, Ini's 'one-talk', was still at Maravovo, but later went to Pawa before joining the Brotherhood. Ini had previously been in touch with one or two villages in the bush, but when the Brothers actually arrived they were not given the hearing which Brother Ini had been promised. The Brothers were taken aback and somewhat disappointed by the reception they initially received, especially at Malañgo on the Tenaru River, where the 'heathen' did not want them. In one place, the chief said he would not try the new way until neighbouring villages had done so, and even gave some money to the Brothers at a feast he gave for them, asking that it be given to the Bishop and the Governor of the Protectorate "because he did not wish to receive the religion." Brother Moffat reported that the Brothers did not accept the money "because he did not give it with goodwill." The people there even appealed to the British District Officer at Aola on the coast, asking to be left alone! He supported them in their request. In another village, where it was thought the new teaching might interfere with labour conditions and so prevent money being raised for the Government tax, the chief was willing, but the people were not. They were afraid of offending the 'ghosts' – the spirits of the dead, to whom they felt they were accountable.

At the second Chapter, held at Veranaaso (Maravovo School), which was delayed until All Saints' Day, November 1, by the non-arrival of the Bishop, fresh plans were made. Brother Ini was able to report news from another part of Guadalcanal he had visited, where a number of villages had expressed willingness to receive the Brothers. The Bishop agreed to the new plan. The ship taking Daniel Sade to Pawa that November dropped Brothers at Koilotumuria where they stayed with Oliver Bato, a teacher who had trained at Norfolk Island. From there they went out in pairs in Ruavatu District. They had picked up John Patteson Ñaña at Marasa on the weather coast of Guadalcanal and he joined them straight away, with no training other than what he would receive from being with Brother Ini, as was the custom at the beginning of the Brotherhood. The novice, called *Tiñqoro* or 'disciple' in Mota, would usually make his vows before the Bishop at the next visit he made, if Ini duly presented him. John Patteson made his on the *Southern Cross*!

The reception received by the Brothers in this new area in late 1926 was very different. The non-Christians were more welcoming and the Brothers were able to prepare the way for a teacher from Santa Ysabel, Joses Para, to be stationed at the village of Reko. They then moved on to Aola (the District Officer's base) and Susu. There were only a few Christians in Aola then. In all, four villages in the Tasiboko area welcomed them[7] and "sought from them the way of Life."[8] Some of the young men wanted to build houses for them and a schoolhouse. The Brothers found also that they could go out from there to contact other villages, some of which received them, but some refused or wavered.

When the Brothers met in Chapter in October 1927 they were full of hope for the future. Invitations had been received from Marau Sound, in the far east of Guadalcanal, where Ini was known because of his former work as a policeman and where the Brothers had been welcomed at Simeruka. One of the children there at that time was Andrew Riropo. Brother Ini, Brother Ben Pupolo from Guadalcanal and Brother Hugo Holun from the Russell Islands came and preached to the people, who were all still 'heathen'. At first, the people were frightened, but when they heard the stories the Brothers told, they loved them. After the stories, the Brothers shared the people's food and betelnut. The children were attracted to the Brothers and came to them first, as happened in many other places later. The people whom the Brothers converted at Simeruka then converted Andrew Riropo. He said: "How was I converted? The Holy Spirit worked. I heard the message and was converted .... Before, there was no peace. We were prisoners of fear. We feared one another and practised magic between one another.... After the Brothers, the catechist used to come. I remember our catechist came from South Malaita. There were not many priests at that time." One day he was playing naked on the beach when the *Southern Cross* arrived with a white priest on board. He asked Andrew's father if he could take him to Maravovo School. He also gave him a fathom of calico – black with white spots. He wore half and put the other half in his custom umbrella. He was happy to go to school, but he saw his sister crying and running along the beach as the ship left, sad he was going away, as their mother had already died. Many years later, that boy was ordained priest![9]

Ini was very insistent on the rule that the Brothers should go two by two. John Patteson Ñaña reported that he was the eighth Brother to make his promises and "in those days we always went two by two everywhere; you even went for a swim and wash two by two. I went with Moffat Ohigita. When we arrived in a heathen place, we would explain to the people that we came to do God's work. We would teach the children. We would build a house and pray with the children. The big men respected us, but it was a long time before they would join our prayer. Ini Kopuria made us keep a notebook and write down a record of our life. If we did wrong or missed prayer, we must write it down. Then every three months we would go through this record with our Brothers in a confession meeting. Ini Kopuria was a kind man, a man of humility. He was hard working too and people always obeyed him."[10]

At the end of his first year in the Brotherhood, John Patteson, who was at Aola, received a letter saying that his mother was sick at Marasa. Ini let him go back there, but he had to walk all the way. When he arrived, he found his mother had already died. When Bishop Steward visited Marasa with Dr Montague Maybury, the doctor suggested that John should train as a dresser at Siota, which he did.[11] Later he also became a priest. He remembered his time as a Brother as hard. "We walked for long distances We used to follow the rivers and often slept in the bush. I remember I was often hungry. And we were often among strangers. But I learnt many things...."

Ben Bokoe only stayed one year, too. He was one of the first group of pupils to open the Senior School in 1920. It was called Pawa only when it moved to Ugi from Siota in 1922. Ini had come to the school and asked for him, and Dr Fox had let him go. He had already finished Standard 4. He remembered the Brothers' first tour, journeying up the Matanigo River[12] to a place called Belaga, where there were already a few Christians. At Lokea the people were not interested, so they went on to a 'real heathen place', Ngichungichu, where the chief was angry with them and sent them away. Then a message was received from Lokea that they wanted the Brothers back, but it became clear to them that this was untrue. They had hoped that Lokea would be the first 'heathen' village in those parts to be converted by them, but the people told them: "We don't like to become Christians. If we were trying to become Christians, our devils will get cross and we shall all die. So don't bother us to become Christians, but leave us and go away!" That night there was an earthquake after the Brothers had left for Belaga and they heard that Lokea had been destroyed. They then left Belaga for Aola. There Ben heard his sister had died. His mother had died already while he was at Pawa, so he asked to be released from his vows. However, he became a catechist in a newly converted village in the bush, among the hills above Aola, and he never married.[13] So he offered himself to build on the work the Brothers had begun. Many Brothers in later years became catechists or priests, thus providing the Anglican Church with committed ordained and lay ministers.

Brother Dudley Bale and Brother Moffat Ohigita on one of their journeys in the mountains of Guadalcanal (which rise to 8,000 feet) climbed a steep cliff, "dragging themselves up by creepers" and found a 'heathen' village at the top. Brother Dudley told Charles Fox later that "they were well received by the chief, but next morning things were different. The chief told them that the village's [heathen] priest had come to him in the night and said to him, 'Drive them out. I have seen a third Brother with them whose face shines and terrifies me. Let us have nothing to do with them.' So out they were driven."[14] Their next work was to be far away, in Fiji, part of the Diocese of Polynesia, among immigrant communities from the Solomons and New Hebrides.

The first experience of the Brothers on Guadalcanal had been rather disappointing. Bishop Baddeley wrote in the *Southern Cross Log* of July 1, 1939: "They felt they could make no headway. They were received for one night only in most villages. They came back and told the Bishop they thought perhaps they had made a mistake. He said, 'Surely you have not come to that conclusion so soon. If the call is from God, he will bless it and later show you the way.' He then took them away to Santa Cruz, the hardest nut in the evangelistic work in the whole of Melanesia."

NOTES

[1] According to Hugo Holun.

[2] Also known then as Cape Marsh, the local name being Laube or Laumbe.

[3] *Southern Cross Log*, July 1, 1926.

[4] This area later became the site of a very large American camp during the Second World War, later adopted as the site of the new capital, Honiara, when the war was over, and this led to the concentration of economic development on the north coast of Guadalcanal, including the plains. Honiara is a shortening of *Nahoniara*, 'the place facing the east wind.'

[5] Information from Dudley Bale.

[6] *Southern Cross Log*, October 1, 1926.

[7] The Brothers worked as follows: at Rako, Cecil and Hugo; at Gurubusu and Gainiviti, Moffat and Ben; at Aola, Ini and Patteson; at Susu, Dudley and Maurice. All these villages wanted teachers and an appeal for them appeared in *O Sala Ususur* (see *Southern Cross Log*, November, 1927).

[8] M.Lycett: *Brothers*, p.35.

[9] Interview with Fr Andrew Riropo by Fr Richard Carter, Chaplain of the Brotherhood.

[10] Personal communication to Fr Richard Carter.

[11] Dr Maybury established the hospital at Fauabu on North Malaita and remained John Patteson's friend for life. He lived from 1900 to 1971 and arrived in Melanesia in 1928. See Hilliard: *God's Gentlemen*, pp.268-270. Two of his sons, John and David, became priests in England and Scotland respectively.

[12] Usually spelt Mataniko ('the eye of the water'), but spelt by Bokoe *Matanigo*. The river now passes through the capital, Honiara, and has come to be spelt Matanikau.

[13] Interview with Ben Bokoe by the author at Ben's home near Najilagu, west of Honiara, in 1979. It was unusual in Melanesia to remain unmarried when not under vows.

[14] Fox: *Kakamora*, p.72.

CHAPTER FOUR

Sending out of Brothers from Tabalia.

Class for novices in two languages at Tabalia.

Maravovo School (Guadalcanal) Football Team with Fr. George Warren second from the left in the back row. He was at Maravovo School from 1920 to 1938.

Maravovo School Band with Mr. Fred Isom, the "Mission Printer" who served for 43 years as Lay Missionary and whose printing press was at Hautabu near Maravovo before the Second World War and later at Taroaniara, Gela.

Southern Cross VII at Port Said, Egypt, on her maiden voyage to the Solomons in 1933, replacing Southern Cross VI, wrecked in the New Hebrides in 1932 with two Brothers on board.

CHAPTER FOUR

TABALIA: HEADQUARTERS AND MOTHER HOUSE

After their first missionary journey, Brother Ini stayed at Aola while the six Brothers went back to Tabalia to do some more clearing of the station and planting of the gardens. There had been no village there before, but some of the land belonged to Ini's line. Brother Ini had obtained permission from the chief, Samuel Lengo, and two teachers at Tabulivu, Wilson Lualome from Gela and a local man, Robin Koropi, to use the schoolroom at Tabulivu until the house at Tabalia was ready. Originally there was only one house at Tabalia, built by the Tabulivu people and the Brothers. A small area had been cleared before building started. It was not until 1927 that the station was blessed. While the Brothers were staying at Tabulivu, they and the teachers used to teach the children in the old church of St Mark.[1] This was later rebuilt, but was then destroyed by a cyclone. Ini needed more land, as he had plans to bring people to school nearer to the Brothers' station. He asked Baptista Ulu to let him have some land nearby and paid him £30, having been able to obtain £50 from Lawrence Kibo while he was still a policeman at Aola. On that extra land he established his school and it was given the Maori name Kohimarama,[2] 'focus of light', in memory of the first Melanesian school of that name, established by Bishop George Augustus Selwyn in New Zealand. Children from 'heathen' villages in Guadalcanal came to it, including Billy Tetega. There were also some Polynesians from the island of Bellona. One old chief from there called Sogogo also came to stay for a while and the Brothers used to take him round with them to keep him quiet!

On the station, discipline was strict. Ini's word was "accepted without question". He had a "dominating personality".[3] If Brothers infringed the rules, they sometimes had to do work on the station as a 'penance'. While in the police, Ini had been expected to whip any prisoner who escaped, so he could be tough and on occasions appear to be hard. However, this was not resented, as those who came to Tabalia felt that he loved them and that the discipline was for their own good. Sometimes he would set people to work at night! Brother Hugo Holun remembered that the rising bell at Tabalia was at 6 a.m. and Matins (Morning Prayer) at 6.30 a.m. As there was no priest resident at first, there was no Eucharist except on Sundays, at Maravovo School. However, at 9 a.m. there was the 'Daily Memorial' (versicles and responses and the Brotherhood Prayer), after which there was work up to 11 a.m. The midday office was at 12 noon. There was more work between 1.30 p.m. and 4 p.m., when the bell was rung for 'swimming' (a bath in the river). Evensong (Evening Prayer) was at 5.30 p.m., after which they went into the dining hall for their meal, which would be followed by a 'rest hour'. At 9 p.m. each one said Compline on his own. Sometimes there was 'bed prayer' led by Ini.

As many who joined the Brotherhood could not write, and might at first have some difficulty in reading Mota, Ini taught them the rules, or they recited them in order to learn them by heart. If a Brother did something against the rules, Brother Ini would usually just take him aside to talk to him and advise him. However, if he had done something wrong publicly, he would call the Brothers together to talk about it and discuss whether they should release the Brother from his vows or receive him back into the community. Ini was insistent that the Brothers always travel in pairs, two by two. Not only was this a pattern established by Our Lord but it meant often that Brothers from *different* islands went together, itself a sign of Christian love and brotherhood. It was also useful for protection, security and mutual encouragement, as well as for avoiding temptation and keeping to the rules!

At Tabalia, Ini told the Brothers that they should respect the whole station, not just a particular place within it, like the chapel (when it was built). He stressed that it was a valuable place for them *and* the people. Also that they should respect each other and those with whom they came into contact. Much of his teaching was done by example, although he stressed the need for respect, obedience and a sense of responsibility on the part of all the Brothers, otherwise they would not gain the respect of the people. Ini's emphasis on these three things soon bore fruit, as the Brothers came to be widely respected by the Anglican Christian people, who regarded the Brotherhood as a precious gift by God to Melanesia, particularly as it had been started by a Melanesian.[4] The Brothers themselves respected him greatly, particularly as he was the founder of their Brotherhood. Times of prayer were observed carefully, with great stress being placed on being in church in good time before the service. They had only the four times of prayer during the day, but they kept these times of prayer with great reverence. Ini himself was recognised by his Brothers as a man of prayer, stressing to them that it was the centre of their community life. If ever he had to miss a prayer time because of pressing business, or was unavoidably late, he would pray the service privately in his office or in chapel. Others followed his example. He was also known to say his own personal prayers, which encouraged others to do the same, although little was said about it.

There was then little formal training and Ini's gifts were leadership and administration rather than teaching. He was not intellectual, although he was very intelligent.[5] Boys from Pawa School who were considered suitable postulants were admitted almost immediately and learnt from Ini as they worked together among the 'heathen'. However, unschooled boys from the bush had to do a six month or one year noviciate. If they did not already know it, they had to learn Mota, and sometimes also the language of the people to whom they would be sent. Ini would teach them about the life, work and rules of the Brotherhood and what *not* to do, as well as ABC (reading) and the Catechism, which they would later teach the people.

At Tabalia, perhaps because of his police experience, Ini decided to raise and lower a Brotherhood flag daily, and taught the Brothers to show proper respect to it and also to the large cross which was eventually erected on the spot where he had made his life vow, and where the Brotherhood could be said to have begun. Before the cross was the area where the Brothers made their own vows – 'St Simon and St Jude's Square.' The vows were 'open' – for no set length of time was stipulated as the term of service as a Brother – although at that time, the vows were renewed annually.

As part of his training of the Brothers, Ini insisted on the Headquarters Station at Tabalia being treated with special respect. All who came had to comply with the rule of the station, as it was a Religious House and 'holy ground'. As ex-Brother John Still Ritau expressed it: "The land is blessed and dedicated simply to train obedient servants of God." In early days there was a boundary where visitors, whoever they were, had to remove their footwear (*if* they wore anything on their feet) as well as their hats. The station was to be kept holy by being used only for prayer and teaching, not for other activities; this was to show visitors what the Brothers were and how they were called to live an 'orderly and obedient life.' The Square of St Simon and St Jude was not to be entered by anybody, even to be cleaned. Only the Brothers were to enter it on their feast day. The Brothers treated it like 'custom ground', as it showed where the 'power of the station' was kept. (The 'holiness' of the place was such that the Brothers believed even the birds would respect it by not flying over it; some even claimed that a group of birds that did fly over it fell down dead!) They also believed that *God's* beauty would fill the place and that it should not be touched to beautify it according to earthly ideas. Various customs and ideas also came to be associated with the flag. When it was raised in the morning, the Brothers had to get up and stand. It was lowered to half-mast when a Brother died and to the ground if a Brother broke his promises. Some believed the flag itself would indicate when something was wrong and the Brother who had 'fallen' would then confess what he had done wrong to his fellow Brothers. The Brothers were strictly ordered not to tell dirty stories. Their bodies were to be treated as holy and not to be touched, even by their fellow Brothers, and never by girls. To guard themselves from temptation and lying and unhelpful storytelling, they were warned not to speak too much with 'outside people' and given guidance about the right ways and means of approaching people. They were, however, expected to greet all they met on their travels and to show 'love and respect to all Brothers and all people', especially to those who visited them in their houses.[6]

Ini had his own way of wearing the 'uniform', Guadalcanal style, with the *malo* (calico loincloth) right over his chest and down to his feet.[7] In early days the Brothers had *four* kinds of uniform. A blue *lavalava* or *malo* with a yellow sash was worn when travelling on mission. The blue represented the land and yellow the beach dividing land and sea. A white *malo* was worn with a black sash during worship in the Brothers' station or among other people after they had been converted. This meant 'conversion to glory', darkness to light. A red *malo* was worn with a white sash during training, to remind them that representing the light of Christ to people could be dangerous. A black *malo* with a white sash was worn as a sign of mourning, if a relative of one of the Brothers had died.[8]

Whatever the colour being worn, it was the rule always to have the sash as part of the uniform. It represented obedience to authority, doing the Master's will and not one's own will, without counting the cost. The other thing that always had to be worn with the uniform was the medal. Originally this was round, with a cross in the middle and the words 'Jesus died on the cross' inscribed around it, to remind Brothers that they must be willing to follow Christ even to death. It was to be hung over the heart. If the Brothers were to be attacked with bows and arrows and one of them was hit, they were to pray and then return home. However, if an arrow hit the medal it was to be seen as a 'sign of victory' and the Brothers were to say a prayer of thanksgiving and advance towards the 'heathen' village. The Brothers saw the medal as a 'breastplate for protection' from temptation as well as arrows.

On tour, the Brothers carried walking sticks as an aid, so the stick was seen as representing Christ, who would be their support in time of need and their guide when confused or lost. It could be touched or used only by the Brothers and had to be properly cared for as they travelled.[9] Uniforms were blessed at the service of admission (profession) and so had to be respected. This meant they had to be hung up when not being worn and not left on the ground or on the bed or anywhere else. No one else could wear the uniform and it could not be washed by women or girls. Anyone who broke this rule, set by the founder, was disciplined. Outside their own station, the Brothers always had to wear their uniform and respect it and this gained them the respect of others. Wearing the uniform made them feel humble, but also gave them a feeling of inner holiness.[10]

Ini was very conscious of the fact that the Brotherhood had to feel like a *Melanesian* community. Included in the programme were various social activities, in which he would always try and join. He had a gift for mixing with his Brothers easily, but he would take time to study the character and behaviour of newcomers before contacting them personally. At night, he would sometimes lead them in songs in the Mota language. He also liked to 'make fun' with the Brothers, in order to make them feel that "they were in a Melanesian community, rather than just staying boring in the community", as Hugo Holun expressed it.[11]

On one occasion he got all the Brothers up in the middle of the night and ran them down to the river, pretending it was 5.30 a.m., the time they normally rose and washed![12] He also taught them some sporting skills, especially those of football (soccer) and cricket, which were his favourite games. In the early days, there were no other activities except 'holy drama', which Ini excelled at. Although there were then no big feasts and no custom dancing at Tabalia itself, Brother Ini was good at dancing, especially the local dances of his own people, and he would join in if they were organising a big occasion in the area.[13] Occasionally the Brothers would organise a small feast and invite others to join them, or go for a picnic. On Fridays, they would go to Maravovo to play games and come back on Sunday after the Eucharist there. They kept two special festivals at Tabalia-St Simon and St Jude's Day, when Brothers were 'admitted' (professed), and St Mark's Day, the patronal festival of the chapel there. These days were marked by the celebration of the Holy Eucharist, followed by breakfast; then the Brothers had one or two free days as a holiday. At the beginning there were only a few of them, so that they were unable to organise a large feast or other activities. There were 15 Brothers by 1928, but the Mother House had no Chaplain or Tutor. Much depended on Ini himself and on the Elder Brother at Tabalia, who took over some duties from him when his other responsibilities grew, and as the Brotherhood extended its work further afield. Elder Brothers, starting with Hugo Holun, wore a silver medal, but Ini continued to wear a bronze one. Hugo was the first Elder Brother at Tabalia. He was appointed by Ini, who himself became Head Brother (*Tuaga*) until 1940.[14]

Ini tried to keep a record of everything the Brotherhood did. After the day's work, he typed. When he was sick, he still worked. The Brothers considered him to be hardworking and tough. He could talk a lot – but calmly – when things went wrong, but he was generally a quiet and thoughtful person. He was always with the Brothers in what they were doing, unless he had to do something urgent in the office. To the Brothers, he appeared to be humble, as he worked *with* them, rather than telling them what they had to do, or forcing them, or making them rush things. He was also very open with his fellow Brothers, which made them happy. Only in the matter of the Brothers' evangelistic work did he reserve some decisions to himself, although he sometimes put up his plans on a notice-board for the Brothers to think about and discuss, and then asked for their views. Any major plans would also have to be discussed with the Bishop of Melanesia, as Father of the Brotherhood.

Dr Fox described the 'special meeting' which the Brothers held when they came together for their Conference, and which came to be held weekly in the Households. "When all were gathered together, with Ini at the head, our rule had it that Ini, beginning with the most junior, should ask each in turn if he had anything against any Brother or his conduct. Our rule forbade the criticism of any Brother except when all met together, and then we must not be silent. If there was a charge, that Brother replied and then we all discussed it and it was soon clear who was in the wrong and he expressed his sorrow. At these times Ini was wonderfully understanding."[15] These meetings came to be known as 'confession meetings' and often took up many hours at Conference time as the Brotherhood grew. They were a great strength to the community, enabling unity and peace to be encouraged and, usually, maintained among those from increasingly diverse ethnic, racial and linguistic background with often varied cultures and customs.

As well as taking seriously the injunction of St James in his Epistle

(5:16) to "confess your sins to one another and pray for one another that you may be healed," some specific commands of Jesus were made part of the Brotherhood's regular practice. Because anger could easily turn to hatred or even violence, Brothers were expected to take literally the words of St Paul, "Let not the sun go down upon your anger," and to quickly tell the Brother or Novice or other person how he or she had upset him, and try to sort the matter out. Thus difficult situations and misunderstandings could be avoided or at least made less.

Moreover, Ini had the gift of being able to make friends, if he wished, with anybody, from European to 'heathen' people in the Malaita bush. He also had a great knowledge of native customs and magic, which helped him deal with many problems with wisdom and understanding.

The Brothers were not allowed any 'holidays', only 'home visits'. Brothers would be allowed to travel with the Bishop on his tour and visit their homes and parents, but they had to continue with the Bishop and not stay. They were always to be 'on mission'. Brother Ini also ordered that no Brother should be allowed to go home to see his dead parents. They could be free only to go back to see the grave or serve their surviving parents, when the time they had covenanted to serve in the Brotherhood had been completed. This was understood by the parents when young men joined the Brotherhood and accepted by them. However, the Brothers were expected to pray for their parents daily. This rule of 'no holiday, no visiting of dead parents' was seen as a 'sacrifice to God's service as a Brother'. Similarly, parents of the Novices were not invited to witness the 'admission' or profession of new Brothers, as this was observed as an internal or 'secret' event of the Brotherhood in its early days, only witnessed by the Bishop and the Brothers, and those being taught by the Brothers at Kohimarama. This custom emphasised the idea that the leaders of the Brotherhood were 'parents' to the members while they were Brothers, while the Brothers would feel they wholly belonged to the Brotherhood and would thus be encouraged to follow all its customs and rules. They were reminded of the need for total commitment and self-giving. Their call to mission was stressed by the solemn blessing of their uniforms and walking sticks at the service, to be used in their task of evangelism. The early Brothers believed that the Brotherhood, because it was Melanesian, was (and should always remain) unique in its life, tradition, custom, rule and ministry, and that what was initiated by the founder should remain unchangeable. Ex-Brother John Still Ritau believed: "This is the secret of what makes the Brotherhood the real spearhead of the Church" and "a real postlight of the Church to the world."

Originally the Order of Companions of the Brothers, as it was called, was established in about 1930 by Ini on his own initiative to help the Brothers by their prayers and giving, and it was he who wrote their rules, which were translated into a number of different languages. Men and women (and, later, young people) could join, after renewing their baptismal promises or 'vow' in church. His idea was that they would be organised in 'Households', like the Brothers, with eight to twelve members in each. So in large villages there might be more than one 'Household'. Later the word 'group' was used instead. Each 'Household' would have a leader and the 'Households' would be organised in Districts, with a District Leader. St James's Day was chosen as the day on which they would meet to discuss their affairs. They could be represented at the Brothers' Conferences, and the Brothers would try to visit them to encourage them in their prayers and work and to report to them on the work of the Brotherhood. The Companions would care for the Brothers when they passed through their District. However, they were not there just to help the Brotherhood, but to provide support, spiritual and material, for their local church. Each was to do something for his or her local village. Often it was the Companions who cleaned the church or looked after the church grounds and cemetery, sometimes with members of the Mothers' Union, some of whom might be Companions as well. They would serve at the Eucharist, visit the sick and get firewood for old people who could not get it for themselves. Although many of the Companions just prayed for the Brothers each day, Ini got the Companions at Tabulivu to help in many practical ways also. They prayed twice a day, and when they were not at prayer, Ini would ring the bell for them to come and provide assistance with planting, weeding, house building or other things that needed to be done on the station. When they prayed, they used the collects for the Brothers, the Heathen and the Companions. The leader read the Litany for the Heathen on Fridays.[16] That became a pattern for the Companions in many places. Dr Fox reported in the 1960s that the Companions usually met every Friday, one week to pray for the Brothers and the second week to pray for the Church in their own village.

They could be a real force for good, especially where the priest supported them or where he himself was a Companion. Some clergy, however, were afraid that the Companions might consider themselves holier than others (including, perhaps, the clergy!).[17] By 1941, Companions' groups had probably been established on Guadalcanal, Malaita, Makira (San Cristoval), Lord Howe, Sikaiana, the Eastern Outer Islands, the New Hebrides, Fiji and New Britain – all the places where the Brothers had worked.

What started in such a small way grew into a great organisation of Companions, with many people throughout the Pacific and beyond becoming Companions, particularly if they came in touch with the Brothers or were inspired by their work. By the 1960s it was reckoned that there were about 2,000 of them. Brother Ini had said, "I want the Brotherhood to rest on Melanesians, not Europeans, but they must be keen Christians." Their gifts of money for the Brotherhood, collected on St James's Day at each group's annual meeting or at a district meeting, increasingly began to help the work the Brothers felt God was calling them to do.[18]

At one of the Brothers' Conferences, the Companions discussed having a uniform in the same colours as the Brothers and considered the best shape for their medal. The idea of a uniform – one which also attracted the members of the Mothers' Union – did not catch on, but in the 1990s the Brotherhood produced a special T-shirt for the Companions.[19]

Ex-Brother Albert Thavero summed up his experience of being in the Brotherhood as "very hard, very happy and very easy!" The hardness of the work was balanced by the happiness of working together in God's service and by experiencing in practice the words of Jesus: "The yoke I will give you is easy and the load I will put on you is light."

Brother Hugo Holun, after eight years and six months in the Brotherhood, felt that the time had come to leave, but his experiences remained with him and he continued to be very conscious of them. He felt that God was always present with him, that "the Spirit was with him, moving him to get through that problem or these problems." Because of his experiences in the Brotherhood, he had "courage to go on", as he had faith in the spiritual experiences he had had. Many of his fellow Brothers served for a much shorter time, some for only two years or one year – a few for only some months.[20] Others in the Brotherhood had begged Hugo to carry on, especially as he was one of the original group who understood the life of the Brotherhood so well, and indeed he did stay longer than most Brothers at that period.

Brother Joshua Halumae, on a tour of the New Hebrides in the 1960s, compared the Brothers to the *apostles* (the word originally meant 'those sent') and the Companions to the *friends* of Jesus. Some saints were apostles, others were friends of the Lord. "When he was crucified only his friends stood at the foot of the cross. The apostles had all fled; only the friends who loved him stood there." He believed, like Ini, that without the prayers of the Companions, the Brothers' work among the 'heathen' would not succeed. "Their prayers are to go before the Brothers to kill the heathen ways, then the Brothers come after; the prayer has already prepared the heathens' minds. Whatever the Brothers say, they listen to. If they (the heathen) don't want to come into church, they still listen. So prayer helps. We also hear our Lord's word, 'The harvest is plentiful, but the labourers are few. Pray the Lord of the harvest that he may send forth labourers into the harvest.'"[21]

In *The Response of Melanesia to the Holy Spirit*, a Melanesian Mission leaflet published in England in the early 1930s, the writer claimed that "the native lay Brothers, enduring hardness for Christ's sake, renouncing what to them is the world, and patiently suffering for the truth's sake, are winning many to righteousness and are manifesting the fruit of the Spirit."[22] Dr Fox wrote: "Instances of faith, courage, endurance, patience. Plenty, but they will never tell them. I know of Brothers going without food for four or five days, but only they could tell, and won't."[23]

NOTES

1 Later a man called Michael was sent by the Brothers to Maravovo to train, and he returned to teach at Tabulivu in 1936, later going to Ngalimoata near Verahue to teach for three years. Local boys who attended the Brothers' school at Kohimarama included Paul Kopuria from Leosa, as well as Matthew Belamatanga and other Roman Catholics.

2 The Bishop Patteson Theological College is now on this site. Kohimarama is now the name of a suburb of Auckland, which includes Mission Bay, where the Melanesian School was situated. The street names there are of people and places associated with Melanesia and the local church includes windows and other items commemorating the work of the Mission.

3 Personal communication to the author by Dr Fox in the 1970s.

4 This was certainly the view of ex-Brother Hugo Holun, interviewed by Brother Patrick Tagini in 1978.

5 Personal communication to the author by Dr Fox in the 1970s.

6 According to John Still Ritau, an ex-Brother.

7 According to Dr Fox.

8 The meanings accorded to the 'uniforms' are as explained by John Still Ritau.

9 According to John Still Ritau.

10 According to John Still Ritau.

11 Interview with Brother Patrick Tagini in 1978.

12 As recounted by Dr Fox.

13 Information supplied by ex-Brother Albert Thavero of Kolomala, Mariñe District, Santa Ysabel, who was a Brother from 1938 to 1942, interviewed by Novice Ernest Farimae in 1979.

14 Sometimes the term 'Head Brother' was also used instead of 'Elder Brother' to describe Brothers in charge of different areas, e.g. the New Hebrides.

15 *Southern Cross Log*, March 1962.

16 Information supplied, in an interview with the author, by ex-Brother Ben Bokoe and Mr Michael Takutili on April 28, 1979.

17 See Fox: *Kakamora*, pages 77-78.
18 See Dr Fox's article on the Brotherhood in *Southern Cross Log*, March 1962.
19 The T-shirt had the design of the Companions' medal on the chest.
20 There was not a set period of commitment, and it seems that some were not really called to the Religious Life and did not stay long.
21 *Southern Cross Log*, June 1963. Brother Joshua Halumae and Brother Peter Ruim were on a tour of the New Hebrides encouraging people to be Companions, when he is reported to have said these words. The Brothers had found Companions in the schools on Ambae (Aoba), but wanted groups to be formed in the villages also.
22 *Melanesian Mission Leaflet*, No.4 (no date), writer anonymous.
23 Letter from Dr Fox to Fr Ernest Ball SSM, chaplain and tutor at Tabalia, dated July 17, 1964.

CHAPTER FIVE

Boys from Santa Cruz Island
Outer Eastern Solomons.

The men who built this church
on Utupua Island, Outer Eastern
Solomon Islands.
Willie, Ramoni and Silas
wearing their "medals".

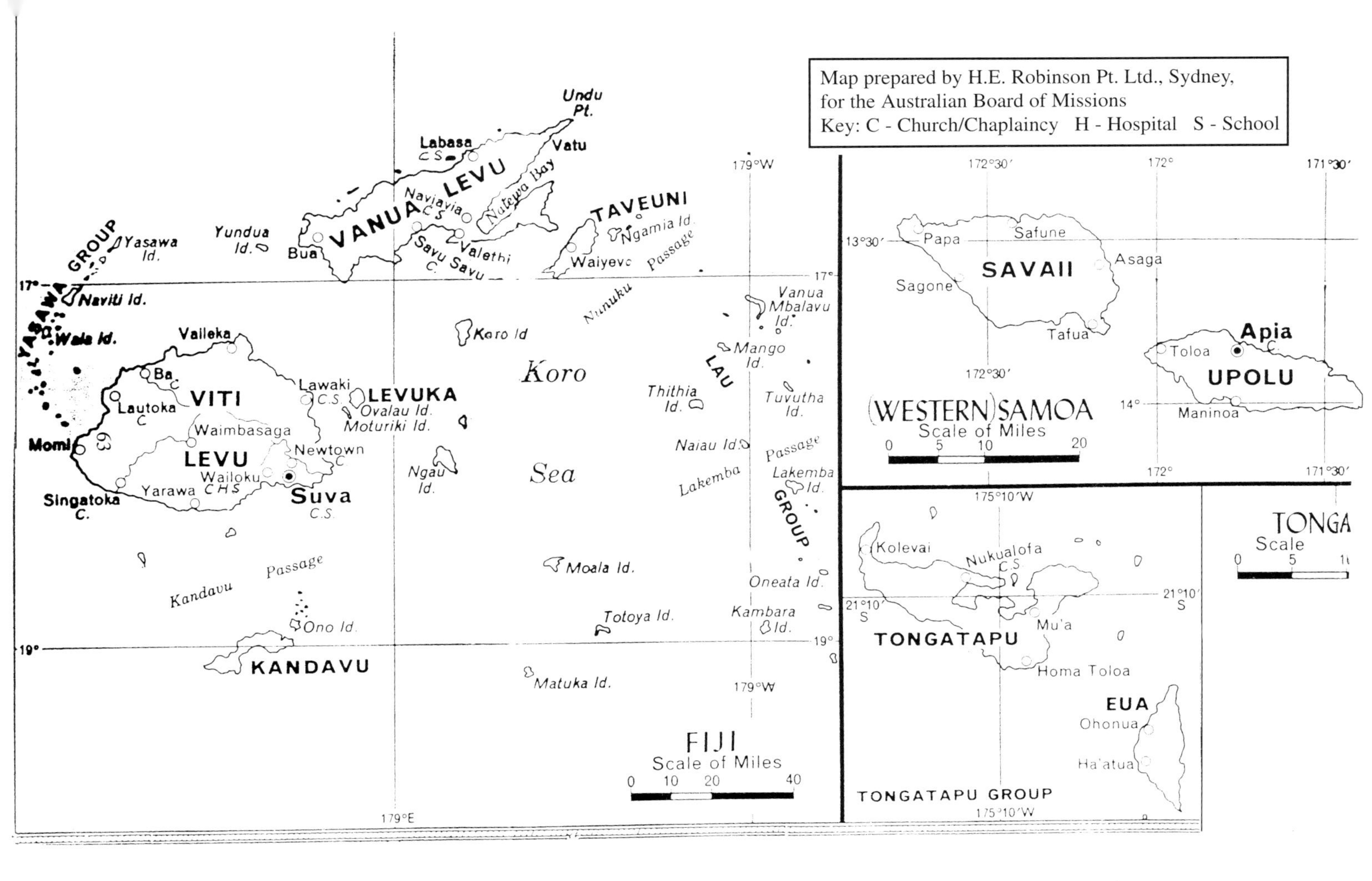

Map prepared by H.E. Robinson Pt. Ltd., Sydney,
for the Australian Board of Missions
Key: C - Church/Chaplaincy H - Hospital S - School
FIJI
Scale of Miles
0 10 20 40
VANUA LEVU
Undu Pt.
Vatu
Labasa C S
Naviavia C S
Natewa Bay
Savu Savu C.
Valethi
Bua
TAVEUNI
Ngamia Id.
Waiyevo
Passage
Nanuku
Yundua Id.
Yasawa Id.
YASAWA GROUP
Naviti Id.
Waia Id.
VITI LEVU
Vaileka
Ba C
Lautoka C
Momi
Singatoka C.
Waimbasaga
Wailoku C H S
Yarawa
Lawaki C.S.
Newtown C
Suva C.S.
LEVUKA
Ovalau Id.
Moturiki Id.
Ngau Id.
Koro Id
Koro Sea
Kandavu Passage
Ono Id.
KANDAVU
Moala Id.
Totoya Id.
Matuka Id.
LAU GROUP
Vanua Mbalavu Id.
Mango Id.
Thithia Id.
Tuvutha Id.
Naiau Id.
Lakemba Passage
Lakemba Id.
Oneata Id.
Kambara Id.
17°
19°
179°W
179°E
(WESTERN) SAMOA
Scale of Miles
0 5 10 20
SAVAII
Papa
Safune
Asaga
Sagone
Tafua
UPOLU
Apia C.
Toloa
Maninoa
13°30′
14°
172°30′
172°
171°30′
TONGA
Scale
0 5
TONGATAPU GROUP
TONGATAPU
Kolevai
Nukualofa C.S
Mu'a
Homa Toloa
EUA
Ohonua
Ha'atua
175°10′W
21°10′ S
63

Church workers in Fiji: George Vaniqa, Bro. Moffatt and Brother Dudley.

St. John's School, Suva, Fiji.

Bishop Baddeley with three Brothers in Sydney, Australia 1932 (In the middle, Bro. Dudley, on the right, Bro. Moffatt).

CHAPTER FIVE

BEYOND GUADALCANAL: SANTA CRUZ TO FIJI

In 1927 Bishop Steward went for a time to Pawa School on Ugi island in the Eastern Solomons while the headmaster, Charles Fox, was away. Brother Ini and all the Brothers took a cutter from Marau at the south east end of Guadalcanal and went to see him at Pawa. They asked him if some of the boys then at Pawa could join them. They then talked privately to some of them after they had had their conference with the Bishop. The Bishop also preached about the Brotherhood and this made many of the boys think seriously about it. Bishop Steward thought that Daniel Sade from Maravovo should join, but Ini knew that Dan's father had already paid the 'bride price' for him to marry. Sometimes he and Daniel were described as brothers, but they were not really related, although they came from the same village. But Daniel's grandmother and Ini's mother were great friends and they, with another woman, shared the feeding at the breast of their various children. In October 1928 Bishop Steward returned to Maravovo village to put up a large crucifix which had been made by himself, Daniel Sade and Frank Bollen Toke, to commemorate the coming of the Christian Church to Guadalcanal.[1]

Bishop Steward received the 'promises' (vows) of 26 young men at Pawa School who wanted to join the Brotherhood.[2] Fr Warren, headmaster at Maravovo, wanted two other pupils, Daniel Sade and Alan Tinoni, to come from Pawa School to teach at Maravovo in the Mota language. They arrived there in November. However, Daniel then decided that he also should become a Brother, and Willie Parapolo from Gela took his place. So Daniel made his 'promise' at Kodovele near Tabalia in December, 1928 and was sent to Aola.[3] With him being professed were Patrick Bugotu and Barnabas Babau, and they all went together to serve with Brother Cecil Lujagathaga, Elder Brother at Aola.[4]

With the growing number of Brothers, it was possible to plan work in other islands, and up until 1941, when the Pacific became involved in the Second World War, the Brothers' work spread to Malaita, Makira (San Cristoval), Lord Howe (Ontong Java), Sikaiana, the Eastern Outer Islands of the Solomons, the New Hebrides (now Vanuatu) and the island of New Britain in the Mandated Territory of New Guinea (administered by Australia), which eventually became part of Papua New Guinea. By the early 1940s there were about 150 Brothers, and Ini had started the Order of Companions of the Brothers, as he wanted the Brotherhood to be supported by the Melanesian Church and not to rely on others.[5] Ini wrote the rules of the Companions himself and these were translated into different languages and printed. Both men and women could join as well as young people, especially those in Church schools. When possible, representatives of Companions would attend the Brothers' annual meeting and, on their return home, pass on information about the Brothers' work and other matters discussed. By the early 1960s, Dr Fox estimated that 2,000 Melanesians had been admitted as Companions and so provided support for the Brothers. Many more joined later from different countries.

At the Conference at Pawa School in 1927, the Brothers discussed with the Bishop matters concerning friends of the Brothers, such as the Companions, and about shirts and trousers and a flag, all in black and white, which would signify 'light going into darkness' – and many kinds of rules. They then returned to work on Guadalcanal in the districts of Marau Sound, Aola and Gainiviti in increased numbers. However, Brother Moffat Ohigita[6] went to start the Brothers' work in Santa Cruz in the Eastern Outer Islands. This was where the first martyrs of the Melanesian Mission, two young men from the Pitcairn Island community on Norfolk Island, Edwin Nobbs and Fisher Young, had been killed in 1864. The work had been started on the island by Mano Wadrokal, who had been put there with his wife at Nelua on the north coast by Bishop John Selwyn in 1880. Wadrokal was from the island of Mare in the Loyalty Islands near New Caledonia and had been trained by Patteson, but he was ordained, after the Bishop's death, in 1875. He became ill and left the island in 1885. Other missionaries, Melanesian and European, came for periods of time. For thirteen months a group of three white missionaries, two priests and a layman, encouraged by Bishop Wilson and calling themselves the Santa Cruz Brotherhood, had sought a response from the people. When they were withdrawn after one of them had died, schools and church services ceased on Santa Cruz Island in 1911. No missionary was sent back to live there until 1925. So the arrival of a Brothers' Household in 1927 was indeed significant.[7] They were able to build on the work of George West, a former carpenter in the Mission who had returned to New Zealand to train for ordination at St John's College, Auckland, and was then put in charge of the work in the Santa Cruz Group from 1925. In 1937 he was drowned at Utupua, caught in a cyclone. He had built himself a house in the Reef Islands and travelled to Santa Cruz and other islands from there. A priest from Ysabel, Lionel Longarata, was based on Santa Cruz with his wife, while Lloyd Francis did medical work there. With the arrival of the Brothers in Graciosa Bay, Santa Cruz, where the Spanish explorer Mendaña had tried to establish the first European settlement in the Pacific Islands in 1595, a strong team of Christian workers was able to change the situation dramatically. The people had been dying out, the schools had all been closed, the villages had become dirty and the people were often unwell. But the Church began to grow from the 1930s onwards. Fox wrote: "The native Brotherhood sent Households of Brothers who transformed the Church in Graciosa Bay."[8] The first Santa Cruz priest, Brown Beu, was ordained in 1952. One of the Brothers sent there, Thomas Peo, was shot and killed by an arrow – another martyr.[9]

While Brother Moffat went to Santa Cruz to establish the Household there, with the help of Brother Ini,[10] Brother Dudley went back to Guadalcanal and then on holiday to Santa Ysabel. In 1928 the two of them went in the old *Southern Cross* to New Zealand. When they reached the Torres Islands, the northernmost islands of the New Hebrides Condominium, the ship's boiler broke. However, the captain and chief engineer were able to temporarily mend the hole, but the voyage continued rather slowly the rest of the way to New Zealand.[11] There the Bishop of Melanesia, Frederick Molyneux, joined the ship and he went with him to Fiji. The Brothers stayed there till 1932, when they returned to the Solomons. They assisted with the work which became known as 'The Melanesian Mission' of the Diocese of Polynesia. This was confusing to people until it was explained that it referred to the work among the Melanesians from the Solomons and the New Hebrides who had been brought there as labourers or were descendants of those brought. Most of the Fijians were 'Melanesians' too, but an agreement with the Methodists meant that the Anglican Church did not attempt to work among them, though some did join the Anglican Church later. Often Solomon Island and New Hebridean men had married local Fijian women, but their children were not considered to have any rights to land. Although the Fijians are predominantly Melanesian by race and language, they have been influenced greatly by Polynesian immigration into the eastern parts of the Fiji group, and so the *Solomoni* (as they came to be known) were, and are, a distinct community.

The Reverend William Floyd, an Irishman from County Wexford, arrived in Fiji from Melbourne, Australia in 1870, to be the first Anglican chaplain there. He based himself at Levuka, then the capital, on the island of Ovalau. The active jurisdiction of the Bishop of Melanesia had not then reached there, but Floyd found quite large numbers of immigrant labourers from the Solomon Islands and New Hebrides who had come from the Bishop's sphere of work. So Floyd wrote to Bishop Patteson inviting him to visit Fiji, both to see what should be done to help them and to carry out episcopal acts, such as confirmation. The Bishop was intending to visit Fiji after his voyage to the Solomons in 1871, but was murdered on the island of Nukapu in the outer Reef Islands on September 20.

In 1874 Fiji was ceded to Queen Victoria by King Cakobau and the Paramount Chiefs and thus became a Crown Colony. Thereafter the chaplain was accredited to the Bishop of London, whose jurisdiction extended to the high seas and any Anglican chaplain unattached to a Province or Diocese. However, contacts with the Diocese of Melanesia continued and in 1875 the Reverend Edward Wogale, originally from Mota in the Banks Islands and brother of George Sarawia, the first Melanesian priest, went as a deacon to assist Floyd for three years.[12] Between 1863 and 1914 about 100,000 Melanesians were engaged as indentured labourers for Queensland, Fiji, Samoa and New Caledonia. Of these, at least a half came from the islands where the Melanesian Mission was then working. The Reverend Dr Henry Codrington visited Melanesian labourers on the plantations in Queensland while he was Administrator of the Diocese of Melanesia from 1871 (after Bishop Patteson's death) until 1877. He found that "absolutely nothing is done by the Church."[13] It was therefore considered necessary to assist with the work among Melanesians in both Queensland and Fiji, but little was achieved.[14] There was, however, considerable concern about the continued recruiting of these islanders and legislation was eventually passed in England, Queensland and Fiji to control it more effectively, partly as a result of the killing of Bishop Patteson in 1871. He had been murdered by a man with a grievance, because five islanders from Nukapu had been stolen to work on cotton plantations in Fiji.

In 1882, Bishop John Selwyn of Melanesia came and ordained Mr T Poole as a deacon to work in Suva and Rewa to assist Mr Floyd. He also formally established the 'Melanesian Mission' in Fiji. The Diocese of Polynesia was founded in 1908 as a missionary diocese of the Church of the Province of New Zealand, with its own bishop. William Floyd, made Archdeacon of Fiji, died in 1909. In 1923 the Reverend Leonard Stanley

Kempthorne, MA, succeeded Bishop T C Twitchell as the second Bishop of the diocese.[15] So it was in Bishop Kempthorne's time that the Brothers were invited to work there. From the beginning of Anglican work in Polynesia, as in Melanesia, it was agreed that the work of other missionary bodies would be respected. It was accepted that the Methodists and Roman Catholics would work among the indigenous Fijians. The Anglican Church established 'missions' to other social groups, so within the diocese were to be found the Indian Mission (particularly on the island of Vanua Levu), the Chinese Mission and the Tongan Mission (in the neighbouring Kingdom of Tonga) as well as the Melanesian Mission. The Melanesian Mission worked among the contract labourers and their families, who were found mostly in and around the town of Suva, at Levuka on Ovalau,[16] and on Vanua Levu Island. Suva, in the south of Viti Levu island, became the capital in 1882. At Levuka, the Solomoni settled mainly at Nasoga and Wailailai and worked mostly on the wharves, loading cotton and copra on to ocean going vessels. Later, numbers of them moved to the Suva area and settled in small villages.

The 'Melanesian Mission' building, a combined school and church dedicated to St John the Baptist, was established in Suva in 1886 as a memorial to Bishop Patteson. By about 1928 the Mission was considered by the Vicar of Suva to be in serious decline. Reporting to the Diocesan Synod in 1931, the Archdeacon of Fiji, W J Hands, who had known the situation for seven years, wrote: "There are a few hundred of the original Melanesian immigrants still in Fiji and about as many of their children, most of whom are Fijian on their mother's side. Numbers of children do not appear to know to whom they really belong, and our efforts to straighten out and put upon a Christian and legal basis various irregular alliances have met with little success.... A further handicap lies in their ignorance, very few being able to read or write, and many are still ruled by primitive instincts and superstitions. Under the circumstances, we have long felt that our main hope of influencing these people is through their children." St John's, Suva, therefore, became the chief centre of the work, while at Levuka off the east coast of Viti Levu and at Lautoka in the north of the island work was undertaken by the local Vicars. Translations into Fijian of services and hymns were made, as the Melanesians mostly used Fijian to communicate, but at that time only a few could read. Between 25 and 80 of them worshipped at St John's Church in Suva.

When the Brothers arrived, they assisted the wife of the Archdeacon,

Mrs Edith Hands, who was running St John's day school. This had a roll of "30 to 50 more or less regular scholars." The pupils were found to be "equal in intelligence to the average Fijian." In 1929 a hostel for boarders was established and during 1930 thirteen boys between the ages of 9 and 15 were accommodated there. The Brothers had charge of the hostel, taught in the school and worked in the 'Melanesian' villages.[17] Brother Dudley Bale wrote: "We worked with Archdeacon Hands for all the Melanesians there in Fiji. The Melanesians there were good friends and we were happy with our one-talks there. We went round many villages preaching the Word of God. The Melanesians learned good English in the school."[18] The transport in and around Suva was very difficult, so the Brothers usually walked through the bush each week to visit and conduct about five village services, walking eight to ten miles in all. There were 17 'Melanesian' villages around Suva, "many being several miles from a main road, accessible only by tortuous footpaths, which are difficult going at the best."

St John's Melanesian Church was used for school as well, with the sanctuary being curtained off during school days. The Brothers learned Fijian and Moffat spoke it fluently. The Reverend Canon Samisoni Meke, one of the pupils then, remembered that Dudley was "a man of pleasing mind and loved to play with youngsters. Moffatt was also of the same quality, but a bit rough at times."[19] When he was sick with fever, he used to throw a spear at the children if they made a noise in school. They believed it had a poisoned tip! Later he had a kidney removed and somebody told him that his 'fashion' would change – and it did. Both of them were good at football, while Moffat was also a good carver and made a cross inlaid with shell. They taught in the school from Monday to Friday and were free on Saturdays to prepare for Sunday services. After school they took part in games and sports or worked in the food gardens. Moffat was very interested in boxing and got some of the students from the Fiji Medical School to help him run a boxing club in the hostel. This was a building 30 by 20 feet with a verandah, on which the boxing was held if it was wet; otherwise, it was held under the mango tree. Some of the students who helped were from Fiji, including Aseri Manulevu and Macu Salato,[20] and some from the Solomons, including Henry Kuper and Norman Wheatley, who all became doctors, or 'native medical practitioners' (NMPs) as they were then called. Moffat was also a good fisherman and would take the schoolboys out fishing on the reef. He showed them how to make lime from coral and change the colour of their hair with it! Every day there was an inspection of the schoolboys for scabies, ringworm and lice. Those who were found to have these were scrubbed by the Brothers with carbolic soap.[21] They visited Lautoka and the Vicar, the Reverend A Stackhouse, committed George Vaniqa into their care. He later trained at the Methodist Centre, Davuilevu, and they visited him there.

When they left for the Solomons in 1932, they travelled first to New Zealand on the old *Mariposa*[22], where they were met by Dr Fox, who showed them round Auckland. They had with them a boy of 15 who had finished his studies at St John's School and was hoping to go to Pawa Senior School in the Solomons and then join the Brotherhood. After gaining experience in teaching, he expected to return to Fiji and minister to his own people. He was a Fijian who had been adopted by a Solomoni from Caubati village and was called Melicio Batidua.[23] They were to travel back to the Solomons on a new mission ship, the sixth in the line of those called the *Southern Cross*. She had reached Auckland in mid-October and, after being blessed by the Archbishop, left with the Brothers and their young companion, Melicio, two weeks later. At 3.17 a.m. on October 31 she ran on a reef at the island of Aneityum in the southern New Hebrides, began to break up and soon sank. The two Brothers were able to swim ashore with a rope. However, Melicio, who was seasick, was washed overboard by a wave and was saved by Brother Moffat, who dived after him. Otherwise he would probably have drowned. All on board reached shore safely. The captain, mate and second mate were assisted by a trader who sent them with two of his 'boys' to Malekula, from where they were able to send a wireless message before proceeding to Vila, the capital. The Brothers were picked up by a ship from Sydney, which took them also to Vila. They stayed two weeks there while a court case was heard, but Captain Stanton won the case. The Brothers then travelled on a French ship from Vila to Sydney; they were the only black people among the eighteen men on board.

Walter Hubert Baddeley, MC, DSO, a distinguished soldier in the First World War, had been chosen as the seventh Bishop of Melanesia after Bishop Frederick Merivale Molyneux had resigned. He was consecrated in St Mary's, Auckland, on St Andrew's Day, 1932. He had come out from England to take up the post after doing parish work in Yorkshire. The Brothers were able to travel back with him to the Solomons on the *Mataramu* and he left them at Tulagi, then the capital, off Gela Island (Florida). This introduction to the Melanesian Brotherhood must have impressed him, for Fox later wrote: "The Bishop was deeply missionary-hearted. This he showed especially in the keen interest he took in the Melanesian Brotherhood.... It had seemed rather to wither, but under his inspiration it flourished and grew from 20 to 150 Brothers."[24] He was to become particularly concerned with the work in New Britain, which had become the northernmost area of the Diocese of Melanesia in 1925, and where he soon established priests and Brothers. However, his concern for the 'Melanesian' community in Fiji continued. He sent Brother Dudley Bale to Siota to train for the priesthood. Melicio went to Pawa School, but died of malaria on July 22, 1933, "deeply regretted by his fellow students and all who knew him."[25] There was no malaria in Fiji.

Brother Moffat returned to Fiji, arriving with Brother Alfred Penny Lobu,[26] on September 4, 1933. The Reverend R F Geddes, Vicar of Holy Trinity Pro-Cathedral in Suva and Vicar-General of the Diocese reported in the *Church Gazette* in November 1933: "We had a splendid service in St John's on the Sunday after the Brothers arrived, when the church was well filled with Melanesians from the distant villages. There was a special offering towards the travelling expenses of the Brothers, which came to the very generous amount of £16." Brother Moffat was appointed as Assistant Teacher in St John's School and went out to the villages on Sundays after the 'early communion' at 7.30 a.m. Usually one Brother went to the Newtown (Flagstaff) area, the other to the Tamavuaiwai area.

Brother Alfred had been born about 1900 and had trained at Norfolk Island. He was older than the other Brothers and was very intelligent. He spoke English well, but was slow at learning Fijian. He had learned to play the organ either on Norfolk Island or in New Zealand – perhaps in both places – and played an old 'paddle' organ in St John's Church for Evensong, as well as playing the organ sometimes in Holy Trinity Pro-Cathedral, which was attended every Sunday by the Melanesian boys. He was a skilled soccer player and carpenter. He could also shoot mangoes off the tree with his bow and arrows and would then give them to the boys. He was very kind and the people appreciated the loving attitude he showed to everybody. He spent weekends in the villages of Caubati, Laqere, Tamavuaiwai and Tacirua, taking prayers on Friday evening, Saturday evening (after house visiting), and Sunday morning, before returning to Suva in the afternoon.[27] There was great sorrow when, after a year's work, he was taken ill with filarial fever followed by two strokes and died at Christmas time, 1934. He was buried in the old Suva cemetery at Lovonilase. He had been married and had joined the Brotherhood after the death of his wife, and he left behind him a daughter and another child in the Solomons. Archdeacon Harris wrote to the staff of the Melanesian Mission: "Everything possible was done for him by the hospital authorities, who seemed as anxious as we were that he should recover .... His loss is a grievous one for he is a very beautiful Christian character and his influence among the Solomon people here has been wonderful."[28]

Brother Moffat also suffered from illness, was admitted to hospital in Suva and had two operations, but he carried on the work. In 1938 there were boys in the hostel from Caubati (5 miles from Suva), Laqere (7 miles), Tamavuaiwai (3 miles), Navua (25 miles away, near Deuba), Navutu (near Lautoka on the north coast) and Wailailai (near Levuka). There were also boys who travelled in daily from Vunidilo (2 miles from Suva and about a mile from the Colonial War Memorial Hospital), Flagstaff, Tamavuaiwai, Kalekana, Laqere and Caubati. These were usually older boys, who were able to walk to school.[29] Pupils from that period included Sakiasi Waqanivavalagi, later a minister in the cabinet of Ratu Sir Kamisese Mara, Father Luke Oli and Ratu Kini Viliami, who became a sergeant in the army.[30] John Qarani went on to Queen Victoria School, originally founded for the sons of Fijian chiefs, and then to Medical School, but he did not complete his course. The opportunities given to Melanesian and part-Melanesian boys, therefore, gradually transformed the prospects for the community and helped to integrate them into the life of the country.

In 1936 Brother Moffat returned to the Solomons. While there, he met a visiting New Zealand journalist, Eric Ramsden, who was impressed to meet "men of the stamp of Moffatt, his colleagues Ini and Henry (and others of 'The Brothers' bank of workers)." He considered that "the native clergy are extending the sphere of British influence in the Pacific" – although that was certainly not one of the aims of the Brotherhood, and was his personal opinion. He compared those he met with outstanding Maori in New Zealand and commented: "One is so accustomed to the more publicised cultural accomplishments of the Polynesians that I must admit it came as a shock to meet an educated Melanesian." He described Moffat by writing: "I have known many Maoris darker than Moffatt in complexion. In appearance he looks less than his thirty years. In stature, like many of his countrymen, he is small. But his head is well-modelled, his brow wide and ample, and his expression keen and intelligent. In Moffat's accent there are definite traces of the Oxonian English accent of his teachers. His vowels, for instance, are always clearly enunciated. There is nothing slipshod in his speech. It is a joy to hear him say 'year'!"[31]

Moffat brought back with him to Fiji Brother Patteson Gatu, a dark, wiry and active Brother from the Weathercoast, the southern coast of Guadalcanal, which faces the prevailing wind. He was a very good teacher and a strict disciplinarian, in and out of class. His favourite punishment was a flick on the head with a finger held back by a finger of the other hand![32] The people noted that this Brother was named after the 'Bishop who was killed in the Solomons'. The Brothers continued the evangelisation by Anglicans among the Melanesians. If they had not come, most of them would probably have become Roman Catholics or Methodists. As it was, people originally from Guadalcanal, who named their village Kalekana to remind them of their home island, had indeed become Methodists, as had those at Tacirua, while most of those from the New Hebrides, settled at Manikoso near Laqere, had become Roman Catholics.

After three years the Brothers returned to the Solomons and took with them another pupil from St John's School, Malakai Umai. He too hoped eventually to join the Brotherhood. He was also known as Vavunua and came from Veiwakau, between Newtown and Laqere.[33] He was back in Fiji within a year because of malaria, but his excuse for returning so quickly was that his father wanted him to come back – although his father could not write.[34] He later went to Vatukoula, the site of a gold mine, and worked as a Lay Reader among the Solomoni people there. He died at Naviavia, where he worked as a Reader, about 1965, and was buried by Luke Oli, who was still a Lay Reader[35] and not yet ordained. Luke Oli, Tome Enikosuna and Samisoni Meke (later a Canon) all went on to Queen Victoria School from St John's and later trained at the Methodist Teachers' Training Institution at Davuilevu near Suva. Others followed their example later. For the three Provinces on Vanua Levu, the second most important island in the Fiji Group, there was only one Provincial High School, but this was restricted to Fijians, so 'Melanesians' had to get High School education elsewhere.

In 1934 the notice in the *Church Gazette* of August referred to 'the Church of St John the Baptist (Mission to Solomon Islanders), Ellery Street, Suva.' By then the Melanesians who had become Anglicans were nearly all of Solomon Island origin or descent and so increasingly became known in Fijian as Solomoni. The services on Sunday at St John's were: 9.30 a.m. Morning Prayer, 4 p.m. Evening Prayer, 2nd Sunday in the month Holy Communion. Evensong in the Melanesian villages, however, was usually conducted by the Brothers at 2 p.m., after they had taken a morning service in another village at 10 a.m. The reason for the early afternoon service was because they had to be home before dark – at that time, it was forbidden to walk about in the town of Suva in the dark![36] Some Melanesians had settled on Rabi Island off the west coast of Vanua Levu, but they moved to join other Melanesians on Vanua Levu.[37] There were therefore Melanesians scattered all round the Fiji Group of islands. Moffat was very concerned that conditions in many of the villages were not good, the people were widely dispersed and the children on Viti Levu had to travel into Suva for school. He had encouraged the people to build churches in their villages wherever possible, and traditional style buildings (Fijian *bure*) had been erected in Caubati, Wainimarama (Nasinu) and Wairua near Tamavuaiwai.[38] Many of the people had been confirmed, but Moffat was not satisfied. He had the idea of bringing the people closer together in a Melanesian settlement, where they could get education for their children and be closer to Suva. He spoke about his scheme on the radio. He got together the village chiefs (the *turaga-ni-koro*, chosen by the people) from Tamavua-i-wai, Flagstaff, Kalekana, Caubati, Laqere, Navua and Navutu. They took their suggestions to the Bishop after they had contacted the Melanesian *turanga buli*(district headmen) and had met together a number of times. They had decided to meet regularly, usually once a month, and started collecting subscriptions from every village to establish a school and church, after a place for the settlement had been found.[39] Eventually the Government allowed the 'Melanesian Mission' to rent 254 acres of good land near Suva from the native owners at 3 shillings per acre. St John's Church and school were moved to the new site. It was called 'Wailoku' after the river there, meaning 'to play with water', as in the Tamavua valley two branches of a stream meet. The people were able to have two acres for each family, on which they could build a home and plant a garden.[40] The establishment of the settlement led to the Melanesians on Vanua Levu asking that something similar be done for them. Friends of Archdeacon Floyd had left property to 'the Bishop of Fiji', possibly expecting him to eventually fulfil that rôle. One of these estates was made available for the settlement of the Solomoni people, the settlers paying rent to the trustees in accordance with the terms of the trust deed.[41] The Fiji Government went even further with the 'settlement' idea. It established a settlement for Fijians, mostly from the outer islands, who had come to work in Suva. But there they had to pay only for rubbish collection, not being required to pay rent or rates.[42]

Also the Western Pacific High Commission settled the Banaban people from the mined-out phosphate island of Banaba or Ocean Island, near the Gilbert Islands, on Rabi Island.

The settlement at Wailoku was named after John Coleridge Patteson, the martyred Bishop of Melanesia. It was about six miles from Suva and many of the Melanesian community eventually moved there. Brother Moffat returned once more to the Solomons with training for ordination now a possibility, and went to the 'Native Theological College' at Maka, Malaita. When he returned in 1940 it was to Wailoku, where the Reverend C Stanley Bull had been appointed superintendent.[43] He was helped by his wife Lucy, who soon became ill and died. In her memory was built the Lucy Bull Hospital to serve the Melanesian community there. Fr Bull had been Vicar of Lautoku from 1936 to 1939 and after leave he was asked by Bishop Kempthorne to establish the new settlement. Brother Moffat was with him from the beginning. He was then the only Brother in Fiji. Fr Bull continued Moffat's training for Holy Orders and he was made a deacon in Suva Pro-Cathedral at Epiphany, 1941 and Fr Bull preached.[44] He was the first Melanesian to be ordained in the Diocese of Polynesia. Two years later he was ordained priest by Bishop Kempthorne – the first indigenous priest in the diocese - but later there were other Melanesians, as well as Fijians, Indians, Tongans, Samoans and some white people, ordained in the diocese to serve its many communities. Other former Brothers were later ordained in different parts of the Pacific as well, thus adding many to the indigenous priesthood of the Anglican Church.

Moffat left the Brotherhood and married Sereana, a part-Fijian, part-Solomoni girl, at Wailoku, and they had one child, John Qaramo, who eventually decided to go back to the Solomons. It was Moffat's wish one day to return to the Solomons, but the Pacific War prevented it. He went to Vanua Levu and other islands during his many touring visits to scattered Melanesian families. Maika Mua, from Kwara'ae, Malaita, in the Solomons, had settled at Naisoño on Ovalau Island and helped to build up the Church of the Holy Redeemer at Levuka on that island. Four families from that area then moved across to Vanua Levu and the men went to work at Matadamu. Maika married a woman called Sera from Wainunu and was allowed four acres of land by her relatives. Later the other families moved there also. It became the village of Nubu-ni-kadamu ('Pool of the red fish') and became an Anglican village after Fr Maurice Basden visited it.

Maika's grandson, Ilai, was six in 1941 when Fr Moffat visited them. He took Moffat down to the creek to bathe and there he showed the small child the scar of an operation. He had had two operations and one of his kidneys had been removed. He had had to come to Nubu-ni-kadamu from Labasa by boat, as there were then no roads in the area, and it had taken him two days. He had stayed in Ilai's father's house and it was due to this 'blessing' that Ilai believed he was later led to ordination.[45]

Wailoku's 'Patteson Settlement' was not fully operational until 1941, because of the war and its effect on Suva. Five hundred Melanesians from different islands and backgrounds then began to move in. Fr Bull wrote: "Moffatt was a tower of strength to me for without him the task of getting the various ethnic groups assembled would have been most difficult.... Moffatt was indeed a 'fine' man. I would perhaps describe him as a saintly man. I thank God for every remembrance of him."[46] At Wailoku he was more concerned with his priestly, pastoral work than with teaching in the school.[47] Sadly, it was not to be for long. He died on the second anniversary of his ordination to the priesthood, of pneumonia, at the end of one of his tours in the wet season.[48] Canon Meke wrote: "Fr Moffatt's sudden death was a shock to me at Wailoku."[49] Thus his work was cut short, but a few years later Fr Manoah Tepa from Santa Ysabel, the home island of both Brothers Moffat and Dudley, arrived with his wife Nora and a stepson Lazarus. He was then a deacon and had come to help at Wailoku for a while.

John Stanley Qaromo (also spelt Garomu), Moffat's son, went to school first at Wailoku; then he was sent to the Solomons for his later schooling at Maravovo and the Government Secondary School, King George VI. He returned to Fiji to study in the Derrick Technical Institute. He married a girl called Anna Moli, daughter of Nephtali from Marata, a village of people associated with Areare, Malaita and a part of the Wailoku Settlement. His mother also had come from there. He did not stay in Fiji. In 1972 he went to Honiara, the capital of the Solomons, to work in a garage. It was not till 1962 that the Brothers themselves returned to Fiji and then it was to begin a new kind of evangelistic work among rural Indian people, as well as to renew links with the Solomoni people.

Canon Meke wrote of the Brothers' earlier work among his people: "The Brothers had done a tremendous amount of work in their ministry and each time 'more were added to their number' (Acts 2:47)." Fr Dudley Bale wrote about his fellow Brothers: "Brother Moffatt and Brother Alfred.... laid down their lives for their Melanesian friends in Fiji."[50]

NOTES

1 Personal communication from Dr Fox to the author.

2 Personal communication from Dr Fox to the author.

3 Personal communication from Dr Fox to the author.

4 According to a written account by ex-Brother Daniel Sade.

5 Fox: *Kakamora*, pp. 77 onwards.

6 Sometimes spelt Moffatt, especially when he worked in Fiji.

7 Hilliard; *God's Gentlemen*, pp. 187, 230.

8 Fox: *Lord of the Southern Isles*, p. 207. In 1999, a Santa Cruz priest, Fr John Ini Lapli, was elected Governor-General of the Solomon Islands and knighted by HM Queen Elizabeth II.

9 Letter to the author from Dr Fox, September 7, 1965.

10 *Southern Cross Log*, July, 1937.

11 Personal communication by the Reverend Dudley Bale. According to Aduru Kuva: *The Solomons Community in Fiji*, (South Pacific Social Sciences Association, no date) Dudley and Moffat were students of Dr Fox at Pawa School.

12 Hilliard: *God's Gentlemen*, p. 106

13 Hilliard: *God's Gentlemen*, p. 106

14 Recruiting for Queensland began in 1863 and for Fiji in 1864. See R A Derrick: *A History of Fiji*, Pt I, Vol I (Government Press, Suva, 1963) and Aduru Kuva: *The Solomons Community in Fiji*. For Anglican work among labourers in Queensland, see David Wetherall: *Reluctant Mission: The Anglican Church in Papua New Guinea, 1891-1942* (University of Queensland Press, St Lucia, 1977.

15 Bishop Kempthorne was an Englishman with a Master of Arts degree and was a friend of the Reverend Professor Leonard Hodgson of Oxford, who supported the Polynesia Diocesan Association in England. Bishop Kempthorne was awarded the CBE for his long service in the Pacific.

16 See C W Whonsbon-Aston: *Levuka Days, or A Parson in Polynesia*, SPCK and SPG, 1936, especially chapter 4, and *Polynesia Patchwork*, p. 36.

17 See the *Church Gazette* of the Diocese of Polynesia, Synod Number (26), Suva, February 1931.

18 Personal account by Fr Dudley Bale written in Solomons Pijin, sent to the author and translated by him.

19 Personal communication by Canon Meke to the author.

20 Dr Salato was later a prominent layman in the Diocese of Polynesia.

21 A personal recollection by Fr Luke Oli and Mr George Robo, interviewed by the author.

22 According to George Vaniqa.

23 Sometimes called Melisio in references to him in certain communications.

24 Fox: *Lord of the Southern Isles*, p. 85.

25 *Church Gazette*, Diocese of Polynesia, November, 1933, p. 8.

26 Named after the Reverend Alfred Penny, who had worked on Gela (Nggela), Solomon Islands

27 Personal communication to the author by Fr Luke Oli and Mr George Robo.

28 *Southern Cross Log*, April, 1936.

29 Violet J Taylor wrote in the *Church Gazette* of August, 1934: "The rain makes the tracks ….almost impassable in bad weather, so that our daily attendance is greatly affected."

30 Information provided by Fr Luke Oli and Mr George Robo.

31 *Southern Cross Log*, April, 1936.

32 Information provided by Fr Luke Oli and Mr George Robo. According to George Vaniqa, Brother Patteson was once arrested in Suva on his way to Tamavua-i-wai, as he was wearing only his 'underwear' - although he was carrying a Bible! There were stricter dress codes in Fiji than in the Solomons!

33 According to Fr Luke Oli and Mr G Robo.

34 According to Canon S Meke.

35 Information provided by Fr Luke Oli. Tome Enikosuna became teacher at the school for Melanesians at Natoavatu settlement, near Savusavu, Vanua Levu.

36 Personal communication to the author by a Melanesian in Fiji.
37 Rabi Island was later occupied by the Banabans from Banaba (Ocean Island), once HQ of the Gilbert and Ellice Islands colony, as their home island was mined for phosphate by the British Phosphate Commissioners. The people were moved by the British colonial administration.
38 Information from a Melanesian informant interviewed by the author (name unknown).
39 ditto.
40 Whonsbon-Aston: *Polynesia Patchwork*, pp. 46-47. The first service there was in April, 1941 and the settlement formally opened in August, 1942.
41 ditto.
42 According to Fr Luke Oli and Mr George Robo.
43 The Reverend C S Bull, ThL, FRGS, JP, later worked on Gela, Solomon Islands. He wrote about Wailoku in *Ebony Exiles* (printed privately).
44 According to *Southern Cross Log*, July, 1940, it was earlier, in St John's Church, in the presence of the Governor of Fiji and many Solomon Island people!
45 Personal communication by Fr Ilai to the author.
46 From a letter to the author dated February 18, 1971.
47 According to Fr Bull, he also tried to introduce betel-nut because he was concerned about the over-consumption of kava (*yanggona*), the traditional drink made from the roots of a plant, *Piper methysticum.* Kava is drunk in Vanuatu, but Solomon Islanders in their homeland do not use it.
48 Whonsbon-Aston: *Polynesia Patchwork*, p. 47.
49 Personal communication to the author.
50 Both Canon Meke and Fr Dudley Bale recorded their opinions in writing for this history. When the South Pacific Social Sciences Association published Aduru Kuva's small book: *The Solomons Community in Fiji* in the 1970s, it was estimated that there were then about 8,000 people descended from the indentured Solomon Islanders who came to work in Fiji.

CHAPTER SIX

Sisters of the Cross at Siota, Gela, about 1933
T. Anne. Sr.Madeleine T. Marie
Sr. Gwen M. Margaret Sr. Veronica
T. Ruth T. Mary Magdalen T. Nesta
('T' stands for 'Taina', used as a title for the native Sisters.)

Bishop Baddeley with Brothers at Tabalia,
Bro. Ini being second from the left.

St. Andrew's – Sikaiana.

Sikaiana children.

Sikaiana: May 1936.

A group of people from Sikaiana (Stewart Islands).

Harry Bullen, Secretary of the Melanesian Mission based in Auckland, New Zealand, with a Sikaiana girl.

CHAPTER SIX

SIKAIANA, SOLOMON ISLANDS TO PENTECOST, NEW HEBRIDES

The people of Sikaiana, an atoll about 60 miles north-east of the island of Malaita in the Solomon Islands, are Polynesian and originally worshipped the same gods as the Polynesian people of other islands like Lord Howe (Ontong Java) and Nukumanu[1] to the north-west. These two larger atolls are separated by the border between the country of Solomon Islands and the North Solomons Province of Papua New Guinea. By comparison, Sikaiana is much smaller and more isolated, having a total area of less than two square kilometres. It is about six miles from one end to the other and four miles wide at its widest point. Sikaiana island itself, built up from a large extinct volcano, is on the east side, while there are three raised islets on its west side, Matuiloto, Tehaolei and Matuavi.[2] They can be reached by canoe, or, at low tide, by about an hour's walk. There the people can fish, cut copra, kill birds to eat, camp for a few days or go to live.[3]

In their traditional religion, there was a special time to go and worship the statues in the large '*tabu* house'.[4] Everybody had a conch shell to blow inside this house, and when they had all come inside, the chief, who also acted as priest, addressed the people in their own language before speaking in a special language to the gods. Then everybody blew the conch shells. After the prayer, the chief moved his chair outside. This chair was a special one, made out of one piece of wood with four legs. He then sat down and spoke to the people, with the number two chief beside him, about the feast which was about to take place. There was no 'play' associated with such a feast at that time.

About 1926 a Scottish trader, Mr Buchanan,[5] arrived at Sikaiana with his first wife, a 'half caste' from Papua New Guinea called Maggie. They lived there till after the Brothers arrived and they destroyed the god the people mainly worshipped. So the islanders turned to their ancestors who were buried there and worshipped them instead, especially their 'great-great-grandfather'. In 1927 a Roman Catholic Dutchman arrived. The people did not agree with him and he went back to Fiji with a wife from the island.[6] Another trader called Mr Beaver had married a Polynesian woman from Tokelau and they came to Sikaiana and set up a store where people could buy trade goods. He would buy copra from the people and take it down to Australia each year and come back with cargo for the island.

One year, however, the ship and all in her were lost in a storm and Taupule, Mr Beaver's widow, married a Sikaiana man. She bore a number of children, including Caroline Vovo, who later became the mother of Alan Piva, the first Christian priest from Sikaiana.

One day, Taupule spoke to Semalu, the headman, and his son, Tuana, and said: "I want you to find a missionary who will teach you and our people in the truth." However, nothing happened until Tuana succeeded his father as headman.[7] By then, some young men from Sikaiana had become members of the crew of the British Resident Commissioner's ship, the *Ranandi.* This was based at Tulagi on Gela[8] (Florida) Island, then the capital of the British Solomon Islands Protectorate. Tuana and his people had begun to wonder if there was any mission that could help them. He contacted the Sikaiana men at Tulagi and asked them to look around and see which of the missions could come and assist them – the Melanesian Mission (Anglican), the Roman Catholics, or the Seventh Day Adventists. Gilbert Teilapiti and Eheo, in particular, were asked to make enquiries there and report back. The mission ship, *Southern Cross V*, arrived about that time at Tulagi. It was 1927 and on board were Bishop Steward, Assistant Bishop Molyneux and Brother Ini Kopuria. Gilbert went to the two Bishops and asked them whether it would be possible to put a teacher on the island of Sikaiana and they agreed that it would. There were then about 300 people on the island.[9]

The *Southern Cross* used to call at the island every six months and on its next visit Bishop Steward asked various questions,[10] including one about whether they needed some people to come and stay with them and teach them about the Christian way of life. They said they did and they wanted those people to come quickly as their 'devils' were trying to destroy some of them. They believed that these 'devils' had the power to eat people's hearts, or to say words which would destroy people, pigs, dogs, fowls or other creatures. The Bishop promised them that after he had been to New Zealand, the ship would return with some missionaries.

On December 4, 1928, Bishop Molyneux had received the profession as Brothers of Patrick Aubugotu,[11] Barnabas Babau and Daniel Sade, who had been Head Boy at Pawa School when Dr Fox was headmaster. They first went to Aola Household on Guadalcanal where Cecil Lujagathaga, one of the original Brothers, was Elder Brother. In July 1929 Brother Daniel was called back to Tabalia by Brother Ini and in November he went with him and Novice Valentine Pitivotu[12] to Sikaiana, arriving on November

22.[13] The Brothers had to spend their first night in the Court House and on Sunday, November 24, they began to take prayers there. The place was always full for Morning and Evening Prayer. They also started a school in the Court House for the children, which some adults also attended. At first they stayed with Tuana who was both the traditional chief and also Government Headman. At the end of six months, they moved into a house which the people had constructed for them. The men had erected the posts and the women had woven dry coconut leaves which had fallen from the trees. The land was given by Tuana to the Mission and it became the site for the priest's house later on. The people provided them with bedding, tobacco and other things they needed, and each household took it in turn to feed them, as they had no garden.[14] They were all together in one village, but not everyone accepted them. They found that the people were divided about whether they wanted Christianity or not. However, with the support they received, they were able to build a church which was in use for prayer by Christmas. Before Christmas, Brother Ini asked those who had been supportive of the Brothers, if they would be willing to prepare a Christmas feast. However, when those who opposed them heard about it, they said: "We the heathen people are going to confound your Church which has just come. This is what we are going to do. We shall put away all our old spirits and get new ones which are more powerful, and we shall ask them to pour rain on you when you sit down to have your Christmas feast." When the Brothers heard this, they asked the people to prepare a lot of food, and they produced enough to fill one small house. They then started their celebrations on Christmas Day with a feast at about 6 p.m. and continued for a week. During the first feast a big cloud came up and the 'heathen' who were standing by laughed. Ini told the people not to worry, but to put the remaining food in the house. The 'heathen' called on their gods to bring rain down, but no rain came.[15] They felt very ashamed and said they would try again at Easter (but the result then was the same!), so they left for the islets the day after Christmas.

About Christmas 1929, Naphtali Evio, father of Veronica Teutalei (the future wife of Leslie Piva, son of Alan Piva) burned down the '*tabu* house'. By New Year 1930, the three people who had rejected Christianity had gone to the other end of Sikaiana, known as Muliakau. Kaetu and Teika, a fisherman,[16] continued to worship their 'devils' or spirits on Tehaolei, and Pakik on Matuiloto. According to Mrs Bennett, formerly Sister Ruth of the Sisters of the Cross (born on the island and then a teenager), one day in April 1930, a man named Vatia became drunk on the local fermented coconut drink or toddy, called *kaleve pulau.* He then took a conch shell in one hand and a knife in the other, together with a bar used for spearing pigs, and went down the road blowing the shell and calling out constantly: "Where is Tasiu Ini? I am going to kill him with this knife." He was cross because the Church had stopped them drinking toddy, had destroyed all their heathen gods, and had forbidden 'immorality'. Ini had already gone to bed, so the man stood at the door of the house and called for him. Brother Ini replied, "I am here." Vatia said: "We do not like you to stay here. You have brought your god here to spoil our gods." But he did not go in. Instead, he turned round and went back. Ini had in fact made various rules for the people, to establish a new way of life on Christian lines.He had said that food should be prepared on Saturdays and eaten cold on Sundays, so that little work was required on the Lord's Day, and that there should be no fishing on Sundays till after midnight. This established Sunday as a different day from the rest of the week.

When the people were freed from what they considered 'heathen' influences, the Brothers were able to run a school which was held every day after morning prayers. When breakfast was over, there were three classes for the men and then another three classes for the women. There was then a break until 3.30 p.m., when there was a class for the children until 4.30 p.m. At 5.30 p.m. they had evening prayers and at 7 p.m. there was another hour's class for the children. The children were very happy to be with the Brothers, but they also respected them very much. They would not go inside the Brothers' house or make a noise nearby.

In May 1930, the *Southern Cross V* arrived with Father Richard C Rudgard on board, and Brother Ini asked him if Patrick Kupa of Guadalcanal could help with the school. It was the influence of the Brothers which led the people to agree to their children leaving the island for further schooling. Previously they had been unwilling for people to leave the island, except for the few who had gone to Tulagi. Ini Kopuria thought about who should go. As a result, Timothy Tenai, Caspar Kaipoia, Henry Halepouli and John Lautalo went to Pawa School in the Eastern Solomons, while Alan Piva, Comins Katava, George Kaitemalu, Patrick Paisu, Silas Vailama and Daniel Enui went to Veranaaso, near Maravovo village on Guadalcanal (later called Maravovo School). Brother Ini prepared a small edition of a *Book of Prayer and Praise* in the Sikaiana language, which was printed at the Mission Press.[17]

By the middle of 1930 the whole of the population of Sikaiana, except for seven who had doubts,[18] had become Christian. This was seen as one of the most significant fruits of the early ministry of the Brothers, and especially of Brother Ini and Brother Daniel Sade. Among those baptised were two girls, Ann and her cousin Marie. Before her baptism, Ann Takaua, then about 18, had asked Brother Ini: “Are there Sisters in the Mission?” He told her that two Sisters had just arrived from England, Margaret and Gwen, who had come to establish the Community of the Sisters of the Cross. Ann said: “That’s what I want.” Amazingly, her mother supported her, and about two years later she and Marie went to test their vocation, first at Siota and then at Buñana Island on Gela. Another five girls, all about 15 or 16, went later to Buñana, including Marietta Teurulata, who eventually became Sister Nesta,[19] and others who became Sister Mary Magdalene and Sister Ruth (later Mrs Bennett). Nesta had first heard of Sisters when she was dancing naked around the fire and a European trader who was visiting the island had spoken about the SMSM (Roman Catholic Missionary Sisters of the Society of Mary) in Fiji and how they cared for the lepers. When the Brothers arrived, she was delighted and said, “If there are brown Brothers, there must be brown Sisters too!”[20] Ruth Poitini, who became Sister Ruth, daughter of William Mouna, the brother of Gilbert, was about thirteen when the Brothers arrived.

The people wanted the Brothers because they believed that their Christian God was stronger than their island gods. They were also impressed by the spiritual power or *mana* which the Brothers seemed to have. This often helped them in their work of evangelisation. The Brothers had prayed for the second wife of William Mouna, Hannah Emuko, who was apparently barren, and she had given birth to a child, Samuel. Those who were sick had been healed after the Brothers had prayed for them. All this confirmed the people’s faith and showed them that there was a real spiritual reason for the acceptance of Christianity. The Brothers themselves brought the Gospel, simple teaching and a Christian way of life. However, they were not strict with the people concerning their traditional customs, as some Christian Missions were. They waited for them to decide what they wanted to do away with and when they really wanted to become ‘true Christians’. They taught the people clearly, but did not attempt to use the Mota language of the Banks Islands, which was then used generally throughout the Mission and the Brotherhood, but instead, used Pidgin or the local language. In their own Household, the Brotherhood rules were carefully observed, and the people admired the way they set a good example. They prepared the people for Baptism, Confirmation and Holy Communion, so that they could report to the Bishop when he came, who was ready to be baptised, or baptised and confirmed. Those who opposed the Brothers said they believed that they were trying to destroy them all; but their opposition came to nothing, except that it brought pain for themselves. The people indeed developed a great respect for the Brothers and after prayer, or at other times, would call them to come and have a meal or a smoke. The Brothers themselves were aware of the importance of stressing the spiritual reasons for their being there. When some Brothers had asked other Solomon Islanders why they wanted to become Anglicans, rather than join another Church, they had been told: "The Melanesian Mission has the largest ship and gives out the most tobacco and soap, and therefore it must have the most, and be the most important Church!"[21] However, the people of Sikaiana had, unlike Lord Howe Atoll, experienced the work of no other Church. They appear to have become Anglican Christians because they felt the 'devils' they worshipped had been trying to destroy them. They therefore needed the Brothers to be with them to drive out their 'devils', so that they could receive power from the God whom the Brothers believed in, worshipped and preached.

In October 1930, the *Southern Cross* arrived to take four of the Brotherhood workers to the Brothers' meeting at Tabalia, which would include the observance of the Feast of St Simon and St Jude, when the Brothers renewed their vows. After the meeting, Brother Ini went back to Sikaiana with three Brothers, leaving Brother Daniel Sade as Elder Brother at Tabalia with Brother Valentine, to look after the station and the four novices there. Brother Daniel taught them and also five 'teachers' from a place just opened by the Brothers.[22] Brother Henry Kafa was appointed by Bishop Molyneux in his place when Daniel accompanied the Bishop in June 1931 to Rabaul and West New Britain in the Mandated Territory of New Guinea, which was then in the Diocese of Melanesia, before returning to the Solomons and going on to the New Hebrides.

There he trained six novices who were picked up at Lolowai and taken to Qatnapni in Central Pentecost to be with Fr Simeon Langlangmele and there he established a Household.[23] Two more young men joined them there, making a total of seven from Raga, the north end of the island of Pentecost, and one from the central district of Qatnapni or Bwatnapni. Brother Daniel taught the novices for just over three months and then

Bishop Molyneux received them as Brothers when he returned in early October on the *Southern Cross.* They made their promises at Lamalanga. Brother Ben Bani was appointed Elder Brother with Brother Judah Ruruhi as his assistant. The other Brothers were John Binihi, Matthias Tabe, Harper Liñi, Leotabetabe Viradoro, Thomas Malau and Leonard Bokokon.[24]

Brother Daniel returned to Tabalia for the Brothers' meeting in October 1931, when he was appointed as Elder Brother on Sikaiana to succeed Brother Ini. He was accompanied there by Brother Percival Buri,[25] his assistant, Clement Mapolu and Valentine Pitivotu. They stayed two years,[26] as the *Southern Cross* did not come for them as expected. This was because a staff conference of the Mission personnel in 1931 had decided that as the *Southern Cross* was very expensive to run, it should be replaced with two smaller ships, one for the Solomons and one for the New Hebrides. The old *Southern Cross* had been in service since 1903 and had become known simply as *akanina* ('our ship' in the Mota language).[27] Its withdrawal meant a long wait for the Brothers, and they missed the Brothers' meeting in 1932 and received little news of other happenings in the Mission or the Brotherhood. A new ship, *Southern Cross VI*, [28] was dedicated in London in July 1932 for service in the Solomons by the Archbishop of Canterbury, Dr Cosmo Gordon Lang, but on October 31 it struck a reef on Aneityum in the Southern New Hebrides on the way to the Solomons.[29] So the next visit by Mission personnel was in June 1933 on the Burns Philp ship, the *Mitiaro.* The Brothers were surprised to find that Bishop Molyneux had had to resign in November 1931 and that their new Bishop, Walter Hubert Baddeley, was on board, accompanied by Brother Ini. With them were a Brother from Santa Cruz and the great friend of the Brotherhood, Dr Charles Fox. Much to their amazement, however, they discovered that in 1932 he had become a Brother too – the first 'white man' to join, although he considered himself to be more Melanesian than European! The Reverend Richard Rudgard had become headmaster of Pawa School in Dr Fox's place and he also was with them on board. Father Rudgard baptised forty people during the visit and the Bishop confirmed six. Ten boys were sent to Maravovo School, six girls to Buñana School and four girls eventually went to join the Sisters of the Cross as *taina* ('Sister' in the Sikaiana language). Among those confirmed were Ann Takaua and her cousin Marie. Ann's mother,[30] Notana, was baptised Zipporah and her step-father was also baptised during this visit.

When the Brothers arrived back at Tabalia in June 1933, there was a meeting of Households and it was decided to send Frank Bollen Toke to Sikaiana as catechist, with his children, but to send the Brothers to nearby Households only. Brothers Ini and Daniel, together with Dudley Bale, remained at Tabalia to be tutored on alternate days, from July to October, by Brother Charles Fox and Fr Jim Edwards (who lived with the Brothers for a year) in preparation for their ordination as deacons. That took place after the Brothers' Conference that year. All the Brothers went down to St Mary's School, Maravovo, at Veranaaso on October 31, and on November 1, the Feast of All Saints, Brothers Ini and Daniel were made deacons, along with the missionary W B (Bill) Seaton, a master at St Mary's School itself. The Gospel was sung by the new deacons in three languages, two Melanesian ones and English. At 3.30 p.m. the Brothers played the school at football and won. Then the Brothers were sent out to all the Households, after they returned to Tabalia. Daniel became Assistant Head Brother. Until 1936 there were still Brothers living on Sikaiana, replacing each other from time to time. They included Wilson Liña, Luke Labahi, Ralph Hatamae and Percival Buri, together with the novices John Mark and Patrick Kupe.[31]

One of those who went away to Pawa School, Timothy Tenai, returned to Sikaiana before the Brothers left and was trained by them to take prayers and to give some teaching to the people. He became 'head teacher' (catechist) until his death. Caspar Kaipoia and Henry Halepouli joined the Brotherhood and led the Household that 'opened' or started the work on Lord Howe Atoll. They were joined there by another Brother from Sikaiana, Philip Hakapuloto. John Lautalo, another of the boys who went to Pawa School, died there.

From the six who went to Maravovo School, Alan Piva[32] was ordained deacon in Brisbane after training there at St Francis College, and became the first priest from Sikaiana. His son, Leslie Piva, was later ordained also, after training at St Peter's College, Siota and St John's College, Auckland, New Zealand. Daniel Enui returned to Sikaiana as a teacher and became a lay member of the Diocese of Melanesia Synod. Silas Vailama became the steward of the High Commissioner of the Western Pacific in Honiara. Comins was taken sick at school and died in Tulagi Hospital in 1931. Patrick Paisu and George Kaitemalu both returned to Sikaiana after leaving school and died there.[33] By the 1970s all had changed on Sikaiana because of the coming of Christianity and the dispersal of the people.

When the Brothers left, Deacon Nelson Tegua came from Santa Ysabel[34] and Togana,[35] one of the Sikaiana men, became a catechist. While Alan

Piva was serving elsewhere, first as a deacon, then as a priest, two priests from Malaita served on Sikaiana, Fr James and Fr Henry Maabe. Fr Alan Piva eventually came back to serve his own people.[36] He had been headmaster of Maravovo School for a while. A group of Companions was started, but it did not grow, as many people left the island because of shortage of land or of work opportunities.[37] Because of a rapid increase in population after Christianisation,[38] Sikaiana settlements were established on other islands, including Santa Ysabel and Guadalcanal, and Sikaiana people worked in the post-war capital, Honiara, and at Auki on Malaita, Tulagi, Yandina in the Russell Islands, Gizo in Western District, and elsewhere in the Solomons and overseas. Daniel Maile, a policeman, and Veronica Teutalei, a teacher, went to train in England in 1963. She married Leslie Piva on his return from New Zealand.[39] She was the first Solomon Islands woman to train in the United Kingdom. John Kilatu became a doctor. There were others who became teachers, nurses and dressers, as well as those who became Brothers. Some of the women became members of the Mothers Union. Joanna Tolohi married a New Zealander, Peter Thompson, the Archdeacon of Malaita.[40] His archdeaconry included Sikaiana and Lord Howe island.

Reflecting on his work on Sikaiana, when he wrote an account of it in the 1960s,[41] Father Daniel Sade stated: "We thank God that He still continues to pour down His grace on the people of Sikaiana. Let us honestly pray for them that the seed which was planted by the Brothers among them in 1929 will continue to grow." It was significant that the Brothers' work on Sikaiana led to a number of young women entering the Community of the Sisters of the Cross. It provided a link between that community and the Brotherhood, and remained as a memory which led the Brothers to welcome other Sisterhoods many years later – the Community of the Sisters of the Church and their own parallel Sisterhood which grew out of the Companions of the Brotherhood, the Community of the Sisters of Melanesia. The Sisters of the Cross joined the Roman Catholic Church in 1950 after disagreements which Bishop Baddeley and, later, Bishop S G Caulton had had with the superior, Mother Margaret of the Cross (Margaret Wilson). She had come to the Solomons to found her own community after being a member of a community in Bombay, India. She was accompanied by another sister who had served there, Sister Gwen (Gwen Shaw).[42] They had been training the first members of an Indian sisterhood for the ancient Syrian Church of Malabar and had been invited to start a sisterhood for Melanesia after Mother Margaret had met Fr George Warren, one of the Mission priests, on a ship to England in 1925.[43] Bishop Palmer of Bombay had blessed this enterprise, not least because his father had been at school with Bishop Patteson. The Sisters had established themselves at Siota on Gela, then the headquarters of the Mission, only three months before the Brothers set off from there to Sikaiana. So the Brothers knew about them and their work.

When Ann Takaua and Marie were confirmed in 1933, the Bishop was informed that they wanted to become Sisters. On St Benedict's Day 1934 they arrived at Siota and Ann was already suffering from her first attack of malaria. There was no malaria on Sikaiana. When she recovered, there were flashes of a radiance which marked her character and which became constant towards the end of her life.[44] After their arrival, more aspirants came from Sikaiana less than a year later. Marie did not stay, but about half of those who came from other islands did. Taina Ann was professed eventually as the first 'Melanesian' sister. She was a wonderful example and inspiration to others. On Sikaiana, she had been at first forbidden to go to school by her mother and step-father. After she had wept continuously day and night, they relented. Having heard about the Sisters, she refused to get married and eventually was allowed to go and test her vocation as a Sister. This inspired other island girls who came to St Hilda's School, which was taken over and run by the Sisters from 1936 on the small island of Buñana, off the south coast of Gela. Among the Sikaiana Sisters were Nesta, Mary Magdalene, Ruth Poitini and Maria Laumua, Ruth's first cousin. Ruth and Marie were also cousins of Ann.[45] They made a great contribution to the Sisterhood, but eventually Ann died, Ruth left and married Bill Bennett (who in the 1970s ran the Solomon Islands Broadcasting Service), while Maria was a Sister for 17 years before leaving and marrying Catechist Daniel Enui.[46] Their daughter Hilda eventually married Mr Page, an Englishman, and settled in England. Hilda's mother and father had Gilbertese blood. Daniel and Maria were sent by Bishop Baddeley to serve the Sikaiana community at Maranatabu, Santa Ysabel, although before marrying Daniel was due to go abroad to train for ordination.[47]

When there were no longer any Sikaiana Sisters in the Community, the Sisters stopped using the word *Taina* and adopted the English words: Helper, Novice and Sister.

The first part of the spiritual journey which led the Sisters into the Roman

Catholic Church was when Mother Margaret was on her journey back by ship to New Zealand after visiting England, where she had addressed the Melanesian Mission Annual Meeting at Mary Sumner House in Westminster, London. The meeting had been chaired by the Archbishop of Canterbury, Dr Geoffrey Fisher, who had been surprised to discover then that Mother Margaret was distantly related to his wife.[48] A fellow passenger on the ship was the Mother General of the Roman Catholic Sisters of Mercy, who introduced her to the Roman Catholic Archbishop of Wellington, Mgr Liston, on arrival in New Zealand. As a result, she eventually became convinced that she should lead her Sisters, five Europeans and seven 'Melanesians', into the Roman Catholic Church; but as Roman Catholics, they were not allowed to remain together as a community. The Sisters who remained under vows joined different orders. Mother Margaret and Sister Petronella from Sikaiana eventually became Sisters of Mercy in New Zealand.[49] Sister Madeleine became a Carmelite in Tauranga, New Zealand. Sister Gwen went to work with the SMSM in Fiji.[50] Sister Veronica, who had written about their work at Buñana in a booklet entitled *The School Island*, (published in 1949, to mark the Centenary of the Melanesian Mission), went to work in New Zealand and became known as Sister Dismas.[51]

In 1942, Mother Margaret had gone for a period to run Selwyn School, Torgil, on the island of Aoba (Ambae) in the New Hebrides, and so there were New Hebridean Sisters in the Community. After Mother Margaret became a Roman Catholic, some of the Melanesian Sisters became Roman Catholics too and they stayed with her for a while. Then three New Hebridean Sisters, including Victoria, joined the Daughters of Mary Immaculate, the Roman Catholic native Sisterhood with its mother house at Visale, West Guadalcanal, not far from Tabalia,[52] the headquarters of the Brotherhood. They rejoiced to be able to maintain some contact with the Melanesian Brothers over the succeeding years. Also Philomena from Gela, who had been with the Sisters, married a Guadalcanal man and moved to live near Tangarare. She had been cared for by the Sisters from the age of 12. The Sisters had also cared for babies whose mothers had died, usually in childbirth.

It was the Sikaiana Sisters who had led the way in the Religious Life for Anglican women from Melanesia. Taina Ann was a peaceful, happy person, wonderful with children. However, three years or so before the Second World War reached the Solomons, she developed tuberculosis, which may have been picked up on Sikaiana. The doctor at Tulagi said she would have to leave Buñana, but he later relented when a small house by the sea was provided for her to live in on her own. Old and young visited her for "counsel and comfort and peace."[53] Her mother came to visit her and they grew closer than ever before. She loved the gramophone and listened to great church music on records, which drew crowds of listeners around her hut. She usually ended these sessions with a record of the Hallelujah Chorus. When the Japanese arrived, she and Taina Ruth were sent with Philomena to the Sikaiana settlement at Maranatabu in South Ysabel. She died about a week before the Japanese arrived there. She said to Taina Ruth: "Our Lord is coming for me today. Don't tell the people, for it is a lovely day for fishing." She then dictated a letter to Taina Ruth, which went to Mother Margaret in the New Hebrides, to whom she was also very close. She thanked God for everything, ending with thanks to the little girl Philomena for saying 'Good morning' and 'Good evening' to her every day. She then closed her eyes and died with a smile.[54] She was one of the most wonderful fruits of the Brothers' work on Sikaiana.

NOTES

1 Nukumanu or Tasman Island is one of a number of islands in Papua New Guinea, mostly outlying atolls, peopled by Polynesians, which include Taku or Mortlock Island.

2 There are also two artificial islands, Te Palena and Hakatai'atata.

3 According to David Harcombe, *Lonely Planet Guide to Solomon Islands*, 1988, there were villages on Matuiloto and Matuavi in 1988; Brother Edward Das MBH, in an account of the Brothers' work there in 1978 mentions people also going there to camp.

4 The account which follows is based on an account of the Brothers' original work on Sikaiana written by ex-Brother (Father) Daniel Sade about 1964. Supplementary information was provided by Brother Edward Das.

5 According to Brother Edward Das.

6 According to Brother Edward Das.

7 Later, Vaioma was due to become Headman, but, as he was considered unsuitable, Simeon Telakia was appointed.

8 Officially spelt Nggela, especially on later maps.

9 Fox, *Lord of the Southern Isles*, p. 210

10 According to Brother Edward Das, who gives an account of this visit.

11 Brother Patrick stayed in the Brotherhood all his life, dying on his island of Ysabel, according to Dr Fox in a personal communication to the author.

12 According to Jessie Sade, Daniel Sade's widow, interviewed by the author at Maravovo village in October, 1995. Valentine (or Valentino) was from Tabulivu, West Guadalcanal; she said that he cried when the ship left Guadalcanal, as he had been told to come, but did not want to go.

13 According to Brother Edward Das.

14 According to Brother Edward Das.

15 According to Daniel Sade, Brother Ini said to those eating, "Don't worry. After eating, put everything in the small house you have made for it, then it can rain." And so it happened!

16 His granddaughter Hilda married an Englishman, became Mrs Page and settled in England. Her father

was Daniel Enui and one of her grandfathers gave the land for the cemetery on the island.
17 See *The Response of the Melanesians to the Holy Spirit*, leaflet produced by the Melanesian Mission, London in the 1930s, undated.
18 According to Brother Edward Das.
19 Sometimes spelt *Nester.*
20 Personal communication to the author by Sister Gwen, formerly of the Sisters of the Cross.
21 According to Sister Gwen.
22 According to an account by Fr Daniel Sade in the 1970s, translated by Bishop Derek Rawcliffe from Mota. In this account Henry Kafa is referred to as Father Henry Kafa.
23 Fr Daniel Sade's account refers (in Mota) to Judah Ruruhi as 'youngest brother', probably meaning 'assistant elder brother'.
24 Some of these Brothers were later ordained as priests. Fr Ben Bani's son John was also ordained and eventually became the fourth President of the Republic of Vanuatu. Harper Liñi was not ordained but his son Walter Hadye Liñi was, and became the first Prime Minister of the Republic on its independence in 1980. Only in Vanuatu have Anglican priests held these posts, although Anglican clergy have held the post of Governor-General in New Zealand, Solomon Islands and Australia.
25 Probably the person called Vasiholo Buri by Jessie Sade in a conversation with the author in October 1995: he was from Verahue, Guadalcanal.
26 Two years and eight months, according to Fr Daniel Sade, although this does not agree with other dates given for their arrival and departure. Perhaps this represented his total time on the island.
27 See Hilliard: *God's Gentlemen*, pp. 250-251.
28 The sixth of this name.
29 See Hilliard: *God's Gentlemen*, p. 293.
30 Notana's first husband had deserted her before Ann was born, but she insisted on keeping the baby.
31 According to Brother Edward Das.
32 Alan Piva was part Micronesian, as his father's family were from Pohnpei (Ponape) in the Caroline Islands, now part of the Federated States of Micronesia.
33 Probably in the 1930s, according to Hilda Page.
34 According to Brother Edward Das.
35 Also known as Michael Tokana. It was he who gave the land for the church building and whose relative, Robert Sisilo, became Solomon Islands Ambassador and High Commissioner in Europe and the UK in the 1990s.
36 By the 1970s the resident priest had been accepted as leader of the community on Sikaiana.
37 According to Brother Edward Das.
38 See *Southern Cross Log*, April 1934.
39 Leslie and Veronica Piva and their four sons emigrated to Australia when he became ill and required kidney dialysis which was not available in Solomon Islands. He worked for the Australian Board of Missions in Victoria, then as chaplain to the Brothers in Carpentaria. The author had been his best man at their wedding, which had been held in the old All Saints Cathedral in Honiara, an American quonset building converted to a church after the Second World War. The Sikaiana settlement at Red Beach on Guadalcanal gave the author, then Vicar-General of the Diocese of Central Melanesia, a farewell feast when he left the Solomons for the New Hebrides in 1978.
40 The Thompson family moved to Australia after Fr Thompson ceased to be a Minister in the Solomon Islands Government. There he worked as a parish priest, mostly in Western Australia.
41 Written in Mota and probably translated into English by Dr Fox.
42 They arrived in 1929 in the second year of the episcopate of Bishop F M Molyneux as Diocesan Bishop (1928-1931).
43 Bishop Steward had asked him to seek for Sisters in England willing to work among women and girls in Melanesia. See the booklet *Community of the Cross*, published by the Melanesian Mission, London (no date).
44 See Sister Veronica of the Cross: *The School Island*, Melanesian Mission and SPCK, 1949, p.58
45 According to Hilda Page, Maria was also known as Muriel. Her parents were of Gilbertese (Micronesian)

descent. Ruth died about 1997.

46 Daniel contracted leprosy and spent some time at the Leper Hospital run by the Diocese at Fauabu on Malaita Island.

47 Information supplied by Hilda Page to the author.

48 Personal reminiscence of the author, who was present at the meeting.

49 Hugh Laracy: *Marists and Melanesians: A History of Catholic Missions in the Solomon Islands*, Australian National University Press, Canberra, 1976, pp. 162-3 and p. 184, note 9.

50 Interviewed by the author in Fiji in the 1980s. She later went to Lourdes Convent, Killara, New South Wales.

51 See Laracy: *Marists and Melanesians* (see note 49).

52 The Sisterhood had been founded by Bishop L Raucaz in 1932 and the first two Sisters were professed in 1935. Bishop Raucaz was Vicar Apostolic of the Vicariate of the South Solomons, which existed from 1912 to 1966. The Roman Catholic Dioceses of Honiara and Gizo were established in 1967 and later an Archdiocese with an Archbishop for the dioceses in the Solomon Islands. The professed DMI Sisters numbered twelve in 1942, but had increased in number to 82 in 1972. See Laracy: *Marists and Melanesians*, pp. 107 and 159. There were also SMSM and Dominican Sisters in the Solomon Islands.

53 See Sister Veronica: *The School Island*, p. 60.

54 Personal reminiscences of Sister Veronica (Sister Dismas in New Zealand), given to the author.

CHAPTER SEVEN

Tasiu Charles Fox and some Brothers on board ship.

CHAPTER SEVEN

ONGTONG JAVA ATOLL, SOLOMON ISLANDS

Ongtong Java or Lord Howe Atoll is the largest atoll in the Solomon Islands, and one of the largest in the Pacific. It is the northernmost island of the country, lying just south of the Equator and about 180 miles north of Santa Ysabel. It is about 40 miles long from north to south and almost as wide at its base. Its two main settlements are Luañiua[1] in the south east and Pelau in the north, at opposite ends of the atoll, and with different chiefs. Nukumanu, the nearest island, peopled with Polynesians like those of Ongtong Java, lies about 45 miles to the north-west of Pelau in Papua New Guinea. Luañiua is the larger settlement. The name Ongtong Java was given by the Dutch explorer Abel Tasman in 1643: *Untung* is Malay for luck, and apparently 'Java luck' was an expression of good fortune in those days among the Dutch. In 1791 the first European to come ashore, John Hunter, gave it the alternative name 'Lord Howe'.[2] In the 1890s, the part-American part-Samoan trader Emma Forsayth (née Coe)[3] was still based in Rabaul, East New Britain. She had married her second husband Paul Kolbe in 1893. Some of her employees went to establish a trading post at Luañiua, which lasted from about 1899 to 1907.[4] These contacts caused considerable sickness among the unprotected population.[5] There was an estimated population of 5,500 in 1907, which dropped to below 600 in 1939[6], causing the British Solomon Islands Government to close the atoll to foreigners in that year. Emma Forsayth's' interests on Ongtong Java were sold to Levers. The Germans had administered Ongtong Java from 1893, but in 1899 the British made an agreement with them to take over the island. Nuku-manu continued under the Germans with Bougainville and Buka, the most western of the chain of Solomon Islands, but Ongtong Java was included in the Western District of the British Solomon Islands Pro-tectorate, with the District Magistrate based at Gizo. It was later transferred to Malaita District.

The Anglican Church, through the Melanesian Mission, had started work with Solomon Islanders in 1850, after the earlier Roman Catholic mission had been withdrawn temporarily. The Roman Catholics, whose Bishop had been killed on Santa Ysabel soon after they arrived in 1845, had held out on Makira (San Cristoval) till 1847. After the establishment of the British Protectorate in part of the Solomons in 1893, they returned in 1898. The policy of C M Woodford, the Resident Commissioner from

1896, was basically to encourage the Missions, in the hope that they would help to pacify the local people. Mr Woodford in fact welcomed missions because of their 'civilising' influence, and wanted them to start work all over the Protectorate. The Melanesian Mission had by then scarcely touched the Western Solomons and outlying places like Ongtong Java. When the district missionary on Santa Ysabel, the Reverend Dr Henry Welchman, was approached by Woodford concerning mission work on Ongtong Java, he visited the atoll with him, but later declined the invitation to start work there, through lack of resources.[7] The Roman Catholics were concentrated in the Central Solomons and around Gizo. The Methodists, who were particularly numerous in Tonga and Fiji, and also had a large following in Samoa, were concerned to emulate the Congregationalists (LMS), who had initiated missionary work in the Torres Straits Islands and Papua in 1871.

The Reverend Dr George Brown, outstanding promoter of Australian Methodist Missions overseas, established the Methodist Mission – led by the Reverend J F Goldie with the help of European and Pacific Islander missionaries – in the Western Solomons in 1902. He was invited by Woodford to visit Ongtong Java, and Woodford even made the government ship available for him to use.[8] Brown was enthusiastic about starting mission work there, noting that the language was "very closely allied to the Tongan, Samoan and Savage [Niue] Islands." He also noted, "The chiefs here have great power, much as the old Fijian chiefs used to have."[9] J F Goldie visited in 1904, and in 1906 he tried to station Semisi Nau, a Tongan catechist, and Isikeli Polonga, a Samoan, and their families at Luañiua. Because of the opposition there, however, the families returned to the Western Solomons, leaving the two Pacific Islands men to fend for themselves, living for months in a boat off the beach! After 97 days, they moved to Pelau, and were welcomed. Eventually, after the intervention of the district magistrate from Gizo, Western Solomons, Semisi Nau was allowed ashore at Luañiua. Although 'flu may have originally been introduced by the visit of the mission ship in 1906, the chiefs and people may have seen the sickness as having been caused not by that visit but by their rejection of Semisi, and so have agreed to allow him ashore. He himself, however, became sick ashore, and was treated with local remedies.

Later, the introduction of a European Methodist probationary minister from Australia, Ernest Shackell, sent to replace the Polynesian missionaries, led to confrontation between him and the chiefs and people, and to his withdrawal. Shackell was working on the atoll from February 1909 until December 1910, but he claimed that the traders had encouraged King Keapea, the priests and some of the people, to ask for him to be removed.[10] This was because he had struck two men, but, he claimed, *they* had been hitting girls, children and a woman. He had also struck with an axe the "principal figure in the temple, to show that the god had no power." Dr Brown was sent to investigate as commissioner of the Board of Methodist Overseas Missions, and it was decided to send Semisi back to Ongtong Java. Keapea offered a bribe to Mr Woodford to prevent Semisi returning, although he had told Dr Brown he could come back on certain conditions. Semisi did return eventually in July 1911 with other 'teachers' and Koke, the chief at Pelau, was baptised and given the name Uzziah. The mission was therefore widely accepted at Pelau, but, because of increased sickness, Keapea in Luañiua was again antagonistic. After a visit to Tonga, Semisi was once again stationed at Luañiua, but those who had become Christians continued to be ill-treated there. The *Missionary Review* in February, 1915 printed a photograph of a "group of Lord Howe natives, who have suffered persecution for their faith."[11]

While Semisi was in Tonga, his colleague Polonga had taken charge at Luañiua, but had returned to Pelau after he too had encountered opposition. J C Barley, district officer at Gizo from 1912 to 1915, reported that Polonga "was from all accounts a veritable firebrand" and that "he was evidently strongly imbued with the intolerant persecuting spirit of an earlier era of Christianity."[12] However, his work at Pelau was so accepted there that the people refused "to supply an ounce of copra to one opponent of the *lotu*, because of his opposition, and because he had a hand in getting the white missionaries and teachers removed."[13] At Luañiua, however, the traders were able to buy copra, although Keapea wanted only Mr Gillan of Lever's Pacific Plantations to be able to do so – probably the very man that the people of Pelau were objecting to! Polonga left the Solomons in 1914 and later went with his wife to the Methodist Papuan Islands District, where they worked for some years. The Acting Resident Commissioner, F J Barnett, when he visited in 1916 was able to get Keapea to agree to the observance of Sunday 'as a day of rest' and he instructed Semisi that "he must not interfere .... if his followers wish to follow out their tribal customs." Barnett reported this to the High Commissioner for the Western Pacific.[14]

With the death of Keapea, Semisi still faced troubles until a new chief was appointed. In August 1915 Barley reported from Luañiua that the majority there "still adhere to the old heathen ideas and customs .... with which the King's authority is inextricably bound up."[15] His death, however, meant there was less control of some troublemakers. Two opposing factions put forward individuals to succeed Keapea. Barley visited Luañiua in May 1917 and appointed Makaike, who was sympathetic to the Mission but tolerant towards traditional customs. From 1915 to 1916, Barley had special responsibility for Ongtong Java as its district officer because of troubles there, although he was not resident permanently. The Reverend Mr Goldie, the Chairman of the Solomon Islands Methodist District, visited in 1918 and found "the Group quiet and prospering under a Christian king." He dedicated a new church at a service which even the 'heathen priests' attended. He also reported to a fellow missionary that "the Christian king of Pelau and his people are visiting Lua Niua for their festivities for the first time in the memory of living men. Peace has come at last!"[16] Semisi and his wonderful wife Matilika left for Tonga in 1919. Sadly, the Methodist Mission was unable to replace him with another minister.

In 1923, because of depopulation, it was forbidden to recruit labour from Ongtong Java. In 1921 there was a lay missionary there, but he left, and in 1922 responsibility for supporting the Methodist Mission passed to the New Zealand Methodist Church, which was facing severe financial problems. By 1925 Goldie had begun to consider whether the Methodists should give up "and let the other missionary society which is anxious to go take up the work."[17] By 1928 the population had dropped to about a thousand, and Methodist resources were severely stretched. Bishop Baddeley estimated the population in 1933 at about 750 and decided to take up the challenge of continuing the Christian work there. The Methodists raised no objection. The LMS had handed over their work in the Torres Straits Islands to the Anglicans, but this was the only occasion on which a field of work in the Pacific Islands was inherited by the Anglicans from the Methodists after their withdrawal.[18] In other parts of the Solomons, people sometimes joined the Roman Catholic Church or the South Sea Evangelical Mission, because of lack of follow-up after the Brothers' initial visits. Ongtong Java was different. There it was the Brothers who were asked by the Bishop to take over and build on the work of other Pacific Islander missionaries.[19] The Bishop claimed in 1934 that "it would almost be correct to say that the whole population are already under our influence, if not actually under instruction for baptism." Medical care was recognised as of great importance, so the mission ship paid a number of visits, and the chief "asked for advice and direction in certain native customs which already he feels to be contrary to Christian teaching."[20] At the same time, the Government stopped Melanesian native teachers going to Rennell and Bellona, Polynesian islands south of Guadalcanal, as it objected to Melanesians living in Polynesian communities. The Bishop had Polynesian Brothers ready to go there, but that did not happen for another sixty years, after various appeals (starting in the 1970s) from people on Bellona who had been educated in Anglican schools[21] or admired the work of the Brothers in other places. Whatever the Government policy, both Polynesian and Melanesian Brothers and, later, clergy, worked on Ongtong Java.

The traditional religion which had been followed by the people of Ongtong Java included a group of gods who were worshipped in the temple (*haleiku*). Chief among these was Puemakua (or Puemaka), who was the most important, his name being made up of two words: *pue* 'protect' and *makua* 'first one'. Next in importance was Aialii (or Aeali'i), who was the one who controlled the spirits. If these two gods were angry, it was believed they could inflict illness on the people; if they were pleased, no one would be ill. Bisiola and Kibu were lesser gods who had charge of the children. The god Ae was responsible for the fruitfulness of the land, and had children called Gumuli and Sakia. Lolohenua was a god whose name meant 'earthquake'. Paeva was the one who controlled the sea and produced fish. Luahine was female; *lua* appears to have meant 'two in one' and *hine* 'a woman'. She was believed to have instituted tattooing, so the women tattooed their faces and their bodies.[22] Two gods had figures outside the temple: Keni was responsible for the land and what it produced, while Hee controlled thc wind and the sea.[23]

Semisi Nau wrote in *The Story of my Life*: "Each of these spirits was represented by a man. These men were called sacred men and were supposed to control the spirits. There were many lesser spirits which were not represented by any sacred man. The man who represented Puemakua was named Kua, and his work was supposed to be of the greatest importance. At certain seasons he had to come to Luanuia[24] to awaken Puemakua. He would awaken it at break of day and put it to sleep again at night. To awaken the spirit he would first call it by name and then say: "Exalt, exalt, exalt all the great chiefs. Awake, O spirit. Take care of the place so that people will live. Carry away from here all sickness. Cause the coconuts to grow so that one bunch will yield a hundred nuts. Look upon the water so that we will get plenty of fish. Enlarge the root of the taro so that people may eat and live. At Luanuia the sacred man was changed every six months; one would go away and another come and take his place."[25]

In the *Southern Cross Log* of July 1939, the Bishop wrote of his earlier experiences on Ongtong Java, where he arrived with Brother Charles Fox, six other Brothers and a nurse. The chief 'Makiki' (Makaike) invites the Bishop to sit beside him. When asked if he knows why the Bishop has come, he points to his pectoral cross and says 'Mission'. He goes on to say, 'We are unwilling that the customs of our fathers should be changed.' While the Bishop goes off to visit the impressive graveyards and wander around the village, Brother Charles is pointing to objects and getting a group of men to tell him their names in their language. He is thus making contact, as the other Brothers are doing in different ways, and the nurse is investigating the medical situation. The Bishop asks the chief if the Brothers can spend the night ashore and permission is given. This provides an opportunity for the Brothers to make contact with the young people, talking late into the night. In the morning the local youth ask the chief if the Brothers can stay, and he gives them leave. The people then see them praying and ask: 'What are you doing?' They reply: 'We are talking to our Father.' 'Who is He?' The Brothers reply: 'Our older Brother told us about Him.' 'Who is your older Brother? Is he a white man?' 'No, he was a coloured man. But it was the white man who came and told us about him. We have a book about him, and one day you will be able to read it when it is printed in your own language. He has taught us to help the sick, to help women, that all men everywhere are to live and work together as brothers.' The Bishop added: "So, little by little, they have their opportunity of revealing the Gospel they have come to preach, and usually to the young men first."[26]

It had been in early 1934 that Brother Charles Fox and two other Brothers came to Luañiua in a trading ship belonging to the Burns Philp Company.[27] He went to the Chief Makaike and talked with him about the Anglican Church. He spent a week there. An agreement was reached, and Brothers arrived on March 12, 1934. They were Patrick Kupe, John Bosamata, Casper Kaepoi and Philip Hakopuloto. They left after about two years. The second group to come were John Bosamata, Ben Tumu, Valentino Poi and Tasikala. They stayed for about one and a half years. A third group then were sent, namely Brothers Matthias, Allen and Selwyn. Fourthly, Hugo Maelasi came, and he took a boy from Luañiua to accompany him to Nukumanu. The third and fourth visits were for only one year each. John Bosamata spent about four years there as a Brother, then later returned as Catechist and Teacher.[28]

The people provided them with a house, but, as they had no gardens, they were also supplied with food. Other necessities such as bedding were also provided for them. The Brothers encouraged and honoured the good customs, but opposed the bad ones. They went to all the places where the people told them there were 'bad spirits' and cleansed them, going out morning and evening to do so. They gave good teaching and preached effectively, but they did not prepare people for baptism and confirmation. Only in the case of one man, Mao, who was ready to die and wanted to be a Christian, did they actually baptise. The people responded well to the Brothers' teaching, but it was left to others to formally bring them into the Christian Church and to establish the Companions and Mothers Union. Father Eric came after the Brothers, as a deacon, and he was followed by a priest, Fr Dudley Bale, one of the first Brothers. Catechist teachers followed him – first John Mark, then John Muia. They were all from other islands, but eventually local catechists took over – Joel Keñohe, Joseph Kumuli, George Kumomoe and Patrick Keopo. Eventually also, the atoll welcomed one of their own people back as a priest. In 1952 Fr Casper Kakaese returned as priest and teacher. He started the school at Luañiua. He was followed by Fr Drummond Ama from Santa Ysabel, who started the Companions and Mothers Union in both Pelau and Luañiua. Ex-Brother John Bosamata returned, this time as their priest and he died there in 1961. (One of the Brothers also died there and was buried on the beach.) Fr Bosamata was replaced by Fr Alan Piva from Sikaiana, the other Polynesian priest already ordained at that time. Two priests from Malaita were his successors: first, Fr Willie Au and then Fr Henry Nuntaloa in 1967. Fr Casper was then sent back and he remained as district priest until his retirement, when he was replaced by yet another Malaita man, Fr William Fakaia, who had been Head Brother. Various local men became catechists during this period.

The Brothers' connection with the atoll did not cease completely. In 1966, Brother Codrington Tolenglenga and Brother James Baddeley Tule spent a year there, and in 1978 a group arrived to do revival work and research the history of Christian missions on the island. The group included Brothers Ellison Vahi, Moffat Pehewa, Benjamin Filei, Justin Andriu, Paul

Neremana, Mark Naebola and a Brother from Fiji, Edward Das, who concentrated on the research. They found only one man who was still following the pre-Christian religion. He insisted that if people went fishing with him, they were to follow the old rules he observed. By pointing the end of a coconut branch out to sea, he believed he could send back the fishing devil (the rainbow fish). If people with him wanted the toilet, he insisted that they returned to shore!

Brother Edward Das found that the people had become split into two groups, one group siding with Fr Casper and another following their own affairs and not respecting the teaching of the Church. He worked with both sides, giving them what help he could, and those who had been estranged from the Church said they were happy with what he had done. He wrote: "I brought them again to the Lord in his Church."[29]

Before the arrival of Christian missionaries, the people of Pelau at the other end of the atoll, had a special house where they prayed called *Haleiku*.[30] Inside were two carved gods they called Keali'i. These were of dead people, a man and a woman, known as Apio and Alei. Sick people were brought to worship there and to touch the statues. Every evening the priests of the special house had to go and lay the statues down to sleep, and in the morning they would have to wake them up and watch with them till the people woke up. The people would pray to their gods ('devils') to grant them plenty of fruit in their gardens.

The first missionary there was the Methodist from Samoa called Polonga or Poroga.[31] The second Chief of Pelau called Apakeia asked Polonga not to do anything too quickly about the 'devil house', but on the Sunday in his first week there, he went inside the *haleiku* with his Bible. He called on the Gali'i (Keali'i) three times, then he opened the door and ordered them to go out. He then went to the central post of the house, opened the Bible and prayed. After that, he got hold of the two statues and burned them in a big fire. That was the end of that kind of 'devil' worshipping.

He had been their only resident Christian missionary until Bishop Walter Baddeley visited and promised them that the Brothers would come; so they invited them to work there. They arrived before the Second World War. Those who came were Casper Kaepoi (Kaipoia) and Kepuga of Sikaiana, John Bosamata of Gela and Patrick Kupe of Guadalcanal, who had been on Sikaiana as a Brother. They conducted prayers and taught the people, who provided them with a house. They ate the local food with the people. When mosquitoes were bad, they moved with the people to other islets, like Avaha. They sometimes travelled by canoe across the lagoon from Pelau to the other main settlement on the atoll at Luañiua.

The Brothers stayed for about four years at Pelau. They respected the people's customs. They had language problems in communicating with the people, as some of the Brothers could use only Pidgin and Mota, but the people found their preaching and teaching good and clear. The people were impressed and filled with awe when the Brothers healed the sick and did other 'mighty works', as well as helping the needy. After daily prayer in the morning, the Brothers would either assist people who needed help, or teach others the rules of the Christian Church. When they began to understand the Christian faith better, they stopped worshipping their 'devils' and eventually all except two or three became believers. Before the Brothers left, a priest and catechist-teacher arrived. The Brothers had chosen two men to take their place (Gogiho and Govolo) who kept the people faithful. When the Brothers left, twelve priests and 21 catechists had ministered there up to 1978. Sixteen Brothers had worked there. A Companions Group had been started, and they continued to operate and develop their work.

NOTES

1 Also spelt Luangiua, Luanguia, Luañuia or Liuaniua by different writers and on different maps. Sikaiana people pronounce it Lua*n*iua, not Lua*ng*iua.

2 See D Harcombe: *Solomon Islands: A Travel Survival Kit*, Lonely Planet, 1988 (1st edition).

3 Popularly known as 'Queen Emma'. See biography so titled by R W Robson, Pacific Publications, Sydney, 1965.

4 Significantly, Forsayth's store in Bougainville had been destroyed in 1897 by local people, and a Chinese trader killed. See Robson: *Queen Emma*, p. 233.

5 The 'flu epidemic in 1906 is said to have caused 30 to 40 deaths a day while it lasted. See *Semisi Nau: The Story of my Life: A Tongan Missionary at Ongtong Java*, p. 30, edited by Allan K Davidson, Suva, Fiji, Institute of Pacific Studies, The University of the South Pacific, 1996.

6 It was probably about 750 when the Brothers arrived in 1933. See Davidson: *Semisi Nau*, p.64.

7 See Davidson: *Semisi Nau*, p.25.

8 See Davidson: *Semisi Nau*, p.25. Brown was General Secretary of the Australasian Methodist Overseas Missions until 1903.

9 See *The Australasian Methodist Missionary Review* for September 8, 1902, cited by A K Davidson in *Semisi Nau*, pp.26-27.

10 See *Semisi Nau*, p.40.

11 See *Semisi Nau*, p.53.

12 See *Semisi Nau*, p.55.

13 See *Semisi Nau*, p.55.

14 See *Semisi Nau*, p.58.

15 See *Semisi Nau*, p.58.

16 See *Semisi Nau*, p.60.

17 See *Semisi Nau*, p.62, John Goldie to a fellow missionary. His district ship was also not in good

condition.

18 In the 1990s the Brothers were asked to take over the Christian work in the district of Kerema in Papua New Guinea after the Roman Catholics and United Church had given up and withdrawn, (according to Head Brother Harry Gereniu in May 2000, in a communication to the author).

19 Dr Fox and two Brothers paid a short visit, and the Chief then asked for the Brothers to come. After the 1933 October Conference, a group arrived and there was "progress made." See *Southern Cross Log*, July 1934.

20 See *Semisi Nau*, p.64.

21 See *Southern Cross Log*, July 1934.

22 Noella Kakapena, an Ongtong Java girl, who had a full forehead tattoo, was in 1964 sent to school in New Zealand, where only the *old* women (*kuia*) still had tattoos, normally on the chin. The author was present in the old All Saints Cathedral in Honiara when Noella was blessed by Bishop Hill before leaving for New Zealand.

23 See *Semisi Nau*, p.102 and p.124, note 76. According to Arthur, the school teacher at Luañiua in 1978, in a written account for Brother Edward Das, the chief gods of Luañiua before the coming of Christianity were Pohulumole, Loaku, Ahine and Sakia. They had children called Akipu and Siola. They were placed as figures in a special house called *Haleiku*. Pohulumole and Loaku were thought to be particularly dangerous as they could kill a person in one or two days, whereas Ahine and Sakia were thought to be kind. These two gods were brought out of the *haleiku* at times of celebration, and they remained outside during the whole period. One of the *namakua* (heathen priests) would say *Lakakaio* (Stand!) to the gods when they were placed in an empty space and then say *Loku* (prayer) to introduce the prayers. The priests were assisted by others: *Napule* (helpers), *Nakaala* (the sharer of food), *Naahi* (the fire-lighter). The priests were Kepae, Keila and Kaloma; the helpers were Ako, Keuolei, Akaha, Maau and Kemalu.

24 Note the spelling!

25 Quoted from *Semisi Nau*, p.64.

26 See *Southern Cross Log*, July 1939. This appears to refer to the group taken there earlier, see Note 19.

27 Information about Luañiua is from the written account by Arthur, the schoolteacher there, given to Brother Edward Das in 1978.

28 See *Southern Cross Log*, December 1960. Brother Martin Fiia stated he was Elder Brother there, 1935-1936, although not mentioned in Arthur's account.

29 In a letter to the author from the Melanesian Brotherhood, Malaita Section, dated September 6, 1978.

30 The account which follows was recorded by Brother Edward Das, from Fiji, in 1978 at a gathering of the people at Pelau with Catechist John.

31 Semisi Nau referred to him as Buloña or Pologa (which in Tongan would be pronounced Polonga). Poroga could be the spelling used by Brother Edward Das, based on what he heard the Pelau people say.

CHAPTER EIGHT

Bishop Baddeley with Tasiu Dr. Fox, 1938.

The Brothers (left) and others in canoes coming to meet the Southern Cross at Fouia, Malaita, Solomon Islands.

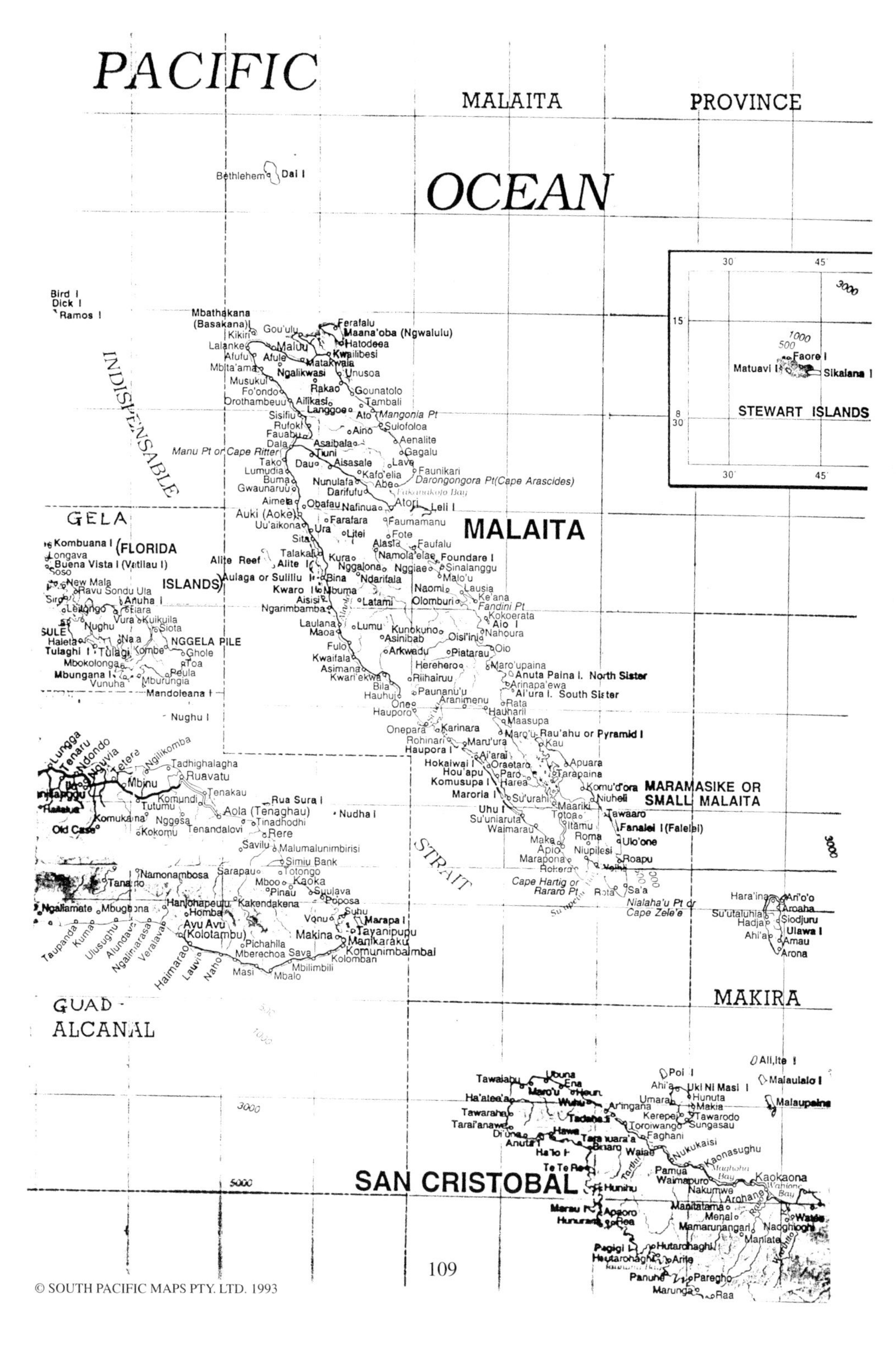
PACIFIC
OCEAN
MALAITA PROVINCE
Bethlehem
Dai I
Bird I
Dick I
Ramos I
INDISPENSABLE
STEWART ISLANDS
Faore I
Matuavi I
Sikaiana I
Mbathakana (Basakana) I
Gou'ulu
Ferafalu
Maana'oba (Ngwalulu)
Hatodeea
Kwailibesi
Kikiri
Lalanke
Maluu
Afufu
Afule
Matakwala
Mbita'ama
Ngalikwasi
Unusoa
Musukul
Fo'ondo
Rakao
Gounatolo
Orothambeuu
Ailikasi
Tambali
Langgoe
Sisifiu
Ato
Mangonia Pt
Rufoki
Aino
Sulofoloa
Fauabu
Aenalite
Dala
Asaibala
Manu Pt or Cape Ritter
Tiuni
Gagalu
Tako
Dau
Aisasale
Lave
Faunikari
Lumudia
Kafo'elia
Darongongora Pt(Cape Arascides)
Buma
Nunulafa
Abe
Gwaunaruu
Darifufu
Fakanakolo Bay
Aimela
Obafau
Nafinua
Atori
Leli I
GELA
Auki (Aoke)
Farafara
Faumamanu
MALAITA
Uu'aikona
Ura
Litei
Sita
Fote
Kombuana I
(FLORIDA
Alasta
Faufalu
Longava
Buena Vista I (Vatilau I)
Alite Reef
Talakali
Kura
Namola'elae
Foundare I
Soso
Alite I
Nggalona
Nggiae
Sinalanggu
Aulaga or Sulillu I
Bina
Ndarifala
Malo'u
New Mala
ISLANDS)
Kwaro I
Mbuma
Naomi
Lausia
Ravu Sondu Ula
Aisisi
Ke'ana
Anuha I
Latami
Olomburi
Fandini Pt
Leitongo
Fiara
Ngarimbamba
Kokoerata
Vura
Kuikuila
Laulana
Lumu
Kunokuno
Aio I
Nughu
Siota
Maoa
Asinibab
Oisi'ini
Nahoura
SULE
Haleta
Naa
NGGELA PILE
Fulo
Arkwadu
Piatarau
Oio
Tulaghi I
Tulagi
Kombe
Ghole
Kwaifala
Hereheroo
Maro'upaina
Mbokolonga
Toa
Asimana
Riihairuu
Anuta Paina I. North Sister
Mbungana I
Reula
Kwari'ekwa
Arinapa'ewa
Vunuha
Mburungia
Bila
Paunanu'u
Ai'ura I. South Sister
Mandoleana I
Hauhui
Aranimenu
One
Rata
Hauporo
Hauharii
Nughu I
Maasupa
Onepara
Karinara
Rau'ahu or Pyramid I
Rohinari
Maru'ura
Kau
Haupora I
Ai'arai
Apuara
Lungga
Tenaru
Ndondo
Nguvia
Tetere
Ngilikomba
Hokaiwai I
Oraetaro
Tarapaina
Tadhighalagha
Hou'apu
Paro
Ruavatu
Komusupa I
Harea
Komu'd'ora
MARAMASIKE OR
Mbinu
Tenakau
Maroria I
Su'urahi
Niuheli
SMALL MALAITA
Komundi
Rua Sura I
Tutumu
Maariki
Aola (Tenaghau)
Nudha I
Uhu I
Totoa
Tawaaro
Komukaina
Nggesa
Tinadhodhi
Su'uniaruta
Itamu
Fanalei I (Falelei)
Old Case
Kokomu
Tenandalovi
Rere
Waimarau
Roma
Savilu
Malumalunimbirisi
Maka
Ulo'one
STRAIT
Apio
Niupilesi
Simiu Bank
Marapona
Roapu
Namonambosa
Sarapau
Totongo
Tanaro
Mboo
Kaoka
Cape Hartig or
Rararo Pt
Rota
Sa'a
Pinau
Suulava
Hara'ina
Ari'o'o
Poposa
Nialaha'u Pt or
Cape Zele'e
Aroaha
Hanjohapeuu
Kakendakena
Ngaliamate
Mbugbona
Homba
Su'utaluhia
Siodjuru
Suhu
Vonu
Marapa I
Hadja
Ulawa I
Avu Avu
(Kolotambu)
Tayanipupu
Ahi'a
Amau
Makina
Manikaraku
Taupanda
Kuma
Ulusughu
Alundavo
Ngalimarasap
Veralava
Pichahila
Komunimbaimbai
Arona
Mberechoa
Sava
Kolomban
Haimarao
Lauvi
Naho
Mbilimbili
Masi
Mbalo
MAKIRA
GUAD-
ALCANAL
Ali,Ite I
Poi I
Ubuna
Tawaiabu
Ena
Ahi'a
Uki Ni Masi I
Malaulalo I
Ha'atee'a
Maro'u
Heuru
Umara
Hunuta
Wuhu
Ari'ingana
Makia
Malaupaina
Tawaraha
Kerepei
Tawarodo
Tadahe I
Tarai'anawa
Toroiwango
Sungasau
Di'ona
Hawa
Faghani
Anuta
Waiae
Nukukaisi
Ha'lo I
Kaonasughu
Te Te Rei
Pamua
Haghoha Bay
Kaokaona
SAN CRISTOBAL
Hunihu
Waimapuro
Nakumwe
Wahiona Bay
Marau I
Manitatama
Arohane
Apaoro
Waiata
Hunuranu
Rea
Menalo
Mamarunangari
Naghoghi
Maniate
Pagigi I
Hutarohaghi
Hautarohaghi
Arite
Panuhe
Pareghe
Marunga
Raa
30'
45'
15'
8
30
3000
1000
500
5000

Canoes at Kumbun, West New Britain, New Guinea.

Kumbun Village, New Britain.

The Bishop and local women at Kauptimeti, New Britain, territory of New Guinea.

CHAPTER EIGHT

PROGRESS IN THE NEW HEBRIDES, MALAITA, NEW BRITAIN

A notice appeared in the *Southern Cross Log* of October, 1929 about the publication of a booklet entitled *The Brothers*, written by Bishop Steward, who had retired in August 1928. It stated: "A simple constitution has been developed on lines which may lead on in time to a permanent religious community." In the booklet itself, Bishop Steward described Ini Kopuria as 'the founder'. The writer of the notice continued: "The whole movement is remarkable as an evident growth of the Mission work, and a leading of the Holy Spirit toward a following of the Divine method, as typified by the first sending forth of evangelists by Our Lord." In 1930 the new Diocesan Bishop, F.M.Molyneux, was not available for a while, and the *Log* stated that the Reverend G W Warren – who was headmaster at 'Verana'aso School' – was to act as 'Father' of the Brotherhood temporarily.[1] Appeals were made in New Zealand for materials for black and white *malos* (loin-cloths) for the Brothers, as well as mosquito nets. Bishop Molyneux had suggested that they also be equipped with rucksacks "for carrying their few belongings and keeping them dry."[2] The Bishop resigned in November 1931 (and Bishop Walter Hubert Baddeley did not arrive until the end of 1932), but there were important developments during his short time as Bishop.

From 1928 sickness had been affecting the Brothers' work, and in 1929 John Pihavaka was picked up by the *Southern Cross* and taken from Santa Cruz, where he had been working, to try and recover in Bugotu District in his home island of Ysabel. The Bishop asked him where he would want to work when next picked up by the ship. "He said he would work anywhere where I thought he was most wanted." However he died soon afterwards – the first to die as a member of the Brotherhood, although there were a number of others over the years. The Bishop wrote: "He leaves behind him the example of a very humble and single-hearted Brother, whose one desire was to go where he was sent."[3] The Brothers had by then started work in about a dozen villages in Santa Cruz, as well as two areas of Guadalcanal. As a result, a school was started at Tabalia for young men from those places, and there they learned first of all to read well, in the hope that they might become catechist-teachers ("or, at any rate, readers") to follow up the work of the Brothers. There were five young Santa Cruzians to start off with, and the school was run by Brother Ini for the first year, in

1928.[4] Thus the Brotherhood began the idea of training other people for mission – something which led much later to the establishment of a Catechist School (and then College) called Kohimarama.

Another development was the appointment of Brother Barnabas Babau to be in charge of the leper village (named Qaibaita) on Malaita, acting as both Chief and Teacher. He had himself been in Tulagi Hospital on Gela receiving treatment for eighteen months. The Medical Superintendant at Fauabu Hospital on Malaita, Dr Maybury, was very grateful for his appointment and write: "We have already realised what a difference a leader makes."[5]

Bishop Molyneux broadcast on the BBC a 'Missionary Travel Talk' prior to his resignation, and so made the existence of the Brothers known to a wider audience. During it, he said: "They have already done some splendid work, generally amongst people speaking languages different from their own and in islands far away from their homes."[6]

Three Brothers, including Dan Sade, had accompanied Bishop Molyneux on a visit to the Mandated Territory of New Guinea, touring New Britain from Rabaul in the east to Sagsag in the west. The Bishop wrote: "It was felt it would be helpful to the natives of New Britain to see something of the enthusiasm for Christ of those who are of their own Melanesian race, who have been for some time in Mission schools."[7]

In 1931, four young men from Raga, or North Pentecost, in the New Hebrides,[8] established a household in Qatnapni (Bwatnapni) District in Central Pentecost, with the help of Brother Daniel Sade. They were Brothers Ben Bani, Judah Ruruhi, Matthias Tabeleo (a young chief) and John Binihi. The situation they had to face was very difficult for them, as most of the people there worshipped their 'idols'. People from other islands, or even the same district, were not allowed to enter a village area unless there was an invitation for a special occasion from the chief. There was much fighting and some cannibalism. The chiefs took many wives, and polygamy was common. (Bride price was usually three pigs and twenty custom mats.) Bows and arrows were used in their fights and for fishing. What they wore was made out of pandanus leaves. They were still following the traditional ways of life, including marriages arranged by the parents of the bride and bridegroom, as well as making axes out of a special stone and knives out of a sea shell. Bamboos were used to carry and store fresh water or sea water (for salt). Cooking was done in clay pots on fires or on hot stones. When a person died, a heap of stones was raised over the body, or it was sometimes wrapped in a special red mat (*sesetememe*) and kept in a special house, as the bones would eventually be used as poisoned arrows to fight with.

There were some from that area who had been taken to Queensland to work on plantations there, and among them were those who had learned a little about the Christian faith while there, and had taught about it in their own villages on their return. This had prepared the way for the Brothers. They kept a household there for ten years, until the impact of the Second World War scattered them in 1942. The Brothers had to establish gardens quickly in order to feed themselves. They befriended the people and learned as much as they could about their customs, before trying to distinguish between what was in accord with Christian teaching and practice, and what was not. They then tried to convert the people to God and to following Christian ways, instead of those ways which they thought were bad. At the same time, they were teaching people the Mota language and how to pray in it. However, they could sometimes be understood when using the Raga language. They also taught the people singing. They were generally well received in the villages, although some villages rejected them. The Christians always gave them a warm welcome. They went out two by two to heathen villages, and would visit for two or three weeks before returning to their headquarters. When they were invited to stay in a village, four of them might go for three or four months, and then others would replace them. This was possible when numbers in the household increased. They would be replaced by a catechist when their work was done in any village, and he would prepare the people for baptism, confirmation and Holy Communion. Over a hundred people had been converted by the time the Brothers left, and the number was constantly increasing. The evangelistic work was done under the general direction of the District Priest, Fr Henry Tavoa. Some of the people, however, joined the Roman Catholic Church or the Churches of Christ, whose missionaries had originally come from the Australian branch of that denomination, founded in the United States of America. Others attached themselves to a sect established by a man called Daniel. His followers, named ‘Danielites’, wanted what they considered to be a purer form of Christianity. Eventually most of the Danielites returned to the Anglican Church. Companions’ groups were established after the Brothers left the area.

The Brothers also started work in North Mala (Malaita) in the Solomon Islands. Following on the outstanding work of the Reverend Arthur Hopkins from 1903 to 1914 in that part of Malaita island, the Anglican Church had gradually grown in numbers under his successors, with the assistance of some outstanding Melanesian teachers, some of whom were later ordained. In 1918 there were 588 Christians belonging to the Anglican Church, but three of the teachers had been murdered by non-Christians. The first Malaita man to be ordained was Jack Talofuila, who had attended the Melanesian Mission school for the labourers in Queensland, run by Mrs Robinson. He had established a school at Fouia on his own land opposite the artificial islands in the Tae Lagoon, and by the time of his death 850 people on the nearest island, Sulufou, where he came from, had become Christians. A white missionary priest, Fr Nind, was eventually based at Fouia, and the Brothers followed up the work established by Talofuila and Nind by making 'further openings'. Brother Ini visited both villages and instructed the households.[9] Teachers were asked for in several artificial islands in the area. Arthur Hopkins wrote a short biography of Jack Talofuila entitled *From Heathen Boy to Christian Priest*, published by SPCK in 1949.

A leaflet produced by the London Office of the Melanesian Mission about 1932, entitled *The Response of Melanesia to the Holy Spirit*,[10] reported on the work in Malaita as follows:

"During Holy Week in 1932 the Brothers on North Mala, with the aid of native Christians, performed a pageant depicting the events of the last week of our Lord's earthly life. On Palm Sunday the Christ came to His Temple, the little Christian church down by the beach. A figure came down the path from the forest, clad in scarlet and wearing a crown, and two little figures in white held up his train with one hand, while the other hand held a palm branch. The people strewed the path with branches broken off from the trees and coco-palms alongside. Children clad in white came out to meet Him crying 'Hosanna', while the people around knelt in adoration. And so the pageant proceeded from day to day; and at the end of each day the Head Brother explained to the crowd of onlookers, who were mostly Heathen, what was the meaning of the things which they had seen. The Brother who related the doings of this week states that his eyes nearly started out of his head when he saw an angel, with wings, in the garden during the portrayal of the Agony. The effect of all this on the minds of the Heathen watchers must indeed have been tremendous. And those sacred scenes were enacted in a land that but a little while ago ran with blood.

"The native lay Brothers, enduring hardness for Christ's sake, renouncing what to them is the world, and patiently suffering for the truth's sake, are winning many to righteousness, and are manifesting the fruit of the Spirit, love, joy, peace, long-suffering, kindness, goodness, faithfulness, meekness, self-control."

George Basilei was part of this household at Fouau, which was the first on Malaita.

The Brotherhood had been steadily increasing: by 1928 there were sixteen Brothers, in 1931 twenty eight, and in 1932 forty. These increases were largely due to groups of boys and young men joining from All Hallows School, Pawa, Ugi,[11] following Charles Fox. These were more educated than the earlier Brothers and included George Basilei, Willie Masura'a, Henry Maabe, Martin Fiia and John Bosamata, all later ordained, and Bartholomew Beve, who later worked for many years on the *Southern Cross*, the Bishop's ship.[12] Martin Qañafiia (or Fiia), when released in 1937, also worked on the *Southern Cross* till 1938, when he returned to his village as a catechist and was later ordained.

However, in 1933 there was a significant change. Numbers swelled to 64, largely because young men were now also coming from villages in which the Brothers had worked. Fourteen new Brothers,[13] who had been trained at Tabalia, a work largely undertaken by Tasiu Charles Fox, were admitted on St Simon and St Jude's Day, 1932, at the Mother House at Tabalia. They included Martin Fiia, who stayed there to help teach the Novices.[14] As Chaplain at Tabalia, the first the Brothers had had, Brother Charles introduced a daily Eucharist, with preparation the night before, in addition to the saying of the Daily Offices. Also fruit and vegetable farming were taught.

Ini used to choose the Elder Brothers after consulting Brother Charles Fox. Fox knew that at the Norfolk Island School, the Headmaster, Thomas Cullwick, used to choose the Head Boy and Assistant Head Boy himself. They then chose whom they wished to work with them, leaving the laziest boys to be chosen last! Fox therefore suggested that each Elder Brother should choose his own Assistant Elder Brother – who would always be from a different island– and then the rest of his household. For this ceremony, the Brothers would not sit at the long table in the dining hall, but would gather at one end and be called up one by one by the newly appointed Elder Brother. Thus they picked their 'teams' to go out and do their work.[15]

At the annual conference in 1933, the fourteen Brothers then working in the New Hebrides were represented by Brothers Ben and Matthias. There were, by then, three households established there, on Pentecost and Aoba islands – the latter is now known as Ambae. It was reported at the conference that two Brothers had bravely walked across Malaita at a point where it was most difficult (and considered unsafe by the District Officer). However, they had been well received, and in the two largest of the forty villages visited, they had been asked to start 'schools'. They had suffered much from the cold in the high mountains, and Brother Paul died at Verana'aso on November 14.

Other Brothers had visited villages in Guadalcanal, making a total of 150 villages in all. Generally they found that the old men did not want to become Christians, but were willing for their children to go to school and become Christian. Their responses to the situation were: "Christianity is like an epidemic; there is no escape from it," or, "We are like fish in a net."[16] Although they may have felt resentful about it, they believed that their children would benefit. In 1934 there were missionary households for work among the 'heathen' at four places on Malaita: Fouia and Maanaere in the north, Fouau in the centre and Takataka in the south, and there was a plan to open a training school at Maka in the south for youth from the villages contacted by the Brothers, to be run by Fr Jim Edwards. There were two households on Guadalcanal, at Bima and Marau, with a plan for visiting 3,000 'heathen' people.

On Gela three Brothers were based at Halavo, to make contact with the seven hundred 'workboys' associated with the Protectorate Government Headquarters at Tulagi and the bases of Messrs Burns Philp and Messrs Levers, as well as the hospital and the prison. The *Southern Cross Log*[17] commented: "Coming, as it does, under the notice of a large number of Europeans, it will be a testimony to the work of the Mission." A church was established on the small island of Gavutu, and conversions increased among the largely 'heathen' work force.

At one Annual Conference, when the report of this household was being delivered by the Elder Brother, he omitted to mention the prison. The Brothers asked why. Pretending to be sad, he replied: "You see, Brothers, in the gaol we are only allowed to visit Anglicans, and we are grieved to say that this year there have been no Anglicans in gaol – but we hope next year …." This answer was received with a roar of laughter – which was a feature of many of the Brothers' gatherings.[18]

Brother Charles Fox and five Brothers were at Tabalia, and twenty novices were in training from 1933 to 1934 on a one year course. They were known as *tinqoro*, or 'disciples' (hearers), while on profession they became *Tasiu* or 'Brothers'. The Elder Brothers of households were known as *Moemera* and the Head Brother as *Tuaga* – all words taken from the Mota language. At this time there were about 300 Companions, who were called *pulsala* (friends) in the Mota language. They met together once a week to pray for the Brothers, and they supported them in kind and with money. They were organised in bands of eight to twelve, each with a leader, and when admitted renewed their baptismal vows. Dr Fox (Tasiu Charles) wrote in 1934: "We hope to have 2,000 of them to support us."[19]

Meanwhile, the new Bishop, Walter Baddeley, had arranged for Brother Ini and three other Brothers to start work in New Britain, and in his annual report for 1933-34[20] he wrote: "Maybe the 'new' tribes in the heart of New Guinea will be evangelised by the Melanesian Brothers." This was a vision not realised till 1956, after the Second World War, although Brother Ini himself had visions of the Brothers extending their work even further, into Indonesia. The Bishop took Tasiu Charles Fox with him on a tour in 1934 and several youths from the island of Tikopia in the Outer Eastern Solomons were brought back to train at Tabalia, in the hope that they might become evangelists, and work as Brothers on the other islands of the Solomons which were peopled by Polynesians like themselves. Although the Government was still not allowing 'native teachers' to go to the islands of Rennell and Bellona with their Polynesian inhabitants, the Bishop hoped that Polynesian Brothers *would* be allowed to go, as there were believed to be 4,000 'heathen' there. In the event, the SSEM and SDA were able to start work there, and the Brothers did not go until the 1990s, at the request of some who wanted the Anglican Church in Bellona.

The plan for the New Hebrides was eventually to put Brothers in the Banks Islands. There was a local meeting of the Brothers held at Lolowai in 1934 with the Bishop and Tasiu Daniel Sade, who had accompanied him on the ship from the Solomons. Two Brothers were chosen to go to Tabalia to strengthen the links with the Brothers working in the South, while two others were to do a course in teaching method at the Sisters' School at Siota. The hope was for them to do more missions in the villages and run central schools in the districts in the larger islands of that country, the New Hebrides.

In 1934, the station at Tabalia was beautifully laid out, and a large cross carved from bush timber by Fr Elias Sau was placed on the spot where Ini had made his vows, while another cross marked the spot on the beach from which the original seven had set out on their first journey with a blessing from Bishop Steward. Tasiu Charles, who loved bushes and flowers, had had them planted around the station and the 'square'. Elias Sau was the first priest from San Cristoval, ordained in 1932, and a fine artist and craftsman, whose work had already appeared in some churches on his own island.[21]

In July 1935, two Brothers were placed on Mota in the Banks Islands, where the first Christian village in Melanesia had been established in 1869 by the Reverend George Sarawia.[22]

In 1935, the Brothers were also working on the island of Utupua in the Outer Eastern Solomons, and the Bishop reported that "all five villages are now re-established." He dedicated a church at Nimbu. Later in the year 81 Brothers from the Solomons and two from the New Hebrides gathered for the annual conference at Tabalia. The report in the *Southern Cross Log* stated: "This wonderful native movement, or perhaps it would be more readily understood if one refers to it as a Bush Brotherhood, has grown almost beyond one's most sanguine hopes." In September, Tasiu Charles Fox was asked if he would take in some boys from the overcrowded school at Maravovo (Verana'aso), especially those who had had no previous schooling. Some were from Rennell Island. Overnight, he took in 35, and the land behind the Mother House was cleared and two buildings erected, one large enough to accommodate 50 boys and the other a kitchen. Instruction was given by the Brothers on the Mota language and the Bible. The school was to be supported by the Companions, of whom there were already about 1,000 in 100 groups. It was hoped that each group would support a boy at the school, on the basis of each boy costing £1 a year. The boys would go on to Maravovo, where they would be taught more English and other subjects. The school was another example of something 'purely Melanesian'. Those attending the conference would have been impressed and encouraged. A good football field as well had been created out of the bush; Tasiu Charles was keen on sport!

The Brotherhood had now risen in numbers to 128 in ten years. Fifteen Brothers were working in New Britain, and the rest were working in the Solomons, Fiji or the New Hebrides. The islands producing the most Brothers were Malaita with 45 Solomon Islanders and Pentecost (Raga) with 22 New Hebrideans. There were three New Hebrideans from other islands in that group! Numbers from other islands in the Solomons were as follows: Bugotu (Ysabel) 13, Guadalcanal 11, New Britain 9, San Cristoval (Makira) 8, Reef Islands 8, Ulawa 5, Gela 4, Savo 2, Sikaiana 1.

It was significant that it was generally the islands where the Brothers were working among the local population which produced the most Brothers, with the exception of Bugotu, a largely Christian island which produced many missionaries, in spite of having no household there then.

After his ordination, Brother Daniel Sade,[23] who had been elected as Elder Brother at Tabalia by the household there during his period of preparation, was appointed as Assistant Head Brother, with the task of visiting households. Charles Fox was elected as Elder Brother in his place. At that time, according to Dr Fox, it was the custom to *elect* the Elder Brother at the 'Headquarters'.

At the beginning of 1934, Brother Daniel went with some of the Brothers to Malaita, being put down at Maka with Fr Jim Edwards, Fr Hipkin and some schoolboys. The Brothers paddled to Takataka in Areare District and established a new household at Wehuu. Bishop Baddeley sent Brother Daniel Sade and Brother Moses Lufifolota to Sydney from August to December, then Daniel returned to Malaita in 1935 and visited all the households in Kwara'ae, Fataleka, Koio, Lau and To'abaita Districts. Christmas was spent at Ataa before visits to Sinaranggu, Aio, Takataka and Ngwalade. From Lau they travelled by canoe, via Ngwalade, to Maka, leaving there at 2 a.m. and arriving at Marau Sound on Guadalcanal at 2 p.m.

From there Brother Daniel travelled with a novice to Longgu and Binu households, then back to Tabalia and Maravovo. Companions from Maravovo and Taburiu then took him by canoe to Savo, and Companions from Hagalu took him to Gela where he visited the Brothers and Companions in Halavo District, before travelling by the *Mavis* from Siota to Fauabu. The Brothers' meeting was held that year (1936) at Alangaula on Ugi, and Brother Daniel was released from his vows after eight years' service.

In thc late 1930s, Brother Alfred Kejoa went to be Elder Brother at Sineranggu Household, then, in 1937, there was a meeting of the Brothers at Fauabu and it was decided to open a household at One'e, North Malaita. There were four households on Malaita then.[24]

In 1935, the Melanesian Brothers began work at Marou, by the sea in Areare District. The household consisted of Brothers Charles Fox, Ini Kopuria, Daniel Sade and Willie Masura'a, but there were no heathen villages converted, although the Brothers worked hard to spread the word of God. For seven years there was no catechist at Marou, although the church there had been established by the Brothers. From 1941 to 1944 there were no Brothers or priest in the area. However, Samuel Su'unorua (born in 1935) had come in contact with the Brothers and been taught the Lord's Prayer. In 1946 the Brothers 'opened' various villages in Areare, South Malaita: Taranaasi, Tanimama, Waiaha, Wairokai, Tawanaora and Potaniu. From then onwards, many catechists came to the villages there, including Marou. Samuel Su'unorua went to various schools (including Pawa), and joined the Brotherhood in 1953, becoming Elder Brother at Tabalia in 1954, before going to Papua New Guinea. He returned in 1958 and became a catechist among his people, spending three years teaching 'heathen' children in the bush at a place newly opened by the Brothers. After three years at Siota he was ordained priest in 1964 and returned to Marou.[25]

Brother Charles Fox did a tour of Malaita in Fr Mason's whale-boat, using an outboard motor, and doing four knots. They visited Manawai, where Fox kept awake at night and found people creeping into the house to kill them. At Sineranggu, he went up to see the people who had been involved in plotting the murder of William R Bell, the District Officer, and his party, in 1927, but who had not been among the six hanged for it. They visited other places to see where the Brothers might establish themselves. On another occasion, Fox with three others from his household walked from Maka to Ngongorefou (Ngorefou).[26]

In Central Malaita, Brother Henry Maabe and another Brother went up twelve miles into the bush and found a boy with sores all over his body and unable to walk. They were talking with him in the house when his father, the chief, returned. He was about to rush in and kill the strangers with his spear when the boy called out, "No, father, they are friends!" The Brothers then offered to carry the boy down to their house on the coast. They carried him in turn on their backs, which they found was very unpleasant, because of the boy's tropical ulcers. However, they were able to heal him and then take him back to his village, where they were then asked if they would open a school.[27] Brother Henry was later ordained.

In early 1939, Brother Misael Misakel[28] and other Brothers went to Su'u and found that there was much quarrelling among the denominations, Anglican, Roman Catholic and South Sea Evangelical. In Su'u District, Brother Ini was able to convert only two families, right up in the bush. They had built their homes near a river, and these houses were later destroyed in a flood. However, the houses were rebuilt by the Brothers, who also put up a church building for the people there.

In 1939, Bishop Baddeley was planning to visit New Britain and asked for four Brothers to accompany him. However, the announcement that the Second World War had begun meant that the Protectorate Government stopped him going, and the Brothers were sent to Fouau on Malaita instead. From there they walked across the island for two days and made a new settlement at Lama and contacted Uru village. They were led by Elder Brother Johnson Tome. While the Brothers stayed at Alasi, Uru, they found it hard to make a garden, and had no support from the people. Therefore two Brothers walked across to South Malaita to ask the Companions for help. Fr Mason was there and gave them whatever they needed. In Uru, Maefili was senior of two chiefs; neither came to church, but their children did. In 1940 groups of Companions were formed in Ngorefou, Fouia, Gwounatolo and One'e (Malu'u District) by the Brothers – Johnson Tome, John Afa, Paul Bobo, Reuben Hulaña and Misael Misakel – and another household was established at Gwanatolo. Other Brothers working on Malaita at that time were Elder Brother Joseph, Brother William Vañarugu, Brother Reuben Male and Brother Timothy. The meeting in 1940 was held at Siota, and Brother Misael was 'released' and went to work on the *Mavis*, a small launch belonging to the Mission.

After the 1935 conference, Tasiu Charles Fox wrote: "From the beginning Bishop Steward and Tasiu Ini had in mind two sorts of Brothers: 1. Those who would join and work for a year or two before getting married and settling down to teach in their villages, probably the great majority for a long time. 2. Those who would become Brothers permanently, some maybe for life, of whom we could not expect many for some time."

"Now ten years have passed and it was agreed to invite any who desired to be Brothers permanently to take a longer vow – for three years. There proved to be eight such, and they were formed into a household at the Brotherhood Headquarters, Tabalia, there to live the Brotherhood life, to become, if possible, a hot centre, to go out from time to time for short periods to visit and strengthen their brethren, to visit and strengthen the Companions, to teach the novices and the Brothers' school of small heathen boys, to hold retreats and perhaps to take missions in church villages, to do translating work in the languages of the people now becoming Christian, and generally to be a stronghold to the whole Brotherhood." His report appeared in the *Southern Cross Log,* the magazine of the Melanesian Mission, published in both New Zealand and Britain, in January, 1936.

As the Brothers were taxed by the Government, many at £1 a year, the basic cost of a Brother was 30 shillings a year, and they wanted to be self-supporting. So another way of serving as a Brother was introduced, some earning money for the Brotherhood while working on the mission's plantations or the *Southern Cross*, the mission ship, or at the hospital, or in the schools. Their evangelism could still be done among non-Christian crew members or hospital patients, or at places visited by the ship. Many Brothers spent their last year in the Brotherhood raising financial support in these ways for the others' work.

By 1936 two villages on Mota which had lapsed from the practice of the faith were reported by the Brothers there to be showing signs of renewed life. In that year also, the Reverend John Barge, en route to the island of New Britain, where the Brothers were working, found that Saungongo, a 'heathen' minor chief from Rennell, had been staying at Tabalia for some months to check on the Brothers' school, where his son was studying, and to see what 'The Brothers' were about and what their teaching was. "A big, burly, heavily tattooed man," he appeared well satisfied with everything. John Barge also was very interested in the Brothers' school, as he would be working in an island (New Britain) where there were still non-Christians and people with little or no schooling, although East New Britain had been largely evangelised by the Roman Catholics and the Methodists. He said of his visit to Tabalia that he had "spent one of the happiest and merriest afternoons since arriving in the Solomons." Bishop Baddeley tried to strengthen the weak Anglican work in the Mandated Territory of New Guinea, with an Archdeacon and a parish in Rabaul, and six small stations scattered along the Arawe coast in the south-west of New Britain between Gasmata and Sagsag. John Barge, although English, was recruited from Australia; other priests came from there and from England. The first few Anglican converts in New Britain had been baptised in 1933. However, in 1936 the Australian Mandated Territory administration created more difficulties for the Bishop, as it insisted on the withdrawal of all 'foreign' teachers brought in from the Solomon Islands.[29] Only a few 'local natives' were allowed to go to the Solomons for training. This made training of Brothers and 'teachers' to follow up their work increasingly difficult. Promised schools could not be provided. Local converts had to be hastily trained to do what they could.

Fr John Barge worked first in Rabaul, the chief town of New Britain, among the young men working there. He used the service book of the Brothers, which the 'boys' found easy to follow and which had been adopted in a number of places in Melanesia where local people used

English. One of the young men working there later went back to his village of Au near Gasmata to work with the Reverend G Voss. John Barge went on to Kumbun to work with Fr Thompson, then returned to the Solomons to be trained in medical work at the Hospital at Fauabu, before he moved to Maka for two years to help the Reverend Jim Edwards, who was now training men for the ordained ministry in a college there. He also helped with the training of a group of native teachers from New Britain brought to the Solomon Islands for some simple instruction in their work.[30]

John Barge returned to New Britain in April 1939, by which time 560 people had been baptised. Brother Ini and a household of Brothers were established at Au for a while, and the Bishop placed a second household along the coast. Brother Ini also worked in Sagsag, where a white lay missionary (later ordained) had started the work. After his two years working in New Britain, Brother Ini went to New Zealand where he spent part of his time at St John's College with Stephen Talu, as they were both preparing for ordination as deacons.[31]

Tasiu Dr Fox was present with Brother Ini when those he had prepared for baptism at Sagsag were baptised in a river. He wrote: "One of my memories is of that baptism, when Ini and I stood waist deep in the very cold water of that mountain river for several hours, while streams of people came to us from the heathen side, were baptised by us and passed over to the Christian side, where the Bishop sat in his chair on a high grassy bank with the few already Christian around him. There the newly-baptised dressed in white loin-cloths, and finally a great procession, led by the cross, set off for the church, a procession so long that they were singing different hymns in different parts without realising it, or caring either, so joyful did they feel .....What great days those were!"[32]

Dr Fox had been picked up at Tabalia by Bishop Baddeley and had been told by him to come on board 'just as he was'. He had on a singlet and his *malo* (loin-cloth) and nothing on his feet. When they arrived at Rabaul, Brother Charles was introduced to the Governor and a famous anthropologist working there, dressed like that. He felt it was like Mahatma Gandhi calling on the King! As they travelled along the south coast, they looked out for a likely spot, and Brother Charles Fox landed and spoke with the chief. He allowed two Brothers to land, and they were left on the shore, 'looking very lonely'. However, when the ship made its annual visit a year later, they were waiting on the shore with a group of people who wanted to be baptised.[33]

The early work in New Britain also owed much to Brother George Basilei[34] from Maravovo village on Guadalcanal. He was chosen by the Brothers in 1935 to go there to take Brother Ini's place at Sagsag in the extreme west of New Britain, so that he could return. He went with the Bishop to New Britain on the *Southern Cross*, having expressed his willingness to work with Brothers from that island. He was there for fifteen months during the two years 1936 and 1937, and trained the first Brothers from New Britain, Hosea Sakira, Jacob Kono and Bertie[35] from Isega in the Sagsag area. He knew nothing of the local languages, but that did not deter him. He started another household at Man-of-War Passage on the island of Apugi in the Arawe area on the south coast and built the Church of St Mary there. He built another on the main island at Kidron, dedicated to St Francis. He opened schools in two villages in the bush above Kumbun, as one of the chiefs in the area had been impressed by the school there. As a result, the Bishop was able to baptise fifteen people, who became the 'first-fruits' of a wide area. Brother George also persuaded the people to rebuild their houses well off the ground, and practise some elements of hygiene. He also obtained medical supplies from Rabaul and improved the general health of the district. The new Brothers were admitted by Bishop Baddeley at Apugi, after they had completed their training.

Brother George returned to the Solomons and was released at the 1937 conference, as the Bishop wanted him as his helper. Brother Ini and Brother Charles Fox wanted him to stay in the Brotherhood, but he felt that he had to respect the Bishop's wishes, as he was Father of the Brotherhood. He acted as lay chaplain on the Bishop's tours and as 'cabin boy' on the *Southern Cross* during 1938 and 1939. When he travelled to New Zealand, he and members of the crew saw a conjuror, who produced endless bits of cloth from three handkerchiefs. He whispered to Harry Bullen, the Secretary of the Diocese of Melanesia, "Tell him to get me some blankets!" Mr Bullen was based in Auckland: he had come out from the parish of South Bank in Middlesborough, where Bishop Baddeley had been parish priest, in Yorkshire, England.

The Bishop's wife gave George some instruction to prepare him to attend Te Aute Maori College, where he spent 1940 and 1941. He returned to the Solomons from New Zealand in 1942, after the arrival of the Japanese. He was sent to assist Fr Alfred Hill, Headmaster of Pawa School in the Eastern Solomons (which the Japanese had not reached), and was ordained as deacon there in 1942, followed by his ordination as priest in the chapel in 1947.

Through the ministry of the Brothers 45 villages became Christian in the 1930s inland and along the south coast of New Britain, but catechist-teachers were often unavailable to follow up their work, so many of the converts joined other Churches.[36] However, about 1940, twenty more were baptised at Asar. By 1940 three of the mission stations were unstaffed, and the island was occupied by the Japanese from 1942 to 1944.

The supervision of the 'double district' of Ilak-Moewe (later called Pulie-Kandrian) was shared by Fr John Barge and Fr Bernard Moore, who had joined the Melanesian Mission in 1936 and had served first at Pawa School, Ugi. They and the Melanesian Brothers worked together. By the time of the Japanese occupation in 1942, they were the only two white Anglican priests left in New Britain, as John Barge had refused to leave his pastoral and medical work, and Bernard Moore his friend had followed his example. They were both killed by the Japanese, John Barge being captured while down from the bush at the mission house at Pomete near Kandrian on the coast, carrying on his work as usual. He was told by the Japanese he was being taken away to Kandrian in Moewe Harbour nearby, to get medical supplies, but there he was brought ashore and beheaded. Unknown to the Japanese, the killing was witnessed by local Christians hiding in the bush, and they buried him there, at a spot known as Vivilo.[37] Pomete became the headquarters of the Brothers in the Diocese of New Guinea after the Second World War, and John Barge's memory was kept alive there, both by them and the local people he had served so lovingly and bravely. Bishop Baddeley wrote: "He might have left and saved himself. That kind of death is not death but a glorious victory."[38]

By 1936 eleven Brothers had died "after splendid service in the cause of the Master."[39] In New Britain and elsewhere the number of Brothers had been rising, but some missionaries in New Guinea were already aware of an increasing threat from Japan to the north. Archdeacon Romney Gill of the Diocese of New Guinea, whose Mamba District in Papua (on the mainland) bordered the Mandated Territory to the north, returned after leave in England and met Bishop Baddeley at Salemua in that Territory in January 1935. The Bishop was waiting to contact Fr Sherwin, who had been assigned to start Anglican work in the Highlands of New Guinea, which had just been penetrated by white explorers for the first time. Romney considered Baddeley "a very loveable man and great company." The two of them made an agreement, and the Bishop paid a visit to Romney Gill in his district the following August.[40] He brought with him on the *Southern*

Cross Brother Charles Fox and some other Melanesian Brothers. The Bishop and Brother Charles told Gill something of "that great venture of faith and self-dedication which is now being made by means of the Melanesian Native Brotherhood," as the Archdeacon wrote in an article for the *ABM Review*, published by the Australian Board of Missions, which provided Australian Anglican support for both Melanesia and New Guinea. Romney Gill wondered whether the Brotherhood could be reproduced in the Diocese of New Guinea, particularly as he was later convinced that single clergy under vows of some sort would be one of the most effective ways of operating in rural Papua. He was also interested in the methods used by the Brotherhood, as there were similarities with his own method of 'organising local people to evangelise local villages,' as it was later described.[41]

In 1936, Fr James Benson, formerly a fellow missionary in the Diocese of New Guinea, wrote to Fr Gill suggesting "a rule for Oblates of the Community of the Ascension, based on the rule of the Melanesian Brotherhood, so that a chapter of at least four oblates could be formed among members of the Mission. The rule of life would consist of a simple rule of poverty, chastity and obedience, renewable each year." He had noted that the Archbishop of Canterbury had called for celibate priests to serve in missions such as that in New Guinea.[42] The proposal came to nothing as far as the white clergy were concerned, but the Melanesian Brotherhood and the Society of St Francis later started work in the Diocese of New Guinea.

However, Bishop Baddeley's plans for a mission by the Brothers in the Highlands came to nothing at that time, as, soon after his visits, a Roman Catholic missionary was killed, and this caused the Administration to ban missionary work in the Highlands, and it became possible only some time after the Second World War. It was then that the Brothers were at last able to begin a notable work among the tribes of that part of the great island of New Guinea. But the war itself was to have a devastating effect on the Brotherhood and would threaten its very existence and continuation.

NOTES

1 *Southern Cross Log* (Staff and Other Notes), January 1930.

2 *Southern Cross Log*, October 1928, July 1929 and January 1930.

3 *Southern Cross Log,* April 1929.

4 *Southern Cross Log*, July 1929 (Bishop's Report for 1928).

5 *Southern Cross Log*, October 1929 and January 1931 (Hospital Report for Third Quarter, 1930).

6 *Southern Cross Log*, August 1931.

7 *Southern Cross Log*, October 1931 (Bishop's Report on his visit to the Mandated Territory).

8 The New Hebrides became the Republic of Vanuatu at independence in 1980. The information about the Brothers' work in Qatnapni District is from an interview with Mr Levi Bule conducted by Brothers Shadrach and Austin in September 1979.

9 *Southern Cross Log*, July 1937.

10 Leaflet No 4, p.4.

11 Originally supported by All Hallows Church, Hampstead, London.

12 According to Dr Fox, in a letter to the author dated March 22, 1970.

13 Brother Robert Raeriara from Maranuhu, Arosi One, Makira, (San Cristoval) was admitted at this Conference and stayed a Brother for fourteen years.

14 According to Martin Fiia's own notes about his time in the Brotherhood, in the author's possession.

15 Personal communication by Dr Fox to the author in the 1970s.

16 *Southern Cross Log*, April 1934 (*The Retatasiu*, written by Tasiu Charles [Fox])

17 *Southern Cross Log*, April 1934.

18 See *Southern Cross Log*, March 1962, in which there is an article by Dr Fox on the Brotherhood.

19 *Southern Cross Log*, April 1934.

20 *Southern Cross Log*, July 1934 (Bishop's Annual Report, 1933-34).

21 See Fox: *Lord of the Southern Isles*, p.162.

22 The first Melanesian to be ordained, he was made deacon by Bishop Patteson in December 1868 and ordained priest in Auckland in 1873.

23 The account of ex-Brother Daniel Sade's touring and release was written by him in Mota and translated by Bishop Derek Rawcliffe for this book.

24 According to Fr Alfred Kejoa, in an account written in the late 1970s.

25 This account of the development of the Anglican Church in Areare and Koio districts was written by Fr Samuel Su'unorua in December 1999 and presented to Bishop Terry Brown, the Bishop of Malaita (a Canadian by nationality), fourth Bishop of that diocese.

26 Personal communication by Dr Fox to the author.

27 Personal communication by Dr Fox to the author.

28 Information about his time in the Brotherhood was written by ex-Brother Misael Misakel in the 1970s.

29 See Hilliard: *God's Gentlemen*, pp.277-279.

30 See *The Road to Gona* by Dorothea Tomkins and Brian Hughes (Angus & Robertson, Sydney, 1969), pp. 64-67.

31 *Southern Cross Log*, July 1937.

32 *Southern Cross Log*, June 1940, included a tribute to Brother Ini from Dr Fox, from which these words are quoted.

33 Reminiscences of Dr Fox in an interview with the author.

34 The account which follows is based on one written by Fr George Basilei on October 29, 1974. Harry Bullen was born in 1909 and died on April 30, 1974 and his ashes were buried at Honiara Cathedral. His widow, Peggy, died on December 20, 2001.

35 Referred to as 'Obed' in a personal interview with the author in October 1995 at Maravovo village, shortly before Fr George died.

36 See Timothy Kinapan: *A Church is Born: A History of the Anglican Church in Papua New Guinea, 1891-1991* (ACPNG, 1990) and *A Study in Apparent Failure*, BTh thesis by James Ayong from Sagsag, subsequently elected Archbishop of Papua New Guinea.

37 George Basilei claimed that John Barge was killed inside the church George had built at Yemelo, during an interview with the author in October 1995.

38 See Fox: *Lord of the Southern Isles*, pp. 213-214.

39 *Southern Cross Log*, April 1936.

40 See *Romney Gill, Missionary 'Genius' and Craftsman*: Christopher Garland (Christians Aware, Leicester, England, 2000), pp.281-282. Romney Gill was brother of Eric Gill, well-known English sculptor, writer and craftsman, who became a Roman Catholic and Christian Socialist and had a considerable influence on his younger brothers. He was a Dominican oblate and formed a community at Ditchling, in Sussex, England.

41 *Romney Gill*, p.282.

42 *Romney Gill*, p.245.

CHAPTER NINE

JOHN BARGE
Priest and Martyr of the NG Islands.

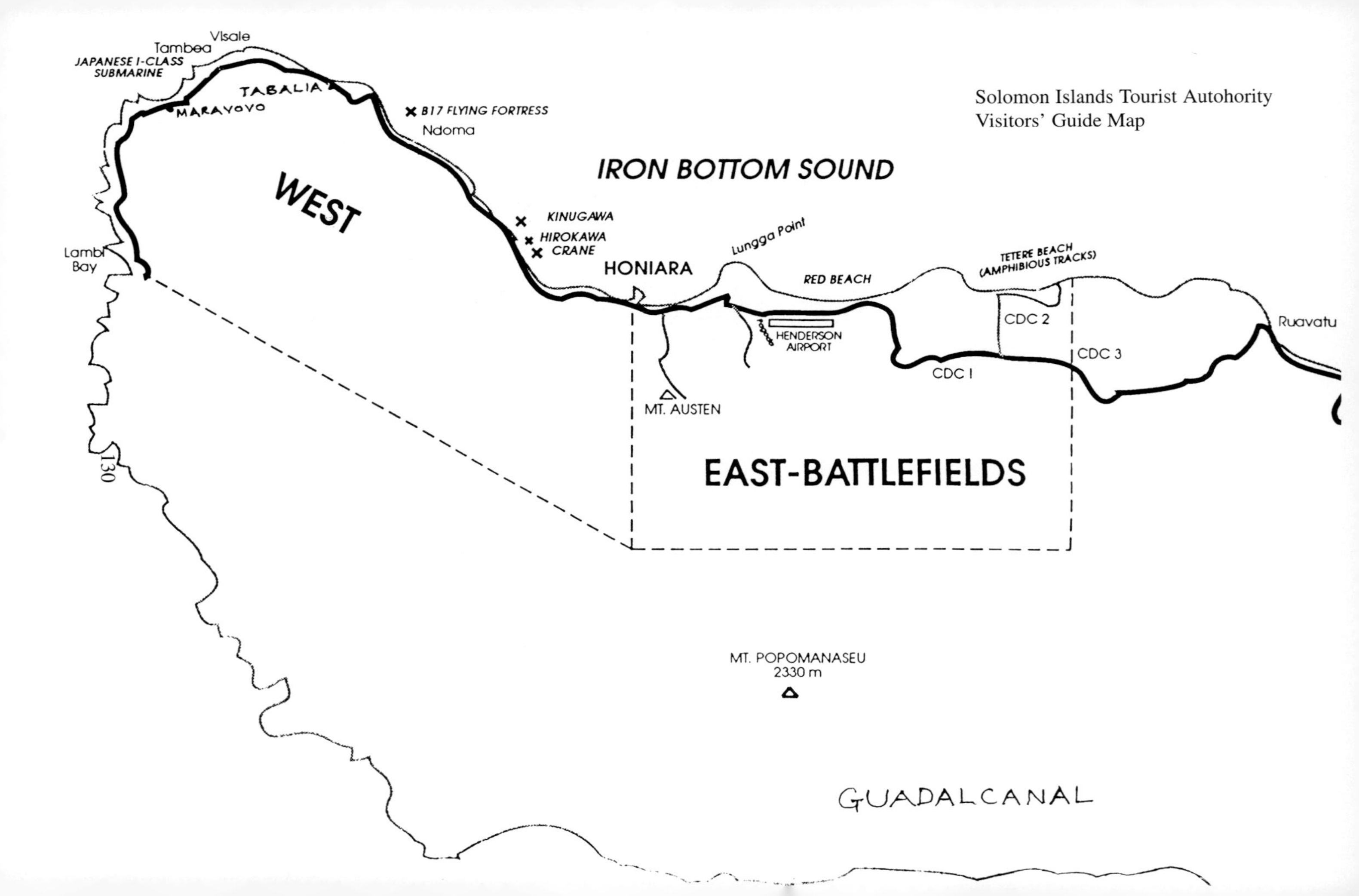
Solomon Islands Tourist Autohority
Visitors' Guide Map
IRON BOTTOM SOUND
WEST
EAST-BATTLEFIELDS
GUADALCANAL
JAPANESE I-CLASS
SUBMARINE
Tambea
Visale
TABALIA
MARAVOVO
B17 FLYING FORTRESS
Ndoma
KINUGAWA
HIROKAWA
CRANE
HONIARA
Lungga Point
RED BEACH
TETERE BEACH
(AMPHIBIOUS TRACKS)
Ruavatu
CDC 2
CDC 3
CDC 1
Pagoda
HENDERSON
AIRPORT
MT. AUSTEN
MT. POPOMANASEU
2330 m
Lambi
Bay

CHAPTER NINE

CONSOLIDATION AND COLLAPSE

By 1936 the Brotherhood had established itself as a powerful spiritual force in the Diocese of Melanesia, working throughout the length and breadth of the Diocese, from New Britain in the north to the town of Vila, capital of the New Hebrides, in the south. However, already the original plan of evangelism was being challenged by the lack of persons to follow up the work of the Brothers. Those converted to Christianity needed teaching and pastoral care, worship and the sacraments. Often there were no catechist-teachers ready and willing to go into the areas 'opened up' by the Brothers, and sometimes it was ex-Brothers who saw the need and took up the challenge. Sometimes the 'teachers' were ill-trained and ill-equipped for the work. The clergy had large districts to cover and were sometimes finding it difficult to provide sacramental ministrations to the Brothers, let alone the new converts. In some places, what the people really wanted was education for their children, something the Brothers themselves tried to supply in a basic way at Tabalia, but that was not what the Brotherhood was founded to do originally. The Brothers were being asked to do many kinds of work which were not just evangelistic, and finding ways of funding the now greatly increased Brotherhood had become a big issue. Not only that, but the more experienced Brothers were being gathered together at Tabalia to act as a resource, not just for their fellow Brothers, but for the Church as a whole. Increasingly, they were being asked to work among Christians, whether lapsed or nominal or in need of instruction, and to serve the Church in ways associated with the more established religious orders. The nature of the vows taken and their length was under review, and there was the prospect of other Brothers, in addition to the founder, eventually taking a life vow. In the wider Church, questions about the character of the community had not been resolved. Some saw the Brotherhood as being in the Franciscan tradition, others as a uniquely Melanesian form of the religious life in community. Some viewed it as more like the Australian 'Bush Brotherhoods' with their temporary vows and specific task in the outback. The Bush Brotherhood of St Barnabas, consisting of priests serving scattered Christian communities in North Queensland, was founded in 1902 and is no longer operating.

At this stage, it appears that the Brotherhood was a mixture of all of these, but the questions of its nature and its true role would take years to resolve. Meanwhile it seemed to be going from strength to strength under the inspiring leadership of Brothers like Ini Kopuria, Daniel Sade, Moffatt Ohigita and Charles Fox.

The Brothers had asked John Steward if he could come back and help them, particularly in the light of the new developments which had been envisaged by the Conference of 1935. He felt that would not be right, but he did present a very beautiful chalice, paten and cruets for use in the chapel at Tabalia.[1]

At the Conference held in 1936 at Lolowai, the headquarters of the Archdeaconry of Southern Melanesia (New Hebrides), Alfred Teall, the Archdeacon, had gathered the Melanesian clergy and Brothers together to discuss their work. The presence of clergy as well as Brothers in these gatherings was a significant aspect of the way the Brothers had decided to operate. Their work was always to be part of the wider strategy of the Church and wherever possible the Diocesan Bishop was Chairman of their conferences. On this occasion Bishop Baddeley brought with him Brother Charles Fox "to guide their discussions,"[2] which resulted in the New Hebridean Brothers agreeing to man the households in the Outer Eastern Solomon Islands on Utupua and Santa Cruz "to relieve the pressure on the Solomon Island Brothers." Brothers had started work at Vila and had offered to work on Vanua Lava in the Banks Islands "until a priest was available to work there." The number of New Hebridean Brothers in 1936 rose to 29. At this Conference, the clergy agreed to start Companions' groups in their districts.

In the Solomons, some 'well-taught young men' had joined the Brotherhood, and, after the example of the school at Tabalia, several 'preliminary schools' were opened and staffed by the Brotherhood. The first had, in fact, been started on Raga in the New Hebrides, but soon afterwards had closed. Another, however, later grew into a Mission Junior School, then a training school for teachers and eventually, after the Second World War, a Senior Primary School.[3] This was the one established in 1936 at Alangaula (Alangakaula)[4] on Ugi Island in the Eastern Solomons, where boys from the Polynesian islands of the Solomons were taught. These islands included Sikaiana, Lord Howe (Ongtong Java), Rennell, Tikopia and parts of the Reef Islands. The school was supervised by Brother Charles Fox, assisted in 1936 by Martin Fiia and Henry Maabe. Novices also were trained at Alangaula for a while as it was felt that a second noviciate was required, and indeed there were not enough houses for all the novices at

Tabalia. With Dr Fox there in 1937 were Brothers Maabe, Male and Tara. The novices came from the Solomons and New Guinea, and spent a year training; their training included some visits to Makira (San Cristoval) in the middle of 1937. The Brothers were admitted at Tabalia at the end of their noviciate. Plans were made for a similar school on North Malaita under the guidance of the Reverend Howard Hipkin. The Brothers on Ugi had a whaleboat to get to their coconut plantation to make copra on Bio Island nearby, and they helped establish a 'women's station' and a 'native house' for a hospital from which medical tours could be made.[5]

Vila was in the part of the New Hebrides which Anglicans had agreed they would not work in. The agreement had been made with the Presbyterians in 1881 and had been largely respected by both sides, in spite of the objections raised by the Reverend Peter Milne, a Presbyterian missionary who had eventually to withdraw from proposed work in Aoba in the Anglican 'area'. However, Anglicans moving to the island of Efate to work on the plantations there needed help from their Church. The Bishop approached the Presbyterian Synod and formal permission was given for Anglican 'teachers' to be placed there. Two Brothers were sent with the aim of providing worship, instruction for adults and children, and the example of a Christian way of life. Mr Ballard, an Anglican working with the Government (which had British, French and Condominium administrations), agreed to try and find a piece of land for a church and a house to be "the spiritual centre and home for our exiles in Vila," as Archdeacon Teall put it. Meanwhile, Brothers James Mesana and Ambrose Gigiri (both from Pentecost Island) stayed with a man from the Torres Islands in the far north of the country. This Willie Taraumera and his wife Mirian had a house on the outskirts of the town at Tebakor. In 1936 Brother James wrote: "We have started work and six boys come to our school every day, and on Sunday about 50 adults from the nearby plantation come to the services, but we want help, that is, prayer, that we may be strengthened in our work and that we may set a good example among the people in this place." Sadly, in mid-July, having returned to Lolowai on Aoba (Ambae) to report to the 'Head Brother' there, he became ill and died at Lamalanga on Raga, Pentecost, on February 15, 1937. The Brothers had already built a temporary church in leaf, but with the generous help of Mr Ballard, by 1937 land had been obtained, and a permanent church was being built.[6] By 1938, Mr B C Ballard, MA, LLB, of the Law Office in the Lands Court, had been licensed as a lay reader and had learned Mota, to assist with the work.[7]

Brother Ambrose died in Vila, as did Willie Taraumera, in 1941. Both were buried at Fila Island in Vila Harbour. Some Anglicans had been living there, but the islanders asked them to move out as they wanted their land back, so they were established at Tagabe, two miles to the west of the town. A permanent church was built there by ex-Brother Harper Liñi, father of the future Prime Minister, Fr Walter Liñi.

In 1937 the number of Brothers was over 130, but only 80 were able to get to the Annual Conference. Forty novices were then admitted as Brothers. Some Brothers 'withdrew'. About thirty Brothers renewed their vows. At the end of the Conference came the ceremony which had become customary. Each Elder Brother, on behalf of his household, came forward to the sanctuary step and received a candle, which had been blessed on the altar. The Bishop then lit each candle with the words: "Let your light so shine before men ....."[8] Numbers had risen to over 140 in 1938. Bishop Baddeley said in New Zealand, at St Mary's Cathedral, Auckland: "Numbers are not everything, but here in the hands of the Bishop is a striking force."[9] In 1937, one Brother on the hospital staff at Fauabu, Walter, while playing football without boots, which was usual, broke his toe. This burst, and he died of tetanus.

Brother Charles Fox visited New Britain and gave the Brothers daily teaching and instruction during the period of a Staff Conference there with Bishop Baddeley. At that time, early 1938, there were ten Brothers working in that island, four at Sagsag in the extreme west, led by Brother Meshak, two led by Brother John at Kavele, two led by Brother Bertie (recently left at Meleglo among rather hostile or indifferent folk whose language they did not know), and two led by Brother Jacob at Au.[10] In the New Hebrides, four Brothers had gone to the extreme south of Pentecost Island.

In 1938, the Bishop in Polynesia had been visiting Ocean Island, the headquarters of the Gilbert and Ellice Islands Colony, on HMS *Wellington*, which had been diverted to Tikopia on the way, to check on lights seen by a passing ship. He had been able to go ashore and meet the five Brothers working there and the New Hebridean priest, Fr Ellison Tergortok, and also visit six of the village churches.[11] Ellison had come as a teacher in 1902 and had married a Tikopian woman. He had been ordained in 1935.[12] Tikopia island, peopled by Polynesians originally from Samoa, Tonga, Rotuma and other islands, lies 150 miles east of all the other islands of the Solomons. An anthropologist who went to work on Tikopia told Dr Fox that "the real change on the island from heathenism to Christianity came when a Household of Brothers went there."[13] Another Polynesian island, Anuta (Anudha) lies 70 miles further away and is the most easterly of the inhabited Solomon Islands and has only a small population. It was evangelised by Christians from Tikopia.

After the 1937 Conference five Brothers had been chosen to go to Tikopia: Elder Brother John Kona and Brothers Alan Otai, Mark Maneaba, Christian Siota and Misael Misakel. The island was ruled by four chiefs, at that time being Pataumarako, No.1 Chief, Patafua, No.2 Chief, Pakafika, No.3 Chief, and Pafañarere, No.4 Chief. It was No.2 Chief, Patafua, who accepted the Christian teaching, but the others did not. When he died, his son, of the same name, continued his policy.

Only a few of the people had become Christians, although they had already built five churches. The Brothers found their first two months very difficult, especially as the people were experiencing a famine. However, early in 1938 Chief Pafañarere as well as Chief Patafua had been converted. The other two chiefs were angry that some of their own people had also been converted by the Brothers, and so No.1 Chief planned to kill the Brothers when they came to build a church in his area. However, on the day they were to begin, there was heavy rain, and the two Chiefs who were against the Brothers fell into a heavy sleep and nothing was done. Some people took this as a sign, and it made them believe they should become Christians. Others were still very fearful of the two Chiefs, so the Brothers did not visit those people during the daytime. After dark, however, "they visited every night and preached the good news of the Lord Jesus." A church was then built at Namo village and dedicated to St Paul. The Brothers returned for the Annual Conference at Tabalia in 1938.

Bishop Baddeley paid tribute in the *Southern Cross Log* of July, 1939 to Brother Charles Fox, saying that he had served in Melanesia "for more than thirty years." He had in fact arrived at Norfolk Island in 1903! The Bishop wrote that Brother Charles was giving "the last years of his life in the training of these Brothers." The Bishop considerably underestimated the Brother. He did not leave the islands till he was 96, and only then because of his health and the need for care that he required. (Matron Woods at Taroaniara, where he had lived on Gela for many years, felt there were none prepared to look after him there.) He promised that he would be back! Doctors in New Zealand much earlier had once underestimated his stamina. He had originally been warned that he might not be fit enough for the tropics, when he first offered himself for service in the islands. He was, in fact, to give over another thirty years service to Melanesia after the Conference of 1938, even rejoining the Brotherhood in his late 90s when living in New Zealand. He always objected to being called 'retired'.

The follow-up to the Brothers' work in many places was not the only problem. The Brotherhood had to face up to the challenge of Ini's release from his life vow. He had led the Brotherhood for fifteen years and his solemn vow had deeply impressed those who had been inspired and trained by him. It was hoped that others might follow his example of lifetime dedication to the work. But it was not to be. Apparently the strain of celibacy, or perhaps the desire to undertake work as a district priest rather than care for an increasingly diverse religious community, had become too much for him to ignore or resist. In other communities for men, both Anglican and Roman Catholic (as well as in the Roman Catholic priesthood in the Pacific Islands) islanders for various reasons sometimes have found it difficult to keep a lifetime vow of celibacy, although some have succeeded. Many have given some years of devoted service as celibates and then married. Such was the case with Ini Kopuria. Surprisingly, all that Bishop Baddeley wrote in his *Letter from the Bishop* in the *Southern Cross Log* of April, 1941 was that the Brothers "no longer have the services of Ini Kopuria, who, after fifteen years with the Brothers, with a rich experience of work in all parts of Melanesia, and a great record of faithful service, is now betrothed, and after his marriage, will work as a district priest." As it happened, things worked out very differently, and he was never ordained priest.

A young woman called Laisa Loe[14] was living at Gaimali. Ini had come by boat to Volonavua and had then taken Daniel Nunuvia, Ben Bokoe, Joseph Rukalee and Christian Botokoli, as well as Laisa, to Veranaaso. As they had just been blessed as Companions, Brother Ini gave them further instruction there. However, he also became interested in Laisa as a future wife, and took the opportunity of asking Joseph Rukalee for his daughter. Joseph was cross and said: "You are a holy man; why do you want to get married?" Ini got carried away and said: "If you do not let me have Laisa, I shall ask the sharks and crocodiles to eat you two!" Joseph was furious and said: "You are not God!" and took his knife to try and cut Ini's throat. Fortunately Ñelevaina was able to stop him killing Ini. Joseph then sent Ini with Laisa's brother, Christian Botokoli, to see Bishop Baddeley at Taroaniara. Although he spent five days there, he did not manage to see the Bishop. He then came back and may have lied to Joseph, so that he would let him marry Laisa.[15] Ini's mother and Joseph Rukalee were cousins, and in custom Rukalee was Ini's 'uncle', and so he should not have asked to marry his daughter – which may explain why Ini went to such lengths to get agreement. Laisa also knew that Ini had made a promise of celibacy and commitment to the work of the Brotherhood 'before God at the cross', and she was afraid – in any case, she was only 18 years of age, and did not want to marry him. When the Brothers heard that he wanted to marry Laisa they decided to send him off to Wanderer Bay on the weather coast of Guadalcanal to run a school. (But this school never started because of something which eventually affected them all – the entry of the Japanese into the Second World War, and thus the beginning of the war in the Pacific.) Before going to Wanderer Bay to build a house for himself and Laisa, Ini insisted that he would stay with Joseph and her.[16] He had been on a tour with other Brothers when he and Christian Botokoli went off to Taroaniara. Brother Joseph Lavena of Malaita and another Brother then stayed in Joseph's house, while the other Brothers left Ini and scattered to different places. On Ini's return from Taroaniara, Joseph would not let him stay in his house. So he went to stay with Daniel Nunuvia at Rou, until Daniel's line had raised the 'bride price' for Laisa, which would have to be handed over before they could get married. Laisa then went to school at Siota, where the Sisters of the Cross taught 100 girls from Ugi, Makira, Malaita, Gela, Guadalcanal, Savo and Ysabel. The boys there were taught by John Bulemelu. Ini had temporary 'leave' but rejoined the Brothers from June to October, 1940, when he was released from his vows.[17]

After Ini's release, he had a custom marriage to Laisa three months later and went to live inland from Maravovo village. He then ceased to take any services and sat on the back seat of the church – a sign of being under church discipline (which he may have imposed upon himself). However, he did not give up his prayer life.

The departure of Ini from the Brotherhood, and especially the way it had happened, was a shock to the Brotherhood, but not a disaster. It showed that the Brotherhood could continue without his leadership, and that there were some whom he had inspired, and others whom he had trained, who could carry on the work. The Second World War had not yet begun to affect their work, although it would have a big impact when it reached the Solomon Islands with the Japanese invasion of the Northern Solomons in April 1942. The Japanese had already advanced southward after bombing

Pearl Harbor in Hawaii on December 7, 1941. This brought the Americans as well as the Japanese into the War.

One of the households on New Britain had been affected by severe flooding in 1940, during which the Brothers' house "went out to sea in a new watercourse which had formed right down the middle of the station."[18] The work on Malaita had been extended in 1935 to the district of Areare. Brother Ini with Brothers Charles Fox, Daniel Sade and Willie Masura'a (later a priest and Canon of Honiara Cathedral) had established themselves at Marou, but from 1935 to 1944 no heathen villages were converted in that area, in spite of their original hard work. At Marou itself there was no catechist for seven years in the church started by the Brothers, and from 1941 to 1944 during the War there were no Brothers, catechists or priest in the area, and no visit by the Bishop, so that some of the new Anglicans joined the Roman Catholic Church.[19]

By 1941 Brother Charles Fox was with a household of Brothers at Gwounatolo near Fouia on the edge of the Tae Lagoon in North Malaita. The Bishop wrote: "The Brothers have a hard job round here, and it is good to have Tasiu Charles' long experience of all sorts and conditions of Melanesians at their disposal."[20] However, when he returned to Tabalia next, the District Officer informed him that he could not stay there as the Protectorate Government had passed a law forbidding white men from spending even one night on native land, unless they were Government officers. Brother Charles Fox was indignant. Earlier regulations which he objected to included one which said every Melanesian had to have a number – so in protest he had worn a metal disc with a number on it round his neck. There had been another which forbade Melanesians to wear European dress. Bishop Steward had protested about that one and had got it withdrawn. So Fox took the matter of the new law to the Vicar-General, Gething Caulton (later Bishop of Melanesia) and was not impressed when Fr Caulton, instead of protesting on Brother Charles Fox's behalf, weakly apologised to Resident Commissioner Ashley for what the Brother had done. He then offered Brother Charles a cabin on the *Southern Cross*, from which he did the work of visiting Companions for a while. Solomon Islanders were also restricted. They were not allowed to move from one area to another without going to the Government station first and paying one shilling. Brother Charles Fox felt that this lack of consideration for the feelings and conditions of the people may have been one of the things which led to the protest movement after the Second World War, starting on Malaita, which was known as 'Marching Rule'.[21] After the war, he spent four months at Siota on Gela with US Navy 'Seebees', then went to Fiu on Malaita for some years, where followers of Marching Rule threatened Archdeacon Reynolds, but not him.[22]

The Movement was properly called Maasinga Rulu, *Maasinga* being an Areare word meaning 'brotherhood', and was an attempt at self-determination by the Malaita people, with anti-European overtones (or, at least, anti-Colonial Government ones). Fr Willie Masura'a's response was to form the 'Church Association' with an emphasis on Melanesians supporting *their* Church, rather than 'the Mission' constantly directing and providing.

Another missionary priest, the Reverend Howard Hipkin, had worked with the Brothers in the 1930s as they travelled through the tribal areas of the Koio (Kwaio), Areare and Kwara'ae peoples on Malaita. Their journey took about one year and was difficult. They slept on grass mats in native houses and ate taro, yams and coconuts. Some of the villages were high in the mountains where the rainfall was 300 inches a year and "the dense tropical bush, deep flowing rivers and mosquito infected swamps were almost impregnable." They suffered from malaria and other tropical ailments. Fr Hipkin was warned by the Resident Commissioner that they had to be cautious when visiting the Sineranggu and Uru tribes, because it was in their area that two white District Officers and fifteen Solomon Islander policemen had previously been massacred. Although they sometimes received a hostile reception, even being "stoned back into the bush," they were usually well received and were able to give people medical attention and get agreement for two Brothers to stay and begin simple teaching. Among the Brothers accompanying Fr Hipkin were Ini Kopuria, Willie Masura'a and Frederick Añii.[23]

In the New Hebrides, where there were 24 Brothers in 1939, they were divided by the Bishop into two groups, one to work at Qatnapni (Bwatnapni) and the other to return with him to the Solomons to work on Malaita. From their headquarters at Qatnapni on the island of Pentecost they taught boys and made visits to the 'heathen' villages inland. They were led by Brother John Binihi, who had been in the Brotherhood for ten years, and included a priest, Simeon Langlangmele, who had previously been a District Priest on the island. He had been ordained in 1926 and had also worked in the Solomons. He died on February 10, 1943. Ex-Brother Matthias Tabe was ordained on April 16 in that same year. Dan Sade left the Brotherhood after eight or nine years. He married a girl from the island of Savo near Guadalcanal and worked for a time in Moli District on Guadalcanal. On St Mark's Day, 1941, in the newly dedicated chapel of St Peter at the College at Maka on Malaita, he was ordained priest. The departure of Dan Sade as well as Ini Kopuria meant that the leadership passed to Tasiu Dr Charles Fox, who in 1941 toured the households, including Kopuria Household on Gela (near Tulagi, the capital) and Tabalia. There was then another household looking after the Brotherhood's coconut plantation on Bio island (off Ugi in the Eastern Solomons), where a new church was dedicated in 1942. At Kopuria Household they used 'pidgin' to communicate with the workers from many different islands, but the Bishop refused to use it when conducting confirmations. On Malaita, the Brothers had opened a school at Gwounatolo for sixty children from the artificial islands, where some of them were working. Indeed, Brother Bartholomew Beve and another Brother had had to sleep on one of these islands in a pigsty! The Bishop, however, wrote of him that he was "a lad who is always clean and proud of his appearance." The school did not last very long as there were "so many counter attractions." The Bishop commented, "Money is their God in Tai" (that is, in the Tae Lagoon area, where the artificial islands were situated behind the barrier reef).[24]

At the end of the year 1942 Brother Charles Fox was released by Bishop Baddeley from his vows. Dr Fox "loved and admired that very great bishop", but they disagreed about a number of things.[25] Brother Charles objected to the Bishop saying to good-looking boys he met anywhere: "Come along and be a Brother", even though the young men might have no vocation to the life. When the Bishop decided to ordain some of the Brothers, Brother Charles wanted some to stay in the Brotherhood. But the Bishop said, "the districts needed them too much," and Brother Charles asked to be released, although it did not happen then. Brother Charles hoped that one day there would be a Melanesian Priest-Brother as Tutor. He himself saw how important it was for the Brothers to be properly trained, and for them to have Holy Communion regularly in their training. When he taught at Tabalia, the Brothers got several hours of teaching a day for the first time, including his fine teaching of the New Testament. When he had joined, he had recognised that there were many weaknesses, which Brother Ini also was concerned about. Bishop Baddeley indeed thought it had become rather lifeless and might not have lasted if Charles Fox had not joined when he did. He had a hard time as a Novice, living on the same food as the others, as he had grown used to a better diet for nine years as Headmaster of Pawa School. However, what was important to him was that the people had recognised the Brotherhood as truly Melanesian, and loved it. He rejoiced to work under Brother Ini, when he ruled it, as he had a great admiration for him. One result of his joining the Brotherhood was that many of the boys at Pawa had followed him into it, and so it began to include much better educated Brothers who had been taught by him, such as George Basilei, Willie Masura'a, Henry Maabe, Martin Fiia and John Bosamata, who died at Lord Howe (Ongtong Java) – in his opinion, the best Brother of them all. In Charles Fox's time as a Brother, the number of Brothers increased ten-fold – but then came the War.

When Charles Fox left the Brotherhood, he did not leave Malaita. He had offered himself and had been accepted as a 'Coastwatcher', to warn the British Administration (which Bishop Baddeley had persuaded to stay[26]) about the movements of the Japanese troops. He was given the status of a Second Lieutenant and was stationed in the Tae Lagoon, where he had the assistance of Brother Bartholomew Beve. The Japanese settled fifteen miles to the north of them. Bartholomew offered to go and count them, under the pretext of selling them bananas – a brave thing to do. He went in one day and came back with information about their numbers and gun positions. The next day, Dr Fox sent this information by runners across the hills to Auki and the Government.[27] Later the Japanese came to search for him, but Dr Fox had already gone up into the hills. The Japanese were afraid to go there, as they had heard that the people were fierce cannibals – although they were in fact friends of Dr Fox! Barnabas had buried Dr Fox's books, without any covering, and heavy rain for a week meant that there was nothing left of them when he came to dig them up. Not only that, but 500 books he left in cases at Siota were all burnt by the Japanese.[28] Unlike Ini, Brother Charles Fox was not fearless. On one occasion, he went up into the bush and stayed with a chief who, after a time, asked him to leave – as "the Japanese might not like it." So Brother Charles left!

At Tabalia on Guadalcanal on Good Fridays, the Brothers usually did a play about the crucifixion and put up a cross on a small hill, which came to be known as 'Calvary'. It was close to their piggery. On it grew wild bamboo and it was there that the Brothers constructed a small house when the Japanese came.[29] One day they were coming from the sea up the bank of the river which runs through their gardens when they came across a party of Japanese with their rifles stacked against a tree. The Japanese rushed to take up their rifles. One Brother jumped into a pool in the river and lay on the bottom pretending to be dead. The other three fled. After glancing at the Brother in the river, the Japanese chased after the others, who ran down to the sea and swam out. The Japanese stood on the beach and fired at them, killing Brother Simon Sigai of San Cristoval. A bullet passed through Brother Alan Suta's hat, "making a deep hollow as it shaved a line through his hair," and leaving a mark.[30] The Japanese also called for their planes to come and strafe the Brothers. However, the two survivors swam four or five miles down the coast, landed and got safely back to Tabalia. There was fierce fighting on the road from the sea to Tabalia, where the church and books were burnt, the houses destroyed and the gold chalice and paten given by Bishop Steward (hidden in bamboos) carried off. Michael Takutili, who had taught at Tabulivu, was hiding in the hills behind Aruligo (Aruligho) and came down to see what had happened, but finding Japanese still in the area, he went back.

The household on Gela was closed and most of the Brothers resigned without being properly released, whether they were in the Solomons, New Britain or the New Hebrides. Some fled, some went to work to raise money for the Brotherhood, and some returned after working for the Americans,[31] who had arrived in force on Guadalcanal and Tulagi on August 7, 1942. By February 1943, the Japanese had been driven off Guadalcanal, but they had retreated further west, making their base at Munda on New Georgia island, and further battles took place in that area between June 24 and October 9, 1943.[32] In 1943 only eight Brothers were left in one household at Gwounatolo. Brother Charles Fox had earlier appointed Brother Patrick Kupe from Guadalcanal to be Elder Brother, but in a few months he got engaged to Dorah Manaboe from Fouia and offered his resignation to the Bishop, who then appointed Brother James Vasethe. The Bishop took the remaining seven Brothers with him to Fauabu on the other side of Malaita on the *Mavis* in 1944 to stay with Mr C R Buffett, the carpenter.[33] Then they were moved again by the ship to Taroaniara on Gela to stay with the Bishop. On October 28, 1944, the Feast of St Simon and St Jude, three more Brothers left, but six boys from Alangaula School came to join. Alan Suta was readmitted, and Mark from Gwounatafu, who had become a Novice at Fauabu, was professed. Two households were to be reopened, Tabalia and Maka, with Brother James Vasethe at Tabalia and Alan Suta at Maka as Elder Brothers, but Tabalia was not available then, and so the Brothers went to Maravovo village instead.

Meanwhile, Ini Kopuria had seen the destruction wrought by the Japanese and heard of the resignation and dispersal of the Brothers, and he thought that the Brotherhood was finished. He had not been there to help them in their hour of need! However he had finished the house at Wanderer Bay and returned to Gaimali to Daniel Nunuvia's house to collect Laisa, who had been brought back (after only four months) from Siota by the *Mavis* because of the Japanese threat. The Brothers who had stayed with her father had dug holes and hid in them when the Japanese came. Ini and Laisa moved from place to place until they reached Komulee, where Ini built a house, and where they settled. Laisa became pregnant and Ini went off to work for the Americans in the Labour Corps. They called him 'Chief Ini', and greatly admired his organisation of the labourers who helped them.[34] He came back for one week for the birth of the baby. However, the baby, Mary, died in the third week after her birth. Ini came back again for two weeks, at the end of which he took his wife to stay with her uncle, Daniel Poru, at Bokonidua on the Guadalcanal Plains. He then came to visit her from time to time bringing rations. Laisa gave birth to their second child, May, at Gaviga, while Ini was in prison for two months. After that, Fr Dan Sade invited them to Maravovo at the end of the war in the Solomons. There were already Brothers stationed there, as they had found that the Americans were using the Tabalia area for exercises, and so it was very dangerous to go there. They made gardens at Maravovo in order to get food for their eventual return to Tabalia. It was then discovered that Deacon Ini was suffering from tuberculosis and in a few months the sickness grew worse. He was brought by his wife and the six Brothers there to the main part of the village, where the Brothers looked after him by rotation day and night, two by two. Tragically the second child had died when she was twelve months old. Fr Dan Sade told Ini that it was because he had not been properly released from the Brotherhood at the time when he had arranged for Laisa to be his wife. It was eight months after that when Ini started to spit blood and got worse. He then grew angry and said, "Do you think it is hard for me to die?" He had seen his beloved Tabalia destroyed, his Brotherhood nearly disappear and both of his children die. But he had reflected on Daniel Sade's words and said to his wife: "It is good that Fr Sade was cross with us because our children have died." He then felt deeply sorry and repentant for what he had done wrong. Dr Fox said his repentance was "deeper than St Peter's."[35] On the day of his death, he sent Laisa to get some hot water, washed his whole body, changed his 'calico' (his *malo* or long loin-cloth), laid himself down again on his bed to read his Bible, then died.

Brother Robert Raeriara reported that his death was like that of a child, as he said nothing to the Brothers or even his wife, except to ask for certain things to be brought to him, which he then threw away. He even asked for the Brothers and his wife and two villagers to leave him, but they did not. The Brothers felt that his sad and disturbing death was the result of his breaking his life vow, and Ini's attitude and actions suggest that he had the same feeling.[36]

Laisa sent the husband of Ini's sister to tell the Reverend F A Rowley, a deacon who was then Headmaster of Maravovo School. Ini had died about 7 p.m. on June 6, 1945,[37] and he was buried in the cemetery of Maravovo village at 1 p.m. the next day.[38] Brother James Vasethe and Brother Robert Raeriara were there, but other Brothers were prevented by heavy rain from attending. The two Brothers had been to see Fr Rowley during the night.

Laisa was left a widow, but she always remembered Ini's kindness to her and their child at Maravovo, letting her go everywhere and never being jealous, although he himself felt lonely and unhappy. It was a sad end to a wonderfully creative life, but the Brotherhood was not dead! Stories circulated about him. It was believed that he had had a vision of angels coming to tell him to go to heaven. His miracles became the stuff of legend. He was said to have travelled on the backs of crocodiles and to have dried up the waters of the Mataniko River on Guadalcanal by striking them with his walking stick, when he and another Brother wished to cross.[39] In Rabaul, one man was supposed to have tried to kill him when his back was turned, but his arm froze in the striking position until Ini released him.

Another story passed down tells of when he was in the Territory of New Guinea and an old man asked him to climb up a coconut tree for a nut, but Ini told him his leg was no good and that he would have to do it himself. The old man refused. So Ini pointed his stick at the coconut and it fell down. The 'heathen' man said in Pidgin: "*Wat kaen devol ia? Mi laekem devol olsem!*" ("What kind of spirit can do that? I would like to have him!"). Ini replied, "*Sapos iu wandem, iu save tekem*" ("If you want it, you can have it"). It seems that in this way he tried to illustrate the power of God.[40]

As the work of the Brotherhood gradually grew again until by the 1970s it had almost returned to its previous strength (and had indeed extended its work as far as the New Guinea Highlands), the Chaplain, Fr Brian

Macdonald-Milne, went to check on Ini's grave at Maravovo and found it in a poor state. This had been reported earlier, in the 1966 Conference, by Brother James Herbert. The Brothers then renewed and beautified it. A special service was introduced in the Companions Book to be used on the day of his death, both at Maravovo – to which the Brothers decided to process yearly from Tabalia on foot – and throughout the islands. A special hymn was written by the Chaplain which could be used at any time in memory of Ini.

A great Melanesian had died in tragic circumstances, but his legacy was in the Brotherhood which lived on, and in the thousands of people throughout the Pacific who had by then found new life in Christ. Ini's name was included among the Commemorations in the new Church of England Calendar in 1997, to be remembered on June 6. Fr Hipkin wrote: "Ini Kopuria was a proud and arrogant man, admired by some people, disliked by others, dedicated to his service for Christ, a trusted and faithful friend, and undoubtedly a leading personality in the Melanesian Church."[41]

Dr Fox wrote in his tribute in the *Southern Cross Log*:[42] "He was, I think, one of the ablest Melanesians I have known, the other two being Clement Marau and Hugo Hebala...... No Brother ever questioned his absolute authority, not because he was the Founder, but because of the force of his personality." The things that impressed Dr Fox were Ini's spirituality – "he was the most reverent Melanesian I have known"; his joyousness – "he was almost always in high spirits"; his deep understanding of the thoughts of his fellow Melanesians – "he always knew who was really in the wrong"; and his commonsense – "he always knew what was practicable." Dr Fox also recognised that "he was not popular with the white staff who thought him conceited" – "there was a little truth in this, for he felt his own gifts, though I don't think the conceit went deep; but also was he very sensitive to colour feeling. He thought it all wrong that *every* Melanesian, because of his colour, should be inferior to *every* white man because of his colour, yet he felt there was this feeling even *within* the Mission." Steward and Fox appreciated what Ini stood for and respected him for that, and in return they gained *his* lasting respect too – but his respect had to be earned, it was not automatically given. He stood for the right of Melanesians to become leaders in their own Church.[43]

His influence has been continuous and strong. When John Ashwin Wetelwur became Head Brother in the 1960s, he discovered words of Brother Ini which inspired him and which he hoped would inspire others to join the work of the Brotherhood – or would at least encourage the clergy to look for suitable better educated aspirants. He quoted them in the Newsletter of St Peter's Theological College in 1968:

"All you young fellows, awake! Here are great thoughts; young men of Melanesia see clearly. If you want to join the Brotherhood, make up your mind to devote all your powers to the work. You must not be like young boys who went early in the morning with their father to the garden. When they reached the garden and began to work, what the boys did was to find the shade of the tree and lie there and rest. Young men, what if we are to follow our father to the garden, are we to do the same thing? When it's a matter of making new gardens, there is no room for idlers and grumblers and slackers; everything in regard to this sort of work calls for keen workers only. The Father's heart warms over his garden. The boy's heart must be warm too! There is no time to complain and waste. The work is all to be done in the spirit of joy and gladness. This is the standard of our work! Often we hear people say, 'He has ended his work or life.' But in that they are wrong, for the work done is not the end, but the beginning. For we need more workers for the garden, Bishops, priests, catechists, brothers, teachers, readers, healers, workers of miracles, interpreters and so on, who shall continue to water and prune the fields in the country and beyond, working with the Master."[44]

Ex-Brother Robert Raerirua, who in 1998 was the only one of the six Brothers present at Ini's deathbed to be still alive, considered that only the title 'Father' (Daddy) was suitable for Melanesians to use of him. He was "the first Melanesian to be outstanding in the time of great conversion. He is to be called 'Father' as a respect for his great work in Melanesia. He is the first Melanesian to start a community in the Church, that is now beginning to be recognised globally...." "He was a man of prayer, play and work. His love for his Brothers was great; though at times hard on his Brothers, he was still one with them as Brother.... I have never in my life seen a man like Father Ini.... He was a man of will and vision." "Through our love and respect for him we have done with our whole heart the service he had begun for us." He added (in the hope that the Brotherhood would remain true to Ini's vision) that a 'real' Brother was "one who gives up himself and commits his whole being to his service, more especially by getting down to know the depths of Father Ini's aim."[45]

NOTES

1 The chalice and paten appear to have been stolen by Japanese soldiers. See *Lord of the Southern Isles*, p. 195

2 *Southern Cross Log*, January 1937. Brother Charles Fox spent six months on Pentecost as well. According to Frank Bollen Qealav in an account written in 1979, Brother Ini was also present, and clergy present included Fr Mackenzie Mumeg (North Nduindui District, West Ambae), Fr Wilson Rong (Lombaha District, East Ambae), Fr Stephen Wetelwur (Gaua, Banks Islands), Fr Harry Vanva (Merlav, Banks Islands) and Fr Adams (Torres Islands). Fr Vanva died in 1937. Companions also spread to other islands.

3 When the Senior Primary School closed, it was handed over for a while to the Society of St Francis for training purposes.

4 The land at Alangaula was leased by Bishop Baddeley with money previously used to pay Dr Fox's stipend, which he no longer received as a Brother. However, the Bishop did not think Brother Charles was eating well enough and allowed him about £20 for extra food to augment his diet.

5 *Southern Cross Log*, October 1937.

6 This second church was built using biscuit tins! See *Southern Cross Log*, July 1937. A church in more permanent materials was built in 1961 at Tagabe on the road to the airport.

7 *Southern Cross Log*, July 1938.

8 *Southern Cross Log*, January 1938,

9 *Southern Cross Log*, October 1938.

10 *Southern Cross Log*, April 1938.

11 *Southern Cross Log*, April 1938.

12 *Lord of the Southern Isles*, p. 209.

13 Fox: *Kakamora*, p. 78. In Raymond Firth's study, *We, The Tikopia* (George Allen & Unwin, London), first published in 1936, he mentions a visit by the *Southern Cross* in 1857, but says, "it was over half a century before any converts resulted from the fleeting periodic calls." He also writes: "In many respects the Christianity of the Tikopia is only superficial. That the old gods still exist is never questioned by the [first Christian] chief or his people; they are merely latent, and from time to time make their presence felt with startling effect" (pp. 4-5). Professor Firth spent twelve months on Tikopia from July 1928 to July 1929. See also his *History and Traditions of Tikopia*, published in 1961 by The Polynesian Society (Incorporated), Wellington, New Zealand. Dr Firth became Reader in Anthropology, then Professor, in the University of London, and was knighted. In 2000 he celebrated his 100th birthday, and died soon afterwards.

14 The account of Laisa Loe's relationship with Ini Kopuria is based on an interview on Guadalcanal with her by the author in the 1970s. Two young men accompanied her and would not let the author see her privately. They indeed appeared to contribute negative comments at a distance from time to time, for reasons which were not clear, and these were apparently somewhat distressing to her. The author had to be as sensitive as possible with his questions in the circumstances.

15 If this is true, it is out of character, as Dr Fox wrote that he had never known Ini to lie.

16 When criticised for this, he replied: "Well, Joseph lived with the Virgin Mary, didn't he?" (This, to the author, indicates Ini's rather unbalanced state of mind at the time.) This piece of information was passed on by Dr Fox to the author.

17 The information about Brother Ini's release and marriage was given to Brother Michael Ripotia by ex-Brother Robert Raeriara on February 25, 1998.

18 *Southern Cross Log*, January 1941.

19 Information from a written account by the ex-Brother, Fr Samuel Su'unorua, communicated by the Bishop of Malaita, Terry Brown, to the author in 1999.

20 *Southern Cross Log*, April 1941.

21 See *Pacific Protest: The Maasinga Rule Movement, Solomon Islands, 1944-1952*, edited by Hugh Laracy. Published by the Institute of Pacific Studies, University of the South Pacific, Suva, Fiji, 1983.

22 Personal communication by Dr Fox to the author in the 1970s.

23 This account is taken from a written communication to the author in the 1970s.

24 This account is taken from a written communication to the author in the 1970s.

25 From a letter written by Dr Fox to the author dated March 22, 1970.

26 Baddeley had done distinguished service as an officer in the First World War and had the MC with bar and DSO. He was awarded the US Medal of Freedom in 1945.

27 Bishop Baddeley and Sister Christine Woods were at Tañtalau nearby. Sister Woods started work on Ugi in 1937 and was later awarded the MBE and then the OBE.

28 This information was included in an account written by Dr Fox for the author.

29 The account of events at Tabalia was given to the author on April 28, 1979, during an interview with ex-Brother Ben Bokoe and Mr Michael Takutili, then living near Najilanggu, east of Honiara. See also Fox: *Kakamora*, pp. 78-79.

30 Fox: *Kakamora*, p. 79.

31 According to ex-Brother Robert Raeriara, the Brotherhood's work was disrupted for thirteen months.

32 See D C Horton: *New Georgia: Pattern for Victory* (The Pan/Ballantine Illustrated History of World War II, London, August 1972, first published in the USA, July 1971). This includes an account of the Coastwatchers, which had been set up by the Royal Australian Naval Intelligence Division.

33 According to James Vasethe, there were two from Santa Ysabel, three from San Cristoval, one from North Malaita and one from Sikaiana.

34 See Dr Fox, writing in the *Southern Cross Log*, March 1962.

35 A personal communication to the author.

36 This account is from ex-Brother Robert Raeriara, who was present.

37 According to a written account by some of the Brothers, probably recorded by Fr James Vasethe, entitled *History of the Melanesian Brotherhood, 1943-45*, in the author's possession.

38 He *may* have been buried by F A Rowley. Subsequently in 1966, the Head Brother asked the Bishop if his bones could be moved to Tabalia, but the request was not granted. Ex-Brother Robert claimed a missionary teacher called Patrick buried him, as no priest was available.

39 A story told by Brother Patrick Aubugotu.

40 Personal communication to the author by ex-Brother Ben Bokoe and Michael Takutili on April 28, 1979.

41 Personal communication to the author, undated.

42 *Southern Cross Log*, June 1946. See also *Exciting Holiness* edited by Brother Tristam SSF (Canterbury Press, Norwich, England, 1997); *The Saints of the Anglican Calendar*, Kathleen Jones (Canterbury Press, Norwich, 2000); and *Love's Redeeming Work: The Anglican Quest for Holiness*, compiled by Bishops Geoffrey Rowell and Kenneth Stevenson and Archbishop Rowan Williams (Oxford University Press, 2001).

43 His day, June 6, has increasingly been observed throughout Melanesia. Many are named after him, including Fr John Ini Lapli, elected Governor-General of Solomon Islands in 1999. He appears in a stained glass window above the altar in the Chapel at Tabalia, commissioned by the Companions and ordered in London by Fr Brian Macdonald-Milne while on leave as Chaplain of the Brotherhood. This is probably the only stained glass window in any Anglican Church in Melanesia. On either side of Ini appear a New Guinea Highlander and a woman Companion reading her Companions' Book – a design suggested by the Chaplain and approved by the Brothers. When Matron Woods visited Tabalia and was shown the window by the Chaplain, she looked at the likeness of Ini and said, "Nothing like him!" This was probably because he was very dark, but the window had to show him with a lighter skin colour so that the light could shine through. She herself appeared to be somewhat critical of Ini. Also, on board ship once with the Chaplain, she said of a Brother dressed for prayer in his white singlet and loincloth ('calico'), "He looks like a servant!" (Those at Government House then dressed similarly.) The Chaplain replied: "Surely that is indeed what a Brother is meant to be!"

44 As quoted in the 1968 Newsletter of St Peter's Theological College, Siota, commemorating the centenary of the ordination of the first Melanesian deacon. John Ashwin was later ordained.

45 These comments were made to Brother Michael Ripotia in February 1998.

CHAPTER TEN

The Brothers in front and the novices standing outside the School House, Tabalia.

Map prepared by H. E. Robinson Pty. Ltd., Sydney for the Australian Board of Missions
Key: A - Air C - Church H - Hospital S - School T - Teacher Training

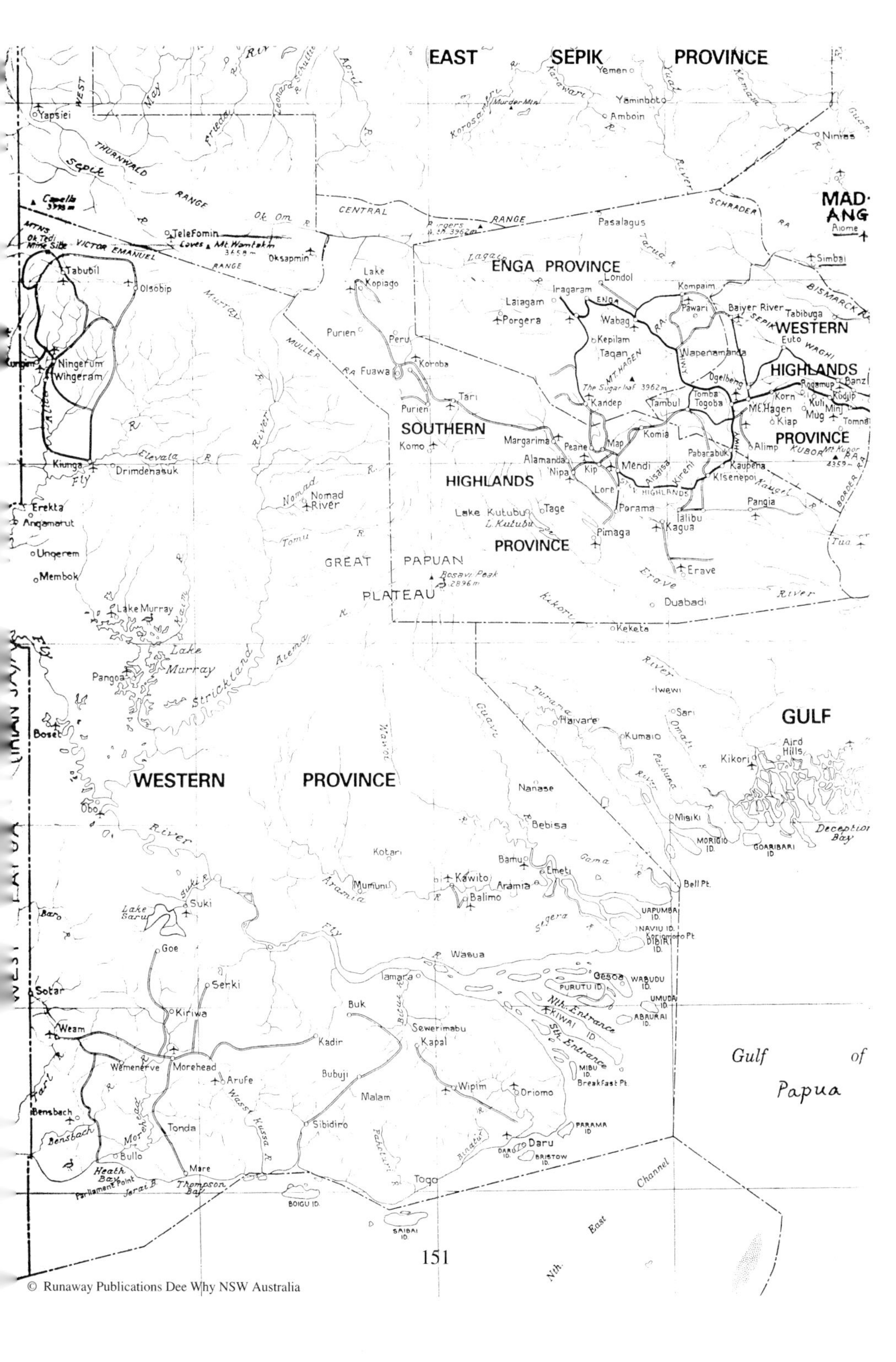
EAST SEPIK PROVINCE
ENGA PROVINCE
SOUTHERN HIGHLANDS PROVINCE
WESTERN HIGHLANDS PROVINCE
WESTERN PROVINCE
GULF
GREAT PAPUAN PLATEAU
CENTRAL RANGE
THURNWALD RANGE
VICTOR EMANUEL RANGE
MULLER RA
SCHRADER RA
BISMARCK RA
KUBOR RA
Gulf of Papua
Yapsiei
Yemen
Yaminboto
Amboin
Ninias
Simbai
Aiome
Telefomin
Oksapmin
Mt. Wamtakin 3658 m
Ok Tedi Mine Site
Tabubil
Olsobip
Ningerum
Wingeram
Kiunga
Drimdenasuk
Erekta
Angamarut
Ungerem
Membok
Lake Murray
Pangoa
Boset
Obo
Lake Kopiago
Purien
Peru
Koroba
Fuawa
Tari
Komo
Margarima
Nomad River
Bosavi Peak 2896 m
Lake Kutubu
Tage
Pimaga
Pasalagus
Londol
Iragaram
Laiagam
Porgera
Wabag
Kepilam
Tagan
Mt. Hagen
The Sugarloaf 3962 m
Kandep
Tambul
Kompaim
Pawari
Baiyer River
Tabibuga
Wapenamanda
Ogelbeng
Tomba
Togoba
Euto
Banz
Korn
Kuli
Mug
Minj
Kiap
Tomnal
Alimp
Mt Kubor 4359 m
Komia
Map
Peare
Alamanda
Nipa
Kip
Mendi
Pabarabuk
Kaupena
Kisenepoi
Lore
Porama
Ialibu
Kagua
Pangia
Erave
Duabadi
Keketa
Iwewi
Sari
Haivare
Kumaio
Kikori
Aird Hills
Nanase
Bebisa
Migiki
Morigio ID.
Goaribari ID.
Deception Bay
Kotari
Bamu
Emeti
Kawito
Mumuri
Aramia
Balimo
Bell Pt.
Urapumba ID.
Naviu ID.
Koriomoto Pt
Dibiri ID.
Suki
Lake Saru
Baro
Goe
Wasua
Iamara
Gesoa
Purutu ID.
Wabudu ID.
Umuda ID.
Abaurai ID.
Kiwai ID.
Nth. Entrance
Sth. Entrance
Mibu ID.
Breakfast Pt.
Sehki
Sotar
Kiriwa
Buk
Sewerimabu
Kapal
Weam
Kadir
Wemenerve
Morehead
Arufe
Bubuji
Wipim
Oriomo
Malam
Bensbach
Tonda
Sibidiro
Parama ID
Daru
Bristow ID.
Bullo
Mare
Heath Bay
Parliament Point
Jerai B.
Thompson Bay
Togo
Boigu ID.
Saibai ID.
East Channel
Fly River
Strickland
Elevala R
Aramia
Kikori River
Turama
Purari
Erave
Nth.

CHAPTER TEN

RESURRECTION: MELANESIA AND NEW GUINEA

At the end of the War, the Brotherhood was a shadow of its former self. It had become small and insignificant, but it had the backing of the Bishop and the devoted loyalty of the few remaining Brothers. They had to start again, almost from scratch.

After the death of Brother Ini, the Bishop collected the Brothers a few weeks later and took them to stay with him at Taroaniara on Gela, his headquarters, from where he was reorganising the Diocese. They stayed for three weeks. Then, on August 23, 1945, the Bishop and Brother James Vasethe travelled to Maravovo village for its church festival on August 24, St Bartholomew's Day. After the Eucharist and feast, they went on to Tabalia and took the big wooden cross from there, which had been damaged in the war, to be repaired at Taroaniara. A few days later, the MV *Gwen* took the six Brothers to Maravovo village to collect their things, and then it dropped them at Tabalia and sailed away. It was near the end of August. What the Brothers found when they walked up from the beach to the station was "a very dangerous and fearful sight."[1] Brother James remembered that "it was very thick bush, the bones of the dead bodies lying all about, bombs, hand-bombs, shells and the cartridges." It had been bombed by the Americans.[2] The Brothers cleared a small area and put up a tent to sleep in, using stretchers as beds. Then they started on building a house, cleared paths to the river and the seacoast and "made a little garden". It was very dangerous to light any fire or burn any rubbish, because of the bombs. They got their food from the gardens they had planted at Maravovo village. The house and garden had, however, been completed by the time they went for their Annual Conference, held that year at Taroaniara, on the Feast of St Simon and St Jude, October 28.[3] Four senior Brothers were released then, but some boys from Alangaula School joined to be trained as Novices. Brother Alan Suta became Elder Brother at Tabalia and Brother Cecil Riumana at Maka on Malaita. Brother James went to teach at Taroaniara Junior Primary School. By 1947 many *tinqoro* were in training again at Tabalia, and two more ex-Brothers had been ordained at Pawa on January 24 – George Basilei to the priesthood and Christian Rouikera to the diaconate.[4] Bishop Baddeley then resigned and paid his final visits, including one to Tabalia, before returning to England to become firstly Bishop Suffragan of Whitby in York Diocese, and then, in 1954, Bishop of the Diocese of Blackburn, where he died in office in 1960.[5] He was famous for his loud voice, and his widow felt it was very appropriate, when a new Cathedral was built later in Honiara, that the bell in its tower, sounding out over the capital, should be in his memory.[6] He was succeeded as Bishop of Melanesia by Sidney Gething Caulton, consecrated on February 2, 1948, in New Zealand.

The Annual Brothers' Conference continued to be arranged. It was held at Pawa in 1950, and the various priests from the districts where the Brothers were at work reported favourably on the Brothers' work. It was said that there was "evidence of the real missionary spirit" among the Brothers.[7] In 1951 the Conference was held at Tabalia and Brother Maurice[8] Maneae was elected as Head Brother, while households were established at Malu'u and Ataa on Malaita, and Gorobau and Marau on Guadalcanal. At a Staff Conference of the Diocese it had been decided to establish a new Catechists' School at Tabalia in 1950, to be started by Dr Fox. He stayed at Tabalia, where he found many mosquitos and rats and a wet earth floor to sleep on, but he also thought the four Brothers there, including the Head Brother, "splendid".[9] He took over the instruction of the fourteen Novices (first teaching them the Mota language), while seven young men from Fiu on Malaita prepared the site for the school. They also rebuilt the road to Tabalia, through a swamp. It had been destroyed by the Japanese with their jeeps and tanks. They also constructed a new road 500 yards long to the site of the new Catechists' School, which Dr Fox decided to call St Andrew's, Kohimarama, in memory of the Melanesian School in New Zealand run by Bishop Patteson. The Brothers built Dr Fox a small house, 15 feet by 15 feet, with a palm floor; "most snug and comfortable, though somewhat small," he wrote.[10]

In 1951 there were altogether 35 Brothers and 20 Novices. In 1952 there were 33 Brothers at work on Malaita and Guadalcanal, and 33 Novices. 20 Novices became Brothers at the 1952 Annual Conference and 18 Brothers renewed their yearly vows, making a total of 38 Brothers. The Conference decided to put a new household in Areare in South Malaita and establish another one for Santa Ana and Santa Catalina Islands, at the eastern end of the main Solomon chain of islands. There would be two households on North Malaita and one on Guadalcanal, in addition to Tabalia itself. The Areare District had been strongly affected by the native movement known as *Maasinga Rulu* or 'Marching Rule', with its rejection of European influence and control. The Brothers would be working with

Fr Willie Au, who would take over half the area, and Fr Willie Masura'a, an ex-Brother. These two priests were deeply concerned about the way Marching Rule was turning some people away from the Anglican Church, and Fr Willie Masura'a had a vision of an alternative organisation, based on Church principles, and enlisted the support of Fr Willie Au and others. It was approved by the Bishop (and the District Commissioner of Malaita District), was formally launched as the 'Church Association' in 1953, and was supported by Synod.[11] The people of Areare were mostly nomadic, living with their pigs, and it was difficult to persuade them to live in villages.[12] But the clergy and Brothers persevered.

John Still Ritau[13] served in the Brotherhood from 1943 to 1958, and part of that time was spent under George Anagnafu[14] of Ysabel after he had been elected Head Brother. He served in various places in the Solomons, but mostly on Malaita. He was originally from Abiria village in Arosi One District on Makira (San Cristoval). He had had no formal education but became a dedicated Brother and served for fifteen years. He described the life of the Brothers in this period as "very holy and full of grace. Life was lived with a blind trust in God by faith." He added: "The Brotherhood is the spearhead of the Church and so the Brotherhood should lead a quality of life for the world to follow." He found the life of the Brothers to be very good – "painful .... yet refreshing; hard.... yet miracles will happen." He had been told that there could be effective ministry only "if you could accept orders with a heart full of joy and the will to serve God's people.... like Christ who so willingly obeyed his Father's will." Their only aim was "to convert and to build God's kingdom.... Because we have direct faith in Jesus, all that we do was done for his glory."

It was while he was serving on Malaita that he experienced what he believed was a miracle. He came one day with another Brother to the village of Fiu, not very far from the Government station at Auki. They found members of one tribe there making a sacrifice to their 'heathen god', as they wanted to bring back to life their chief, who had died two days before without appointing a successor to lead the people. Two days of sacrifice had had no effect, so when the Brothers arrived they were asked to bring him back to life. They explained that they believed only God had the power to give life and to take it away. They could not go against his will. However, the people insisted, and even threatened them. The other Brother told Brother John that God could raise the dead chief to life, and then the people would convert to Christianity. So they placed their walking sticks on the man's heart and prayed. They waited in hope and faith for a few minutes, and then the man sat up, without saying a word. They prayed again and God opened his mouth and he began to speak. He then told everyone to gather round him, chose a man to replace him as chief, and gave him his orders: "You are appointed to be the next chief, not to lead the people to our heathen god, but to lead our people to follow the God of these two Brothers. Their God is the true and living God. I have seen their place called heaven. So follow them."

Star Harbour District had another ex-Brother as District Priest, Dudley Bale. In his district, one of the three villages on Santa Ana was mainly 'heathen', while the island of Santa Catalina was almost entirely 'heathen'.

Harry Reynolds, who had become Archdeacon of the Solomons, had taken a great interest in the Brotherhood and gave them much support, regularly attending the Annual Conference, sometimes acting as secretary, and writing reports for the *Southern Cross Log*. The Bishop, Gething Caulton, though happy with the Brothers' work, felt they needed a good Melanesian priest to lead them, or "better still, a European who could guide the movement in the recognised traditions of community life." He hoped that would be possible one day. He added: "There is a great deal of enthusiasm and keenness, but at present it needs more guidance and oversight."[15]

After the announcement of the resignation of Bishop Caulton, which took effect in March 1954, Alfred Thomas Hill, Headmaster of Pawa School, was the choice of the clergy of the Diocese. A Sacred Synod of clergy with 48 priests from the Diocese, 39 of them Melanesians, elected Fr Hill as their nominee to the Bishops of the Church of the Province of New Zealand, of which Melanesia was then an Associated Missionary Diocese. The Bishops then formally elected him, after meeting a delegation from Melanesia. He had been accepted by Bishop Baddeley in 1936 to serve on the staff of the Diocese in charge of the ship which served the Northern Archdeaconry, especially around New Britain. He had at one time been captain of a large Merchant Navy vessel, as a master-mariner, and then a fulltime lay-reader working in a dockland parish in the East End of London. In 1938 he was appointed by the Bishop as Headmaster of All Hallows School, Pawa, and was ordained deacon. In 1939 at Epiphany he was ordained priest, remaining at his post throughout the Second World War. He was then made a Member of the Order of the British Empire (MBE) in recognition of his services to education in the Solomon Islands. Fr David

Hoey, Headmaster of Maravovo School, wrote of him: "He sees the urgent need of Melanesian leadership, and how essential it is for Melanesians to take a leading part in the affairs of Church and State."[16] For the first time an Anglican Bishop was consecrated in the islands of the Diocese of Melanesia. The Archbishop of New Zealand, the Most Reverend Norman A Lesser, DD, officiated, and Fr Hill was presented to him by the Bishops of Dunedin and New Guinea. Bishop David Hand read the Epistle, and All Saints Pro-Cathedral was packed with people of all races for the service at 7 a.m. on May 30, 1954, the Sunday after Ascension Day. He was installed as Bishop later on the same day at 6 in the evening.[17] The Cathedral, like that of the Roman Catholics, was a converted American Quonset. Both buildings were later replaced by more worthy structures.

The Brothers' 29th Annual Conference was held from October 27 to 30, 1954, with Bishop Hill presiding and Dr Fox present and available to write a report for the *Southern Cross Log*. He wrote:

"One thing that has always surprised me is the completely different attitude towards the Brotherhood of the white staff and the Melanesian people. The first has always been critical; they have been ready (should I say eager) to see faults in individual Brothers of laziness or worse, and attribute them to all the Brothers. On the other hand, the attitude of the Melanesian people has been one of deep respect and warm affection. The Roman catechists respect them more than they do any others of our Church. The South Sea Evangelicals do so also; a sign of this was that they started a similar Brotherhood of their own; they took no vows and it did not, I believe, last very long or have much success. As for our own people, the Brothers get a warm welcome everywhere. It is, I think, a very high honour to be a member of the Retatasiu."[18]

However, Dr Fox was concerned that too many Brothers were leaving after one or two years' service, and that the training of novices had been reduced from two years to only one.

Fr Dan Sade then agreed to undertake the training of the Novices for a year and the Brothers asked the Bishop if a member of the English Franciscan brotherhood, the Society of St Francis, could come for a few years to help them. The number of Brothers had risen to 57 and the Bishop said he was limiting the number to 60. They asked him if a Household might go to New Guinea, an idea that had been welcomed by the Bishop of New Guinea when he had come for Fr Hill's consecration. The Bishop promised to consider this in 1955, saying he hoped the party might be led by a Melanesian priest.

The number of Companions had risen to about a thousand, as they were to be found in the New Hebrides (where they had been introduced in 1935), including the Banks Islands, as well as the Solomons. Companions present at the Conference felt it might be possible for the Companions to bear the whole cost of the Brotherhood, rather than relying on 'The Mission'. Indeed, £82 had been received from Santa Ysabel Companions. The Brothers had ceased to wear their former uniform, partly because of the War, and they agreed to go back to wearing a black loincloth with a white sash. The Bishop had the idea of receiving the new Brothers' vows at the end of the Conference, and of doing it at the foot of the grey 12 foot cross which marked the spot where Ini had made his original vow nearly 30 years before. He held the ceremony at noon and it was very hot, but the idea of having it there instead of in the chapel became the custom of the Brothers. In the 1970s an altar was built at the foot of the cross on a permanent concrete platform to replace one previously carried out from the chapel. There were 26 new Brothers professed in 1954. Two significant decisions were made at the Conference: Brothers could stay more than three months in a place if there was no catechist-teacher to follow them up, and they could go to work in a 'weak' Christian village which had no teacher.[19] Dr Fox, reporting on the Conference, wrote: "These may be the first steps towards a change in the Brotherhood from a purely missionary one to a teaching Brotherhood as well – a development I have always hoped for."[20] Fr Dan Sade, who had been acting as Chaplain for the Brothers and the Catechists School, soon became ill, and was replaced by Fr Matthias Tabe.[21] Brother Clement, who had been released, went on to Siota to train for the priesthood.

The Bishop of New Guinea, Philip Strong, who had invited the SSF Brothers to work in his diocese in urban areas from 1953, gratefully accepted the offer of a Household of Melanesian Brothers as well to help in his diocese. Eight Brothers were selected for a special three to four months course of preparation to be given at Taroaniara by Dr Fox. The Companions started to collect money to pay for them while they were in New Guinea.[22] The Brothers chosen toured the Gela villages for ten days before leaving for New Guinea, preaching to the people, and were given £60 by those who were themselves quite poor.[23] The Brothers were initially to be stationed in the Goroka area of the Highlands among newly discovered tribes, and their coming was given a warm welcome by members of the

New Guinea Mission and by the local Government Officer (*kiap*). Ini, who did not live to see it, would have been delighted. He used to say, "One day we must go on to New Guinea and Indonesia."[24]

There was no Brothers' Conference in 1955 as the Bishop was away in October, and it was transferred to St Paul's Day in January 1956. There was a one-day retreat, followed by three days of conference. The Brothers going to New Guinea were to be led by Brother Andrew Taba'ania, and nine eventually went with him to work under the special care and direction of Bishop David Hand, the Assistant Bishop of New Guinea, who had been consecrated in 1950 in his thirties. The group included David Hokoseni, William Fakaia, William Tobana, Michael Hepepaina, Henry Nuntaloa, Benjamin Kemakeha, Peter Ruim, Charles Arimana and Samuel Su'unorua, who returned to the Solomons in 1958.[25] The Bishop of Melanesia wrote: "They are the first missionaries sent out from Melanesia to serve in another diocese." He also announced: "It is my hope to strengthen this most valuable movement (for it should be remembered there are still some thousands of heathen in Melanesia) by placing the postulants under the tuition and guidance of a priest of Kelham."[26] Thus it was that steps were taken to relate the Brotherhood for the first time to another Anglican Religious Order. The 'Kelham Fathers' from England had established a house at Crafers in South Australia in 1947. Originally founded in 1891 as the Korean Missionary Brotherhood, their name had subsequently been changed to the Society of the Sacred Mission, as their work began to extend far beyond Korea to Africa and other continents.

The total number present at the Brotherhood Conference held early in 1956 was 99. As Brother Andrew Taba'ania was going to New Guinea, Brother Mark Maebea was chosen to take his place as Head Brother. Because of difficulties in follow-up to the Brothers' work, it was proposed that catechist schools be set up on each island. Plans were made for a new church, dining hall and several more leaf houses at Tabalia, as well as larger gardens to enable the Brothers to sell some of their produce to raise funds. Brother Andrew suggested that the Brothers should think again about their method of evangelism. He said he would not ask the people of New Guinea if they wanted a school, but that instead he intended to speak about the God revealed in the Book of Genesis, the God of all people, and tell them Old Testament stories, before speaking of the 'new creation' in Christ, through whom they might have new life and be no longer in darkness. He said that water was not just to touch, but to drink! 23 novices were professed as Brothers at the end of the Conference. The Companions also met separately for their own meeting. "They were giving the Brothers much help in the work of spreading the Gospel of Christ."[27]

The Home Secretary of the Australian Board of Missions, the Reverend T B McCall, on a visit to New Guinea Diocese, was impressed by the Brothers sent there. He noted that Brother Andrew had been in the Brotherhood for twenty years, and two of the others had been trained as teachers. The Brothers sent had been selected from among a group of volunteers, and it was understood that they would have to serve for at least three more years as Brothers, having committed themselves to the work in New Guinea. With Bishop Hand, Fr McCall had visited the Brothers at a heathen village on the top of a mountain, where it was very cold, in the Siane District of the Eastern Highlands. The people there still hunted for their food and fought their enemies with bows and arrows. Bishop Hand preached in Pidgin and the *Luluai* (headman) translated for him into their language. He preached about God "coming on earth in Jesus", and spoke about his death and resurrection. The people fed them with a stew of taro, sweet potato, cabbage and tomatoes, and killed a pig and some fowls in honour of the Bishop's first visit. Fr McCall was, however, even then concerned whether there could be any priest available to care for the needs of the people after the Brothers had gone.[28] After the October Conference in 1956, at which the Bishop introduced "four new rules, which met with some resistance," only four households were sent out, in addition to the two working in New Guinea.[29]

When the Brothers had gone to New Guinea, they had flown from Honiara to Rabaul, then travelled by ship to Madang, where they took another plane to Goroka in the Eastern Highlands. Their flight to Rabaul had been financed by the Companions. However, they had by-passed the main area of Anglican work in Papua, so later Bishop Hand took Brother Andrew and three other Brothers on a tour of Papua to inform the local Christians about the Brothers' life and work, to ask for prayer and giving for the Brothers' work (in the hope that some would become Companions), and to seek for possible recruits for the Brotherhood. The group flew down to Lae with nine schoolboys for St Paul's School, Dogura, from the Siane area, where the Brothers were working. Brother Andrew spoke in various places of Our Lord's words about "launching out into the deep" for a catch, and challenged the Papuan Christians to help the Brothers pull in the nets full of fish in the Highlands. Brother William Tobana spoke about the meaning of the vows and the contrasts between poverty and money-making, chastity and promiscuity, obedience and licence (i.e. doing what you like). At Uiaku the Maisin people gave food, tapa cloths and native ornaments, and £18 in money, and the teacher gave his son, who wanted very much to become an evangelist, to be a postulant. So Prout Moi became one of the first Papuans to join. Frank Oripa became a teacher after leaving Martyrs' School and worked in New Britain, before asking the Bishop to be transferred to the Highlands. He was placed with Brothers William Fakaia and Samuel Su'unorua at Koko Mission on a 7,000 foot peak overlooking the Goroka Valley. After nine months there, he asked to be admitted as a Brother. After instruction by Bishop Hand and Brother Andrew, he was admitted as the first Papuan Novice in Dogura Cathedral on Christmas Day, 1956. Novice Frank then addressed the single girls of St Mary's Guild at Sasembata, and the Bishop commented: "It must have been the first time that any tall and handsome and apparently eligible young Papuan man had ever addressed a crowd of handsome and apparently eligible young Papuan women, challenging them to a life of consecrated celibacy!" A young man called Livingstone was offered as a postulant by his father Elijah at Sasembata too. At Martyrs' School, after a stirring speech by Brother William, Edwy Kaib, who had just finished Standard 9 (the son of a teacher of the same name at Wanigela), offered himself immediately. At Dogura, the Brothers and postulants sang carols, and Canon John Chisholm welcomed them to a beautiful 'friary' he had had built for them.[30] He later became Assistant Bishop of New Guinea, and then Bishop of Melanesia and Father of the Brotherhood – so this was a happy beginning to his relationship with the Order.

In 1959 the Brothers serving in New Guinea were replaced by others, except for two who asked to stay on. At Koko, thirteen people had become Christians, the first Anglicans from the New Guinea Highlands. Bishop Hand consecrated their church in February. At Aiome, a long way from Koko, Elder Brother Charles and his fellows were teaching at Tsugup and Gai. Fr Peter Robin was responsible for that area, and it took the Brothers three nights on the road to reach Gai from where he lived at Aiome. Four Brothers were at Gai and three at Tsugup, in addition to Brother Charles. Brother Ishmael Kapalu wrote in the *Southern Cross Log*: "These two districts, where we are, know nothing of the Government or the Church; the people are still killing each other. You in Melanesia must help us with your prayers so that we can set up the rule of God among them. Pray for us!"[31] In 1959, Brother Ben, who was then the 'Head Brother' of those working in the Highlands, wrote: "The people are not all together....Wherever you go here, you go up, and then you go down, not at all like the Solomons, where you can walk along level country....so sometimes we are homesick for the Solomons, where it may rain but it does not make you feel cold, but you should see what it is like here! We are all well and our work is going well."[32] On their return to the Solomons, Brother Charles and Brother Mostyn visited the Girls' School at Buñana on Gela and taught the girls two plays about the conversion of the heathen in the area of New Guinea.where they had been working – these were very popular.[33]

Brother Joshua Halumae described what they found in the Highlands. The people did not wash; some plastered their hair with mud, then covered it with bark. In other places they cut their hair with bamboo and wore a small hat. A man did not live with his wife or wives – each had her own house. The houses were too low to stand up in, but each had a kitchen, a middle room for the pigs, and a sleeping room. Each pig had its own little cubicle. They covered their sleeping area with rubbish to make it softer to sleep on, as they did not make mats. If someone died, they covered their bodies with mud from head to foot as a sign of mourning, doing the same also if a pig or dog died, as they loved animals. After a period of crying, the body of a person who had died was placed on a platform, and after the flesh had decayed, they would take the bones, if it was a near relative, put a hole through them and hang them round their necks to remind them of the loved one. They might also cut off fingers or a whole hand, dry it in the fire, and hang that round the neck. The Brothers tried to persuade them to give up these customs and to improve their way of living. They were surprised that sometimes women would suckle piglets!

Bishop David Hand and Fr Peter Robin went with them to 'open' new places, but, before doing so, the Bishop had to seek permission from the Government. If so allowed, they asked the chief and people of the village if they wanted the Church. If they did, the Brothers built a house for themselves, a school room and a dormitory. They asked for children to go to school. Some villages sent many, some few, and the children were at school from Monday to Friday and went home for the weekends.

Doing deputation work in 1963 in the New Hebrides, Brother Joshua said:

"Only on Sundays did we call all the people together for prayer. On

Saturdays we went round the villages telling them, 'Tomorrow is Sunday, the day for prayer to God.' They came on Sundays; sometimes they were late, arriving at 11 or 12 midday. When they were all assembled there were many people, sometimes 300 or 400. We did not have prayers in a house, but outside. You understand that not all the Brothers were in one place, but we were sent out two by two to different places. So there would be two of us to take prayers. The way we did it was like this: one Brother would look after the people and the other would take the prayers. These were new people who did not understand prayer, and so, during prayers they would do what they liked, eat, smoke, make their spear or bow and arrows, or anything they liked. One Brother had to go round them and stop them. Perhaps during the prayers one lot would be doing something, and one Brother would go to stop them. When he went to them, those on the other side would start doing something. Sometimes the Brother taking the prayers had to leave off the prayers and go and help his Brother keep order. Then he would come back and go on again with his prayers or with his address. We had to write down all the names of the people in our villages. Then every Sunday, after prayers, we had a roll call, so that we would know who came and who did not. The people behaved like that at the beginning, when they did not yet understand. After four or five months they would begin to understand.

"We were never able to stay quiet in our house. You understand we were living in the midst of heathen. Whatever happened, fighting, quarrelling, even if it was midnight, we must go and see to it. These people are different to us, but we were like that before. We people now have been born into the Church and so we don't know what it was like before. If a man gets angry with his wife, he would kill her with an axe, knife or club. If two men have a row, they will do that too, one could be killed. They quarrelled about anything they wished. So day and night we didn't rest. One of us would be at school, the other going round the people. That is the work we started. Now others have taken our place and are doing it."

In the three years that the group of Brothers were there, they opened up eight stations, each of which had many small villages attached, which they visited during the week, sometimes from Friday to Sunday, when they would return to their own station for prayer. They would teach the people about faith and prayer. When they left, there were 6,649 people related to these eight stations, who were beginning to pray as hearers of the Gospel, but were not yet baptised. Some of the children had been sent to the big schools in Papua. The Brothers suffered from the cold, and Bishop Hand gave them six blankets each and any other things they needed. When they went to Papua, the school children found that there were Papuan priests, and even a Papuan Assistant Bishop, George Ambo, who had been consecrated in 1960![34]

Brother Michael Hepepaina, from Ulawa Island in the Solomon Islands, after six years in the Siane Valley, said he was "tired in body but willing in spirit."[35] He had been working at Miu, which he left because there was no teacher to follow up the work. He was asked to go to Karando on his own by Bishop David, as the Papuan teachers who had been placed there had, according to Brother Michael, "stolen some of the people's things" and made 'trouble' with young girls. They wanted the teachers to go away and said if any 'silly teachers' came to them again, they would kill them. However, Brother Michael they trusted, and many of the catechumens who had considered going back to their own 'heathen ways of life' returned. After his arrival, there were 600 who did so, and some 85 more became catechumens. He prepared them for baptism, prepared those already baptised for confirmation, ran a school for 85 children, and trained some men to be Evangelists among their own people.

At Fikobara, where the Brothers had built the large Church of the Holy Cross, others were ready to be baptised at Easter, 1961. There were another 400 catechumens at Orumba. On his way to teach them and conduct prayers Brother Michael was nearly killed on January 4, when crossing a river, as it suddenly rose and swept him onto rocks. He struggled for three hours, but survived, uninjured but bruised. Altogether he prepared 616 people for baptism in 1961, and one of the six young men whom he had trained as Evangelists, Michael Baira, went to Fiu to look after the 437 catechumens there after the Papuan teachers were removed by the Bishop. As Brother Michael was working on his own – which was supposed to be against the rule of the Brotherhood – his name had been omitted from the list of Households. He was worried that the others would not be praying for him! Later he decided to join the First Order of the Society of St Francis, which had arrived in Papua New Guinea in 1953, and spent some years serving as a Franciscan Brother in Papua New Guinea and the Solomons. He was the first Solomon Islander to join that Order, and so prepared the way for their arrival in the Solomons after John Chisholm became Bishop of Melanesia and decided to invite them to work there.

Brother Andrew Taba'ania served for three years in New Guinea.

Brother Michael Hepepaina visited his household and Andrew found that he "was a great help" to his spiritual life. He also wanted to stay with the Franciscans and asked the Father of the Brotherhood, but the Father felt it was better for him to go to the House of the Society of the Sacred Mission in South Australia. Brother Andrew wrote: "I have sought help from many, that I might help and strengthen the Brotherhood."[36]

In 1960 the Annual Conference was held at St Andrew's tide, as the Bishop was in Australia before that. Archdeacon Reynolds conducted the usual Retreat before the Conference began. He also acted as Secretary. Fr Patteson Gatu had by then become the head of the Catechists School and chaplain at Tabalia as well. There was a good report from Areare on Malaita, where some converts were preparing for baptism. But the other two households on Malaita and the one on Santa Catalina had had less response. A working household had been established on the Mission plantation at Tanaemba near Tabalia to raise money for the rebuilding of the headquarters at Tabalia in permanent materials, and some hundreds of pounds had been raised. But they were not sure if the owners of the land would allow the Diocese to renew the lease. Some had believed that Ini's gift of the use of the land meant that it belonged to the Brotherhood, but this was not legally the case. It was agreed to place 26 Brothers on Malaita and six on Santa Catalina, and to send eleven more Brothers to New Guinea to work in both the Highlands and New Britain, as Bishop Hand had requested. Three of these were replacing Brothers returning to the Solomons after three years' service. Ten would be working in the Highlands and eight following up the earlier work of the Melanesian Mission in what had previously been the Northern Archdeaconry (covering the Territory of New Guinea, not Papua). This had been handed over to the Diocese of New Guinea in 1949. It was also agreed that Head Brother Andrew Taba'ania, with Brother Silas as his companion, would go to gain experience of community life at the House of the Society of the Sacred Mission at Crafers, South Australia, with the possibility that he might take a life vow, being a widower of 45. He had by then served over ten years as a Brother, a requirement for taking such a vow in the Brotherhood. The number of Brothers in total rose to 80, with 20 being newly professed and only four withdrawing. The initial vow was now for three years, the Brothers then having the choice of either withdrawing or renewing their vows annually.[37]

In 1961, Fr Paul Hume of the Society of the Sacred Mission visited the Solomons and did a tour, calling, among other places, at Takataka in Areare on Malaita, and celebrating Holy Communion at the Brothers' Household there.[38] At about the same time, the Bishop of Melanesia was looking for "a single priest of community experience to offer himself to this diocese as a tutor and spiritual adviser to the Brotherhood." He also expressed the hope that the Brotherhood would "ultimately become a teaching Brotherhood within the diocese and capable of conducting missions within and without the diocese."[39] Also in 1961 two Papuan Brothers came to the Solomons to gain experience, and gave "fine service", according to the Bishop. William Fakaia, who had joined in 1955, and who had served in New Guinea, had become Head Brother in 1959. He took forward the programme of rebuilding the headquarters with many improvements, while Brother Andrew was in Australia. On the return of Brother Andrew, Brother William left the Brotherhood in 1963 in order to get married.

Brother William Fakaia's experience of working in the New Guinea Highlands for 3¼ years had stood him in good stead when he was chosen to be Assistant Head Brother on his return to the Solomons in 1958.[40] He was an experienced schoolteacher, having been deputy headmaster at Maravovo School, and was a good musician. He had joined the Brotherhood after having a dream, which he described as follows: "In the beginning of 1955, I was thinking so much about the Melanesian Brotherhood, that one day, if God turned me around, I will be a Brother of that Society. One night I dreamt a dream; I was standing on a shore with a fishing net in my hand, watching a group of men catching fish with a big fishing net. I said to myself, that could be done – no difficulties about catching fish. So I dropped down my net, chasing many different kinds of fishes. To my surprise, when I closed together the ends of the net, the fishes were turned into human beings, adults and children. I then woke up. Next day I made up my resignation. I made another application to the Head Brother of the Brotherhood." In the Conference of 1959 he asked why Tabalia was in such a poor state and why nothing had been done for a long time to improve the housing, narrow roads, the flowers and the gardens. The answer from the Head Brother was that they were 'poor men'. Brother William felt it was wrong to depend so much on the Companions, who were already sending money to pay the fares of Brothers going to New Guinea. He suggested a Working Household at Tanaemba Plantation, on contract to Mr Hill, the manager, and the establishment of projects for poultry and a piggery at Tabalia. There could be ten hardworking Brothers in each Household and the money they raised could go into a Building Fund. Wages were low for the contract labourers, only £7 a month, but they could manage to raise £70 a month for the Fund. Brother William was then chosen as Head Brother.

To improve the station at Tabalia, which could become very muddy, Brother William took three Brothers to tour Tasimboko District on Guadalcanal to ask for help in retrieving steel matting from Koli Point airfield, 1½ miles inland. They stayed at Gaimali village and, with the help of men and women Companions, in two weeks they managed to pull up 200 pieces of matting, each ten feet long, with the help of spades, shovels, bars and knives, working in the hot sun. The Companions hired a ten wheel truck, and five men helped the Brothers to load it and to unload it again at Tabalia. A month later, the Brothers had completed a pig fence 160 feet by 80 feet, with two sections, one for boars and sows and the other for sows to deliver and to care for their piglets. They started with one boar and three big sows and, when a poultry project was completed, they acquired two cocks and ten hens.

Brother William was shocked one day to receive a message from Brother Ini's elder brother Lawrence, who sent his son to tell him he wanted to see him urgently. Apparently he had been told by the District Officer that the land at Tabalia had only been leased for thirty years, so he either had to take it back or renew the lease for 99 years. He said he had decided to take it back. Brother William reminded him of his brother's promises to give the land for the Brotherhood, the cross marking the spot where he had made his life vows could not be moved, and thousands of people had become Christians because of the Brothers' work and witness. After two meetings, Lawrence remained unmoved and demanded his land back at New Year 1961. Brother William said: "You are now determined to do something to us like Ananias and Safira his wife to the apostles in the stories of the Acts of the Apostles in the Holy Book." He told Lawrence he would be forcing William to look for a new site for the Headquarters on Guadalcanal or Gela. William also consulted the Bishop, who told him to look for somewhere else to move to. He searched for two months and the only land offered was at the foot of Tatuvo mountain on Guadalcanal, five miles inland. He felt he had failed and returned to Tabalia, but found out there that Lawrence had fallen seriously ill. One evening Lawrence's wife and daughter arrived to say he was at the point of death. They had been sent by him, and in response William took a few Brothers with him and rushed to Lawrence's home, where they found he could not even speak.

Brother William conducted a healing service with the Brothers standing round. Lawrence then turned his face round, looked up and said: "Are you Brother William?" William replied: "Yes, I am, Lawrence." Lawrence went on: "Have you already prayed for me?" "Yes, Lawrence, we have done it," William answered. "Thank you very much. Good to have you here – and other Brothers," Lawrence said. William responded, "You are right." Ten minutes later Lawrence got up from his bed and sat down, saying: "Listen to me, Brothers. I am now well, and I realise the sickness I had was caused only by my foolishness and silly ways, trying to destroy the Brotherhood. I am now decided that the Brotherhood will have the land again for 99 years, and one day the Head Brother and I will go to the District Officer to fix up this matter." The Brothers thanked him and praised the Lord, and the next day had a service of thanksgiving at Tabalia. The land leased included that used by the Catechist College, which later became the Bishop Patteson Theological College.

Construction could now continue on the new accomodation buildings for the Brothers, which, instead of being dormitories, were designed to have ten small rooms in each, so that Brothers could be quiet for study and meditation on their own when they wished. The two buildings were 60 feet by 25 feet, with concrete floors, and some parts of them were constructed from good local hardwood timbers. There was no architect or carpenter involved, but the Brothers did all the work themselves, led by William. On the station, many holes were filled in and the roads and paths widened, although the Brothers did complain that they were being expected to work both morning and afternoon, whereas, before, other Head Brothers had left them free to do other things in the afternoons. The station was planted with clover and flowers in an orderly way. The Brothers were hardworking, obedient and loyal, which is why Brother William was able to achieve his aim of raising new money for the Brotherhood, making it more self-reliant, and improving the headquarters. He also tried to give an example of faithfulness and keenness. On leaving the Brotherhood in 1963, he got married and went on to train for ordination. He spent part of his ministry as a priest working with and following up the work of the Brothers on Lord Howe Atoll (Ongtong Java).

Brother Andrew wrote on his return from Crafers: "While I stayed there it was good for my soul and for my body. Our worship brought us near to Christ and the life of obedience was a great help to my body and spirit. On my return journey to Melanesia, I visited all Papua and also stayed at the

House of the Franciscans, where once more I had a great desire to remain with them. I have hopes that we might one day be one with the Franciscans or the SSM.... Later, we may be able.... to go to other countries to preach to the heathen whether they be near or far."[41] He felt the Brotherhood needed a tutor from SSM.

About the Brothers' evangelistic work he wrote: "When the Brothers work among the heathen, the chief things to do are to learn the ways and customs of the heathen people, then to compare their heathen beliefs and the Christian faith, so that the heathen may see what is good and what is evil. When they see what is good and what is evil, they put away their heathen ways and establish the truth of the Christian Church. Say to them: 'Death lives in the heathen faith but you did not see it, but now you can see the Truth. Everlasting life abides in Christ and the Church. It is by this faith we have victory.' We the Brothers love the heathen and also the heathen love us, and we see how through the blessing and presence of God we are able to do his work."[42]

After he left the Brotherhood, he wrote: "Any boy who wishes to come to join the Brotherhood I accepted, because he wants to serve Christ and his Church for his glory,not because he has been educated, but, of course, he tries to serve the Church of God and to love him."[43]

Each year a different person was invited to lead the retreat before the Brotherhood Conference. In 1961 it was Fr Peter Thompson, soon to be appointed to the new Archdeaconry of Malaita (which would include Sikaiana and Lord Howe). In 1962 it was Dr Fox, who spoke movingly about vocation. He had written in March, 1962: "Now at 83 I am no longer a Brother, but still a Companion. But my happiest years were when I was one of them."[44] At that Conference Brother Andrew announced that he wished to retire from being Head Brother, a position he had held for nine years.[45] The Bishop said he wished Brother John Ashwin Wetelwur from the Banks Islands, a New Hebridean, to be the new Head Brother, and this was unanimously confirmed by the Brothers. Peter Ruim was elected as Assistant Head Brother in place of Brother William Fakaia. Two new dormitories, a lecture room, a dining hall and kitchen were to be built in permanent materials, largely paid for by money raised by the Brothers working at Tanaemba Plantation. The chapel was to be left till last, as the one made of leaf was still serviceable. An important decision was made about periods of service, as Brothers were now to make a commitment to serve for a minimum of five years, although still renewing their vows annually. The Head Brother was to serve for five years. Requests for households were received from the Archdeacon of Southern Melanesia, Fr Derek Rawcliffe,[46] to work on Pentecost and perhaps on Espiritu Santo island. Two Brothers who had served in New Guinea did deputation work in the Archdeaconry in 1963.[47] The Bishop in Polynesia[48] requested Brothers "to assist the Melanesians and their descendants living in Polynesia," probably from 1963 – thus renewing the link between the Brotherhood and that Diocese. These requests were accepted in principle, for action later. Brother Andrew announced that he wished to take a Life Vow, and this was in line with the Bishop's wish that Brothers should consider the possibility of doing this seriously, to help the Brotherhood grow stronger. However, the Bishop warned that the Community should always maintain its Melanesian character and not try to follow European models, such as the Society of the Sacred Mission. He did, however, announce the coming of Fr Ernest Ball SSM from that Society's mother house at Kelham in England, to act as tutor and adviser to the Brotherhood 'for two years', and said that they were "greatly indebted to this Society for its real assistance to the Church in Melanesia."[49] Later the Bishop wrote: "I am most hopeful that his presence and spiritual leadership will be an important milestone in the further development of this movement which has done so much for the evangelisation of the heathen, not only in Melanesia but for the last seven years in the Diocese of New Guinea."[50] He hoped that the Brotherhood would be prepared eventually to conduct "parochial missions, not only in centres such as Honiara, but also in the Districts."

In the end, Brother Andrew Taba'ania did not carry out his plan to take a life vow in the Brotherhood, in spite of declaring his intention of doing so and of receiving the blessing and encouragement of the Father of the Brotherhood, Bishop Alfred Hill. However, his interest in doing so showed that this was still a possibility for others, and eventually Dr Fox rejoined the Brotherhood towards the end of his life and died a Brother.

NOTES

1 From a written account by some of the Brothers entitled *History of the Melanesian Brotherhood, 1942-1945*, probably prepared by ex-Brother James Vasethe, in the author's possession.

2 *Southern Cross Log*, July 1951. There was a big bomb-pit close to Ini's cross, another by a tank which had been 'knocked out'.

3 There were then Brothers from the following islands: Guadalcanal 1, Santa Ysabel 2, San Cristoval 3, Sikaiana 1, North Malaita 1.

4 *Southern Cross Log*, June 1947.

5 This occurred just before he was due to ordain a large group of deacons, including Brian Macdonald-Milne, whom he had welcomed to the diocese to serve in the parish of Fleetwood (where he later did a course at the Navigation School), in order to prepare for service in Melanesia.
6 Personal recollection of the author.
7 *Southern Cross Log*, January 1951.
8 Sometimes spelt Morice.
9 *Southern Cross Log*, July 1951. He says he considered Brother Michael to be as good as any Head Brother he had known. It is, however, not clear which Brother he is referring to at this point.
10 *Southern Cross Log*, July 1951.
11 See chapter 5 of Darrell Whiteman: *Melanesians and Missionaries: An Ethnohistorical Study of Social and Religious Change in the Southwest Pacific* (William Carey Library, Pasadena, California, USA, 1983). Some Anglican missionaries opposed or criticised Marching Rule, whereas the Roman Catholic (Marist) Mission approved of it and gained many converts as a result, including some Anglicans. The Diocesan Synod met in July 1953, the first to be called since 1928, and, significantly, it had a majority of Melanesians, having 39 Melanesian clergy and only 9 Europeans in attendance. After modifying the rules of the Church Association, it commended them to other islands as well as Malaita. The original rules can be seen in Whiteman's book on pp. 282-289, and the ones approved by the Synod in Appendix VI. See also *Southern Cross Log* (English edition), February 1954, pp. 156-160. Dr Fox added his comments on the Synod version of the Association Rules reported there, saying that it was a movement "of greater importance than any since Ini Kopuria began the Native Brotherhood. It is a movement of self-support, but it is far more than that; for they propose to send out missionaries not only to the remaining heathen parts of Mala, but beyond Melanesia, and to support them themselves" (See Whiteman, p. 282).
12 *Southern Cross Log*, December 1958.
13 An account was given by him to Brother Michael Ripotia and Deacon Francis Tolei, who wrote it down on February 25, 1998, and quotations from it follow.
14 Recorded by Deacon Francis Tolei as *Niapu.*
15 *Southern Cross Log*, March 1954.
16 *Southern Cross Log*, November 1953.
17 *Southern Cross Log*, September 1954.
18 *Southern Cross Log*, May 1955.
19 *Southern Cross Log*, May 1955.
20 *Southern Cross Log*, May 1955.
21 *Southern Cross Log*, March 1956.
22 *Southern Cross Log*, September 1955.
23 Fox: *Kakamora*, p. 78.
24 See Dr Fox's article on the Brotherhood in *Southern Cross Log* of March 1962.
25 He claimed in a paper on *The History of the Church in Areare, etc.* in 1999 that 49,000 people had been converted by the Brothers in New Guinea. It is not known (to the author) how he arrived at this figure, but the numbers were eventually considerable.
26 *Southern Cross Log*, June 1956, part of the *Bishop's Log* in that issue. There were, of course, Brothers in the Diocese of Polynesia in the 1930s!
27 *Southern Cross Log*, June 1956: the report on the Brothers' Conference was written by Albert Jones, the Bishop's secretary.
28 *Southern Cross Log*, December 1956.
29 *Southern Cross Log*, March 1957.
30 *Southern Cross Log*, December 1957, includes a report by Bishop David Hand on the Brothers' tour of Papua entitled *Melanesia's Own Missionaries.*
31 *Southern Cross Log*, June 1959.
32 *Southern Cross Log*, December 1959.
33 *Southern Cross Log*, March 1960.
34 Brother Joshua and Brother Peter Ruim, on their return from New Guinea, toured the New Hebrides to speak about their work, and on one occasion Brother Joshua's talk was transcribed by someone, and this

appeared in the *Southern Cross Log* of June 1963 under the title, *A Missionary Talk.*

35 See his article in the *Southern Cross Log*, September 1961, entitled *New Guinea Story.*

36 *Southern Cross Log*, March 1962. An article for the English *Log* was translated and sent by Archdeacon Reynolds to the General Secretary of the Melanesian Mission, August 6, 1962. See Note 41, below.

37 *Southern Cross Log*, June 1961.

38 *Southern Cross Log*, June 1961.

39 *Southern Cross Log*, September 1961. In the June 1962 *Log*, he hoped the two Papuans would "lay the foundation of a Papuan Brotherhood."

40 *Southern Cross Log*, December 1962. His account which follows was written down by Brother Edward Das on Lord Howe Atoll in 1978.

41 Brother Andrew's words come from an article prepared for the *Southern Cross Log*, translated by Archdeacon Harry Reynolds (presumably from Mota) and sent to the General Secretary of the Melanesian Mission in London, Canon Peter Garrity, on August 6, 1962.

42 In a letter to the author dated May 2, 1971, from Gwa'alalamea village, Malaita.

43 As Note 42.

44 *Southern Cross Log*, March 1962.

45 It is not clear whether he is counting in this the years he was in Australia, when William Fakaia was carrying out the work of Head Brother.

46 Derek Rawcliffe had arrived in Melanesia from England in 1947 and had served in the Solomons from 1947 to 1958. He became an Assistant Bishop in the Diocese of Melanesia in 1974, caring for the New Hebrides and New Caledonia. On the inauguration of the Church of the Province of Melanesia in 1975 he became the first Bishop of the New Hebrides, being succeeded by Harry Tevi, a New Hebridean (*ni – Vanuatu*) in 1980, just before the country gained its independence as Vanuatu and the diocese became that of Vanuatu, not of New Hebrides any more.

47 *Southern Cross Log*, June 1963.

48 The Right Reverend John Charles Vockler, an Australian and a member of the Oratory of the Good Shepherd, resigned in 1968 and joined the Society of St Francis from 1969 to 1990, and was Superior of the Franciscan Order of the Divine Compassion from 1990 to 1998 in the USA.

49 *Southern Cross Log*, December 1962.

50 *Southern Cross Log*, March 1963.

CHAPTER ELEVEN

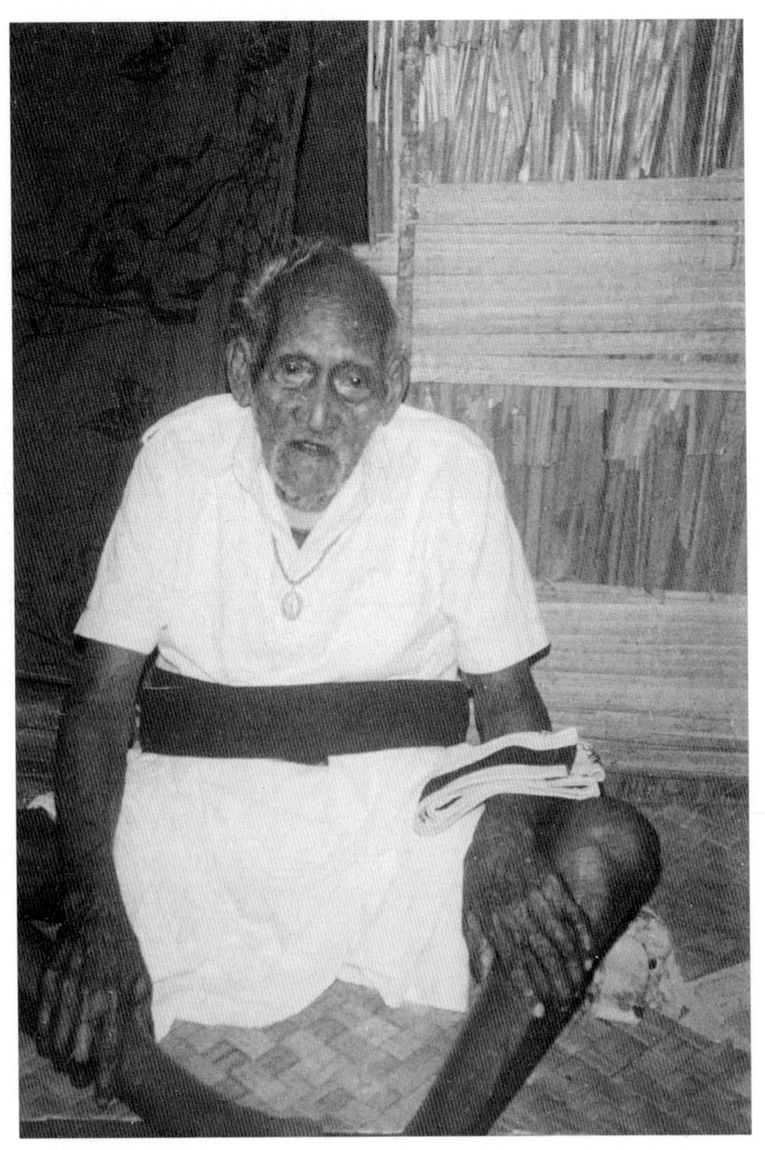

Ex-Brother Maurice Maneae. One of the original group of Brothers and the last to die, in October 1993.
Dressed as a Brother in 1993.

CHAPTER ELEVEN

GROWTH AND RENEWAL

The arrival of Fr Ball at Tabalia marked a new stage in the history of the Brotherhood. Numbers were increasing, and calls were being made for longer and better training to meet the need for work among a more educated population, and to enable the Brothers to conduct teaching missions.[1] At Kohimarama, Fr David Salt had been Principal of the Catechist College and the office of Senior Catechist had been introduced, the idea being that these men (and, perhaps, eventually women) would be a resource for each District, working together with the District Priest and not limited to one village as 'village catechists' were. Fr Ball was a quiet man with a deep spirituality, who had suffered in the Second World War at the hands of the Japanese, and was reported to have only one lung. He had been in the Far East and so was accustomed to the tropics and appeared to love the sun; he delighted in wearing very little, or nothing at all when he went to sunbathe or have his bath in the river at Tabalia. The Brothers were somewhat surprised at this, but saw it admiringly as a way in which he identified with the Melanesian way of life. He wore his habit for services only. His coming meant that the training would be reviewed, the book of offices for daily use be revised and prepared for printing, the Rule of the Brotherhood be turned into a Constitution, and the Companions Book revised and reissued. Quietly and effectively, Fr Ball gave himself to the task of helping the Brothers in these ways. As he was helping to prepare these things for the approval of the Conference of 1963,[2] the Brothers were busy putting up three dormitories in permanent materials, with a little help from some others. Friends in the USA had given money for them to build a combined classroom and library, as a 'partnership' relationship had been established with the Diocese of East Carolina in the State of North Carolina. This was part of a new initiative in the Anglican Communion, agreed at Toronto in Canada, entitled 'Mutual Responsibility and Interdependence' (MRI). However, the Brotherhood then had no reference books, and the library had to be built up from nothing, although later the library at the Bishop Patteson Theological College at Kohimarama was able to supplement what was available at Tabalia. The 1963 Conference was attended by four Papuans, the first to come and train at Tabalia and provide a link with the Brothers in New Guinea, who were increasing in numbers. Not only that, but the invitation to send Brothers back to work in the Diocese of Polynesia, the first since the 1930s, was approved in principle.

In 1964, Fr Brian Macdonald-Milne from England arrived to take up his work as Sub-warden of St Peter's Theological College at Siota on Gela to replace Fr Desmond Probets who was to become Headmaster of Pawa School. He visited the Catechist College and was asked to celebrate Holy Communion at Tabalia, and so began his relationship with the Brotherhood, as, soon after his visit, he became a Companion.

Bishop Hill, in late 1965, visited two of the Households on Malaita. At both Aiofia and Olumburi he met some of the 'heathen' who came down from the hills to see him. At Aiofia, it was children from their school that Brothers brought down to meet the Bishop.[3] Then the first 'Great Conference' of the whole Brotherhood, at which the 'New Guinea Section' with its own 'Section Brother' was set up, was held at Tabalia, followed by the annual conference of the 'Melanesia Section'. At the Great Conference, Ellison Vahi of Ysabel and Ataban Maurilage of Raga, New Hebrides, were elected as Head Brother and Assistant.[4]

In 1965 there were almost as many Brothers working in the Diocese of New Guinea as in the Diocese of Melanesia. With its own noviciate at Pomete in West New Britain and its own Section Brother, it was in some ways self-governing. The Brothers there were admitted by the Bishop of the Diocese. There was a deliberate policy, however, of mixing Brothers from the two dioceses in order to keep the Brotherhood 'united in mind and spirit.' Of the thirty two Brothers working in New Guinea, twenty were from the Diocese of Melanesia, while of the thirty seven in Melanesia, four were from New Guinea. Three Brothers and two Companions leaders had come to the first Great Conference from New Guinea, and there were so many Companions present that it was difficult to accommodate them all. The new Head Brother and Assistant had been educated at Pawa and Vureas Schools respectively. Brother Ellison was a man of great energy, enthusiasm and vision, while Brother Ataban was skilled in practical matters, particularly building and agriculture. It was decided at the Conference to accept aspirants only if they were recommended by their district priests or headmasters, to avoid the problem of people wishing to join from the wrong motives, such as wanting to leave school early or travel to other places. A new Companions' Book was approved, after the Companions had said what they thought of it. It was agreed that two Brothers would go to Santo in the New Hebrides to take a mission, in the hope that other opportunities for mission might arise later. A diocese in

New Zealand had provided money for a new dining hall and kitchen at Tabalia in permanent materials, with concrete floor and walls, and it was being built. It would have an iron roof, off which rain water would be collected in a concrete tank for cooking. Things were improving at the Central Headquarters!

On Malaita, Fr Samuel Su'unorua was district priest in Areare and Kwaio, based at Marou, for eight years from 1964. In his time, the Brothers moved from Maka to Marou. He then resettled them at Su'u Manawai and then Wainiura. Villages converted to Christianity which remained Anglican during this period were Tariaroaro, Tariuna, Su'u Oropuru, Wainiura, Wairaha and Kerenapisi (all in 1965), and Apuala and Apaldo, which were 'opened' in 1966. In 1967 the Brothers 'opened' Uhu village to Christianity.[5]

In 1966 the Chaplain, Fr Ball, had the opportunity to visit New Britain and the New Guinea Highlands, although in New Britain he did not have time to go inland to the places where the Brothers worked. In the Highlands he visited one of their stations and admired the buildings, "beautifully made of local materials with local help and roofed in grass.... linked with neat flower-bordered paths; and close by were the vegetable gardens and a levelled and enclosed area for outdoor services and classes." The buildings were a chapel, living quarters and cook-house, guest house, store room and school. He was amazed by the welcome he received. "What does one do when held in a tight embrace by a naked, dirt-covered man out of the Stone Age? Dirt helps them to keep warm, for it is very cold sometimes, especially at night, and they have no clothes. They sleep on the ground as close as possible to the fires which burn all night in their windowless houses." He noted how they appreciated having razor blades and matches, as well as steel axes to replace their beautiful (but less effective) stone ones. Although used to seeing aeroplanes, they had not before seen a white man who could take out his teeth while doing his 'rather public ablutions.' He wrote: "I had to repeat the performance, amid squeals of amazement, many times both here and in other places: the news soon got round."

Fr Ball was deeply impressed by many aspects of the life and work of the Brotherhood. He admired their adaptibility, or their "ability to find the common human level under the compulsion of Christian love" which gained the trust and affection of 'primitive people' in spite of differences in language and culture. At the time of his visit to New Guinea, the Brothers were working in two adjacent valleys, having handed over the first one they evangelised to the 'ordinary pastoral care of the Church.' He believed that the work called "not only for courage and endurance, but also for a sturdy faith. It cannot be easy for them, with their tribal memories, to resist the dread pressure of heathen superstition. Yet there can be no doubt that serving anywhere and under any conditions as the messengers of God to those the Gospel has never reached is, for these gay and gallant young men, a glorious enterprise."[6]

In March 1967, Fr Ball reported in the *Southern Cross Log* on the 1966 Conference, which he described as a 'reunion' as well as a time of 'refreshment and renewal'. Preparation of gardens and ordering of necessities had to be done months ahead, and just before the Conference hunting parties had to go out to get wild pigs from the bush (which could be dangerous) or fish and turtles from the sea, in readiness for the feast at the close of the Conference. Firewood was cut and dances rehearsed. Some Brothers even arrived with a small black pig, which they referred to as 'a heathen from the bush' who came regularly to chapel and "after running around anxiously looking for his friends settled down quietly beside them." The Retreat was for two days and was conducted by the Rector of Honiara, the Reverend Donald Ferguson. A new dining hall with water tank had been erected with funds from friends in New Zealand under the MRI scheme. A new chapel was the next step – a large bowl had had to be placed on the altar steps of the old chapel to catch rain coming through the leaky roof! A small chapel had already been built by the Brothers for workers on nearby plantations.[7] Later, in 1967, there was a severe cyclone and the chapel at Tabalia was totally destroyed, and a dormitory had to be converted into a temporary one.[8]

The 1966 Conference decided to close two of the three households on Malaita, Maro'u and Aiofia, and instead to have one central one at Onelava, from which the eighteen Brothers would be able to go out on more evangelistic work, rather than spending so much time on buildings and gardens. The Brothers were to be withdrawn from Tanaemba Plantation and other means of financing the Brotherhood were to be explored. One suggestion was for a small house in Honiara: "This would be useful not only for those needing to spend a few days in town, perhaps waiting for a ship to go elsewhere or for hospital treatment, but also for work in the township itself with Companions and others." The Brotherhood had then a membership of 80 Brothers and 30 Novices.

During the Companions' session the instruction of leaders in their duties was the main topic, and it was suggested that Brothers on tour should call district leaders together and explain their duties. The Father of the Brotherhood made it clear that women could be Companions and Members of the Mothers Union at the same time, if they wished.

It was the last Conference to be presided over by Bishop Hill, as he was about to leave. He decided to go to New Britain to live at Apugi in 1968, and became honorary chaplain to the Brothers in the Section there, a decision which endeared him even more to the Brothers. He was indeed returning to the area where he had first begun his service in the South Pacific. Fr Ball wrote: "The Brothers are well aware of all that they owe to his fatherly concern for them and their life and work, and to his wise direction and counsel over the years, and will greatly miss his stimulating visits. But they know that the bond of mutual affection will always remain."[9] Much the same could have been said of Fr Ball himself! Bishop Hill did not live much longer: he died on August 27, 1969.

After the resignation of Bishop Alfred Thomas Hill had been announced, a Sacred Synod of clergy was convened in Honiara, chaired by Archdeacon Harry Reynolds, the Vicar General, who was to be Commissary in charge of the Diocese during the vacancy in the see.[10] The two Melanesian Assistant Bishops, Leonard Alufurai and Dudley Tuti, who had been consecrated in Honiara on St Andrew's Day, November 30, 1963, were present. One of the names proposed was that of John Wallace Chisholm, an Assistant Bishop in the Diocese of New Guinea. However, the majority of the Melanesian clergy voted for a New Zealand priest on the mistaken view that the New Zealand Bishops would agree only to a New Zealander being appointed. But they were told the priest in question was not particularly interested in the work of the Mission. When Archdeacon Reynolds went to New Zealand to convey to the Bishops the name of this priest with the majority vote, they too recognised his unsuitability and asked what other names had been voted on. They then appointed John Chisholm, who had come second, to become the tenth Bishop of Melanesia, at the age of 45. He was an Australian, ordained in the Diocese of London, where he served a curacy at St Stephen's, Rochester Row, Westminster from 1947 to 1951. He had served for fifteen years in the Diocese of New Guinea, mostly at the Cathedral at Dogura in Papua,[11] before being consecrated Assistant Bishop on St Matthias' Day, 1964, at St John's Cathedral, Brisbane. On September 24, 1967, at 7 a.m. he was enthroned by the Melanesian Assistant Bishops as 'Lord Bishop of Melanesia' in the

Cathedral Church of All Saints in Honiara, which was a converted American Quonset Hut from the Second World War (as was also the then Roman Catholic Cathedral in the capital). The service was on the Sunday after Bishop Patteson's Day, a major feast in the Calendar of the Church of Melanesia.

One of his first duties was to chair the Brothers' Conference. A series of Brothers' meetings had been held during most of October, so that everybody understood the issues to be discussed. The Brotherhood had grown so big that the Conference had had to become one of chosen representatives of the Brotherhood, as not all could attend. The retreat this time was conducted by Bishop Dudley Tuti, and the Diocesan Bishop arrived on his first visit to Tabalia immediately after it finished. He was carried shoulder-high in a "rustic flower-decked chair and greeted with shrill cries." This was followed by a song of welcome, a short speech by the Head Brother and an extended round of hand-shaking "with more than ordinary meaning on this occasion." In his address to the Conference, he challenged the Brothers to "rise up and build." The Brothers were able to understand this both spiritually and materially, as another gift from the USA had been received for the construction of a new chapel in permanent materials, and it was hoped to have a generator to provide electricity for both Tabalia and Kohimarama, a long-felt need.[12]

In mid-1967, the Head Brother visited Onelava Household with Brother Christian Makona, while Brothers Frederick Abednego Wes and John Selovana spent several months visiting the Outer Eastern Solomons. The Assistant Head Brother, who also cared for the Solomon Islands Section, visited Longgu Household on Guadalcanal. At the end of July the Head Brother left Honiara by air to visit the Diocese of New Guinea. He attended the Diocesan Synod at Dogura, and while there, the Companions' Leader, John Solomon, told him that they had more than a hundred probationers. He visited the Franciscan Brothers at Jegarata before going on to the Siane Valley in the Highlands, where the Brothers had first worked and were still "gratefully remembered." Reginald, the Companions' leader there, had a large number of Companions and proposed building a chapel for daily prayers in each village, as in the Solomons. The young people originally taught by the Brothers had, in some cases, had further education, and were offering to serve the Church in various ways. The Head Brother then flew from Goroka to Kwanabe and two Brothers met him and took him on a two day journey to Kumbruf in the Simbai valley, where he spent two weeks, having meetings with the Brothers and paying visits to the stations. He had a week at Pomete before returning to the Solomons. As a result of his visit, he was convinced that a central household should be established in the Highlands and the Brothers "allowed to work in their own way." Sometimes the district priest there expected them to work in ways different from what they considered most suitable for them. The Head Brother was convinced that some Brothers admitted at Pomete should gain experience in the Solomons. The people in the Highlands liked the way the Solomon Islanders worked! Head Brother Ellison also felt that Brothers, who wanted to, should be allowed to stay more than three years working in New Guinea.[13]

After the 1967 Conference, as well as the Households in New Guinea, to which ten Brothers were sent in February, 1968, to replace those returning, it was agreed to have one Household with twelve Brothers on Malaita at Onelava, and another at Longgu on Guadalcanal, with two Brothers only. Four Brothers would go to the New Hebrides, two to the Eastern Outer Islands of the Solomons to tour, two to Lord Howe atoll to continue the revival work there, and two to explore the possibility of Brothers going to Fiji to work in a new Household. These two were to be accompanied to Fiji by the Head Brother, Ellison Vahi.[14]

After the Conference the Bishop reviewed the staffing arrangements for the Diocese. Fr Alan Dutton, whose wife Susan came from South Australia, had decided to resign as Warden of the theological college at Siota on Gela, where he had served for many years, and to go to Australia with his family, to be South Australia Secretary of the Australian Board of Missions. Fr Brian Macdonald-Milne was appointed as Acting Warden, but the Bishop told him he wanted him to serve for a year until the arrival of the Reverend Eric Jones from the Pacific Theological College in Fiji, who would take over as Warden, while he would replace Fr Ernest Ball as Chaplain and Tutor of the Brotherhood. The Bishop had decided that Fr Ball, who had originally been sent by the Society of the Sacred Mission for two years, would not be expected to return after his next leave. He had served for five years.

Fr Ball had come to know and love the Brotherhood well and had brought to it the experience of a Religious of mature years and wisdom. He was sorry to leave this post. He had become convinced of two things: the importance of the Brotherhood in the whole Anglican Communion (and thus the need to record its history), and also that its expression of the

Religious Life in community was as valid as that of the more traditional orders, like his own. Some had, over the years, doubted its status as a 'Religious Order', partly because the Brothers did not normally take Life Vows. Taking a Life Vow was indeed seen as a special privilege only open to Brothers who had served ten years, according to the new Constitution which Fr Ball had helped to draft. By the time of his departure on March 19, 1968, the Brotherhood had grown so much that a five-yearly Great Conference had been inaugurated, when the Head Brother, Assistant Head Brother (and later, Regional Head Brothers) would be elected. This enabled Sections (later called Regions) to have their own Conferences in the intervening years. Fr Ball felt that these arrangements might help to commend the Brotherhood to other religious communities in the Anglican Communion, and indeed they led eventually to its admission into the Australasian Advisory Council of Religious Communities (Anglican).

He prepared a paper entitled *The Melanesian Brotherhood – A Religious Community?*[15] in which he wrote: "Some people, if they were asked this question would probably reply, 'No, of course not.' Yet, if they came to know the Brotherhood more intimately, they might revise their opinion." He argued that the Brotherhood met all the definitions of 'Religious State' and 'Religious Community' given in a *Directory of the Religious Life*, published in 1957 by the Advisory Council of Religious Communities in England, including a Constitution, a regulated devotional life with daily offices at prescribed times, and the "spiritual qualities which should specially characterise a religious community." He also stated that no community admitted people into Life Vows without a period of temporary vows first. The Brotherhood had by then adopted an initial period of five years, followed by a period which could be extended. Thus a Brother might serve till he died. In any case, the Constitution did indeed provide for Life Vows under certain conditions. Not only that, but all communities, whether they took Life Vows or not, inevitably lost members for various reasons. He pointed out that terms used in the Brotherhood were equivalent to those employed by other religious communities, so 'Brotherhood' equalled 'Society' or 'Order'; 'Head Brother' was equivalent to 'Superior', 'Section' to 'Province', 'Section Brother' to 'Provincial', 'Household' to 'Priory', 'Elder Brother' to 'Prior', 'Admission' to 'Profession', and 'Conference' to 'Chapter'. The word 'promise' was used instead of 'vow', but had the same significance. The founder's 'life vow' was indeed an indication of his intention, as it was of Bishop Steward's. Some communities had seven offices a day, based on the 119th Psalm, but many were revising their worship patterns to fit in with their work, as the Brotherhood had done. Eventually 'Sections' became the 'Regions' of the Brotherhood, covering Papua New Guinea, the Solomon Islands with Australia, and Vanuatu with Fiji, with each Diocese having a 'Section' of Brothers, all as a result of the reorganisation initiated at that time.

Fr Ball's concern for the history led him to write to Dr Fox, who in turn encouraged ex-Brothers to write down what they could remember of their time in the Brotherhood, as Dr Fox did himself. There the foundation was laid for future work on the archives of the Brotherhood and for ongoing research by different generations of Brothers and Novices and by his successor as Chaplain. Fr Ball envisaged two versions: for 'home consumption' and for 'propaganda'. Presumably, the 'propaganda' was to show people outside Melanesia what the Brotherhood was really like, and to justify his assertion that it was truly 'a Religious Community', offering a non-European version of the traditional 'Religious Life'.

In the mid-1960s Miss Noella Kakapena from Ongtong Java went to continue her education in New Zealand. She had a tattoo right across her forehead, which caused surprise and some amazement among the Maori people in New Zealand, where the tattooing of women had almost ceased. The matter of tattooing was something which concerned the Brothers when they returned to the atoll, as some of them considered it cruel, and unsuitable for Christians to practise.

In the late 1960s, two Brothers went to Lord Howe for a year (1967-68).[16] They found the tattooing was being done by the old men and women. They waited till the children were old enough, then they tattooed the faces of the boys till the blood ran down. When it came to the young women, they started with the face, then moved to the belly and other parts of the body, down as far as the knee. Sometimes children died because they lost too much blood. Brother Codrington Tolengalenga from Raga and Brother James Baddeley Tule, from Merelava in the Banks Islands, persuaded them that it was better to give up the practice.

They also dealt with the problem of drunkenness. As in other Polynesian and Micronesian islands where coconuts are abundant, the people made a toddy from the coconut flower, and all ages drank it, so drunkenness was common and sometimes led to men acting wrongly towards women, especially through sexual misbehaviour. The toddy would be kept for a week by each house which made it, then drunk on a Saturday, until people were completely drunk. The Brothers managed to persuade some people that it was wrong to drink too much. Particularly among 'backsliders' there were problems concerning excessive drinking and dancing all night, especially after someone had died, and this made some of them sick. The Brothers themselves were willing to dance, but only on Tuesdays and Fridays, and to drink in moderation. They gained the respect of the people by their participation, but they joined in so as to persuade them to do all these things in moderation, such as finishing the dancing by midnight.

The Brothers, who were both Melanesians from Vanuatu (New Hebrides), and observed different customs, were surprised to find that if someone died, the family would go and make a shelter over the grave and sleep there in the cemetery. In the case of a child, this would be for about six months, but for an adult it would be for a year or more. The Brothers asked the people what they thought happened to the spirit of the dead person and what death meant to them. After hearing what they believed, they taught about the Christian understanding of death, and, as a result, the people stopped sleeping in the cemeteries. However, when they checked up, the Brothers found that some women were still going to the cemeteries by night – but they gave that up when they realised the Brothers were checking on them! It was hard at first for the people to listen to the Brothers' teaching, but the Brothers were patient and kind and were careful to support good customs they found. In return, the people gradually responded and showed kindness to the Brothers; they came to them with their problems and said they wanted them to stay. They also acted well when they understood the reasons the Brothers gave for changing some of their customs as they were now Christians. The Brothers went on to teach the people how to receive Holy Communion and act reverently in church, especially when to bow, and they taught singing to the children. They taught everyone about the meaning of things in the Church House, such as the altar and the font. When dealing with customs the Brothers thought were wrong, they would find stories in the Bible to teach them from, so that the people would understand that they were being asked to change their customs to accord with the teaching of the Bible, and not with the Brothers' own ideas.

At a later period, when Bishop Willie Alaha Pwaisiho from Sa'a district on Malaita became the second Bishop of Malaita Diocese, in succession to Bishop Leonard Alufurai, he arranged tours from the Airahu Training Centre on Malaita, led by Fr Derek Au, a former teacher, and Fr John

Gerea,[17] a former carpenter, who had specialised after ordination in training village people, especially the youth. The training team would tour round the Diocese, including the outer islands, and would include Brothers and others. They would give training to people to help them be better Companions or Mothers Union members, and concentrate also on the young people. Their emphasis would be on evangelism. The *Southern Cross* would take them; they were usually with the Bishop, but sometimes went without him.

In the mid-1980s, a little church was built on the islet of Avaha, the materials having been ordered by the carpenter through Bishop Willie. They had raised the money there, but when the Bishop arrived on Pentecost Sunday, the weather was so rough they could not unload. This was thought to be a sign, reminding them about not working on the Christian Sabbath! The carpenter, Zephaniah, then trained for ordination and was later ordained by Bishop Willie in the church he had built himself. Fr Casper Kakaese's son was also ordained. Another church was built at the new village established by Johnson Kengalu and Martin Sualeva on the atoll.

Contacts with Nukumanu were maintained. Two Papua New Guinean Brothers were sent to the atoll by Bishop Willie. In 1985 they were withdrawn at the request of the North Solomons Provincial Government, which administered Bougainville and those neighbouring islands politically part of Papua New Guinea. Apparently, some members of the Nukumanu, Tasman Islands, community did not agree with their presence and had complained to the Provincial Premier. However, the Anglican priest at Kieta on Bougainville, Fr John Ewington, had received letters from others, including Kipano, the chief, asking for their return. The Brothers and Fr Ewington therefore had a meeting with the Premier. It was agreed that a meeting should also be held with the people of the atoll to find out at first hand their wishes concerning the involvement of the Anglican Church there. However, there was then a change of government in the Province and it was not until October, 1985 that three Government members and Fr Ewington set out for the island, calling on the way at the Mortlock Islands, another atoll inhabited by Polynesians 195 kilometres NE of Bougainville. The people of the Tasman Islands all live on Nukumanu, just one of the fifteen or so islands which make up the circular atoll about 400 kilometres NE of Bougainville. It was possible for the ship to steam into the lagoon and anchor there. Fr Ewington stayed with Francis, the son of the chief, Kipano, whose whole family had welcomed him on arrival into their home.

The meeting started on October 20 and was followed by a Communion service held in one of the houses, made of pandanus leaf, and it was probably the first time a Eucharist had been celebrated there since the Second World War. At the service, there were also forty baptisms. Many islanders crowded outside because of the lack of space within. Guests and elders gathered at the Chief's house in the evening for food and fellowship and the drinking of the fermented sap of the growing coconut shoot, which they call *karave.* The public meeting, which had previously come to no decisions, continued the next day, and it was decided that three religious bodies should be able to continue their work on the atoll, namely the Anglican Church, the United Church and the Jehovah's Witnesses. The Anglicans would respect the existence of the other two denominations.

The local Anglican lay people had kept the services and prayers going in the absence of the Brothers. The Brothers kept visiting there in the mid 1980s, and Prayer Books, hymn books and Bibles were sent. The Bishop of the New Guinea Islands Diocese (which included Nukumanu) and the Anglican priest on Bougainville island supported these initiatives. The Bishop was Bevan Meredith, who was then Regional Father of the Brothers in Papua New Guinea, and, before retiring to Australia, was also Archbishop of Papua New Guinea for some years. Fr Ewington was able to make a month's visit in 1986 and he called a general meeting of the congregation on January 26. A Church Council was formed with eighteen members, including the four Brothers then working on the island – Joshua, Hamilton, Keith and Robin. (Two of the Brothers were also, from time to time, to go and help Fr Ewington visit Anglicans working on plantations on Bougainville, if his plans worked out.) Three days after this annual general meeting, the Church Council met, and it was decided that the Brothers would lead a weekly fellowship Bible study and look into the possibility of setting up a youth club, as well as starting a Sunday School. The women would consider starting a Women's Fellowship. Other 'Fellowship meetings' were held three times a week while Fr Ewington was there, and some of the United Church girls joined them and taught the Anglicans new choruses! They studied the life of Christ. During his visit, Fr Ewington enjoyed the fishing and learning about the various customs. The people had undertaken to build a church, and later in the year Bishop Bevan Meredith came to conduct baptisms and confirmations. Fr Ewington even got to Ongtong Java and was able to ask the priest at Pelau, Fr John, to go occasionally to Nukumanu to celebrate Holy Communion, as it was not possible for him to go there often himself.

It became the practice for choirs from the two atolls to visit each other for church festivals, which on Ongtong Java were St Peter's Day at Luañiua and St James's Day at Pelau. Canoes would go from Pelau and Nguingui with choirs to Nukumanu for festivals there.[18]

The people of Ongtong Java became strong supporters of the Brotherhood, and more and more Polynesians from outlying islands of the Solomons (or from Polynesian communities who had settled on the larger islands) became members of the Brotherhood.

NOTES

1 *Southern Cross Log*, September 1965.
2 *Southern Cross Log*, June 1964.
3 *Southern Cross Log*, December 1965: *Highlights of the Bishop's Tour*, by Captain Eric Healy, then Master of the *Southern Cross*, the Bishop's vessel.
4 *The Melanesian Messenger* (produced in the Solomon Islands and edited by Dr Fox), December 1965.
5 *History of the Church in Areare and Koio*, an account written by Fr Samuel Su'unorua in 1999.
6 *Southern Cross Log*, December 1966.
7 *Southern Cross Log*, March 1967.
8 *Southern Cross Log*, June 1968.
9 *Southern Cross Log*, March 1967.
10 During this period Bishop Hill went away for two weeks to visit the Brothers in New Guinea. He left the Diocese of Melanesia in June, 1967.
11 He had been Chaplain, Canon and Sub-dean.
12 *Southern Cross Log*, June 1968.
13 *Melanesian Messenger*, August 1967, pp. 11-13. See this issue for a report on the 1966 Conference, including the Companions' one.
14 *Southern Cross Log*, June 1968.
15 In the author's possession.
16 The account of the Brothers' work on Ongtong Java was recorded in an interview with Codrington Tolengalenga, then an ex-Brother, at Vureas High School, Ambae, New Hebrides, where he was working, conducted by Brother Shadrach Vulum in February, 1979. Codrington objected to the tattooing of the children, as he felt they were being 'crucified' and 'cut like a pig or a cow'.
17 Both priests trained at St Peter's College, Siota, when Fr Brian was on the staff.
18 Information about developments on Nukumanu during Fr Ewington's time as parish priest were provided by him to the author in the form of a typed report on his first visit to Tasman Islands dated January 1986, and in an extract from the Spring 1986 edition of his parish magazine, *Holy Cross News*. Information about activities during his episcopate was supplied to the author by Bishop Pwaisiho in 2000 when he was serving as Rector of Gawsworth in Cheshire, England, and Assistant Bishop of Chester, a diocese which had established a strong link with the Church of Melanesia by then.

CHAPTER TWELVE

Fr. Brian Macdonald-Milne, Chaplain (as Vicar-General of the Diocese of Central Melanesia).

The stained-glass window Fr. Brian designed for St. Mark's Chapel at Tabalia, showing a New Guinea Highlander, Bro. Ini, and a woman companion.

The Head Brother's house at Tabalia, including office, library, sewing room and classroom, 1969.

Tabalia Novices 1969.

Elder Brothers of Households 1970-1971.

Brothers from Malaita & Tikopia.

Notice at entrance to the Headquarters of the Papua New Guinea Regional Headquarters at Pomete, West New Britain.

Brothers in the Common Room of the Dormitory at the Papua New Guinea Regional Headquarters at Pomete, West New Britain.

CHAPTER TWELVE

NEW HORIZONS

The Bishop of Melanesia wanted the new Chaplain and Tutor, Brian Macdonald-Milne, who was known as Fr Brian, to do more about training to help the Brotherhood. He was installed at the end of the 1968 Conference, and moved to Tabalia from Siota soon after. He had been involved in theological education and had been in close contact with life in the districts, especially on Gela, where he spoke the language, as well as promoting religious education, for which he was Diocesan Secretary. He had also been a member of the Executive Committee of the Diocese under Bishop Hill, and had, on behalf of the Diocesan Synod, approached other Churches to form the Solomon Islands Christian Association (the National Christian Council), of which he had become the first Secretary. He brought all these concerns with him to Tabalia and also continued to teach Religious Education and Pacific Studies at the Theological College. As Acting Warden, he had worked with the Principal of St Andrew's Catechist College, Kohimarama, Fr Adrian Scott, who had previously been on the staff at Siota, to try to get the two institutions combined on one site at Kohimarama. This idea was taken up by the new Bishop and by Fr Brian's successor at Siota, Fr Eric Jones. Fr Jones managed to move all the people and property of the college in one day in March 1970 on a large amphibious vessel and land them on the beach at Kodovele, near Tabalia. From there, everything was carried on the backs of students, Brothers and Novices up to Kohimarama. Thus the facilities of the theological college were made available for the upgrading of the training of the Brotherhood, and staff of both institutions could help in the teaching of ordinands, lay workers and Novices. The new combined institution was named the Bishop Patteson Theological Centre (later in the 1990s this was changed to 'College', and the title 'Warden' was changed to 'Principal'). Fr Jones was assisted by Fr George Connor, who had been Fr Brian's colleague at Siota, replacing Fr Scott there. He later worked as a superintendant priest among the Maori people in the Diocese of Waiapu in Aotearoa New Zealand, and eventually was consecrated Bishop to serve in the Bay of Plenty in that diocese. Another member of staff at Siota, Peter Atkins, became Bishop of Waiapu and then Dean of St John's College, Auckland.

At the Annual Conference of the Melanesia Section held at Tabalia from October 23 to 25, 1968,[1] the Father of the Brotherhood stated that

Brothers should take part in the work of renewal which was beginning in the new training districts, and stressed that this should include the teaching and training of Companions to be the spiritual helps and leaders in each village and district. They in turn should teach others, and help them to be strong Christians. Such renewal should include an emphasis on prayer and silent waiting upon God. He stressed that it should all be done in cooperation with the district clergy and catechists. He added that the new Chaplain would be able to do much about the planning and the training of the Brothers for all this. The Assistant Head Brother, Ataban Maurilage, reported to the Conference on the problems the Brothers commonly had to deal with in the Solomons. He listed them as: divorce; why children are often sick; why some people have no children; why some married people quarrel often; and what should be done to make the standard of living better. He said the first and the last seemed to be the commonest problems. The Bishop pointed out that only the Bishops can deal with matters concerning divorce and remarriage. On their farm, Brother Ataban stated, the Brothers had grown plenty of cassava, kumara and bananas, and they had pigs, goats and poultry.

Various reports on the Brothers' work followed. During the previous year the Brothers working on Lord Howe had faced opposition from the President of the local council at Luaniua when they suggested that the painful tattooing they practised should be given up. The Bishop advised that the Brothers should be careful not to stop any custom unless it was clearly against Christianity, but to give teaching to the people so that they could decide which customs to keep and which to give up. The Brothers had been taken to the neighbouring atoll of Nukumanu, and had noticed that the Lord Howe people taking them there had not decorated their bodies and their canoes as they had usually done out of fear of a shark. The Brothers had taken the opportunity of preaching Christ to them and said prayers at the place where the shark was normally seen. On Nukumanu (Tasman Island) in Papua New Guinea, they saw how well looked after the people were by their Government, but found that many of them had forgotten about Christianity. They had welcomed the Brothers' visit and their words to them.

In the Guadalcanal bush the Brothers based at Longgu had found one village where the chief wanted them, although he himself wished to remain a 'heathen' and keep his three wives. The Chaplain explained that Fr George Connor and some of the students from Siota had visited some 'heathen' villages in Tasimboko District on Guadalcanal and hoped that the Brothers would be able to follow. The Bishop encouraged them to do so.

Brothers working in the New Hebrides had found that the island where the first Christian village had been established by a Melanesian, Mota in the Banks Islands, was still affected by pre-Christian ideas and customs which were affecting the Christian lives of the people. The local people still believed that evil spirits were to be found in certain places, especially in stones and trees, and they were afraid of the spirits and the places where their ancestors used to worship them. There were still taboos associated with the Salagoro, the place where the men prepared for the custom dances, and during the weeks of preparation they would not attend village prayers. The Brothers had been investigating the possibility of working among the 'heathen' in South Pentecost. The two Brothers working in the Eastern Outer Islands of the Solomons had been asked by one of the priests to speak in the Reef Islands about certain customs which continued, such as tattooing and the piercing of noses and ears. This had caused the Brothers to be criticised. The Bishop said that one of the main problems in that Archdeaconry was the drinking of methylated spirits. In all these places, there seemed to be inadequate teaching of the faith, both for adults, young people and children.

The Chaplain designate, Fr Brian, had been able to visit Fiji in August and to learn about the work of the Brothers in the Solomoni communities at Wailoku and New Town, and the possibility of them beginning work among the non-Christian Indians. He had had discussions with Bishop Vockler, Archdeacon Bryce and some of the Indian clergy, and had received some helpful advice about the sort of preparation required by Brothers before they began the work among Indians in Fiji. The Brothers were to work among rural Indians south of Ba in the north of Viti Levu. He had also made contact in Fiji with Sister Clare Masina, a Tongan, and other Sisters of the Community of the Sacred Name, which had been founded in 1893 at Christchurch in New Zealand – the only other religious order to have been started in the Church of the Province of New Zealand. Fr Brian became a Priest Associate of the Community. The Sisters were delighted that the Brothers were extending their work to Fiji, as the Sisters themselves had just done. They had arrived in the Diocese in 1967, and in 1968 started a Children's Home at Naulu, east of the capital, Suva, for orphans and needy children of all races, and also single mothers.

Numbers in the Brotherhood had increased considerably. After the 1966

Conference there were 80 professed Brothers, with 25 Novices in training at Tabalia, including 12 from the New Hebrides, together with 12 aspirants, and others were training in Papua New Guinea. Brother John Ashwin Wetelwur had gone as a Brother to train at Siota for ordination. This all marked an increase in numbers of about ten per cent over previous years. Fourteen new Brothers were admitted in the Melanesia Section in 1968, and twelve were released. There were then 15 new Novices in the Section, in addition to those in the New Guinea Section.

Part of Bishop Chisholm's plan was to bring Franciscan Brothers of the Society of St Francis (SSF) and Franciscan Sisters of the First Order, called the Community of St Francis, to work in Honiara. He had admired the work the Brothers (also called Friars) had done in Papua New Guinea since 1953, and wanted them to extend their operations to the Solomons. Fr Ball was doubtful about introducing a second Religious Order for men into the country, thinking it might cause confusion in the minds of people, who thought of the Melanesian Brotherhood as *their* Religious Order. However, the Bishop consulted Fr Brian and it became clear that the new Bishop was eager to have both communities working in different ways, to complement each other, particularly as one member of the Melanesian Brotherhood, Brother Michael Davis Hepepaina, had decided to join the SSF and take Life Vows. Bishop Chisholm's idea was that the Franciscans would handle urban mission and the Melanesian Brothers the rural. Patteson House was built in Honiara to accommodate the Friars and Sisters, but the Sisters of the Community of St Francis said they could not spare any members to come. (When the Franciscan Brothers had said this to Bishop Strong of New Guinea after he had invited them there, he replied: "If you do not come, you will not grow!") So the Bishop approached the Community of the Sisters of the Church who had work in Australia, and they responded. Soon there were white Brothers and Sisters established in Honiara, including Brother Daniel from England.

The Sisters established work among the women and children in the town, especially among wives mistreated by their husbands, and they soon attracted Melanesian aspirants. Both communities set up Noviciates on Guadalcanal, the Franciscans at Hautabu near Maravovo and the Sisters of the Church at Tetete ni Kolivuti (Hill of Prayer) on the Guadalcanal Plains. Meanwhile, the Head Brother, Ellison Vahi, approached the Chaplain with the idea of a women's community to be established along the same lines as the Melanesian Brotherhood, with no requirement that the Sisters take life vows. Behind this development was Nesta Tiboe, who in 1967 had had a vision which, she believed, had been a sign from God that she should take the initiative in getting such a religious community established, but only with the agreement and support of the Brotherhood. Fr Brian encouraged Head Brother Ellison Vahi in his efforts to help the women who were interested, especially as two of them, at least, were Companions. Nesta had trained as a village catechist on Guadalcanal. This was still fairly unusual for a woman at that time. One of those interested was Lily Tetehu from Santa Ysabel, who had become the Chief Secretary of the Companions, assisting Fr Brian in his extra role as Chief Chaplain of the Companions. The Community of the Sisters of Melanesia was planned and later Archbishop Palmer gave his encouragement. It came into being in 1980 with the first professions at Buñana, then moved to Vutu in Tasimboko District on Guadalcanal in 1984 and established its permanent headquarters in 1990 at Veranaaso, the site of the former Maravovo School and quite close to Hautabu.

Bishop Chisholm had invited Fr Brian, after he ceased to be Chaplain of the Brotherhood, to be Coordinator of Religious Communities, to encourage them to work together and complement each other and to deal with any problems which might arise. There was a tradition in the Melanesian Brotherhood that it should be accountable to the Church as a whole, and especially to the Companions. The other Communities were also expected to give an account of themselves and of their work, especially to the Provincial and Diocesan Synods, to the Bishops and to their supporters. The Bishop's original plan, however, had to be modified – the Melanesian Brotherhood decided it had to have a house in Honiara too, especially to help Companions in the growing town, and the other Communities increasingly established themselves throughout the country. The Solomon Islands thus became the main centre of growth for the Religious Life in the whole Anglican Communion, as Religious Orders in other parts of the world tended either to be attracting very few new members or were in decline. The SSF eventually also established the 'Third Order' for men and women, single and married, ordained and lay, in Melanesia, as elsewhere. Fr Brian was the first member to be admitted in the Solomon Islands. The admission was by Brother Geoffrey, who was then Minister-General of the whole SSF, as all three of its Orders then had one Minister-General. It took place in the chapel at Tabalia.

In 1969[2] refresher courses for Brothers were held, the new courses for

Novices were begun, two Brothers were prepared for work in Fiji to join the two already there, and a special class for Brothers going to do 'revival work' in the New Hebrides and Lord Howe was arranged. A beautiful little church was built at Sagalu, a small village behind Tabalia, whose members sometimes came to worship on Sundays at Tabalia. Fr Brian went there from time to time to celebrate the Eucharist for them in the Vaturanga language. The Brothers also provided a large picture behind the altar, painted by the Head Brother and Brother John Henry Buffet from the New Hebrides. They also built a large, two-storey Novices' house on the station at Tabalia. Work continued on Guadalcanal at Longgu Household as well. By now the total number of Brothers had risen to over 100, and there had been a second issue of a *Companions Newsletter*. The new Chaplain, Fr Brian, had been encouraged by Fr Ball to take up his idea of writing a history of the Brotherhood and the *Newsletter, No 2*, invited people to send in material which would be useful. Fr Tom Tyler, the new Principal of the Catechist College, and his wife, Tricia, a nurse, also helped the Brotherhood, especially when the Chaplain went on leave in 1969 after visiting New Guinea with the Head Brother.

During the year, the Head Brother and Chaplain visited households on Malaita in May, and also spoke to various schools about vocation. The Brothers had two households on the island, one at Olumburi and the other at Tariaroaro, which was near Harisi in the Areare District, right up in the bush. In June the Head Brother and Chaplain attended and spoke at the Diocesan Conference of the Diocese of New Guinea at Lae and had discussions with the Diocesan Bishop, David Hand, and the Auxiliary Bishop, Bevan Meredith, whose work was in the Northern Archdeaconry, where some of the Brothers were based in the Highlands. From Madang they flew to Simbai in a four-seater Cessna plane, as the station is 3,000 feet above sea level. The journey took about three quarters of an hour. The Brothers from Asai and Kobon Households came to hear what had been discussed in the New Guinea and Melanesia Diocesan Conferences, and Fr Brian was able to meet some of the Highlanders, who appeared to have met few white people before, at Kobon Household. He was greeted with great jubilation and much noise.

In April 1969 Bishop John Holland was enthroned as the new Bishop in Polynesia[3] in Suva. The Brothers were already working with Fr Philip Thirlwell, the parish priest, in the parish of Ba, where land had been acquired and a house for them had been planned. They were learning Hindi, and had as their assistant and translator an Indian, Andrew Susappa Sebastian, who was testing his vocation to the Brotherhood. He later came to Tabalia to train, although in the end he returned to Fiji to do other work, and eventually became a Methodist Minister. The Brothers worked in the sugar plantations and visited the homes of Indian people, speaking to adults and children about the Christian faith. There was much goodwill, but few became Christians. However, through the presence of the Brothers in the Diocese, others from Fiji became Novices and then Brothers over the next few years, and they worked in Fiji and in other countries.

At the Melanesia Section Conference in 1969 it was agreed to increase the number of households by having an extra one on Guadalcanal in Tasimboko District at Tenalinggi (Tenaligi), and extra ones on Malaita at Su'u Manawai, Tariuna, Fouau and Onelava School. Work would also be maintained in the New Hebrides in Qatnapni District with Fr Ephraim Togoro, and in Fiji. There was discussion about plans for the Great Conference in 1970 and the building of the new Chapel in memory of the Founder. The Companions wanted a stained glass window which would include a depiction of him, and which would be paid for by the Companions – possibly the only stained glass window in the Anglican Diocese of Melanesia. The Chaplain had been asked to look into the design and execution of this when he went to Britain on leave in mid-1969. He visited the firm of Whitefriars, discussed the design with them, and asked them to accept the order. He was away from near the end of June till mid-January, 1970, having a holiday and doing deputation and other work. He had had no leave in the United Kingdom since leaving England in early 1964, although he had been in New Zealand for seven months in 1966. His leave there had been extended, as he had an attack of malaria, and he had acted as chaplain at St John's College, Auckland., at the invitation of the Warden, the Reverend Dr Raymond Foster.

In 1970 the new two-year course for Novices was begun. There were sixteen Novices at Tabalia and another ten were training at Pomete in New Britain, the Section Headquarters for New Guinea. There was another household in New Britain at Gimi as well as the two in the Highlands. The Great Conference met in October,[4] with representatives from all the countries where the Brothers were working. A new revised Constitution was approved, in which it was stated that the Brothers could do any kind of work for the Kingdom of God, not just evangelistic work among the 'heathen'. Regions instead of Sections were set up for Papua New Guinea and the Solomons, and a Southern Region was planned for the New Hebrides and Fiji, with its Headquarters in the New Hebrides. A new Head Brother was elected, namely Allen Daniel Borugu from North Raga, Pentecost, in the New Hebrides, who had been Elder Brother in Fiji. The Head Brother was also to be Regional Head Brother for the Solomon Islands Region, and the other two Regional Head Brothers were from then onwards to be elected by the Conference. It was hoped that each Region would have its own Regional Father and Chaplain, and that each Region would be divided into suitable Sections, of which the local Bishop would be Section Father. As membership in the Brotherhood grew over the next few years, it was possible to have at least one Household in each new Diocese in the Solomons and New Hebrides, and it was hoped something similar would happen in Papua New Guinea. Each Region was to have its own Noviciate, although there should still be interchange of Brothers between the Regions when possible.

The Brotherhood in 1970 joined the Advisory Council of Religious Communities in Australasia and the Pacific, which was established for Anglican religious communities on the lines of the 'Advisory Council' and the Communities' Consultative Council (as it was called from 1975) in the United Kingdom. Later the Advisory Council in Australasia became limited to Australia and New Zealand. In England since 1935 there had been an Advisory Council on the Relations of Bishops and Religious Communities, giving official recognition to the Religious Life within the Church of England. Fr Ernest Ball's wish that the Melanesian Brotherhood be formally recognised internationally was fulfilled by its inclusion in the *Anglican Religious Communities Year Book* 2000-2001.

The Companions also had a 'Great Conference', where it was suggested they should be grouped in Areas with their own Chaplains and annual meetings. Associates of the Brotherhood could be Companions, ex-Brothers or any others who were willing to offer themselves for a year or more as volunteers to work without pay under the direction of their Senior Priest. Training courses for Companions' Leaders and Chaplains were discussed, and cooperation with the Mothers Union encouraged.

On All Saints Day, 1970, the new Chapel of St Mark at Tabalia was consecrated, paid for with money from the children of the Episcopal Church of the USA, as the Anglican Church is called there. The new furnishings made by the Brothers were in memory of Bishop Alfred Thomas Hill, Father of the Brotherhood from 1954 to 1967, and then, until his death, Chaplain to the Brothers in New Britain. The cross standing behind the altar was inlaid with shell, showing the symbols of the Resurrection of Jesus – the crown, the rising sun, and the cup of the Eucharist. The actual building work was under the direction of Mr Moses Razak, who was one of the lay missionaries from the Diocese of Polynesia, who had arrived to serve in Melanesia in 1966.

The year 1971, being the centenary of the martyrdom of Bishop Patteson was declared a Holy Year by the Bishop of Melanesia, and it was agreed at the Conference that it would be appropriate for the Brotherhood to mark the year by holding a Mission in the Reef Islands, as Bishop Patteson was killed on Nukapu in the Outer Reef Islands.

Four Brothers and the Chaplain arrived on the *Southern Cross* on July 26 and started their teaching mission at Tuwo on Fenualoa Island, later moving to Otambe on the island of Lomlom. Brother Ellison Vahi, leader of the Brotherhood's Revival Team, took over the running of the mission at Tuwo, and Brother Timothy Vildam, a Reef Islander, that at Otambe, when the Chaplain returned to Tabalia. The Missions took three weeks in each place. Teaching was given to children and young people during the day, and a special sermon was preached each evening, followed by discussion groups for young people, men and women. Clergy, catechists, Companions' leaders and other lay people joined in the work of the Mission Team, and a large meeting was held in Nganyivo School towards the end of the Mission to discuss the follow-up. Training courses for the Companions in the various islands followed. On September 20 the Brothers joined in the Centenary service which was held on the island of Nukapu. The Chaplain accompanied the Bishop and a representative group of people to the island on the *Southern Cross*, Fr Brian being responsible for preparing a programme for Solomons Radio.

The Head Brother and the Chaplain then visited the households on Malaita, and attended the Brothers' meeting at their local headquarters at Su'u Manawai, at which Bishop Leonard presided. At this meeting a question was raised about whether Christians should take off their clothes, if asked to do so out of respect when attending feasts organised by the 'heathen'. The Bishop's response was: "They should keep their clothes on. The heathen are only asking them to take their clothers off to test them, to see whether they are really Christians or not." The Chaplain blessed a church made of leaf materials at Alikata and others in Areare District at Tariuna and Osi. At Tariaroaro he admitted eleven men, women and children as catechumens. He had admitted the first group of catechumens there in 1969, and, with the admission of this second group, the village now consisted of about forty people, some baptised and some preparing for baptism.[5]

The Central Solomons Section Meeting of the Brotherhood took place at Tabalia on October 23 and 24, 1971, preceded by a retreat conducted by Bishop Dudley Tuti. The Brothers by then were doing many different kinds of work: primary evangelism among 'heathens'and non-Christian Indians, district work as part of teams with clergy and catechists, revival work in areas where the Church was weak, visits to plantations, youth work, work in schools and training centres, craftwork, work among Companions, recruiting for the Brotherhood and Companions, translation work, administration of the Brotherhood, and various kinds of manual work, including agriculture, building and carpentry. Novices were being trained at Tabalia for the Solomon Islands Region, at Naone on Maewo island for the Southern Region and at Pomete in New Britain for the Papua New Guinea Region. Fr John Pepela had been asked to go from the Solomons to be Chaplain at Pomete. The Brothers[6] at Ba Section Headquarters in Fiji were responsible for encouraging Companions in Fiji and Tonga. The Southern Region also included some Companions in New Caledonia, while the Solomon Islands Region dealt with Companions in Australia.

In New Zealand, the Christchurch Diocese's Melanesia Committee, whose chairman was the Reverend John Froud, concentrated on Melanesia for its Mission Month in September 1972, and the Head Brother provided a sermon for use throughout the Diocese. In this, he invited people who wanted to support the work of the Brothers to become Companions, as well as to pray. About the work in Fiji, he wrote: "In Fiji, the Brothers live in almost a complete Hindu community, and they become part of the community by what they do. The people are mostly sugar cane farmers, and so the Brothers, according to the season of the crop, do different kinds of work for the farmers and earn their living that way. For example, when the harvest comes, the Brothers join the cane cutters and cut cane and so on. In all these outside works, there are many opportunities of contacting other people and families as they meet in their daily work." He also described how in a household in Melanesia, according to local custom in such a 'heathen' area, a woman was sent out to the bush to deliver her baby. One day, one of the Brothers went out to the bush to look for edible ferns, as the Brothers had nothing for their lunch. While in the bush, he heard the cry of a woman and discovered that the pregnant woman was in labour and was also in great pain and very sorrowful. He helped the woman till the baby was born, then continued to do so secretly, in spite of the strict local 'custom' rules. He brought her medicine and food until she was strong enough to return to her village, and also prayed with her. Because of the great Christian love she had experienced – something she had never even dreamed of before – she later became a Christian, with her baby.

It had been decided at the Great Conference that Brothers should take their first vows for three years, and, if they wished to renew, to do so for at least one year. However, they no longer had to renew annually, as the second vow was for an indefinite period, either until the Brother asked to be released (and was commissioned for other work as a Christian), or until he died. There was provision for a Brother to take a life vow after ten years, but he would have to receive the agreement of the Brotherhood to do this, as it was considered a special privilege, and was normally felt to be appropriate only for a Brother who was a widower. Brothers going to work outside their own country were expected to give an undertaking to remain for a certain number of years.

In 1973 the Chaplain went on leave at the end of his service with the Brothers. He continued as Chief Chaplain of Companions, however. He visited Companions in Fiji and Tonga, and preached about the Brotherhood and Companions in those countries and in Samoa, Tahiti and the USA, where he stayed in the Diocese of East Carolina (in the state of North Carolina) with Mr and Mrs Bill Page, who were Companions there. Mr Page had been involved in establishing a 'Companion Diocese' relationship with the Diocese of Melanesia. He and Mr Walker Taylor Jnr had first visited Melanesia in 1965, to strengthen the connection with East Carolina Diocese. Fr Brian also visited Companions and preached in England – and in New Caledonia and the New Hebrides on his return journey to the Solomons. He had also been asked to preach to a Chinese congregation in Singapore when he passed through there.[7]

Numbers of Companions were increasing in Papua New Guinea. Fr Hubert Prout Moi had started a group in Port Moresby in August 1974 with six members. They had been visited by the Head Brother on his way to a Campus Crusade for Christ training course in Seoul, South Korea, called EXPLO 74, which attracted over 300,000 people. Bishop Leonard Alufurai went too. The Church of Melanesia, through the Department of

Evangelism and Community Education, was willing to cooperate with other evangelistic agencies approved by the Solomon Islands Christian Association, the national Christian Council. These included Campus Crusade for Christ, the Child Evangelism Fellowship and the Billy Graham Evangelistic Association. The Church, although of an Anglican Catholic tradition, thus showed its openness to what it saw as positive aspects of the Evangelical tradition, and the Brotherhood was willing to learn from others and share its own insights. On June 16, 1974, John Solomon came to Holy Name School, Papua New Guinea, and spoke to the girls about the Brotherhood and the Companions. Twenty-one indicated they would like to join the Companions. Soon after, Brother Santus and Brother Isaiah, who were visiting the District, came to the school and talked to the girls again, and as a result more and more girls joined in the work of the Companions group. The Brothers were present when they became full members of the Companions on July 28 in the Cathedral of St Peter and St Paul in Dogura, being admitted by Bishop Henry Kendall. There had been a group in the school in 1971, but it had soon lapsed. The first support given by the revived group was to the Brothers who visited them, to help them in their patrolling. They also raised some money for the Brotherhood by holding a dance and asking girls to pay a small amount in order to attend. Thus $10 was raised and given for the general fund of the Region.[8]

On the Feast of St Simon and St Jude, 1974, at 7 a.m. at an altar placed before the great cross in the open square in front of the new chapel at Tabalia, 23 new Brothers were admitted. Seven Brothers were released (plus two more in the New Hebrides), including Brother Christian Ofamana, who had served for thirteen years. However, he and another Brother retained their vow of celibacy, which meant they had a 'temporary release' for special reasons and could return to full vows in due course if they wished. Of the new Brothers, seven were from the New Hebrides and the rest from the Solomons.

The Assistant Head Brother, who had been elected at the Great Conference, was then Brother Wenceslas Papao from Papua, and there was a Solomoni Novice from Fiji, Kevueli Bogi Oba, who was training at Tabalia. Brother Ellison Vahi was going to Kohimarama daily to study for the priesthood. Brother Philip SSF, another Papuan, had taken over from Fr Brian as Chaplain and Tutor in 1973, thus fulfilling an earlier suggestion that the Franciscans might one day supply a Chaplain for the Brotherhood. He had taken up residence, with Brother Daniel SSF, in the Chaplain's

House at Tabalia, after it had been much improved, with proper ceilings to exclude the rats (which had previously found their way through the leaf ceilings), and with the passage way through the house enclosed at each end. Brother Daniel was the first white student to study at Kohimarama for the priesthood. He was from England and had been sent to the original house in Honiara with the first group of Franciscan Brothers, while Patteson House was being built for the Franciscans and the Sisters of the Church. He was later ordained in Melanesia and in due course became Minister Provincial in the Pacific, then Minister General of the First Order Brothers in the 1990s, remaining a friend of the Melanesian Brotherhood and one who understood it well.

By 1974[9] there were Sections in the Solomon Islands Region covering the Central Solomons, Eastern Solomons (Malaita) and Outer Eastern Solomons, and the Head Brother was still also Regional Head Brother for the Solomon Islands and Southern Regions. There were 28 Brothers and 26 Novices in the Solomon Islands Region. In the Southern Region there was a new Section Headquarters for the New Hebrides Section at Toroulo on Maewo island with four Brothers there and five Brothers at Tombet Household, working among the 'heathen' inland from Big Bay on Santo Island (Espiritu Santo). There were two Brothers also at Nabatolu Household near Ba in Fiji, in the Polynesia Section. Brother William Tedi, who had joined the Brotherhood in 1961, had taken over from Brother Christian Ofamana as Regional Head Brother for the Papua New Guinea Region, and this Region now had two Sections. The Regional Father was Auxiliary Bishop Bevan Meredith, an Australian. In the New Guinea Islands Section, there were thirteen Brothers working in New Britain island, at Pomete Regional Headquarters, Umbi Household near Kandrian and Samaru Household near Au, Gasmata, in West New Britain. In the New Guinea Mainland Section there were sixteen Brothers working in the Highlands in three households: Aganmakuk Section Headquarters (Aiome), Miami Household (Simbai) and Sareb Household (Simbai). Brother David Defe, who, like Brother William Tedi,[10] was a Solomon Islander and had also been admitted as a Brother in 1961, had been chosen for special work at Agaun, Eastern Papua. Brother Edward Pamudi from the Highlands, who had become a Brother after he and his people had been converted through the work of the Brothers, had gone to Newton College to study for the priesthood, while Brother John Ashwin Wetelwur, a New Hebridean, had gone to the Pacific Theological College in Suva, Fiji, to continue his studies there. At the end of its first fifty years, the Brotherhood was in good heart.

NOTES

1 The minutes of the Conference (in the author's possession).

2 See Report of the Chaplain-Tutor to the Diocesan Conference of the Diocese of Melanesia in 1969, and the Minutes of the Brothers' Section Conference held at Tabalia from October 25 to 27, 1969 (after the Companions' Conference on October 24), which covered the work in the Solomons, New Hebrides and Fiji.

3 The title was Bishop *in* Polynesia, in recognition of the late arrival of the Anglicans in that part of the Pacific and the agreement made with the Methodists not to start work among indigenous Fijians.

4 See Minutes of the Great Conference and of the Great Conference of Companions which followed it (October 31-November 1), as well as the Report of the Companions' and Associates' Commission to Great Conference, which made detailed proposals about the organisation, development and training of Companions and Associates. See also the Report by the Brotherhood to the South Pacific Anglican Council, which met in Honiara from January 13 to 21, 1971, and a paper on the Melanesian Brotherhood prepared for the Diocese of Polynesia in February 1971. In 1970 Bishop Halapua, the Assistant Bishop, had dedicated the Church of the True Light for the Brothers' station at Nabatolu. Brother Allen Daniel was replaced by Brother Robert Wobur as Elder Brother. Brother Nelson Gigini remained there until February 1971.

5 An account of the Melanesian Brotherhood's contribution to the Diocese of Melanesia's Holy Year and Patteson Centenary celebration was prepared by the Chaplain-Tutor in September 1971 (in the author's possession).

6 There were three Brothers from the New Hebrides – Robert Wobur (Banks Islands), who was the Section Elder Brother, Ezekiel Tias and Harper Tinge – and one from the Solomons, Selwyn Teodoña (Malaita).

7 The step-mother of the Reverend John Cook, then parish priest at St Peter's, Serangoon Gardens, was a former staff member of the London office of the Melanesian Mission, when single (Miss Mollie Allen).

8 See report by Miss Melva Moi from Holy Name School Companions in the Minutes of the Solomon Islands Region Companions Conference, held on October 26, 1974.

9 The information which follows is contained in intercession lists produced for the Brothers and Companions.

10 Brother William Tedi had led the team of Brothers which cut down trees in the bush near Tabalia to make the altar and the long heavy bench behind it, on which the sacred ministers and servers sat during parts of the Eucharist. The furnishing of the chapel had been planned by the Chaplain and the Head Brother, Allen Daniel, who painted the designs above the vestry doors.

CHAPTER THIRTEEN

SAINT BARNABAS CATHEDRAL, HONIARA
Painting by Barbara House.

The figure of Christ as a Melanesian, made in England of fibre-glass and given by supporters of the Church of Melanesia in the United Kingdom on the inauguration of the Province of Melanesia and placed outside St. Barnabas Cathdral, Honiara, Solomon Islands.

Bishop Derek Rawcliffe, Assistant Bishop of Melanesia from 1974 and first Bishop of the New Hebrides 1975, with his wife at their wedding. Regional Father of the Southern Region of the Brotherhood 1975-1980 and later a Companion in England.

Fiji Indian women among whom the Brothers worked in northern Viti Levu Island, Fiji.

CHAPTER THIRTEEN

NEW VISION

The year 1975 was notable as a year of reflection and change. A Committee appointed by Bishop Chisholm had drawn up a Constitution for a Province of Melanesia which had been accepted by the General Synod of the Church of the Province of New Zealand. The Committee had been composed wholly of Melanesians, except for the Chairman, Fr Brian, who was also Head of the Department of Evangelism and Community Education. The Department encouraged evangelism through the Religious Orders, the Mothers Union, Training Centres, Youth Work and the media, and promoted Christian Stewardship as well as Christian Education in all its forms. Bishop Chisholm had also asked Fr Brian to be Coordinator of the Religious Communities, assisting them to work together and plan their future work. Basil LePine-Williams from England, the Diocesan Secretary of the Diocese of Melanesia, was to become first Provincial Secretary of the new Province.[1]

On Sunday, January 26, the Church of the Province of Melanesia was inaugurated in a great service in the Provincial Cathedral of St Barnabas, Honiara, which Bishop Chisholm had had erected, with a bell-tower containing a large bell which was a memorial to Bishop Baddeley. The SPG, later USPG (United Society for the Propagation of the Gospel), had for many years kept in its chapel in London the mat which had wrapped Bishop Patteson's body after his martyrdom at Nukapu, together with the knotted palm frond which had been placed on his body. These, with other relics, were placed in a specially dedicated area at the entrance to the Cathedral. John Chisholm was installed as first Archbishop of Melanesia and as Bishop of the new Diocese of Central Melanesia. At the same time the other Bishops became diocesan bishops: Dudley Tuti of Ysabel Diocese, Leonard Alufurai of Malaita Diocese, and Derek Rawcliffe of the Diocese of the New Hebrides (which changed its name to the Diocese of Vanuatu when that country became independent in 1980).

This had implications for the Brotherhood, as, although the Archbishop of Melanesia remained as Father of the Brotherhood, more responsibility was now exercised by the other Bishops, who would each need to agree before there could be developments of the Brothers' work in their individual Dioceses. Although the Archbishop remained Regional Father for the Solomon Islands Region, Bishop Derek Rawcliffe became Regional Father for the Southern Region, and Bishop Bevan Meredith Regional Father for the Papua New Guinea Region. However, on John Chisholm's first visit as the new Archbishop in 1975 to his homeland Australia, he was diagnosed as having cancer of the throat, and he died there after some time in hospital. His body was brought back for his funeral, and burial in the Cathedral Garth. Soon after his funeral, when all the Bishops were present, together with the members of the Electoral College from the Diocese of Central Melanesia, the Dean of the Cathedral, Norman Kitchener Palmer, a Solomon Islander from the Western Solomons,[2] of mixed Melanesian and European ancestry, was elected as second Archbishop. Not having been a Bishop before, he was both consecrated and installed in his dual role as Archbishop and Diocesan Bishop in the Provincial Cathedral on November 1, 1975. So it was that at the celebration of the fiftieth anniversary of the Brotherhood on November 2, it was to be a Melanesian Archbishop who would preside as Father of the Brotherhood.

He appointed Fr Brian as his Vicar-General and Diocesan Secretary, responsible for representing him when away from his Diocese, and for running the diocesan administration. The headquarters of the three religious orders were in the Diocese of Central Melanesia, and they were all represented in the Diocesan Synod by representatives they chose. Bishop Caspar Uka from Tikopia was Assistant Bishop of the diocese, and resided on Makira, concentrating on work in the Eastern Solomons.

Brother Philip SSF had ceased to be Chaplain of the Brotherhood on January 1, 1975. The Headquarters at Tabalia now had a truck, partly paid for by the Brothers and partly with money granted by Bishop John Chisholm, who had previously provided a Mini-Moke for Fr Brian when he had been Chaplain. Ex-Novice Willie Huhulu had become Chief Secretary of the Companions, based at Tabalia. This was after the Solomon Islands Regional Conference in October 1974, which had discussed how the fiftieth anniversary should be celebrated. A Planning Committee at Tabalia had then been set up to arrange the Third Great Conference in October, 1975, together with the celebrations at Tabalia and Honiara of the Brotherhood Jubilee. The fifth issue of the Companions' Newsletter was sent out in January, and it was followed by an invitation to clergy and District and Group Leaders of Companions to send one representative from each District (parish) in the Solomons to join others from overseas at the Great Conference to be held from October 23 to 25. This was to be followed by the 50th anniversary service and celebrations at Tabalia on October 28, the Great Conference of Companions in Honiara on November 1, and the Jubilee celebrations in Honiara on November 2. Special Collects, Epistles and Gospels for use at services on special days through the year were made available from the Department of Evangelism to encourage people throughout the Province to mark the Jubilee in appropriate ways, especially by prayer.

At the 1974 Conference, thirty Brothers had been chosen to serve in the Households at the Central Headquarters, at Honiara, and at Tariuna on Malaita. Six went to Temotu Household on Santa Cruz. Ten were sent to the New Hebrides to join Toroulo Household on Maewo and Tombet Household on Santo, while four went to Nabatolu Household in Fiji. Nine Brothers went to New Britain to join the households at Pomete, Umbi and Samavu, while twelve more went to the households in the Highlands at Aganmakuk, Miami and Salep. Four were placed in a household at Param in Papua.

The Head Brother paid a month's visit to New Zealand, beginning on February 19, 1975, followed by visits to the Brothers in Fiji and the New Hebrides. He arrived back in April. It was a year of great activity for him and he was assisted by the Brotherhood Committee (formerly called the Ruling Committee) which consisted of a representative chosen at each Regional Conference: Papua New Guinea Region had chosen Brother David Defe, Solomon Islands Region had chosen Brother Geoffrey Tekuirawa and Southern Region Brother Patteson Ihomana. Brother Patteson had first come to Tabalia after leaving school on Santa Ysabel, and Fr Brian had been asked by the then Head Brother, Ellison Vahi, to give him further teaching. At the age of 16 he had become a Novice and at 18 a Brother.

The Great Conference of the Brotherhood elected new leaders. Brother Robert Tempest Wobur, from the Banks Islands in the northern New Hebrides, succeeded Brother Allen Daniel Borugu, another New Hebridean, as Head Brother. Brother Robert had previously succeeded Brother Allen as Section Elder Brother in Fiji, and both of them had learnt Hindi (as spoken in Fiji) and some Fijian. Brother Patteson Ihomana, then about 21, was elected as Assistant Head Brother, with responsibility also as Regional Head Brother of the Solomon Islands Region. Regional Head Brothers were chosen: for the New Guinea Region it was Giles Livingstone Pondo, and for the Southern Region, Wilson Valiusala. Their duty was to appoint Section Elder Brothers and Elder Brothers of households in their Regions. Torgil on Ambae was to be the new Regional Headquarters for the Southern

Region. Fr Brian was chosen as Adviser to the Companions and Chief Chaplain for the Companions in the Solomon Islands Region and for Companions in parts of the world beyond the three Brotherhood Regions.

The Reverend Dr Charles Elliott Fox, born on October 1, 1878, who had gone to New Zealand because of his health, was invited to become a Brother again at the age of 97! Fr Brian was requested to write to him and ask him if he would be willing to rejoin the Brotherhood, which would mean so much to the Brothers in their fiftieth year. He consented, saying it would be a great honour, and would mean more to him than anything else would have done. He was readmitted as a Brother in New Zealand by the Archbishop of New Zealand, wearing the Brotherhood uniform and the insignia of the CBE (Commander of the Order of the British Empire), with which he had recently been invested there. His MP, Sir Keith Holyoake, former Prime Minister of New Zealand, had been shocked to find that he had received only the MBE on the recommendation of the British Solomon Islands Protectorate Government, in recognition of all his service to the Solomons; he was determined that the New Zealand Government should do better, as he considered Dr Fox as one of the most remarkable New Zealand citizens to have served abroad. Dr Fox, however, really considered himself a Solomon Islander and wrote to the Chief Minister, Peter Kenilorea, to ask if he could receive Solomon Island citizenship when the country became independent, and this was agreed by the MPs. He had already written (jokingly) to congratulate the Solomon Islands Government on choosing his birthday as the National Day – it was also the anniversary of the establishment of self-government! Sadly, he died in 1977 at the age of 99, a year before the Solomon Islands became an independent country, but his body was brought back to Tabalia and a special grave and headstone were prepared for him in the Brothers' graveyard. However, for two years there *had* been a Melanesian Brother in New Zealand!

The Great Conference made some important decisions about the extension of the Brothers' work. In response to a request from the Bishop of Carpentaria, a household was to be established in his diocese, mostly for work among the Aborigines. Brothers William Tedi, Michael Toa and Ellison Vahi were to do this. Formal backing was also given to the establishment of a parallel Community of Sisters, living under a similar rule and Constitution, to be called the Community of the Sisters of Melanesia (CSM). The Archbishop-elect gave this his support.

However, he did not accept a request brought by a representative of Bellona Island, one of two Polynesian islands to the south of Guadalcanal, that the Anglican Church should resume its work there. People from Bellona and Rennell had occasionally come to the main part of the Solomons to attend Anglican schools, or to receive some teaching from the Brothers. However, on their islands there were then only two main denominations, as the Anglican Church had earlier withdrawn, leaving the work to the South Sea Evangelical and Seventh Day Adventist Churches. The Archbishop-elect was concerned about the possibility of further rivalry between denominations if the Anglicans returned there, and he also felt that it was difficult for the Brotherhood to accept further responsibilities when it was going to undertake new work in Australia. He was also concerned about how Brothers working there would be served, as the Province's ships did not go there any more. The Bellonese would have to wait till 1995 to receive the ministrations of the Church that some of them wanted! The Brothers had by then established a household there and been warmly welcomed.

The fiftieth anniversary was marked by the installation of a permanent altar before the great cross on the central grass square at Tabalia, before which the Brothers took or renewed their vows. Companions in the Province of Melanesia paid for it, and a plaque was attached to it with the inscription: IN LOVING MEMORY OF BISHOP JOHN STEWARD FIRST FATHER, WHO HELPED INI KOPURIA TO START THE MELANESIAN BROTHERHOOD IN 1925 - 28 OCTOBER 1925. The altar was blessed on October 27 by the Regional Father of the New Guinea Region, Bishop Bevan Meredith, who later succeeded Archbishops David Hand and George Ambo as third Archbishop of Papua New Guinea.

After the great Jubilee Service at St Barnabas's Cathedral, Honiara, which was held on November 2, the day after the consecration of Archbishop Palmer, a procession of Brothers, Companions, clergy, Bishops and overseas visitors wound its way from the Cathedral porch through part of Honiara and down Mendaña Avenue to an area behind the Provincial Headquarters and in front of Patteson House, where a memorial cross was unveiled and consecrated by Archbishop Palmer – his first public act as Archbishop. The plaque on it had the inscription: IN THANKSGIVING FOR THOSE WHO BROUGHT THE GOOD NEWS OF GOD TO OUR ISLANDS AND IN COMMEMORATION OF THE FIFTIETH ANNIVERSARY OF THE FOUNDING OF THE MELANESIAN

BROTHERHOOD ON GUADALCANAL BY INI KOPURIA ON 28 OCTOBER 1925. PRAISE THE LORD.

Nine new Brothers had been admitted at Tabalia on October 28, including five from the New Hebrides and one from New Guinea. Only three had been released from their vows. After all the celebrations, ten Brothers were sent out from the Solomons to the other Regions or to Australia, some of them after first making 'home visits', as they probably would not see their homes again for some years.

In November the new Head Brother, Robert Wobur, wrote in the Newsletter: "So many friends in and out of the Province have been praying for the Brotherhood, asking especially for God's guidance and help for the future. Whether these prayers have been answered or not, God's way always prevails. The letters and messages of good wishes for the Brotherhood and for myself, the gifts for the Brotherhood for its Jubilee, I humbly acknowledge with sincere thanks. I for one am very much aware at this time of the power of prayer. The number of people who prayed for our Great Conference and Jubilee in the past days is a great source of encouragement to all of us..... may the Glory, the Praise and Honour be to our God for ever and ever."

The ex-Head Brother, Allen Daniel Borugu, continued his involvement with evangelism by becoming, on his release from vows, Head of the Provincial Department of Evangelism and Community Education in succession to Fr Brian, who combined his new appointments with continuing to be the priest at Vura, part of the Cathedral parish. Later, this became a separate parish with its own Church of the Transfiguration, built in memory of Archbishop John Wallace Chisholm.[3]

NOTES

1 Mr LePine-Williams had brought his own boat out from England via the Panama Canal and the Galapagos Islands, and it joined the Church fleet. His wife Anne had been his mate on the voyage and his sons had formed the crew. He made it a priority to train a Melanesian to take over the role of Provincial Secretary after suitable training. He was a great support to the new Archbishop.

2 The majority of people in the Western Solomons had belonged to the Solomon Islands Methodist District, but the Methodist Church in the Solomons and Papua New Guinea had joined with the Papua Ekalesia and the United Church in Port Moresby to form the United Church in Papua New Guinea and the Solomons in 1968. The new Archbishop had been brought up as a Methodist, but because the Japanese invasion had destroyed all the schools in the Western Solomons, he was sent to school at Pawa, where he became an Anglican. His great-grandfather had been one of the powerful head-hunting chiefs of that part of the country. His white grandfather had been an Australian trader, invited to establish his store in the chief's area. However, his plan was to kill the trader and take over the goods in the store for himself. On discovering what her father intended to do, his daughter said to him: "Don't kill him, I'll marry him!" This is what happened, and

their daughter became the mother of the future Archbishop. His father was an Englishman who had come out to work for his grandfather but did not stay in the country. (Information provided to the author verbally by Archbishop Palmer.)

3 Services in Fr Brian's time took place in the local primary school at Vura on weekdays, and the congregation worshipped with others in the Cathedral on Sundays. Fr Brian asked the Province to acquire a piece of land which was then available, in order that a church might one day be erected. He himself lived in Lichfield House, the priest's house at Vura, purchased with money given by the Diocese of Lichfield, where Bishop G A Selwyn became Bishop in 1868, when he returned to England from New Zealand. Bishop Selwyn's splendid tomb, which incorporates scenes from New Zealand and Melanesia, is in Lichfield Cathedral. Fr Brian felt that a church would be an appropriate memorial to Melanesia's first Archbishop. He preached in the newly consecrated church on a return visit to Melanesia in 1990, when he represented the British Friends of Vanuatu at the tenth anniversary of Vanuatu's independence, then paid a visit to the Solomons.

CHAPTER FOURTEEN

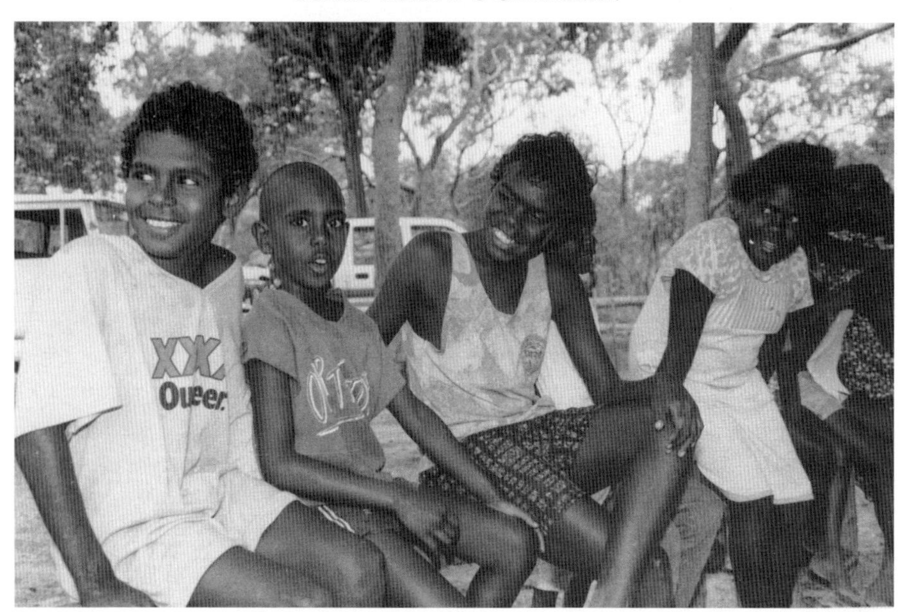

Aboriginal children at the Dedication of the Brotherhood Household at Cutter Creek, Cape York Peninsula, North Queensland, September 1989.

The Brotherhood Household, Cutter Creek.

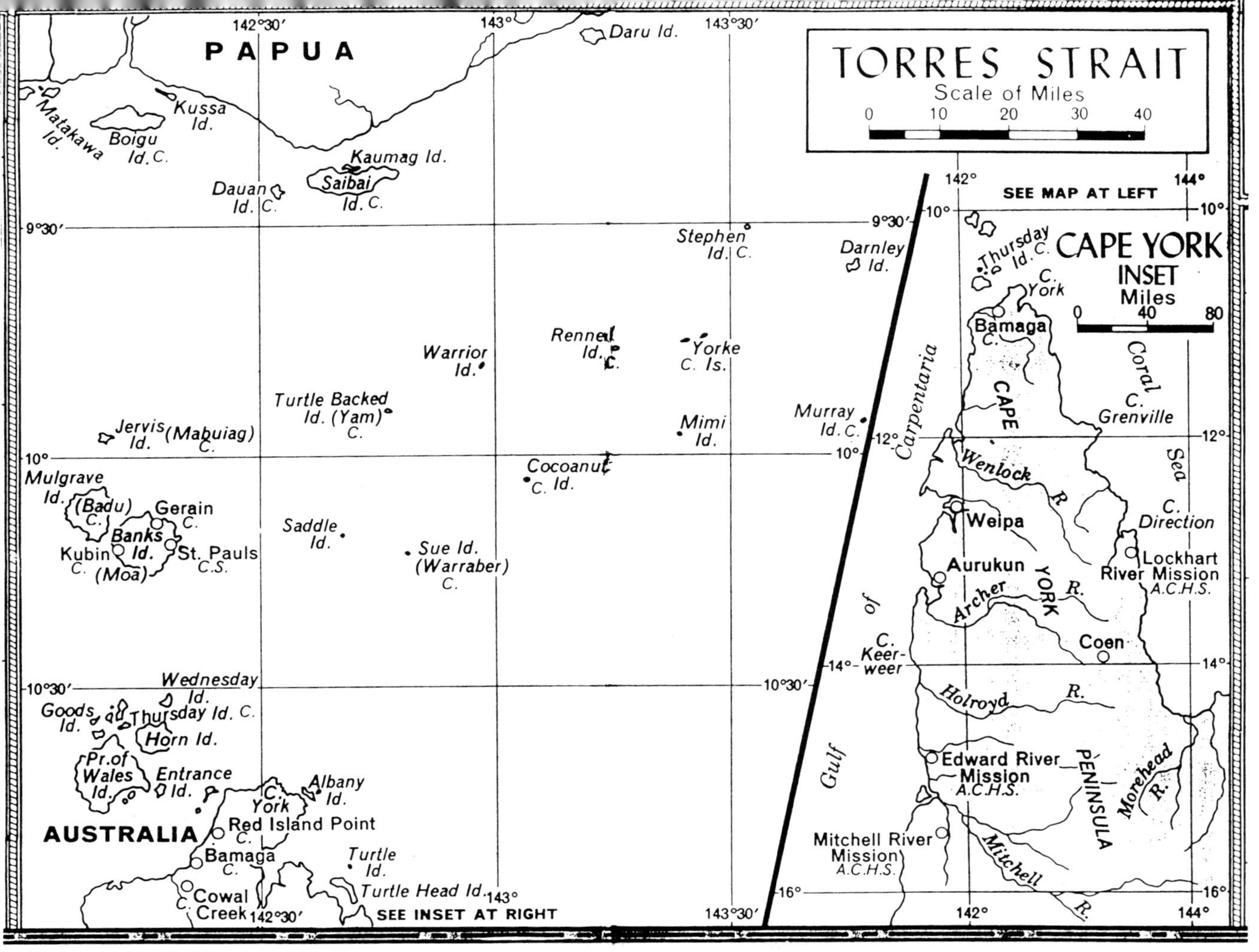

Prepared by H E Robinson Pty. Ltd for the Australian Board of Missions

Key: A - Airstrip C - Church/Chaplaincy H - Hospital S - School

The Bishop of Carpentaria, the Rt. Revd. Hamish Jamieson, prepares the Eucharist following the ordination of Torres Strait Islander, the Revd.Simon Peter, in the Quetta Memorial Church, 'the Cathedral' on Thursday Island. In the picture, from the right are Canon Pat Allen (Bathurst), Revd. Gordon Barnier (Newcastle), Canon Tony Matthews (Rockhampton), the Bishop, Revd. Simon Peter (Torres Strait Islands) and the Revd. Wal Ogle (Grafton).

Photo: Australian Board of Missions

Brother Robert Wobur is seen here teaching scripture at Bamega Primary School in the Diocese of Carpentaria. Their skins are the same colour, but to these Torres Strait Island children Brother Robert is a foreign missionary. Brother Robert was the Head Brother of the Melanesian Brotherhood from the Church of Melanesia and visited Australia early in 1978

Photo: Australian Board of Missions

CHAPTER FOURTEEN

AUSTRALIAN ABORIGINALS AND ISLANDERS

After the Great Conference of 1975, the three Brothers selected to investigate the possibility of working among the Aboriginal people of Australia went first to Thursday Island in the Torres Strait, the headquarters of the Diocese of Carpentaria and the site of its Cathedral. Bishop Eric Hawkey, Bishop of that diocese, had been formerly a staff member of the Australian Board of Missions (ABM), and therefore had been well aware of the work of the Church among the indigenous people in Melanesia and Papua New Guinea. He had retired on August 24, 1974, St Bartholomew's Day – the day when the first Bishop of Carpentaria, Gilbert White, had been consecrated in Sydney in 1900. His successor, Hamish Thomas Jamieson, was an Australian from New South Wales, who had studied for the ordained ministry at St Michael's College, Crafers, in South Australia, run by the Society of the Sacred Mission. He had been ordained in 1956 and had spent the next seven years in the Bush Brotherhood of the Good Shepherd, so he had his own ideas of mission and had experienced 'Brotherhood' life himself as 'Brother Hamish'. He later became Rector of Darwin in the Northern Territory and then a Naval Chaplain, serving in various ships and shore establishments. As the Diocese of Carpentaria included both the Torres Strait Islands, peopled by Melanesians, and Aboriginal communities on Cape York Peninsula (all part of Queensland), he had sometimes to travel by the diocesan boat, the *Torres Herald III* or its replacement, the *Yosepha Tauki*, named after the first two Torres Strait Islanders to be ordained priest. There were at the time of his consecration in Brisbane on November 1, 1975, churches and priests on sixteen of the Torres Strait Islands. He was the seventh Bishop of Carpentaria, which had earlier covered the Northern Territory as well. The border with Papua New Guinea passed through the north of the Torres Strait, so that those islands in the far north of the Diocese were very close to the Papuan coast. A priest from one of these islands, Saibai, was a member of the SSF and served in the Solomon Islands for a time as a First Order Brother, known as Brother Kabay.

Historically, the Church in the Torres Strait had strong links with the coming of Christianity to Papua. The Reverend Samuel McFarlane and the Reverend Archibald Murray of the London Missionary Society had arrived with eight evangelists from the Loyalty Islands and their wives at

Darnley Island on July 1, 1871. Every year this event is still celebrated with services and festivities as 'The Coming of the Light'. The Reverend Albert McLaren, pioneer missionary of the Anglican Mission in Papua, visited Thursday Island the day after a vessel called the *Quetta* had been wrecked on an uncharted rock. He urged the Diocese of North Queensland to appoint a priest on Thursday Island, and later a 'Quetta Memorial Church' was built. This became the Cathedral in 1900, dedicated to All Souls and St Bartholomew. The LMS did work on Cape York, in the other islands of the Torres Strait and on the Papuan mainland, but early in the twentieth century it found that its resources were being stretched, and, as it was in origin an interdenominational mission, it invited the Anglican Diocese to take over its work in all the Torres Strait Islands and the Cape York peninsula. In 1915 the ABM agreed to support the work there and more resources became available.[1] This was the only example of LMS work in the Pacific Islands being handed over to Anglicans, although the Society had previously handed over its work in the New Hebrides to the Presbyterians and its work in the Loyalty Islands off New Caledonia to the Paris Evangelical Missionary Society.

After their arrival at Thursday Island, the Brothers toured some of the islands for a week on *Heron 3*. Then they had a retreat on Moa Island. At the Diocesan Conference, it was decided that they should go first to the towns where the 'Aboriginals'[2] were. They went first to Bamaga, which with Cowal Creek and Red Island Point form the most northerly residential communities on the mainland of Australia, lying at the very tip of Cape York Peninsula. Bamaga is named after the chief tribesman of Saibai Island who brought his people to settle there, both because of their many problems with malarial mosquitoes, and also a fear that their island might become submerged. The Brothers held a mission there for one week before flying in the plane of the Carpentaria Aerial Mission, *Gilbert White II*, to Edward River settlement, half way down the west coast of the Cape York Peninsula, in the Gulf of Carpentaria. Canon Tony Hall-Matthews, son of a former Bishop of Carpentaria, Bishop Searing John Matthews, had been Carpentaria's 'flying priest' for eight years, and piloted the plane all over the area.

Edward River Mission had been founded by Joseph Chapman in 1937, located between the Chapman and Munkam Rivers, but named after the Edward River, nine miles north. It later became known as the Edward River Aboriginal Community and in the mid-1970s was home to about 300

Aborigines. Although largely detribalised because of living in the Community, certain clan taboos persisted among the people. There were two main tribal groups, with four or five dialects spoken within each group. Intermarriage between clans was considered wrong. The Brothers remained there for two weeks. Brother Ellison Vahi then returned to the Solomon Islands. The view of the Brothers was that members of the Melanesian Brotherhood *could* work among Aboriginals, although their customs and attitudes were very different. The Carpentaria Diocesan Synod agreed that the Brothers should work at Edward River and Cowal Creek and relieve the clergy in other places such as Kowanyama (Mitchell River), Lockhart River (on the east coast) and Umagico (Cape York). Provision was made for two more Brothers to be sent, and in 1977 three more Brothers arrived – Moses Keahi (a Polynesian from Lord Howe atoll), Geoffrey Tekuirawa and Paul Neremana. William Tedi became Elder Brother at Edward River with Brother Michael Toa to assist him, while Brother Moses went to Cowal Creek with Brothers Paul and Geoffrey, and became Section Elder Brother of the Section in Australia.

At Edward River, the Brothers found a difference between full-blooded Aborigines and those of mixed race. The full-blooded ones were not interested in jobs or work, as understood by Europeans or Melanesians, and were not used to washing themselves or their clothes or in cleaning their houses or mattresses. They found it difficult to adapt to living in a settled way, as their tradition was nomadic. They worked well with animals and some became stockmen, while others tended to do jobs "without a great deal of responsibility", such as truck drivers, teachers' assistants, carpenters or labourers in workshops. The Brothers were particularly surprised to find that they had very different sexual mores. Girls were willing for many men to go to them in one night, "circling constantly". Over the years there had been gradual improvements. The church building destroyed by cyclone 'Dora' in 1964 had been replaced by another dedicated to Edward the Confessor and Our Lady, and had been consecrated by Bishop Hawkey in 1972. The Bishop had asked Malanggi, an outstanding Aboriginal artist from Milingimbi in Arnhem Land (who had painted the design for the Australian dollar note) to paint a picture for the church in Aboriginal style, and he had done one, showing the Nativity of Our Lord, surrounded by Biblical symbols, and other symbols representing the whole of Creation. The settlement had a school and small hospital, but the road to Cairns, 400 miles away, was often unusable for eight months of the year, because of rain in the 'wet' season and then drying-out problems. The Flying Doctor visited once a month.

The Brothers at Cowal Creek extended their work to Bamaga as well. When they first arrived there, it was one month before a special event[3] brought all the people together from both places. In that area the Torres Strait Islanders had inter-married, in some cases, with Aborigines. The first Aboriginal priest, Patrick Brisbane, had once been priest-in-charge of the Church of St Michael and All Angels, Cowal Creek. He had also worked with Canon Eddie Mosby, a Torres Strait Islander, based at Bamaga. The Reverend Patrick Brisbane had been born on a cattle station 60 miles inland and had lived with his parents in a bush home made from the bark of a tree. His father had died when he was a baby, and his mother had died during the Second World War. Like Canon Mosby, he had become for many years a pearl diver, but felt a call from God which he described as "like a crawling inside." He had died in 1973, and a machine had dug the hole for his grave. However, in 1977, the people had decided to re-inter him in the church. The Manager of Aboriginals and Islanders from the Department of Islander and Aboriginal Affairs, based at Bamaga, wanted to order a bigger machine from Brisbane to dig up the body and transfer it. However, the grave was opened by other means, and all the people who had gathered around moved away when the coffin was revealed, except for Canon Eddie Mosby, Fr Joel Maka (another Islander priest), the Brothers, the Manager and another white man who was present. One relation of the departed priest was willing to go down into the grave, and Brothers Paul and Moses followed. The relative, and a boy who went down with him, wore rubber gloves, but the Brothers refused the offer of some for themselves. However, when the coffin was opened, there were flies everywhere, and the smell from the mixture of black blood and water affected the Brothers' hands when they helped to remove the remains into another coffin – and they went on smelling for four days. Everything was rotten except the dead priest's green stole! The people were afraid to look inside because of their fear of *puripuri*, evil spirits. The body was taken to the church and reburied. Then the relatives and other people, with the Brothers, feasted and danced. The Brothers were offered three hundred Australian dollars by the people, but they said that they had not come to be paid, but to help and teach them, and to show them not to be afraid of evil spirits, as they could overcome their fear through the love of Christ, who had sent the Brothers to them. By 1980, twenty three people had been baptised at Cowal Creek, and twenty three more at Edward River.[4]

A succession of Brothers followed to serve in the households, all of them from the Solomons except Brothers Lawrence Ambeke and Sergius Paulus from Papua. Brother Luke Magiza from Santa Ysabel arrived in 1981 and stayed for six years, leaving in 1987. Brother Francis Mauru from Makira arrived with him and stayed for three and a half years. Others stayed for various periods of time.[5] The Brothers found the Aborigines to be very generous: for example, anyone catching a turtle would share it with anybody else. They found the people slow to understand, but once they believed, to be Christians with a strong faith. Bishop John Matthews had handed over the superintendance of the communities at Edward River, Lockhart River and Kowanyama to the Government, but this had led to the introduction of bars, and drunkenness had led to all kinds of sexual and other excesses. At Lockhart River, where a household had been established, Anglican work had been begun in 1924. But the Queensland Government had taken over the administration in 1967 and moved the site 45 miles further north, as it was so difficult getting supplies into the old site during the 'wet season', although otherwise it was desirable, being near a beach with good fishing. The new site had many modern facilities, including electricity, sewerage and a nearby airstrip, but the people found life much more complicated there, with an elected Council, police and European style ways of doing things. By contrast, however, they still maintained their Bora initiation ceremonies, with their unique ritual and drum, and the children were taught tribal dancing. From the age of 17 upwards the boys went to the Bora ceremony in the taboo ground to be declared mature and able to marry. The Brothers found that leading men, such as chiefs of tribes, were respected, but not the women.

In January 1981, Bishop Jamieson wrote a newsletter to 'Friends' of Carpentaria, in which he asked especially for prayer for the Aboriginal ministry being carried out by the Melanesian Brothers, and for Fr Tony Hall-Matthews and Fr Frank Neubecker, who, he had decided, should be involved in the work too. Fr Tony was to be priest-in-charge at Lockhart River[6] and Fr Frank would live at Edward River and be responsible for Kowanyama as well.[7] The Bishop himself would be Chaplain to the Brothers, as well as their Section Father. He urged 'Friends' in Australia to become Companions of the Brothers, as there were then very few there, and he hoped the Companions would pray and give money to help support the Brothers; their expenses were about $700 a year. Fr Brian had admitted

Donald Shearman, by then Bishop of Grafton, NSW, as a Companion, when he had been General Secretary of the Australian Board of Missions and still a priest. Subsequently, Miss I U McLachlan, originally from England, had applied to Fr Brian through the General Secretary, Donald Shearman, to become a Companion, and had regularly attended Conferences at Tabalia as a representative of Australian Companions. So Bishop Jamieson initiated a drive in 1981 to enrol more. He had also been reflecting on the difficulties which the Brothers had been having in their work, and wrote: "Basically the Aboriginal people are nomadic people living in an artificial-type European existence.... it is quite unsatisfactory, in a spiritual sense, because it is alien to their whole nomadic background, upon which has been spun a rich and sophisticated mythology. This mythology is an interpretation which accounts for every facet of life, but it is far more than a philosophy, it is DREAM TIME, a way of life..... In a real sense Aboriginals are caught in between these two worlds. Such issues as Land Rights and the Makanata are expressions of a protest against an identity being lost and swallowed up by the dominant European culture. For the Brothers, as for Europeans, our background is a village, settled life, in which we tend our houses and animals and gardens. The Aboriginal does not really understand this at all."

He goes on to point out that the background to much of the New Testament and the teaching of Jesus is also an agricultural or pastoral farming existence. So he notes: "How do I identify with the Aboriginal so that I can preach a Gospel which is relevant to his needs, and one which he understands? I personally believe that the answer to that is LOVE, the love that does and can only flow from a 'God who so loved the world that he gave his only begotten Son....' (John 3:16). It is only within the love of God that we can begin to perceive not only our own needs, but how they can be met."

In 1981, Brothers Moses and Michael from the Solomons and Brothers Lawrence Ambeke and Sergius Paulus from Papua New Guinea were working at Kowanyama (Mitchell River). Fr Frank Neubecker was based at Edward River, and Fr Tony Hall-Matthews, Archdeacon of Cape York, was working with Brothers Christopher Hetamana, Patrick Tagini and David Mauriahi (all from the Solomons) at Lockhart River. Brother Paul Neremana had returned to the Solomons at the end of 1980, and the Brothers then ceased their work at Cowal Creek. In Kowanyama the Brothers' main colleague was a woman, Nancy Dick, who was subsequently made deacon.

Two Aboriginal men also became deacons with the encouragement of the Brothers, but their health had been affected by previous alcoholism and they both died. There were some young men from the Diocese who became Novices, but two dropped out because they felt they had waited too long to become Brothers. However, two others from the Torres Strait were eventually professed as Brothers, first Basa Banu and, later, Jonathan Gagae (Kakai).

The Brothers found that the usual way they planned their work, with programmes of instruction at particular times, just did not work in an Aboriginal environment. The efforts made to get the Aboriginals to follow the Brothers' programmes were given up when they realised that they had to fit in with the Aboriginal way of doing things. They had to be very careful about their visiting too. If they went all the time to one family, for however good a reason, that family would start to think of them as theirs, and resent them visiting any other family. This led to rows between families. So they realised they had to visit many families, and eat with them only if the food was there when they called. They eventually worked out a pattern for their ministry, which included visiting, holding Sunday School, seeing children in the evenings (while parents went drinking), preparing people for Confirmation, and training people to lead services.[8]

In 1982, the Bishop chaired a Section meeting at Edward River at which all the Brothers gathered with the two priests who had been working closely with them, Fr Frank and Fr Tony. The big question they faced was, "What do we do with the Novices?" Brother Basa Banu had been sent to Tabalia to train, but there were now two Torres Strait Islander Novices and one part-Aboriginal. The normal training provided in the Solomons or Papua New Guinea fitted the Brothers for work in Melanesian communities, but not with Aborigines. Also, it was not enough for the Novices just to live with the Brothers in their households. Something special was needed in the way of preparation, although the Bishop did not feel that it would be possible to establish a proper Noviciate in Carpentaria. He wrote in his Newsletter: "One of our biggest concerns, as ever, is that of evangelising the Aboriginal .... It seems to me important that we get experienced Brothers who are prepared to stay in this ministry for a fair period of time. It is so vital that our Aboriginal brothers not only hear the Gospel, but respond to it, for it is the only thing that will bring salvation and hope in a desperate time."[9] The Bishop himself had been greatly encouraged by being able to attend a Conference organised by SOMA (Sharing of Ministries

Abroad) in 1980. He wrote in 1981: "I found it an immense confidence-booster or perhaps faith-booster, after talking and ministering non-stop for a fortnight in Borneo." He was therefore determined to continue to give priority to the work among Aboriginal people, and believed the Brothers could be valuable agents in this, if their preparation for it could be improved. He therefore planned to attend the Great Conference at Tabalia in 1983 with his new plan. This would involve the use of St Paul's Mission, Moa Island. Fr Rick Bowie would 'disciple' two Brothers so that they in turn could 'disciple' the four Novices expected. Two other Brothers would then come and take the place of the first two. In this way, training needed for the special work in Carpentaria could be provided. The Bishop was convinced that there should be careful selection of Brothers suitable for the work, with a real sense of vocation both to the Brotherhood and to work among Aboriginal people, special training in evangelism among Aborigines, continuity of Brothers, and at least six year's service by Brothers who came to work in the Diocese. The Bishop was inspired by the Roman Catholic missionary Fr Vincent Donovan's work among the nomadic Masai people in East Africa, and by evangelistic and pastoral experiences there which had led to the writing of his book *Christianity Rediscovered*.[10] He wanted the Brothers to benefit from some of those insights. His plan began, experimentally, early in 1983.

By the end of 1982 there were eight Brothers serving in the Diocese. After a visit to England from January to March 1983, the Bishop travelled to the Solomons on his way home, to attend the Great Conference held in April, at which Brother Moses Keahi, the Section Elder Brother in Carpentaria, was elected as the new Head Brother of the whole Brotherhood. This, the Bishop wrote, meant that "at least he will be on our side." Brother Moses had served in Carpentaria for six years. The Bishop found the Conference "excellent in so many different ways, both from my point of view, and, I hope, theirs." However, later in 1983 he received an invitation to become Bishop of Bunbury in Western Australia, and accepted, being enthroned there on January 4, 1984.

In 1982, when the new arrangement for the Brothers had been discussed, Fr Tony had moved the headquarters of the Carpentaria Aerial Mission from Cooktown to Cairns in the Diocese of North Queensland. But on his election as Bishop he himself had to move to Thursday Island until a Bishop's House was bought in 1990 in Cairns, from where he could fly more easily.

Meanwhile, the Brothers moved to Moa Island on February 2, 1983, where they started building a house. The Household there was to be the new Section Headquarters, where training could be given to any boys or young men thinking of joining the Brotherhood, but at first there was only one aspirant, Jonathan Gagae. There were three Brothers, and they helped Fr Adea Wapau in his ministry work on the island by conducting services and prayer meetings, training young people to take services, and holding Bible Studies, especially in people's homes. They also took religious instruction in the school. Brother David Mauriahe wrote: "We Brothers were very happy..... because we can make gardens and fish and help people in their work."[11] The Brothers with him there were Luke Magiza and Clement Kikia, in addition to the Novices. Brothers Francis Mauru and Wilson Dora Adi were at Lockhart River, and Fr Frank took over as Chaplain to all the Brothers in the Diocese. At the 1984 Diocesan Synod Eucharist, Brother Luke Magiza[12] and Brother Francis Mauru, who was at Lockhart River, renewed their vows, while the new Bishop and the clergy renewed their ordination promises.[13] It looked as if a new chapter was opening in the Brothers' work, especially as they hoped that their new Section Headquarters would enable them to have more contact with the islands in the Torres Strait, which had been difficult when they were all based on the mainland. The Church in the islands was then facing a rapid decrease in population. The previous fifteen years had seen the numbers drop by nearly half to 5,000, while islanders on the mainland had increased in number to 10,000, many going to the towns and cities. In 1984 Brother Michael Uqwerepo took over as Section Elder Brother, based at Moa Island.

1985 saw a new development – ex-Brothers serving as Chaplains to the Aboriginal settlements. Fr John Buffet Wotlimaro from Vanuatu and his wife, Imogen, a white Australian, had settled in at Edward River, and Fr Ellison Vahi and his wife Adelina, both from the Solomons, were at Lockhart River. However, Fr Philip Freier and his wife Joy, a white couple, were at Kowanyama. Fr Frank Neubecker had moved on to be Rector of Cooktown, a very different ministry, serving bush towns, mines and cattle stations. The work continued to be very difficult, with few Christians among the Government administrators in the Aboriginal settlements, and no consultation by them with the Church, or support in its efforts to serve the people and wean them off 'King Grog'. If two planes flew into a settlement, the second might be full of beer! At Kowanyama, "the *nightly* takings for alcohol in the canteen equal the Church's *annual* income," reported the

Reverend Roger Atkins, Chairman of the English Carpentaria Association, after a visit in 1985. At the Aboriginal village of Umagico in Cape York, he noted that the magnificent 'canteen' was almost next door to the church, and that it witnessed to "the terrible toll that the grog takes of the aborigines' dignity, personhood and morals."[14]

The announcement was made in 1986 of the first indigenous Bishop to be consecrated for the Diocese. Canon Kiwani Dai, who had been caring for Darnley Island and its pilgrimage shrine at Kemus, where the first LMS missionaries had arrived, had been chosen as Assistant Bishop. He was from Saibai in the western Torres Strait Islands. In the Diocese of North Queensland Arthur Malcolm had been chosen as the first Aboriginal Bishop, and he would assist there. However, they were both to be available to help Islander and Aboriginal Christians throughout the Australian Church, wherever they were invited. More Aboriginals were studying theology, including a number of women, and Mrs Nancy Dick, who had worked with the Brothers at Kowanyama, was eventually ordained deacon.

The Reverend Stephen Giblet, first Aboriginal deacon at Lockhart River, died in August 1986, but the other deacon, Jimmy Doctor, continued to assist Fr Ellison Vahi at the Settlement. Another priest from Melanesia arrived to serve in the Diocese, Fr Francis Gilu from Vanuatu, who took up his work as Dean of the Cathedral in the late 1980s. The Edward River Aboriginal Settlement changed its name to Pormpuraaw. The name of Cowal Creek was also changed to Injinoo.[15] Meanwhile, a political movement demanding some sort of 'independence' for the Torres Strait Islands was growing. In 1991 Fr Michael Hough took over from Fr Francis Gilu as Dean, while Fr Leslie Piva and his wife Veronica arrived from Broadford Parish in the Diocese of Wangaratta to replace Fr Ellison Vahi and his wife, who had served for six years at Lockhart River. Fr Leslie and Veronica were Polynesians from the island of Sikaiana in the Solomons, and for a time in the early 1980s Fr Leslie had been ABM Secretary in Melbourne, while receiving kidney dialysis treatment. Fr Brian had been his best man when he had married Veronica Teutalei in Honiara Cathedral, after returning from his studies in the 1960s at St John's College, Auckland. Veronica had done further studies in education in Cambridge, England, beginning in about 1963.[16]

The Brothers had established a Household at Cutter Creek, south of Lockhart River, which eventually became Section Headquarters, and Brother Benjamin Vaki served there. He left in 1991 after four years and two Brothers from Papua New Guinea arrived, Barnabas Ram and Lindsey Umbude. The arrangement with Lockhart River was that two Brothers visited there each month from Cutter Creek, and stayed there conducting weekly Bible Studies, religious instruction in the primary school, and pastoral visits among the population of 500. Support also came from other parts of the Australian Church, including Broadford Parish. Fr Piva wrote: "We can support each other since I know we have support – we are not alone." His wife did much with the women, including a regular sewing class, hoping to develop a support structure among them as "women are the key figures in family life here," according to Fr Piva's report.[17] Another Melanesian priest from the Solomons, Fr John Pihavaka, arrived with his wife Helen to serve on Darnley Island in 1992. The people of Pormpuraaw showed their regard for their Chaplain, Fr John Henry Wotlimaro, when the Aboriginal Council there asked him to be their Council Clerk,[18] indicating also their confidence in him and his ability to serve them.

In 1993, Mrs Veronica Piva arranged a local Mothers' Union seminar at Lockhart River, the first time one had been held outside the Torres Strait Islands for members of the Mothers Union in the Diocese. Preparations included catching four turtles and a bullock, and collecting enough containers of fresh oysters and locally grown food to feed the delegates. The theme was 'Home and Family' and the programme was based on one used in North America with Native American and Eskimo communities. (Carpentaria Diocese was twinned with the Diocese of the Arctic!) The Aboriginal parish councils were beginning to exercise more authority, and it became apparent to the Bishop that the next step in their development would be small groups within each parish community, selected from family clan groups. Bishop Tony wrote: "Tribal kinship regulations often prevent even lay readers from ministering to certain members of the clan, e.g. at the time of a funeral." This had created real difficulties for Aboriginals trying to exercise Christian leadership, and the Bishop believed that the small groups could develop an Aboriginal model for parish life. This could be in conjunction with the revived catechumenal process of step-by-step Christian initiation then being encouraged throughout the Australian Church, together with a revival of the traditional ceremonies of Aboriginal initiation into tribal life.[19]

New initiatives began to affect the lives of people in the Diocese. At Pormpuraaw and Lockhart River 'Op Shops' had been opened, and the one at Lockhart River, the largest in the Diocese, raised increasing funds for the Diocese.[20] At Pormpuraaw, Mr Walter Tubuai from Moa Island was running the store and also doing extension studies, in the hope of eventually being ordained deacon, in order to serve the community in *two* ways. St Paul's College, which had formerly been on Moa Island, but had been closed for some years, had been reopened on Thursday Island, offering training for lay and ordained ministry. At Lockhart River, Veronica Piva, Diocesan Overseas Link for Mothers' Union, had encouraged its members to do more weaving of hats, baskets, mats, etc out of pandanus palms, and this was proving a success. Mrs Valerie Hall-Matthews, the Bishop's wife, was Queensland Mothers' Union President, and she visited Lockhart River to learn about the members' efforts in sewing, weaving and gardening, and enjoyed a barbecue arranged by the Pivas and the Brothers, whose policy was to cooperate with the Mothers' Union wherever possible. Mrs Hall-Matthews discussed the Mothers' Union Centenary in Australia, and how it could be celebrated throughout the Diocese in 1992. At Kowanyama an Aboriginal couple were prepared to take on the running of the 'Op Shop'and were trained to do it.[21]

Politically and legally, an important judgement was delivered by the High Court of Australia when Fr Dave Passi, priest-in-charge of Murray Island, was one of three plaintiffs in a court case involving native title to the land there. The court declared that British sovereignty and the subsequent sovereignty of the Australian Government had not extinguished the title of the people to their land. This had implications throughout Australia for the Aborigines also. *Carpentaria Link* commented: "This enables the Aboriginal and Islander people to more firmly establish their identity within the wider Australian community."[22] The Bishop commented: "We have moved into the post-colonial era with the Torres Strait Islanders assertively establishing their identity through expressions of independence. Aboriginal people in the remote communities of Cape York Peninsula have moved from 'Mission time' back in the late 1960s through 'Government time' over the last twenty years, and they now face the responsibilities of 'Community time'. During this period of Community time, the Aboriginal communities are taking on the responsibility of local Government themselves. They do this in the context of cynical criticism by those who don't believe they can do it. However, they do it with the Church still there.... These days members of the Church from elsewhere and from different ethnic and cultural backgrounds are being invited to walk alongside the Aboriginal people as partners."[23]

The Reverend Roger Atkins, formerly stationed on Murray Island, the Chairman of the English Carpentaria Association, wrote in 1992 that the Islanders and Aborigines had till 1963 no vote, and thus only second-class citizenship. They had been paid less than white workers and were kept in reserves where no alcohol was allowed – but that was to keep white people out! – and their movements inside the reserves were restricted, as the Government wanted to know where they were. The white population in a referendum in 1963 voted to give full citizenship to all Australians, with equal pay, no restriction on movement, and Community Councils deciding whether alcohol should be allowed on reserves or not. That solved some problems and created others. The Aborigines in particular had found it hard to settle, rather than to roam their traditional hunting grounds. Regular work and wages were often not attractive to them. They were not accustomed to growing things, and had no experience of alcoholic beverages in their traditional culture. They had lived off their hunting grounds quite successfully for 40,000 years, until these were taken away from them by the white settlers who deemed all land on the continent to belong to 'the Crown'. So they had lost in most places their traditional way of life, and were expected to conform to another which did not attract them. No wonder there were problems! They did not believe they *owned* the land, but that *it* owned them. "It provided for them and sustained them in every way, so they revered it." So the land became their spiritual mother, and their culture and religion arose from their deep relationship with it. Fr Atkins continued: "Cutter Creek, the Lockhart River 'annexe' or outstation, is a small community where the Melanesian Brothers work on the rehabilitation of Aborigines who have fallen foul of drink, the law, etc. But the task is immense, and we very much need to pray for understanding, patience and wisdom for all those who have to do with Aborigines, particularly Government officials and church workers, that with time and hard work their worth may be recognised and their dignity restored. It's mostly our problem, not theirs. Their problem is us."[24] He also acknowledged that some Aborigines had managed to adapt to all the changes very well, but he was concerned for those who had not been able to do so. It was among them that the Brothers had a special ministry.

In 1993 there was to be an 'International Year of Indigenous People'. It was significant that the Aboriginal people had already begun to say what they expected of the Church authorities. Thomas Bruce, Churchwarden of Kowanyama, said they wanted appropriately trained and experienced priests at Kowanyama and Pormpuraaw who could train catechists for the small groups based on clans, which could then become agents of evangelism and pastoral care. The priests would no longer be 'in charge', but be there to serve the community in specific ways for at least three years, to lay the foundation for this kind of community evangelism.[25] Significant decisions were also taken at Diocesan Synod in 1992. Bishop Kiwani Dai had worked hard in the Torres Strait to help his fellow Islanders to overcome their feelings of oppression, and to grasp the emerging opportunities for managing both the Church and the wider community. The Synod decided to form two Regions within the Diocese, the Torres Strait Region and the Cape York Peninsula Region. The Synod also proposed to General Synod the establishment of a national Torres Strait Islander Anglican Council to complement the already established National Aboriginal Anglican Council, and requested that it be centred in the Torres Strait itself. The Bi-centenary of Australia celebrations of 1988 had awakened a sense of their own identity among the Islanders, and Bishop Dai had encouraged the concepts of self-management, self-support and self-growth among them. He was farewelled with deep affection after the Synod, on his retirement, which took effect on September 15, 1992. The Diocesan Synod had been very cautious, for cultural reasons, about the proposed General Synod legislation for the Ordination of Women, although not opposed to it being practised elsewhere in Australia![26]

At the end of 1992 both Pormpuraaw and Kowanyama were without Chaplains: Fr John Wotlimaro had transferred to the mining town of Weipa, and there were only four Brothers left in the Diocese, all at Cutter Creek – Section Elder Brother Barnabas Ram and Brothers Jonathan Gagae, John Teteo and Francis Tawasu. Significantly, the Melanesians of the Torres Straits had begun to take evangelism of their own people dispersed elsewhere very seriously. A mission entitled 'Called to Serve', led by the Principal of St Paul's College, Thursday Island, Canon Gayai Hankin, with twenty of the 'brothers' from the College, went to five parts of urban Queensland, including Townsville and Cairns. This was to bring together the Islanders of the 'Melanesian community' in those places, to strengthen and renew their spiritual life.[27] The College had indeed become the base of a kind of community in which "an appropriate way of ministry training has been discovered within Torres Strait cultural expression." It was called a 'Brotherhood' and its title was the Paulon Mura Tukuipal Community,[28] and missions were also conducted by teams from there, under the direction of the Principal, to islands of the Strait.

The new ways of conducting work among the Aborigines based on the 'catechumenal' process and Aboriginal culture had begun to be implemented at the Aboriginal village of Injinoo (Cowal Creek) at Cape York, and also at Lockhart River by Fr Leslie Piva. Fr Leslie had, however, become sick, but he had carried on manfully. He died in October, 1994, leaving his widow and some of his sons living in Australia. His place was taken by the only Melanesian priest from overseas left in the Diocese, Fr John Pihavaka, who was accompanied by his wife, Helen. The Brothers continued to assist at Lockhart River and Pormpuraaw, but in 1994 Brother Jonathan retired from the work and was replaced by Brother Bernard. The other Torres Strait Islander Brother, Basa Banu, was ordained at Boigu Island on November 27, 1995. In 1995 a new Chaplain arrived at Koyanyama from the Diocese of Polynesia. Peter Bentley was originally from England, but his wife Petisi was from Western Samoa. Thus another link was forged between the peoples of the Carpentaria Diocese and Christians of other parts of the Pacific.[29]

Changes in the Diocese were mirrored in Government. The Torres Strait Regional Authority was set up on July 1, 1994, so that the Torres Strait Islanders would have more say in running their own affairs. Happily, July 1 was the day already celebrated annually in the Torres Strait as the anniversary of 'The Coming of the Light'. In the Church, there were those in the Diocesan Council who felt that there should be a Diocese of the Torres Strait, but Bishop Tony felt that this would not be viable. There were already great financial difficulties, with the decrease in financial support from other parts of the Australian Church, and he felt that the northern dioceses should instead pool their resources so that they could be more self-supporting. The Assistant Bishop could still be appointed for the Torres Strait with considerable authority there. As the meetings of Cape York clergy had to be held in Cairns in the Diocese of North Queensland, where the Bishop and the plane were based, it seemed to suggest that the two dioceses should now be united; this would also enable more effective pastoral care of Aborigines and Islanders in both dioceses. Many had moved from Carpentaria to North Queensland with the easing of restrictions on their movement. Two white staff members and an adviser strongly disagreed with the Bishop, wanting instead a Torres Strait Diocese, with Gayai Hankin as Bishop. This led to the passing of a no confidence motion in the Diocesan Council and a demand for the Bishop to resign. He instead again gave notice of his intention to resign on February 2, 1996, when the Bishop of North Queensland, John Lewis, would also retire to make way for a new united diocese to be formed. Those against the Bishop accused him of financial misdemeanour, which proved to be untrue,[30] so in the Diocesan Synod in September, the Council motion was rescinded, and strong support for the Bishop expressed by the indigenous delegates.[31]

The Bishop flew a chartered plane to Pormpuraaw for Midnight Mass at Christmas. Two of the Brothers were working there. *Carpentaria Link* commented about the Brothers' work at Pormpuraaw and Lockhart River: "Working under the rule of a religious order, the Brothers have responded in obedience to a very difficult challenge." Also in December a national conference entitled *Martung Upah* was called by the Aboriginal and Islander Commission of the Australian Council of Churches to press for a Bill of Rights for all Australians, and for support by all the Churches for the Native Title Bill going through Federal Parliament. The Primate of Australia, the Most Reverend Keith Rayner, who was also Archbishop of Melbourne, had visited Carpentaria Diocese in September and had included a visit to Kowanyama. He said that "the Aboriginal and Islander communities can give a lead on matters relating to a rational and reasonable debate on the Native Title issue to the rest of the Australian community."[32] He also declared that the judgement in the High Court (known as the Mabo judgement) had "given a strong sense of dignity to peoples who had long felt that they were regarded by the Australian community as being of no account." It was, therefore, significant that at the Olympic Games in Sydney in 2000 the Aboriginal and Islander communities took such a prominent part in the opening ceremony, and that the Olympic torch was carried on its last lap in the stadium by an outstanding woman Aboriginal athlete, who later proudly carried both the Australian *and* Aboriginal flags when making a victory lap of honour!

Bishop Tony went on extended leave, which had accrued over a long period, prior to his retirement. He invited Bishop Colin Sheumack (who had retired from being Bishop of Gippsland in the State of Victoria in July 1994) to become Administrator of the Diocese from February 1995, and to initiate a process of consultation throughout the diocese about future developments.[33] An era was coming to an end, and in 1995 the Brothers withdrew from the Diocese after twenty years of ministry. What had they achieved? They had met the challenge of working among people very different in custom, culture and attitudes to themselves. They had enabled

Torres Strait Islanders to experience the life of the Brotherhood, and one of them had later been ordained. They had helped to establish fruitful relationships between the Diocese of Carpentaria and the Provinces of Papua New Guinea and Melanesia. Two ex-Brothers and two other priests originally from the Province of Melanesia had come to work in the Diocese in close cooperation with the Brothers. They had also extended their work beyond the islands of the South Pacific, as their founder had predicted they would, and this had prepared the Brotherhood for the challenge of working in the Philippines. Perhaps they had also helped to inspire people in the Diocese of Carpentaria to accept the challenge of evangelism among their own people with more confidence and hope. Moreover, they had seen the indigenous members of the Church in the Diocese take up responsibility for their own affairs, as their fellow Christians in Melanesia, Papua New Guinea and Polynesia had already done. Sadly, however, there were later developments which divided the Torres Strait Islands. After the union of Carpentaria Diocese with North Queensland, Fr Ted Mosby was chosen and consecrated as Bishop for the Torres Strait, but he died after two years. The movement for a separate diocese grew stronger, and a body called 'The Traditional Anglican Church' was formed, with Gayai Hankin and Dave Passi as Bishops. The Diocese of North Queensland had an 'Administrator' based at Moa Island. So at the end of the twentieth century, the Melanesian Anglicans of Australia were no longer united in one Anglican Church. Although the Diocese of Carpentaria had disappeared, the fruits of its efforts remained among the scattered Aboriginal and Islander communities in the far north of the Commonwealth of Australia. On September 16, 2001, James Randolph Leftwich was consecrated as 'National Aboriginal Bishop' and Assistant Bishop of North Queensland in St Alban's Church, Yarrabah, following the retirement of Bishop Arthur Malcolm.[34]

NOTES

1 The information in the first paragraph of this chapter is taken from an ABM publication, *Introducing the Diocese of Carpentaria*: Information Handbook, 1976 (prepared by the Adelaide Diocesan Board of Education).

2 They were variously known to the white people as Aboriginals or Aborigines.

3 Information about this was given to the author by Brother Moses Keahi, now dead.

4 See the report by Brother William Tedi to the Central Solomons Section Conference, April 1980.

5 They included Michael Ukarepo (South Malaita), Morris Lauba (Reef Islands), Wilson Dora (South Malaita), David Mauriahe (Ugi) and Patrick Tagini (Malaita), all Solomon Islanders.

6 He worked there with Brothers Christopher, Patrick and David.

7 He worked with Brothers Michael, Moses, Lawrence and Sergius Paulus.

8 Information provided by Brother Francis Mauru to the author.
9 *The English Carpentarian* magazine, Autumn, 1982.
10 *Christianity Rediscovered: An Epistle from the Masai*, Vincent J Donovan SCM London 1982 (first published 1978 by Fides/Claretian, Indiana).
11 *The English Carpentarian,* No 87, Winter issue.
12 He appears to have been then at Thursday Island, possibly temporarily, as in 1984 he became Elder Brother at Edward River. Wilson also moved to Edward River in 1984, as did David Mauriahe. Alpheus Tabuira and Morris Leuru were then at Lockhart River. See the *Melanesian Brotherhood Daily Intercession Scheme*, 1984.
13 *The English Carpentarian*, No 89, Autumn 1984.
14 *The English Carpentarian*, No 91, Summer 1985.
15 *The Carpentarian*, No 106, Summer 1990. (The magazine had shortened its title.)
16 She was probably the first woman from the Solomons to do higher studies in the UK, and the author first met her at a meeting in Cambridge before he left for the Solomons by ship in January, 1964
17 *Carpentaria Link* (formerly *The English Carpentarian*), No 111, Winter 1992
18 *Carpentaria Link*, No 112, Summer 1992.
19 *Carpentaria Link*, No 116, Summer 1993.
20 'Opportunity Shops' were established in Islander and Aboriginal communities to produce a flow of internal income, as support from ABM and the Home Mission Fund was progressively decreased.
21 *Carpentaria Link*, No 113, Autumn 1992.
22 *Carpentaria Link*, No 113, Autumn 1992.
23 *Carpentaria Link*, No 112, Summer 1992.
24 *Carpentaria Link*, No 111, Winter 1992.
25 *Carpentaria Link*, No 116, Autumn 1993
26 Women were, however, ordained as deacons in the Diocese in the mid-1990s.
27 *Carpentaria Link*, No 115, Summer 1993.
28 *Carpentaria Link*, No 117, Winter 1994 and No 121, Summer 1995.
29 *Carpentaria Link*, No 120, Winter 1995.
30 There had, apparently, been fraud by another member of staff, *not* the Bishop.
31 *Carpentaria Link*, No 119, Autumn 1994.
32 *Carpentaria Link*, No 117, Winter 1994.
33 *Carpentaria Link*, No 120, Winter 1995.
34 *Anglican World* (the official magazine of the Anglican Communion), Christmas 2001, issue No 104, the Anglican Communion Office, London, England.

CHAPTER FIFTEEN

John Barge Household, Pomete, New Britain, with the dining room and library.

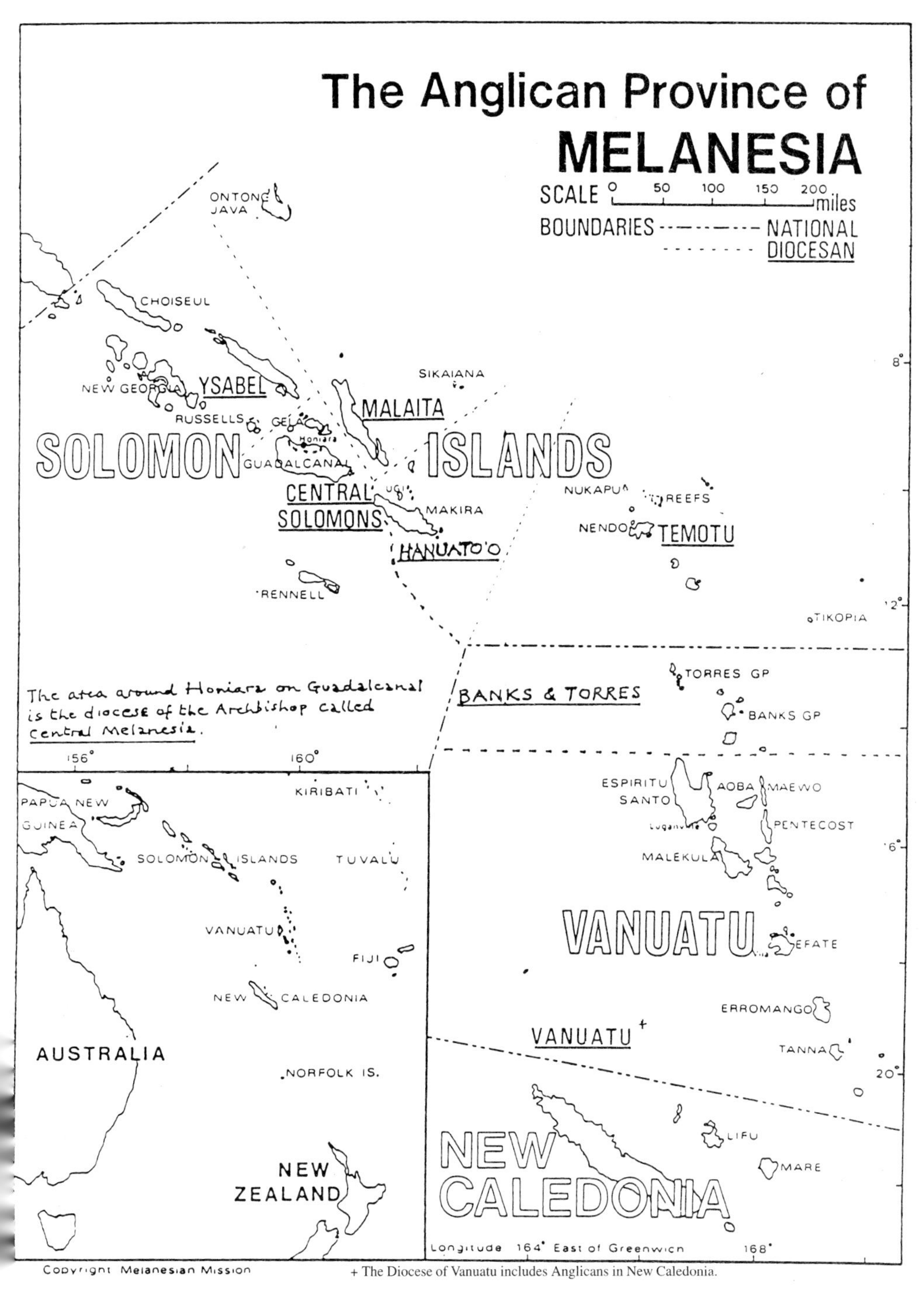

+ The Diocese of Vanuatu includes Anglicans in New Caledonia.

CHAPTER FIFTEEN

FOLLOWING ON – IN FAITH

At the beginning of the second fifty years, there were nearly eighty Brothers at work in the Solomons, New Hebrides, Fiji, Australia and Papua New Guinea. The Brothers had households at Tabalia and Honiara on Guadalcanal and there were 22 Novices in training. The work on Malaita was based at Tariuna Household, and there were seven Brothers in Temotu Household on Santa Cruz in the Eastern Outer Islands. At the two households in the New Hebrides there were eight Brothers, six of them in the bush on Espiritu Santo among the 'heathen'. Brother Wilson Vwaliusala was Regional Head Brother for the Southern Region, which included Nabatolu Household on Viti Levu island, Fiji, with four Brothers there working among the Indians. There were ten Brothers in three households on New Britain, with the Regional Headquarters at Pomete, while ten others worked at three households in the Highlands of New Guinea. Param Household in Papua had four Brothers. Brother Giles Livingstone Pondo was Regional Head Brother for the Papua New Guinea Region. At Pomete a new dormitory and a new dining hall had been erected with iron roofs, and a new chapel had been planned. Money from the Scottish Episcopal Church (Anglican), which supported the Church in Papua New Guinea, had been received, and it was hoped this would pay for the building of the chapel.

The Chief Secretary of Companions was Mr Amos Willy Huhulu, who planned to make an annual tour of Companions Groups and Areas, to encourage them in their work. He wanted also to hold courses on the 'Renewal of our Life', and started with one in the Russell Islands, after a visit to Gizo in the Western Solomons. He wrote in the *Companions' Newsletter* (No 6) in February 1976: "The people are interested in this course about renewal. They are willing to attend the course because something makes their lives new again. Although they feel asleep and their bodies are weak, they never give up." 168 people attended the course, which was based on 'Notes for Companions', prepared by Fr Brian, Companions' Adviser, who had run various courses for Companions in the districts of the Solomons and at Tabalia. The Great Conference had recommended that each Diocese have a Diocesan Chief Chaplain of Companions, one of whose duties would be to arrange courses for Chaplains, Leaders and Companions. Bishop Dudley Tuti of Ysabel

Diocese had a team going around his diocese, giving in each place training to catechists, youth leaders, Companions and members of the Mothers' Union, and increasingly this pattern was adopted in other dioceses also. The Companions in Honiara built up a strong organisation to support the Brothers working there and elsewhere. Their efforts included such activities as a bazaar held at the Cathedral in 1976 and 'Bring and Buy' in 1976 and 1977. Mr Dudley Painetala got support from some Chinese store owners, who provided transport for goods to the Bazaar, while Selwyn College Companions at Najilagu on the Guadalcanal plains helped to collect firewood for sale in Honiara, together with garden produce, to add to bazaar funds. Part of the money raised was to go to Tabalia for the chapel, and part of it to enable Companions' leaders to hold courses in the districts. At the 'Bring and Buy', cooked food was on sale, including rice, traditional puddings and curried meat, fish and chicken. Soft drinks could also be bought. This encouraged many of the urban Companions to work together and to help others outside the town, as well as assisting the Brothers themselves.

In 1977, Lily Tetuhu from Santa Ysabel took over as Chief Secretary of the Companions, based in Honiara, and she produced a joint *Melanesian Brothers and Companions Newsletter.* Brother Ellison Vahi became the 'Touring Chaplain' in July 1977, serving the whole Brotherhood. Fr John Ashwin Wetelwur (a former Head Brother), who had served for four years as Chaplain, went to Selwyn College to be Chaplain there, accompanied by his wife Alice and their little daughter. At Tabalia on July 3, Brother Ellison Vahi was ordained priest.[1] He enlisted the assistance of two ex-Brothers as Tutors, Fr Christian Makona, also to be resident Chaplain and District Priest, and Fr Peter Ruim (a former Assistant Head Brother), who came with their wives and families – just as Fr Leslie Fugui had done when he came as Assistant Chaplain and Tutor to Fr Brian, when Chaplain.[2] Fr Lonsdale Usumae from Makira had become the Chief Chaplain of Companions in place of Fr Brian. The late 1970s thus saw 'local' Melanesian clergy and laity training Novices and Companions in the Solomons.

The Touring Chaplain, Brother Ellison Vahi, recognised a need for more careful selection of aspirants, and suggested that each Diocese should vet applicants to see if they were suitable, whether they had reached the age of 17, and whether they had had or should have some preliminary preparation and training in Diocesan Training Centres, where these existed.

In the past very little notice had been taken of the educational standard reached by applicants, and it was still not intended to stop sincere applicants with little schooling from joining. However, Brother Ellison felt it important for all applicants to know more about their own culture and customs, and so he suggested that, if they had been away at school, it would be good for them to return to their villages for a while. He wrote in the *Brotherhood and Companions Newsletter*: "The important things we looked for in those seeking to join the Brotherhood were: (a) his right belief in God, (b) his own interest and willingness, (c) his simplicity and obedience; and these today are still the most important points for anybody wishing to follow Christ in this ministry."[3] His words were supplemented by an article in the Newsletter on Vocation, submitted by Brother Silas Aberama of Papua New Guinea, which included the following: "Religious Life is a special call by God, to leave the ordinary pursuits of life and come apart to live with Him alone. This involves a complete act of renunciation on the part of the individual. It means leaving home, family, friends, the work for which one has been trained, the hobbies and pleasures to which one is devoted, possessions and hopes of secular happiness; all this in order to live a voluntary life of poverty and self-sacrifice in a completely new environment. A vocation is not the same as a profession. A Religious does not choose to be a Religious, he is called by God and hears the call.... At the back of every call to the Religious Life is presumably a dissatisfaction with what the world has to offer, a longing for something more, for God in some more real sense, a longing to surrender one's whole self to Him to be used in His service." The article goes on to ask: "How does the call come? It may grow naturally from the first with the soul itself, as God has chosen it from the beginning. It may come like a flash of lightning and be supernatural in origin, or develop slowly as a conviction from reading a book or hearing a sermon or even from an opportune conversation. There is no end to the ways in which God may call a soul, but once convinced, the call is answered without delay. Here indeed we see Jesus issuing the same call as in the days of his earthly ministry."

Before the arrival of Brother Ellison as Touring Chaplain and the new Tutors, Tabalia was accepting only about twelve Novices a year for training, but from 1978 it was possible to increase the number to twenty. In 1977 there were thirteen Novices in training at Tabalia, three from Malaita, one from Sikaiana, two from Makira, one from Guadalcanal, three from Santa Ysabel and one each from the Russell Islands, Gela, Savo and Ugi. One of the Novices from Malaita[4] had come from a 'heathen' family and had not been to school; he had spent a year in the household on Malaita as an aspirant. Mr Richard Naramana from Ysabel, a trained teacher, offered his services free for a year before going to Kohimarama, and he did valuable work on planning a curriculum for the training of the Novices.[5]

In January 1977, the Head Brother visited Temotu Region. The Diocese of Central Melanesia then stretched from Guadalcanal to Tikopia, and was divided into Regions, each with a Senior Priest in charge. Makira and Temotu Regions also had an Assistant Bishop serving them, Caspar Uka from Tikopia, who was based on Makira. Fr Ellison Fititei was Senior Priest of Temotu and Chaplain of the Brotherhood Section there. The Brothers' household had existed on Santa Cruz for seven years, and their main work had been "revival work among the backsliders or 'Sunday Christians' or the people who are not faithful to their Christian Faith" (as Novice John Peter Bilive from Santa Cruz described it).[6] The Brothers had gradually built up their station there. The chapel was dedicated to St Nicholas, and they had erected a large cross which had been recently blessed by the Archbishop. They had had problems with food, as rats had invaded their gardens for many years. The Head Brother found that there were many difficulties caused by lack of communications. Some islands in the Region were very isolated and the people received Holy Communion only when the Bishops or Senior Priest were able to visit them. During his visit the Head Brother was accompanied by the Section Elder Brother, George Hiva Huhugu, and they were able to travel on the *MV Southern Cross* with the Assistant Bishop and the Senior Priest. The work of the Brothers had been helped by the provision of a 'Seagull' outboard engine, which had been paid for with money provided by Temotu Region and the Australian Church Union. The Head Brother felt that the needs of the people were great; they were still like new Christians and needed more instruction and help. Many were weak and had 'backslidden'; they were "like little children who would respond 'Amen', sing hymns and reverence in the church." On Tikopia, he found that the 'Second Chief' (No 2), who invited him for breakfast after the service, was one of the leaders of the Companions on that Polynesian island.[7]

At Sarep Household in Papua New Guinea, no priest had been able to get to the household for Holy Communion at Christmas, 1976. However, a service was held to which 123 people came, and afterward all feasted on two pigs and four chickens cooked in earth ovens, together with other food brought by the people. On ordinary days, *instruction* for catechumens and hearers would have followed the service, but on Christmas Day they had a *feast* instead! In early 1977 the work there was due to be taken over by an evangelist, while the Brothers moved on to a new station. They were then entering an area which was considered very difficult, the Sagavi Valley. The Section Elder Brother, Santus Athahage from Ysabel, was based at Aiome.

From New Zealand, Brother Charles Fox, already 99, wrote to the Head Brother from Woburn Hospital, Waipukurau:

Dear Robert Wobur,

I loved your letter, but the Doctor says I shall be blind. So I thought I would send one letter to you all, my Brothers.... I shall pray for all of you. After so long in the Solomons I am at least one of you, and always will be. Well done, my Head Brother, doing a good work and faithful. I would always obey you.

Tasiu Charles Fox[8]

Brother George Thomas Kope was at the Bishop Patteson Theological Centre, Kohimarama, where he had gone to do a four year course in 1975, at the insistence of the then Head Brother, Allen Daniel Borugu. In 1977 he wrote in the *Brotherhood Newsletter*: "Since the Melanesian Brotherhood was founded, I am the third person to be in a Theological College like this. I found my study too complicated at first, because I had no idea at all.... To lead up to this sort of study.... I think it is wise enough for two Brothers to study in a College like this or other places, rather than sending one, as I am now. It is very important to be in pairs, because then you will feel that you are both sharing your lives together, as when you were in the Community of the Melanesian Brotherhood." Brotherhood policy thereafter was for more than one Brother, whenever possible, to be sent for further study at Kohimarama or elsewhere. Members of other Religious Orders also had people in training at the Bishop Patteson Theological Centre, Kohimarama, from time to time, both women and men.

In February 1977, the Bishops of Papua New Guinea, Melanesia and Polynesia met in Port Moresby, the capital of Papua New Guinea, and discussed their cooperation, which was indeed strongly encouraged through the South Pacific Anglican Council. One thing they all appreciated was the work of the Melanesian Brotherhood. After the meeting, Archbishop Palmer and Bishop Derek Rawcliffe went on to Dogura to represent the

Province of Melanesia at the Inauguration of the Anglican Province of Papua New Guinea. The Archbishop of Canterbury, Dr Donald Coggan, was present with his wife, and the visitors were welcomed by dancers, among whom were some of the Melanesian Brothers. Archbishop Palmer and Bishop Derek had a meeting with them and gave them news of Brothers in other places. The former Assistant Head Brother, Wenceslas Papao, was working as an evangelist at Dogura, having been released from the Brotherhood. The new Archbishop of Papua New Guinea was David Hand, and the new dioceses of the Anglican Church were Port Moresby, Dogura, Popondota, the New Guinea Islands and Aipo Rongo (in the Highlands). After the Inauguration, Archbishop Coggan visited the Church of Melanesia. After going to Malaita and Ysabel Dioceses, he visited Tabalia and Kohimarama on Guadalcanal. The Archbishops of Canterbury and Melanesia and their wives were accompanied by the Bishops of Malaita, Isabel and the New Hebrides.

Often, as part of a traditional welcome in the Solomon Islands, there is a pretended ambush or attack by 'wild men', dressed in traditional costume, carrying spears or clubs or other native weapons, sometimes with their bodies painted or smeared with mud. On the road up to Tabalia, the party was greeted by such 'wild men', and the chief wild man asked Dr Coggan, "Do you come with peace?" He answered, "Yes, I come with peace." He and his wife were then placed in chairs, which were carried on their shoulders by Brothers and students from Kohimarama, accompanied by the beating of a drum. After shaking hands with everybody, Archbishop Coggan spoke to the Brothers and students in the College chapel and answered questions. He was presented with a cross from Tabalia and Kohimarama, while Mrs Coggan was given a string of shell money. After a play about Bishop Patteson presented by the students, the party had lunch at Kohimarama before visiting the chapel at Tabalia. The Brothers then joined with the students in singing the Archbishop and Mrs Coggan a farewell song. Archbishop Palmer wrote: "We love him so much for his humility and his dedicated life.... A true man of God."[9]

In contrast with such celebrations, the Brotherhood was very concerned about the magic called *vele* still being practised on Guadalcanal. Novice Malachi Toto wrote that the *vele* man "goes out during the night, and day too. He kills and destroys our people's lives and makes our people unhappy.... As Christian people we must try to help those people who use *vele*. They are hungry and thirsty for God's words, and they haven't seen

God's love in their lives.... In order to stop the harm *vele* gives, we must work closely with our people and teach them about God."

Brother Silas Aberama was in charge of the household of Brothers in Fiji at this time. He and his fellow Brothers had two kinds of work in the Diocese of Polynesia. For ten years they had done 'primary evangelism' among Indians south of Ba, a town on the north west coast of Viti Levu island. He wrote: "The work is not easy. There are times when we are confronted with hardship, loneliness and frustrations. Yet each day is a challenge to fulfil the Great Commission of Our Lord in Matthew 28:19-20. Most of the people among whom we work are Hindus. They are followers of Hinduism, an oldest religion in the world with a history dating back to the sixth century BC. Thank God, in spite of many hardships and problems, he has blessed our work with six baptisms and eight confirmations, bringing the total of Christians to 25 for the ten years of Brotherhood's work. Certainly not a dramatic statistic. But it should be noted that conversion from one religion to another is a long process and it takes time before the individual decides which way to take."[10]

The Brothers were also involved in 'secondary evangelism', as they did not spend all their time at their Section Headquarters at Nabatolu ('Number Three'). They had visited the Solomoni Community settlements. Brothers Andrew and Richard had gone first to Wailoku, the main settlement for the descendants of those who had originally been brought to Fiji as 'labour'.Then Brother Christian and Brother Andrew had gone to Labasa on Vanua Levu island. These experiences underlined for them the feeling that they should be available to answer the call to evangelism in any parish of the Diocese to which they were invited. Brother Silas wrote: "We are here for everybody, irrespective of race, colour, creed, culture, etc, and we hope that the Church here will use us to that advantage in the days ahead." He hoped that parishes which invited them would also be able to meet their 'material and spiritual needs' during such visits. The Brothers were treated very much as staff of the Diocese, being involved in Diocesan Conferences, Retreats and special events. Their 'means of outreach' included taking part in soccer, kava drinking, weddings, parties and funerals (Christian and non-Christian). They paid pastoral visits to farms and shared people's problems. Among the most effective means of reaching people were Sunday Schools and youth groups, run under the supervision of Brother Richard Suiga. One important fruit of their work was some young men wanting to join the Brotherhood. In 1976, six aspirants from Wailoku went to train in Melanesia.

The work of the Brothers in Temotu also bore fruit in more recruits from that area. After the Solomon Islands Regional Conference at Tabalia in April, 1977, four Brothers were admitted from different islands in the Outer Eastern Solomons – one from Santa Cruz, one from the Duff Islands (Taumako) and two from Utupua. The service after the Conference was conducted by the Father of the Brotherhood, Archbishop Norman Palmer, and the retreat before it was conducted by Brother Reginald SSF.

In Honiara town, a Team Ministry had been established. The Cathedral Parish had been divided into three main areas: White River and Rove, cared for by the Archbishop and his Chaplain; All Saints, the area of the former Cathedral in the centre of the town, cared for by the Franciscans and Melanesian Brothers and the Sisters of the Church; and the Cathedral and Vura areas on the east side, cared for by the Dean, the Rector, the Vicar-General (Fr Brian) based at Vura, and others, including some catechists. The team was led by the Dean, assisted by the Rector of Honiara, whose work was mainly pastoral. The Team met weekly and a strong spirit of cooperation between all those involved was thereby established. Brother Christopher Hetamana, Elder Brother of Honiara Household, wrote in the 1977 *Melanesian Brothers and Companions Newsletter*: "All the members of the team are responsible for spreading the Good News about God to all the members of the Church of Melanesia living in town, and to support their spiritual lives. The whole work of the Team is completely under the control and the leadership and under the direction of the Holy Spirit of God who is present and is at work in His Church here in Melanesia." Team meetings allowed for the discussion of problems encountered during visiting and for the arrangement of services, preaching, and cooperation with other denominations. Brother Daniel SSF (from England) had initiated work for the Missions to Seamen in the port, having once worked at sea himself. This urban work led to closer cooperation between the Religious Orders, although some coordination had also been provided through meetings called by Fr Brian, whom Bishop Chisholm had appointed to initiate and encourage this. For the Melanesian Brothers this experience of urban mission widened their concept of the call to evangelism. They were enabled to adopt new strategies, including targetting young men in their homes or lodgings, who were involved in drinking, gambling and other activities which were drawing them away from the Church. Sometimes the Brothers were able to persuade them to have Bible studies or discussion instead of these, and many of them shared their problems with the Brothers. Some of those contacted returned to active Church membership and worship. There were plenty of temptations for the Brothers themselves in this kind of work, and the regular Team meetings and support they thereby received were a great encouragement, and indeed a lifeline in their difficult ministry.

At Tabalia, a rural Team Ministry was established to do evangelistic and pastoral work, first in the villages and institutions around the Central Headquarters, and then in the new settlements and plantations in the area, often peopled by Malaitans. The area had been made into Saghalu Parish,[11] and the Team cooperated with the District Priest who toured the parish four times a month to administer the Sacraments and give counselling. Brothers and Novices followed up Missions conducted by the Team by taking Bible studies and classes for Baptism and Confirmation.

A new method of doing the evangelistic and teaching work of the Church was thus being learnt by clergy and Brothers working together, both in urban and rural areas, and by the Religious Orders discovering how they could complement each other and cooperate in numerous ways. One of the Novices wrote: "The people are hungry for the spiritual food, and this can only be done through Team Ministry work which meets the present need of our people in the rural areas. The people are now beginning to see the way the Church goes in the field of work of Team Ministry."[12]

In the New Hebrides, the Brothers had established their Regional Headquarters at St Mark's Household, Tumsisiro on Aoba (Ambae), not far from St Patrick's School, Vureas, and the Training Centre at Torgil. Nearby was the airstrip which served Lolowai, with its Godden Memorial Hospital, and Longana District. Brother Andrew Letade was Teaching Brother at the Headquarters, and from there Novices went out to do their 'practical'. In May 1978, Brother Andrew took five Novices to Lombaha District, where they conducted various activities to help the people, such as Bible study, Sunday School, singing practice, visiting the sick, calling on people in their houses, assisting them in their work, trying to solve problems, and speaking about the work of the Brotherhood and the Companions. They also called a Companions' meeting, as people had told them that their leader had not been carrying out his duties well. A new leader, Martha Garae, was elected and received at a service conducted by the Assistant Bishop of the New Hebrides, Harry Tevi, from Raga (Pentecost). At a farewell breakfast, choruses were sung, and Novice

Charles Fox wrote: "Six girls came up, facing each of us, bowed their heads, genuflected together, and put on us flowers they have prepared."[13]

The Brothers were invited in 1978 to go to a village in Central Pentecost near where there were forty people who were 'heathens'. The invitation had come from Raton, a Christian village surrounded by smaller 'heathen' villages. In January 1979, Wosak Household was therefore established near Raton, and the Brothers were visited by a heathen chief and his family, eight persons in all. Thereafter, they visited the family twice a week to prepare them for Baptism and Confirmation, and they hoped that all the other 'heathens' might become Christian within eighteen months.

In the Santo Bush, the Brothers had experienced considerable difficulties because their main household at Tombet was not far from Fanafo,[14] the headquarters of the Nagriamel Movement, led by Jimmy Stevens.[15] At that time Nagriamel was one of the two main political parties working for independence in the New Hebrides. The other was the New Hebrides National Party (later called the Vanuaaku Party), which was led by Fr Walter Liñi, an Anglican priest. The two parties were rivals and had quite different ideas about independence. Certain American and French groups, including the French administration, hoped to be able to use Nagriamel for their own ends, one of which was to divide up the country, with separate constitutions for different areas.[16] One of these areas would be Espiritu Santo and nearby islands. The New Hebrides National Party was totally opposed to this and wanted a unitary state. Nagriamel had attracted much support from 'heathens' in Santo island, Malekula (the people called Big Nambas and Small Nambas), Tanna and South Pentecost. The party stressed the importance of 'custom', and suspected the motives of the Anglican and Presbyterian Churches which appeared to be backing the Nationalist Party. None of this made it easy for the Brothers. Elder Brother Robert Kware,[17] who had been working on Santo for two years, found increasing opposition from traditional leaders. In February 1978 he divided the Brothers into three small Households, with two Brothers in each, to work at Tombet, Begine and Vutioro. One of the Nagriamel chiefs visited Brother Robert and threatened him and his Brothers with violence, if they did not leave. The chief said that if the people became Christians their 'custom' would die out. Robert disagreed and said the Brothers would not leave, whatever happened. They stayed in their households and prayed and carried on with their work as best they could. Another chief, Andrew Walling, then called on Brother Robert and told him that the chiefs of Nagriamel wanted to judge him. Robert said he was willing to go with him. Arriving at their Nakamal (men's meeting house), he found ten very angry chiefs, who complained about people becoming Christians, and criticised him very strongly. He remained quiet, then asked if he might speak. He then explained why the Brothers had come and what they were doing. He was amazed that, after this, the chiefs began to say how sorry they were that they had been so rude! The wife of one of the chiefs even took up a long knife in order to kill her husband, but Brother Robert ran to her and took it away. The result of the meeting was the recognition of the Brothers' way of life and work. Brother Robert wrote: "For the sake of the people we are serving, we Brothers visit the heathen villages and talk to the people and their chiefs. Finally we show our love and example and our way of life." By 1979 there were eighty-eight new Christians, and three young men had been trained as village catechists, and conducted morning and evening prayer. As a result, the Brothers were able to withdraw from Begine, and a catechist took over.[18]

The Archbishop of Melanesia, as Father of the Brotherhood, visited the Brothers at their Regional Headquarters in the New Hebrides in early 1978 and took their Retreat. In November 1978, he visited the Regional Headquarters of the Papua New Guinea Region at Pomete, which was named 'St John Barge', after the priest murdered there by the Japanese during the Second World War. There he conducted the Brothers' Retreat and attended part of their Regional Conference. He wrote afterwards: "A life in a Community is not always easy – you have to live together as a family. You have to learn a life of sharing and accepting that way of life. Try to remember that God our Father who has called you will also give you the strength to carry out what He wants you to do."[19]

In 1979, the fourth Great Conference was held at Tabalia from April 19 to 24, starting with a two-day Retreat conducted by the Bishop of Malaita, Leonard Alufurai. Bishop Bevan Meredith of the Diocese of the New Guinea Islands, Regional Father of the Papua New Guinea Region was present, as were some Companions from Australia and Mr Michael Wulump, representing the Diocese of Aipo Rongo in Papua New Guinea. On April 21, the Brotherhood elections were held, and Brother Patteson Ihomana (retiring Assistant Head Brother) was elected as Head Brother, the youngest in the history of the Brotherhood.[20] Brother Patteson Dora from South Malaita was elected as Assistant Head Brother and Regional Head Brother for the Solomons Region (which included Carpentaria). Two other Regional Head Brothers were elected: John Di Adriu from Fiji for the Southern Region, and Michael Toa from the New Hebrides for the Papua New Guinea Region. At the Great Conference which followed, Sister Helen from Canada, serving with the Sisters of the Church at Patteson House in Honiara, who also did secretarial work for the Archbishop, acted as Minutes Secretary.

The Companions' Conference followed on April 23 and 24. They elected a new Chief Secretary to replace Miss Lily Tetehu, who was taking the minutes: Mr John Bosamata Niabo from Luemini village on Santa Cruz. Fr Michael Tavoa, a New Hebridean teaching at Kohimarama, became Chief Chaplain for Companions Overseas, and Fr Willie Pwa'isiho from Malaita, also a lecturer there, became Adviser to the Companions. Fr Brian had filled these two roles, but he had moved to the New Hebrides in 1978 to establish the Pacific Churches Research Centre in Vila, as a staff member of the Pacific Conference of Churches, on secondment from the Church of Melanesia. Before the Conference began, the Reverend John and Mrs Johanna Geoghegan, who had travelled at their own expense from Australia, were admitted as Companions on April 22 in St Mark's Chapel, Tabalia, by Bishop Bevan Meredith, himself an Australian, who was also Father of the Companions in Papua New Guinea. St Mark's Day was celebrated by the admission of eleven new Brothers, including two from Papua New Guinea. The former Head Brother, Robert Wobur, was released from his vows (and later trained for ordination), and so was Brother Santus Athalage from Santa Ysabel, who had been working in Papua New Guinea. Three Brothers were temporarily released from two of their vows, keeping that of celibacy. After all this, everyone went into the church from the square outside, to celebrate the Sung Eucharist. The Archbishop was assisted by twelve priests and one deacon. The Brothers and Novices provided the choir, led by Brother William Piru. Increasingly the Brothers were using traditional Melanesian tunes and a wide range of other music, and this was beginning to influence what was sung in places where they went out to work. After the midday feast, there were dances, as usual, performed by the Brothers and Novices and students from Kohimarama.

Head Brother Patteson Ihomana wrote afterwards: "For me, the work is very new, tough and difficult, as many might have thought of. In fact, I accepted it humbly, the glorious work my Brothers have me to carry, knowing also through your support and prayers, our eternal Father will provide me the strength and the ability to rule and lead the Brotherhood according to His will in these four years."[21] Earlier, as Assistant Head Brother, he had written about the Brotherhood as if it were a child growing up: "I was born as a child to my mother the Church of Melanesia in 1925. My mother, the Church, took me, cared for me, nursed and supplied me with what I needed, in order for me to grow and be as I am today. When I was old enough, my mother gave me a rule to help her. The role she gave me was to 'convert, help and share God's love' with my brothers and sisters who did not yet hear and know God. I began to wander from island to island and from one country to another country, seeking for those who were lost and did not know God and His love. I won some of them. In turn, some of them joined me. 'My role was widely spread and was one of the most important types of work that a man could do', my mother the Church whispered in my ear."[22] What was true for the Brotherhood was also true for Brother Patteson himself; he had been just a young teenager when he first came into the care of the Brothers and the Chaplain at Tabalia!

NOTES

1 *Melanesian Brotherhood Newsletter*, Easter 1977.

2 Fr Christian Makona acted as Resident Chaplain at Tabalia as well as District Priest for Saghalu District, which covered the villages and plantations around Tabalia. The presence of families on Tabalia station added another aspect to the life of the community. Fr Fugui eventually became Chaplain of the University of the South Pacific, Fiji, where he died. He had also helped to teach Pacific Studies at the Bishop Patteson Theological Centre.

3 *Melanesian Brothers and Companions Newsletter*, 1977, Honiara.

4 Peter Sulutu.

5 By 2001 he had become Canon Richard Naramana, Secretary of the Melanesian Board of Mission, which encouraged evangelism and mission in the Province and overseas, and related closely to the work of the four religious orders, continuing work formerly coordinated by the Provincial Department of Evangelism and Community Education.

6 *Melanesian Brotherhood Newsletter*, Easter 1977.

7 The presence of four chiefs leading different groups on the island was probably because of the immigration of people at different times, especially from Samoa and Tonga. It was the only part of the Solomons not to have a Local Council, the chiefs insisting that they *were* the Council.

8 *Melanesian Brotherhood Newsletter*, Easter 1977.

9 *Melanesian Brotherhood Newsletter*, Easter 1977.

10 *Melanesian Brothers and Companions Newsletter*, 1977.

11 This was part of the Honiara Region, of which the Dean of the Cathedral was 'Senior Priest' (a title which replaced 'Rural Dean' when the Province was inaugurated). This was equivalent to 'Archdeacon' in the Province of Aotearoa, New Zealand and Polynesia.

12 Barnabas Buio in the *Melanesian Brothers and Companions Newsletter*, 1977.

13 *Melanesian Brothers and Companions Newsletter* for the year 1979.

14 Jimmy Stevens called it Tanafo, others Fanafo or Vanafo.

15 His father was of mixed European and Tongan ancestry, so he claimed, and his mother was from the Banks Islands. He founded the 'Royal Church of Nagriamel', with perhaps a suggestion of contact with the Tongan Royal Family!

16 Copies of two Constitutions for northern and southern (but not central) areas of the country were given

to the author when he visited Jimmy Stevens with Fr Gregory Manliwos from the Banks Islands, a distant relative of Jimmy Stevens, in about 1979. Jimmy had taken wives from various islands, apparently to try and unite the country through his relations, but as these were often young women, it was difficult to distinguish his latest wives from his older daughters! Subsequently he was arrested and imprisoned.

17 Sometimes spelt Qare.

18 *Melanesian Brothers and Companions Newsletter* for the year 1979.

19 *Melanesian Brothers and Companions Newsletter* for the year 1979.

20 He was about 23 or 24.

21 *Melanesian Brothers and Companions Newsletter* for the year 1979.

22 *Melanesian Brotherhood Newsletter*, Easter 1977.

CHAPTER SIXTEEN

Brother Robert Wobur beside the grave at Tabalia of Brother Charles Fox, missionary in Melanesia for over 60 years.

Brother Robert Tempest Wobur became Head Brother in 1975 after working in Fiji, and was later ordained and became Chaplain for a while to the Brotherhood in Vanuatu.

Brother Luke Magiza (Head Brother 1987-91).

Head Brother Luke outside St. Mark's Chapel, Tabalia.
The large cross marks the spot where Brother Ini made his vow.

CHAPTER SIXTEEN

BROTHERS AND SISTERS

Brother Charles Fox died in New Zealand on October 28, 1977 – the Feast of St Simon and St Jude! While living there as a Brother, he had been visited by Ellison Pogolimana, who had been secretary to the Dean, Norman Palmer, and Fr Brian (when Head of the Department of Evangelism and Community Education), before beginning his studies at St John's College, Auckland. Brother Charles wanted to see any Melanesian visiting New Zealand, and he was delighted when Ellison – a future Father of the Brotherhood, although he could not have known! – managed to visit him. Dressed as a Brother, Charles Fox opened a drawer and showed the student first a medal awarded to him by the Queen on the recommendation of the British Solomon Islands Government, the MBE (Member of the Order of the British Empire). Then he took out another box and showed him the medal awarded to him on the recommendation of the New Zealand Government, the CBE (Commander of the Order of the British Empire). Then he dipped his hand in the drawer again and brought out the medal which he said was the most important one of all – it was his Brother's medal, given him when he rejoined the Brotherhood. On Ellison this made a deep impression, and it became a memory he treasured. Brother Charles Fox was brought back to Tabalia after his death and buried in the Brothers' cemetery near what was originally the Chaplain's house, built for Fr Ernest Ball to occupy. His grave was carefully tended and gradually improved by the addition of a headboard and surround, after work on Brother Ini's grave at Maravovo village had been completed.

On November 15, 1977, the planned Community of the Sisters of Melanesia began its preparations for approval, under the guidance of Miss Nester Atkin Tiboe from Guadalcanal and Miss Lily Tetehu from Santa Ysabel, who was later elected as Head Sister for a short period. The Brotherhood gave the women every support; it was to be a parallel community to their own, following a similar Constitution. At first, the women aspirants were based at Tabalia, in the house formerly used by Brother Ellison Vahi as Chaplain. He had been one of the earliest supporters of the idea of such a Sisterhood, when Head Brother. The women joined in services with the Brothers, worked in their own garden and helped the Brothers in theirs, as well as helping with the communal work and in the Brotherhood 'bush sections'. They went up to Kohimarama to join in the

Women's Club and Mothers Union activities. They also planned a new station with a church, classroom, staff house, dining hall, kitchen and two dormitories, and were seeking help from Church members all over the Solomons. By 1980, 21 young women had applied through their priests to join, but could not be accepted until there was more accomodation. Some of the women attended classes with the Novices, and they all joined in the Bible Study and the singing (hymns and choruses). They supported the local group of the Melanesian Christian Youth Movement (MCYM), which had been started at Tabalia to train Brothers and Novices in youth work.

Fr Brian, whose Provincial Department included Youth Work (promoted there by ex-Brother Clement Savaka) had adopted the idea of the MCYM from the United Church of Papua New Guinea and the Solomon Islands. He had started a group at Vutu on the Guadalcanal Plains, when he was Chaplain at both Tabalia and Selwyn College, Najilagu, the Anglican co-educational secondary school for the Solomons, which had replaced Pawa Boys' School and Pamua Girls' School. This double chaplaincy had lasted for a year, and Fr Brian had spent the weekdays at Tabalia and the weekends at Selwyn College, travelling the 40 miles each way mostly on 'unmade' roads in the Mini-Moke provided by the Diocese of Melanesia. He had been assisted at Selwyn College by Brother Timothy Vildam.

A number of girls at Vutu village had joined MCYM, and the group, including some young men, was supportive of the Sisterhood, which later established a house nearby. The Brothers promoted MCYM in a number of places where they went to work. There was a great need for youth work of various kinds, and the Brothers at Tabalia had also had a Young Farmers Club in the 1970s, in which Novices were trained in agriculture and animal husbandry. The Brothers and Sisters felt a special call to help other young people wherever possible, as both Communities were largely composed of young members, unlike most Communities in the Anglican Communion.

Bishop Derek Rawcliffe resigned as Bishop of the New Hebrides in Februry, 1980, and Bishop Harry Tevi was elected the next day to replace him. He also became Regional Father of the Southern Region, and the first New Hebridean to become a Diocesan Bishop. On the Independence of the New Hebrides as the Republic of Vanuatu on July 30, 1980, the Diocese changed its name to the Diocese of Vanuatu. The members of the Electoral College (who had chosen the new Diocesan Bishop) and leaders of the Church in the New Hebrides were entertained by the Brothers, and the Archbishop visited their headquarters at Tumsisiro. He also paid an official visit to the Brothers and Sisters at Tabalia and met with the Brotherhood Committee. A new Chaplain and Tutor was appointed, Fr John Victor Pepela, who had previously served in a similar capacity at Pomete in New Britain, the Papua New Guinea Regional Headquarters and Noviciate. Fr Christian Makona had left Tabalia and gone to Kohimarama to continue his studies. The Archbishop had chosen ex-Brother George Kope, by then a priest and married, to go as Chaplain and Tutor to Pomete.

The Archbishop visited Temotu Region in May, in preparation for it becoming a Diocese in November. The new Diocesan Headquarters was to be established if possible at Luesalo on Santa Cruz, when the Allardyce Lumber Company moved out, and the Archbishop talked to the Brothers about their future work in the new Diocese. He also launched a programme of 'Outreach and Evangelism' for the whole Church.[1] He wrote: "The work of evangelism has already been carried out by the Brothers, but let us continue and strengthen this work within and outside the Pacific."[2] In this way the whole Church of Melanesia was urged to participate in the work of evangelism and renewal in both Christian and non-Christian areas in Melanesia and beyond, seeing this as the task of the whole Church and not just of the Brothers. This was in line with the thinking of Archbishop Chisholm, when, as Bishop of Melanesia, he had established the Department of Evangelism and Community Education. This renewed emphasis on evangelism as the concern of the whole Church of Melanesia led on to the establishment of the Melanesian Board of Mission. It was no longer just Brothers who were seen to be involved in mission and evangelism, or to be sent to serve outside the Province, but bishops, clergy and lay workers as well. Clergy from Melanesia went to serve in Carpentaria, Papua New Guinea and England in the next two decades, and Brothers of the First Order of the Society of St Francis[3] and the Sisters of the Church, who had established their Noviciate at Tetete ni Kolivuti on the Guadalcanal Plains, would also go to serve in various places outside the Province. Fr Johnson Bana, later Tutor at Tabalia, spent time in England, where he spoke about the work of the Brotherhood when he could.

In the Papua New Guinea Region, a new chapel at Pomete had been dedicated on the Feast of St Simon and St Jude, 1979. The Diocesan Council of the Diocese of the New Guinea Islands had been held at Apugi so that the Council members could be present at the dedication, which was also attended by some Roman Catholics, including the Auxiliary Bishop of Rabaul and Sisters from Tutuk near Kandrian. Brother Giles Livingstone

Pondo had done a design for the wall behind the freestanding concrete altar. Seven new Brothers had been admitted and six released, and there were five Novices in their second year of training. A Section Conference and a Companions Conference for the New Guinea Islands Section was held at the same time. The pattern in most parts of the Brotherhood now was for an annual Section Conference, a Regional Conference every other year, and the Great Conference every four years. Brother Michael Toa arrived in March 1980 and took up his work as Regional Head Brother, visiting the New Guinea Islands and Highlands Sections first. The Regional Father, Bishop Bevan Meredith, was planning to visit the households in Papua: Sakarina in Popondota Diocese and Sirisiri in Dogura Diocese, which had just been opened. The Brothers in New Britain had just been given two bicycles, which helped them to get to the schools in Kandrian to help the Parish Priest with Religious Instruction. In October, 1980, all the Brothers from six households[4] came to Pomete for the Regional Conference Retreat, followed by the admission and release of Brothers. On the Feast of St Simon and St Jude, October 28, the Eucharist was celebrated at the grave of John Barge, Priest and Martyr.[5]

The Brothers at Tabalia, meanwhile, worked to improve the grave of Ini Kopuria, the founder, in Maravovo Churchyard, so that a Eucharist could be held annually there on his day, June 6. The Central Solomons Section meeting was held at Tabalia in April 1980 and the Assistant Bishop of the Diocese of Central Melanesia, Caspar Uka (from Tikopia) presided. Brother Colin SSF, from Malaita, conducted the retreat. Twenty three aspirants were admitted as Novices, six from the Diocese of Ysabel, ten from the Diocese of Central Melanesia[6] (including John Kuvi from Gela), and seven from the Diocese of Malaita. Among the congregation on St Mark's Day, the Patronal Festival of Tabalia, were some Sisters of the Church and also some Roman Catholic Sisters of the Daughters of Mary Immaculate (DMI). There were professions of twenty-two new Brothers, five from Ysabel Diocese, ten from Central Melanesia Diocese, four from Malaita Diocese, two from the New Hebrides Diocese, and Basa Banu from Carpentaria Diocese – the first Australian to be admitted into the Brotherhood. In Temotu Section, eleven aspirants were admitted as Novices by the Section Elder Brother on St Mark's Day, and, following the new training plan, they were to do their first year's training at Luesaleba and their second year at Tabalia. In Malaita Section, a new Section Headquarters was being built at Wainiura in West Areare. This would take the place of the headquarters at Tariuna in East Areare. Work continued at Su'u in Areare. The Brothers had contacts with 'heathen' people at Aio in Koio District, and were planning visits to all of Areare and to South Malaita, as well as to the atolls of Sikaiana and Lord Howe. The work was led by Section Elder Brother Edward Das, who was from Fiji.[7]

In the New Hebrides, first year training of Novices was being undertaken at Tumsisiro. The Brothers and Novices there had their own Chaplain. As well as the training of Novices and doing MCYM, Sunday School and Bible study, they toured the villages and stations, and encouraged the Companions in their life and work. On Sundays, they visited sick people in the Godden Memorial Hospital at Lolowai. Three Brothers were now stationed in Santo Town, and a new house for them had been completed. There they worked closely with the parish priest, both in the town and in the surrounding settlements. In Pentecost, Wosak Household continued its work among the newly-converted, the 'heathens' and the surrounding Christians. The Brothers taught catechism in a Christian village and religious education in a nearby school. Bible study was conducted on Sundays.

In the three households in the Santo Bush, the new Christians still faced difficulties because of political pressures, only some of which were resolved at Independence, although Jimmy Stevens was arrested, tried and imprisoned in the latter part of 1980. The attempt to establish a 'Vemarana Federation' with Jimmy as Prime Minister had failed, and a son of his had been killed on Santo island. In other disturbances on the island of Tanna, a Member of Parliament was killed in a shoot-out. It was a very confusing time for people in the bush, who were trying to understand what Independence meant to them and their island, to their country, and to those who had been putting pressure upon them to support the Nagriamel secessionist movement. Sadly, at that time the Brothers had only three aspirants at Tumsisiro, and so were concerned about how they would maintain and strengthen the work they were trying to do throughout the Diocese of the New Hebrides/Vanuatu. In Fiji, the Brothers were visiting different parishes at the invitation of the parish priests.

For the Brothers and Novices at Tabalia, Brother Ini's Day was celebrated in a very special way in 1980. Instead of just the special service at the grave, with the singing of the Brothers' and Companions' hymn written by Fr Brian, they had for the first time a Sung Eucharist on June 6, after the Pilgrim Walk from Tabalia to Maravovo on June 4. The Brothers and Novices were joined on the walk by the Chaplain, the Tutor, who was Mr Peter Ruim, formerly Assistant Head Brother, and some of the Community of the Sisters of Melanesia. They slept in three villages, including Maravovo, on the nights of June 4 to June 6, and helped to prepare the feast during the day on June 5. Later in that same day, they all gathered round the grave of Ini with some of the villagers, and the Chaplain blessed the improvements, which had been carried out under the direction of Brother William Tedi, who had years before superintended the work on the furnishings of the sanctuary in the new chapel at Tabalia. An altar had been built at the head of the grave, with a three foot cross beyond it. At the base of the cross was a platform, where a preacher could stand. On the front of the altar was a memorial plate carved out of *tubi* wood, with an inscription inlaid with shell and polished. On the other side of the altar was a cross inscribed with the words, "Take up your cross and follow me." On June 6, after First Office and Mattins in the village church, a procession led by a thurifer[8] and crucifer made its way to the grave for the Eucharist. The Chaplain was assisted by four other priests, and Peter Ruim preached about the "birth, life and work of Brother Ini, in relationship with the work and life then and now in Melanesia."[9] The feast and dances followed the service. The Brotherhood had thus paid its tribute to its founder, and thereafter his grave and that of Brother Charles Fox would be constant reminders of those who had played decisive roles in establishing and encouraging what was about to become the largest religious community for men in the Anglican Communion. In 1979 there were already 99 Brothers and 66 Novices in training.[10]

In 1980, four Sisters were professed in the Community of the Sisters of Melanesia and over the next two and a half years the Sisterhood grew rapidly, with more applications to join than the few Sisters could adequately handle. By 1983 they had moved temporarily to Buñana Island off the southern coast of Gela island, and were occupying the former St Hilda's School, where the Sisters of the Cross had been based many years before. They planned to move later to Vutu in Tasimboko District on Guadalcanal. They had seven Sisters, twelve Novices and one aspirant, as well as two girls hoping to join, who were not yet old enough. On September 28, 1983, the number of Sisters rose to eleven. At the weekends they visited villages on Gela to take Bible studies and run Sunday Schools. In 1983 Sister Nesta Tiboe, the Founder, and Sister Elizabeth Sina'a took four Novices to do their 'practical' in Tasimboko District for two months. This followed the pattern established by the Brothers, whereby second-year Novices went out for periods of practical work in different areas of the Solomons. Lily Tetehu, formerly Chief Secretary of the Companions, had been professed as a Sister and was running the Community. They were hoping to extend their work beyond the Diocese of Central Melanesia, as the Community grew larger. This became possible in the years that followed, as the number of Sisters and Novices eventually outgrew all the previous houses they had had, and they were offered the former Maravovo School as their Mother House.

In April 1983, the Great Conference of the Brotherhood met at Tabalia, and Moses Keahi was elected as Head Brother. The Diocesan Council of Carpentaria, where he had faithfully worked for six years, met and passed a unanimous motion of congratulation. They wrote through Bishop Jamieson: "We feel our loss is the gain of the Brotherhood, but also know that we will not lose in the long run."[11] Other changes in leadership occurred. Brother Andrew Letade became Assistant Head Brother and Regional Head Brother for the Solomons Region (including Carpentaria). Brother Luke Rowomana was elected Regional Head Brother for Papua New Guinea Region, and Brother Francis Apoi for the Southern Region. Novice Jackson Ha'apwesi became Companions' Chief Secretary. Fr Michael Henry Tavoa, who, since 1979, had been Chaplain for Overseas Friends and Companions, handed over his responsibility to the Chief Secretary. He wrote: "It has been a wonderful experience, specially in being able to contact our beloved friends and Companions, many of whom I have never met, as well as many of them have not personally visited Melanesia and are real faithful servants of Christ, who have heard of the work of the Melanesian Brotherhood and have responded positively in various different ways to help furthering the Gospel of Christ through the outreach of the Brothers in the Isles of Melanesia – Papua New Guinea, Vanuatu, Fiji, Solomon Islands – and at the moment Australia. This relationship has created a feeling of oneness in our common goal for the sake of the Gospel."[12]

There had indeed been developments among the friends and Companions in Australia. Since 1979 work had progressed in Grafton Diocese in northern New South Wales, where the Bishop, Donald Shearman, already a Companion, had welcomed the establishment of a District of Companions, with himself as Chaplain and Mrs Johanna Geoghegan as District Secretary. Most of the parishes in the diocese had been visited with news of the Brothers, and especially their work in Carpentaria, and prayer requests had been distributed throughout the diocese. A service for admission of new Companions had been held on November 1, 1982, the Feast of All Saints, when five were admitted. In March 1983 two more new Companions joined the group, making ten in all, and others were being prepared for admission.

In February and March 1983 the Head Brother visited Australia at the invitation of the Australian Board of Missions, and with Brother Lawrence Ambeke did deputation work in the Dioceses of Brisbane, Grafton and Armidale. Questions they were often asked included: "Who started the Brotherhood, a white man? Since the Brotherhood started, have any Brothers got killed by the heathen?" The Brothers showed the film *Spearhead* and slides of *Brothers in Action.* Mrs Geoghagan wrote of their one-week visit to Grafton Diocese: "There have been many blessings in the parishes from their visit. Some will have farreaching effect. Some lives have been changed as a result. We praise God for this and all other blessings that happened in this Diocese over the last four years."[13] In November 1983 the Head Brother visited Areare in Malaita to see the Brothers, Companions and Christians there.

Peter Ruim had by now been ordained and become Chaplain at Tabalia. Before he handed over to Fr John Falea in 1984, he wrote that there was a lack of respect for the station at Tabalia as a place of prayer, as it had been in times past. "In the past the station was respected by the people, because of the kind of life it shows. It is the Light of the Church of Melanesia, and because of that those who serve in it must make sure that the station was and still is the Light of our Church." He commended the fact that previously it had been like a 'wilderness', to which people had come to experience the 'Great Silence'. He warned the Brothers that this should remain their aim: "To be quiet and be with God should be one of the fundamental objectives of the Melanesian Brotherhood – a life of prayer." As far as the Novices were concerned, he wrote: "For them to be able to realise that they have been called to serve in the Melanesian Brotherhood would be to spend some of their precious silent time talking with God and listening to God, who will direct them, encourage them and strengthen them."[14]

NOTES

1 This was in line with the later call of the Bishops of the Anglican Communion at the next Lambeth Conference in 1988 for a 'Decade of Evangelism' from 1990 to 2000.

2 *Melanesian Brothers and Companions Newsletter*, 1980.

3 The SSF had established their Noviciate at Hautabu near Maravovo on Guadalcanal.
4 There were households at Pomete and Gasmata in New Britain, Aganmakuk and Aredep in the New Guinea Highlands and two in Papua.
5 *Melanesian Brothers and Companions Newsletter*, 1980.
6 The Diocese still included Makira and Temotu Regions.
7 *Melanesian Brothers and Companions Newsletter*, 1980.
8 Incense made from the sap of a local tree was widely used in Melanesia.
9 *Melanesian Brothers and Companions Newsletter*, 1980.
10 Minutes of the Great Conference, 1979.
11 *Melanesian Brotherhood and Companions Newsletter*, 1984.
12 *Melanesian Brotherhood and Companions Newsletter*, 1984. Fr Michael Tavoa was later elected Bishop of Vanuatu and became Father of the Southern Region of the Brotherhood.
13 *Melanesian Brotherhood and Companions Newsletter*, 1984.
14 *Melanesian Brotherhood and Companions Newsletter*, 1984.

CHAPTER SEVENTEEN

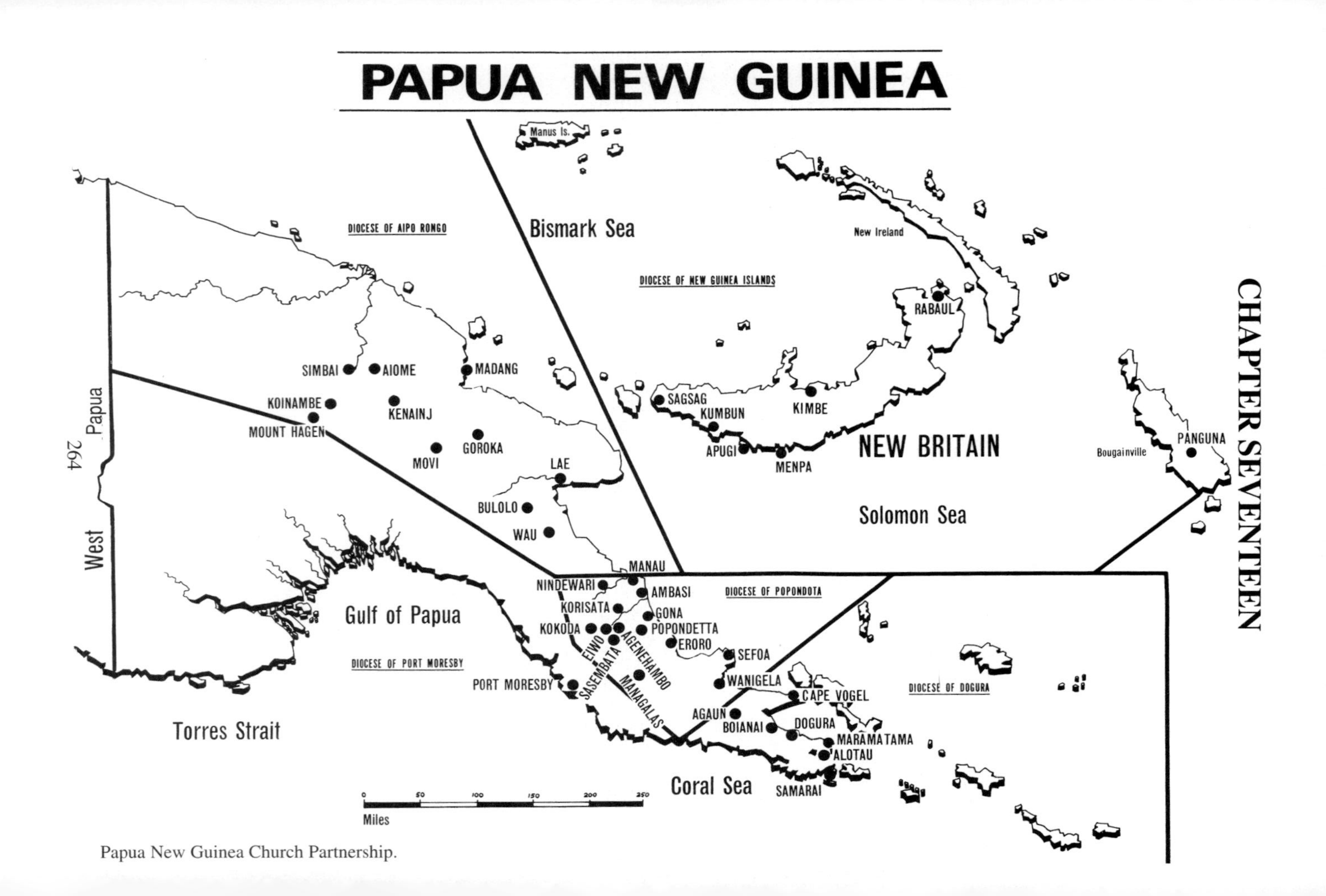

Papua New Guinea Church Partnership.

"May the Peace and Joy of the Lord..."
The Archbishop of Canterbury, Dr. Donald Coggan, blesses the first Archbishop of the new Anglican Province of Papua New Guinea, the Most Revd. David Hand, at the Provincial inauguration ceremonies at the Cathedral, Dogura, on February 27, 1977.
The Anglican Church began in 1891 with the landing of the two Australian Priests, Albert MacLaren and Copland King, at Dogura. Eighty-six years later the inauguration of the Anglican Church of Papua New Guinea can be seen as the culmination of their labours and the faithful work of those who followed them.
Photograph: Australian Board of Missions

1977
The first diocesan bishops of the Province of Papua New Guinea – left to right:
Bishop Rhynold Sanana of the Diocese of Dogura,
Bishop George Ambo of the Diocese of Popondota (later the second Archbishop),
Archbishop David Hand of the Diocese of Port Moresby, Bishop Bevan Meredith of the Diocese of the New Guinea Islands (later the third Archbishop),
Bishop Jeremy Ashton of the Diocese of Aipo Rongo.
Photograph: Australian Board of Missions

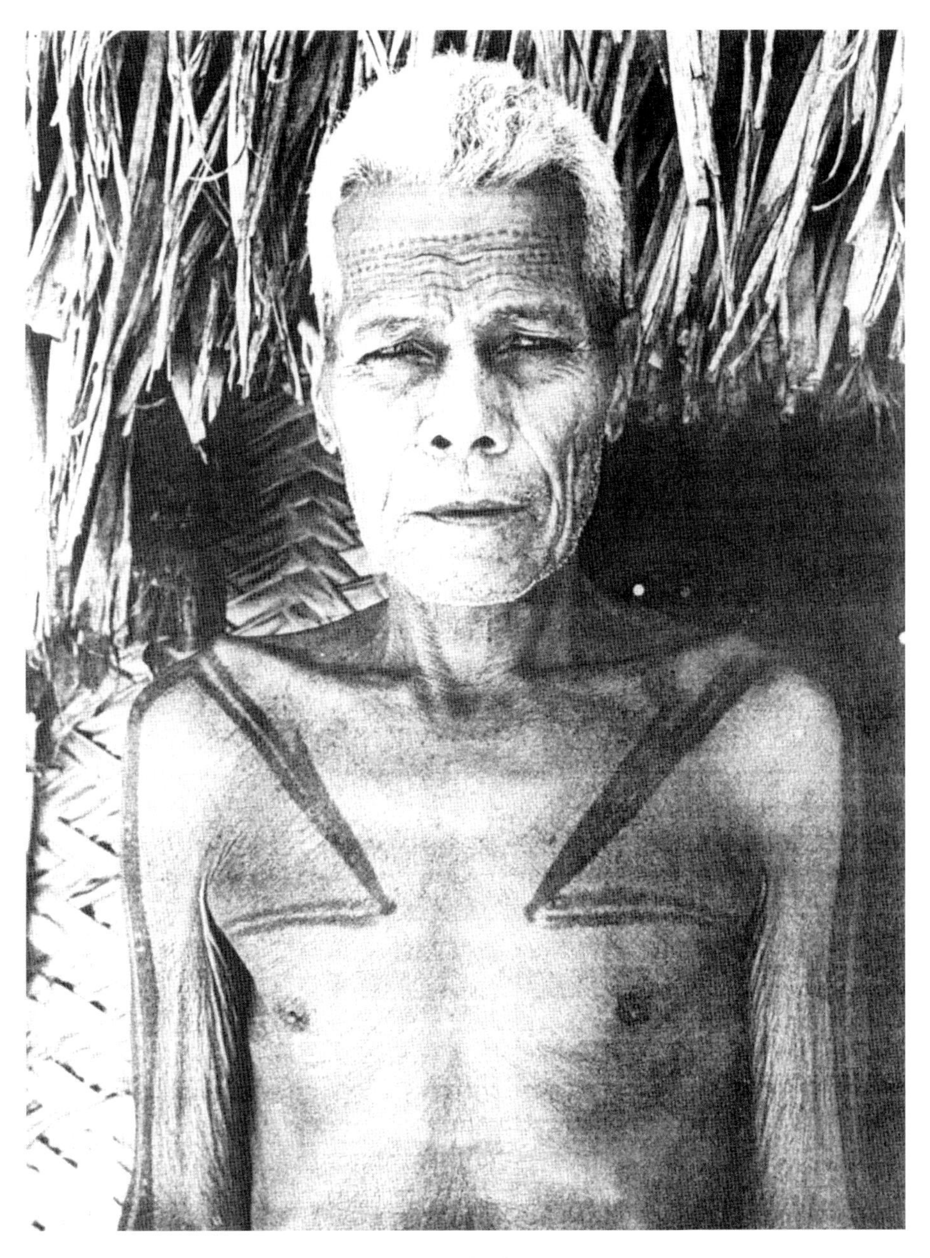

Tasman Islands man
Nukumanu

A woman of Nukumanu, Tasman Islands.
Drawing by Fr. John Ewington

Mother and baby – Tasman Islands (Nukumanu)
Drawing by Fr. John Ewington

Chief Kipano, who asked Fr. John Ewington to send Brothers to Nukumanu, Tasman Islands.

Fr. John Ewington with local women on Ongtong Java Atoll, Solomon Islands.

Fr. John (Ongtong Java) with his wife.

Norman Cruttwell and John Ewington being professed into the Third Order of the Society of St. Francis at Alexishafen.
The six members of S.S.F. taking part in the ceremony are (left to right) Bp. Tony Hall-Matthews, Bro. Philip SSF, Fr. John Ewington, Bp. Meredith Bevan, Fr. Norman Cruttwell, Bp. Jeremy Ashton.
Bishop Chisholm was also a Tertiary Brother.

CHAPTER SEVENTEEN

GROWTH AND DEVELOPMENT

The new decade had started with thirty-two Brothers working in the Solomon Islands Region, twenty-five in the Papua New Guinea Region and twenty-four in the Southern Region. As eleven of these Brothers were at the Central Headquarters, the rest of the Brothers were fairly evenly divided among the Regions, although eight of the Brothers in the Solomon Islands Region were actually working in Australia.

Brother Christian Ofamana, who had served for twenty years, was released early in 1980.[1] Altogether the number of Novices had by then increased to an average of twenty a year at Tabalia alone, while Novices were also being admitted at both Regional and Section Households. Prayer at the Mother House was central: 5.50 a.m. First Office, Mattins and Holy Communion; then breakfast; 8.0 a.m. Morning Office; 12.15 p.m. Midday Office; 1.30 p.m. Afternoon Office; 5.30 p.m. Evensong (6.0 p.m. on Saturdays and Sundays); 9.0 p.m. Last Office (Compline). Money was being raised by Companions in the Solomons to buy a refrigerator for the Brothers' House in Honiara, while Companions' Groups from Gela island and Longgu District on Guadalcanal were providing both materials and labour for the CSM Sisters' station about a mile inland to the south-east of Tabalia.

A great flood had swept over the gardens at Tabalia in February, 1980. The gardens beside the river had been on rotation cropping for more than fifty years and the land was in fact getting infertile, while the number of people to be fed from it was constantly increasing. Taro, cassava and Kumara (sweet potato) were grown, while the fruit they had to eat was usually bananas. After the flood, Companions and Kohimarama students had sent food to feed the Brothers and Novices until the gardens had recovered. The Chief Secretary to Companions, who also acted as Secretary for the Solomon Islands Region and the Central Solomons Section (Guadalcanal, Savo and Gela), had accompanied the Regional Head Brother, Eric Nerei, on a visit to the island of Gela, and was very pleased to discover that in the five Districts there was a total of 807 Companions. Brother Eric and he held short courses and meetings for both the Companions and Mothers' Union in each District and encouraged them in their prayer life and work. He wrote: "In the districts or villages we toured the Companions always asked me if I am paid for the job. Since I am an

Associate of the Melanesian Brotherhood, I've been with the Brothers now for four years. Two years at Luesaleba Household, and then I came down here last year, 1979."[2] 'Associates' were introduced in the 1970s, being volunteers willing to offer their services unpaid, to do any needed work under the auspices of the Brotherhood.[3]

At the 1981 Solomon Islands Regional Conference, it was announced that applicants to join the Brotherhood would have to be twenty years old, as the Brotherhood Committee had found that, increasingly, younger men did not take the Brotherhood work sufficiently seriously, and this had caused problems. The work the Brothers were being asked to undertake was becoming more varied, demanding a higher educational standard and more maturity. Young men, if they wished, could become Associates for a while, doing some worthwhile work to help the Brothers or the local Community before they applied to become Novices. The Regional Conference was chaired by the Bishop of Isabel, Dudley Tuti, Section Father of Isabel Section, who was due to retire in June, 1981. The Archbishop had gone to attend an Anglican Primates' meeting in the USA. Bishop Dudley remarked that "maturity comes at any age, some at an early age of 10 or 15; some at 20, 30 or 40 years old." (The Head Brother, Patteson Ihomana, could have been cited as an example of maturity at an early age.) He also said: "All of us need development. Development is not only 'project' or 'plantation' but also the prophetic message and the life our people live. We are co-workers with God in leading the people to Him, so that the people become more completely human, more like what God intended them to be."[4]

The Household of the Brothers on Santa Cruz had been moved to Makio, near Allardyce. The Brothers had found that the Catechists, Companions' leaders and young people had not responded to their teaching as they had expected. Although the whole Temotu Diocese had originally been completely Anglican, like Ysabel or Gela, some of the people were joining other denominations. Bishop Dudley believed this was because of a lack of pastoral care: "they are hungry.... And they are attracted to new ideas which flow into the country continuously."

During the 1981 Conference there were calls from the Companions and others for the Brothers to establish households on Makira, at Gizo in the western part of the Solomons, and on Gela. New households were agreed for Makira[5] and Gizo, whereas Gela Household was established later. Bishop Dudley, whose Diocese included all the west of the country, said:

"Our people who live in Gizo requested Brothers to work with them. Members of our Church living there are scattered, and they are working people in plantations, companies and offices, coming from Malaita, Gela, Ysabel, Guadalcanal and other islands in the Solomons." The Western Solomons had been an area gradually covered by the work of the Methodist Church from 1902, and the Diocese of Melanesia had agreed with the Methodist Mission to leave that part of the country in its care as far as 'mission work' was concerned. However, developments in government, the fishing and timber industries, and other activities, had drawn people there from other parts of the country, so there was a need for more Anglican ministry. In 1968 the Methodists had become part of the autonomous United Church of Papua New Guinea and the Solomons,[6] and had continued to work closely with the Anglicans in the Solomon Islands Christian Association (established in 1966) and in Honiara and other urban areas. So a ministry to Anglicans in the west by the Bishop of Isabel and Anglican clergy and Brothers was welcomed. One unexpected result, however, was a request from the island of Choiseul by a group of people already Christian to join the Anglican Church. Other Churches working in the west were the Roman Catholics in the Diocese of Gizo, served by the Dominican Orders of Friars and Sisters, the Seventh Day Adventists, who had done evangelistic work in non-Christian areas there from 1914, and the Christian Fellowship Church, which had been established in 1960 by a Methodist catechist, Silas Eto, who became a prophet known as the 'Holy Mama' (Holy Father). He had been disturbed by some developments in the Methodist Church. Working there was a new experience for the Brotherhood! It was different from areas of the Solomons in which they had worked before; it meant they were working in a largely non-Anglican area.

In 1981, Fr John Rufus Pituvaka took over as Chaplain of the Brotherhood, assisted by Deacon Peter Ruim. He was also parish priest for Saghalu Parish, and involved in the Commitment Programme. This was an effort, with the help of an Australian agency, to make the Church of Melanesia more self-reliant, in financial and other ways, which was a special concern of the Provincial Secretary, Basil LePine-Williams. Fr John Rufus had arrived two months before the Regional Conference and took a full part. It was agreed unanimously after discussion that the Great Conference should be moved back to its traditional time in October, but the 1983 one was still held in April, from the 20th to the 22nd! The

Chairman then was the Father of the Brotherhood, Archbishop Palmer, and Bishop Bevan Meredith attended as Regional Father of the Papua New Guinea Region. Two Deputy Fathers were present – Bishop Jamieson of Carpentaria and Bishop Willie Pwaisiho of Malaita. Father Peter Ruim was acting Chaplain, having been ordained priest, and other Chaplains present were Fr John Falea from Malaita Section (Wainiura Section Headquarters) and Fr George Thomas Kope from Papua New Guinea Region (Pomete Regional Headquarters). There were two Companions present from Australia. At the opening service, Fr John Rufus Pituvaka was specially remembered, as he had just died on 9 April.

Before the elections, the Head Brother, Patteson Ihomana, reported that there were 120 professed Brothers and 50 Novices in training. They were working in five countries. He also reported that the Sisters of Melanesia had 7 professed Sisters, 4 Novices and 9 aspirants.[7] One of the matters of great importance tackled in the Conference was the relationship of the Brotherhood and the Sisters of Melanesia, and this was referred to the Brotherhood Committee for consideration. Similarly, proposals to be incorporated in a new Constitution were referred to it, so that the Constitution could be adopted, if agreed, at the next Great Conference. The aim was to provide more flexibility for the Regions to operate in ways which were suitable for them, keeping to the 'spirit of the Brotherhood' rather than detailed rules. Those elected were not only Moses Keahi as Head Brother and Andrew Letade as Assistant Head Brother (and Regional Head Brother of the Solomon Islands Region), but also Luke Konomana as Regional Head Brother for Papua New Guinea Region, and Francis Apoio as Regional Head Brother for the Southern Region. One of the original Brothers, Hugo Holun from the Russell Islands, who had worked with the Founder, sent a message to the Conference, written out by his son as he was now old, blind and had to walk with sticks. It was read by Fr Peter Ruim, who was also from the Russell Islands. It read as follows: "My advice is that never give up hope, let Christ be always your leader, whether in heathen places or Christian countries. Remember the saying which says – 'Let your light so shine before men that they may see your good works and glorify your Father who is in heaven.' With these words I wish you all a bright future. May God bless you all. Your brother in Christ, Hugo Holun."[8]

Important developments since the previous Great Conference were a request from the Diocese of Port Moresby for a household, although not enough Brothers were yet available in Papua New Guinea for that. Representatives of the Anglican Church in Japan had visited the Church in Papua New Guinea, including the Brothers, and they felt this was an important occasion both for the Japanese and for themselves, as a sign of reconciliation and greater understanding between Japan and the Pacific Islands.

In Vanuatu, three villages in the Santo bush had been handed over to catechists to care for, and more than a hundred people had become Christians since the previous Great Conference. A Household had been established at Gaua in 1982, so that there would be Brothers working in the northern islands, the Banks and Torres.[9] It was also hoped to recruit more Novices from there. The Brothers in 1983 had ten Novices in training at Tumsisiro Regional Headquarters and there were seven aspirants. Their Chaplain was also the Warden of the Torgil Training Centre.

In spite of previous discussions, the Conference agreed to April, 1987 for the next Great Conference. Fr Peter Ruim was confirmed as Chaplain, and Fr Saul Ninian, an ex-Brother, was invited to become Tutor, to replace Mr Peter Saul, by the Brotherhood Committee at Tabalia.[10] Brother Wilson Dora'adi took over as Chief Secretary to Companions. A Brotherhood Council had been established, to meet every two years, to comprise the Head Brother, the Assistant Head Brother and the two Regional Head Brothers. With the growth in the number of households, it was agreed that the Head Brother and Assistant Head Brother would share the touring of households, both in the Solomon Islands and other countries, taking it in turns to go.[11] Plans were made in 1983 to build a headquarters for the Community of the Sisters of Melanesia on the Guadalcanal Plains near the village of Vutu with the help of the Brothers. The Sisters had been based at Tabalia and at the Mothers' Union Training Centre on Buñana island, Gela, where they trained Novices.[12]

The new Head Brother's first visit was to the Areare bush on Malaita. The Archbishop and the Bishop of Malaita too both visited the Brothers at Wainiura Section Headquarters in Areare, as questions had been raised in the Great Conference about whether the Brothers should withdraw from there. As this was the area where the Brothers had most contact with the 'heathen', as nearly every other part of the Solomons was now completely Christian, having one or more of the long-established or new denominations, this suggestion was greeted by many with alarm. Some felt the Brothers still had a responsibility to the non-Christians, wherever they were to be found in the Pacific. Some Brothers working in Malaita felt, however, that they had been neglected and largely ignored by the previous Bishop of Malaita. Bishop Pwa'isiho had, by contrast, increased the number of priests working in the Areare and Koio (Kwaio) areas of the Diocese, and the visit of the Archbishop with Bishop Pwa'isiho was a special encouragement to them all.

The Archbishop also visited the Brothers working among the 'heathen' in the bush villages inland from Big Bay on the island of Espiritu Santo in Vanuatu. He wrote in the 1984 *Melanesian Brotherhood and Companions Newsletter*: "Pray especially for follow-up work. We need priests, catechists, teachers and nurses who are prepared to work under the difficulties and isolations."[13]

In 1983 the new Companions' Chief Secretary, Novice Jackson Ha'apwesi, reckoned that the Companions had been in existence for 53 years. The Companions' General Fund which he administered, and which supported the work of the Companions generally, had not received what was expected from the many thousands of Companions in Melanesia and beyond, in spite of constant appeals to Companions' representatives in the various Conferences and meetings, and through reminders from those touring and visiting the Companions throughout the islands. The new Secretary asked for the collection on St Matthias's Day to be increased. The principle had always been that the money should be divided equally between the local organisation and the General Fund. 30c had at one time been suggested as an amount to be given by each Companion on St Matthias's Day when the Group met. The Secretary supported that this be increased to $1.00, half of which would be sent to the Companions' General Fund. The money in the Fund was used to pay for printing of Companions' books, medals, Newsletter, postage, touring by the Secretary, and other expenses such as courses for the Companions. Traditionally, Companions also met on St James's Day, wherever possible, in a District meeting with their District Priest, and members of all the Groups in the District were supposed to come. On that day a collection was taken to support the work of the Brothers, and this was usually sent to the Central or Regional Headquarters. However, with a new emphasis on observing Brother Ini's Day on June 6, many Groups met on that day also and had a collection then for the Brothers, as well as on St James's Day. From time to time, targets were set for amounts to be reached in each island or Section, or special appeals were made for the Great Conference or special projects, to which the Companions responded in money or kind. They saw the Brotherhood as *their* movement!

In Honiara they were well organised, with committees for each area of the Cathedral Parish, as well as an organisation for the whole Area, with its own officers. The Cathedral Parish was eventually divided into four parishes as the town of Honiara doubled in size. The country had achieved by now one of the highest birth rates in the world, half the population was under 15 years of age, malaria eradication had for a while been effective and had prevented many deaths of the old and the very young, primary education had been extended since Independence to the whole population for both boys and girls, and Honiara had become a magnet for people seeking work and town life, with more excitement that they found in their villages. The Melanesian Brothers in Honiara, with members of other Religious Orders, undertook revival work, pastoral care and the visiting done in various institutions such as the Central Hospital. However, increasingly, they were also called upon to be teachers of religious education, both in primary and secondary schools. So the Brothers were teaching at Buvali School, Mbokonavera School, Tuvaruhu School, St John's School and King George VI, the Government secondary school.[14] This was demanding, and led to a decision that selected Brothers should train as primary school teachers, their wages going to support the work of the Brotherhood. This led to some of the Brothers acquiring skills which had been largely absent before, and a further raising of educational standards. The growth of junior secondary schools throughout the Solomons, and of secondary education generally throughout the Pacific, meant that increasingly applicants for the Brotherhood came with some secondary education, and a few with full secondary education, enabling them to take on tasks which had not been considered suitable for them before. It also gave increasing confidence to those Brothers who were chosen to represent the Brotherhood abroad, whether in Australia or New Zealand or, in the 1990s, in England.

In Australia, Companions in the Grafton District of the Companions had been specially concerned for the Brothers in Carpentaria, sending $200.00 to Tabalia, half of which was to be used for the uniforms of the Carpentaria Brothers. They also sent money directly to the Bishop of Carpentaria to help them. Gifts in kind included parcels of food, clothing, Sunday School and Scripture materials, and church linen.

The Brothers at the various Section Headquarters usually tried to build a dormitory, dining room, kitchen and chapel. Sometimes a large cross was erected, to remind them of the one at the Central Headquarters or Mother House, which marked the spot where Ini had made his life vow in 1925. As, increasingly, Novices were admitted in some of the Section Headquarters, a special area or square similar to that at Tabalia would be made in front of the cross. Instead of constantly moving on, it became clear that the Brothers would need a permanent type of headquarters in each diocese where they worked in the South Pacific. From it they would go out to do revival work, together with visits to the Companions and courses for them. During the Archbishop's visit to Wainiura Household on Malaita, he dedicated the square there in honour of the Founder, Brother Ini, and also the large cross and a Brotherhood flag. Fifteen Brothers were based there, some going out to contact the 'heathen', but more being engaged in the revival work. This included weekend visits from the Section Headquarters to five villages to carry out various programmes, which covered teaching on prayer, Bible study, Sunday School and singing, as well as instructing Catechists in the faith of the Church.

Brothers working on Lord Howe Island in the past had had contacts with the people on Nukumanu or Tasman Island, who were Polynesians like those on Lord Howe atoll. The island of Nukumanu was over the border in Papua New Guinea and came within the Anglican Diocese of the New Guinea Islands, of which Bishop Bevan Meredith, later Archbishop of Papua New Guinea, was Diocesan Bishop. He requested that the Brothers undertake some research on Nukumanu to discover the needs of the people there, not least because, if they wished to be Anglicans, they should be the concern of the Anglican priest at Kieta on Bougainville island. Three Brothers were chosen from the Malaita Section after consultation with the Section Father, Bishop Willie Pwa'isiho. Two of them, Brothers Simeon Aina and Joshua Siwawata, were actually Papua New Guineans, but they were accompanied by Brother Gilbert Tenson, a Solomon Islander from Santa Ysabel. They visited Lord Howe as well as Nukumanu. In 1984, the Malaita Section Chaplain was Father Bartholomew Ramoana, based at Wainiura Section Headquarters.

At Makio Household, the Section Headquarters in Temotu Section, one of the Brothers, Peter Warren, acted as Tutor for the first year Novices training there. Makio had been designated as a 'Training Household', as it was so far from Tabalia on Guadalcanal, and transport was usually difficult or expensive. Four Novices were there in 1983 and they went on to Tabalia for their second year of training. Their programme at the household included going out at weekends to visit the parish of Lata, the administrative centre of Temotu Province's government, as well as Church Districts on Santa Cruz. They visited prisoners and the hospital, did counselling, held Bible study groups and Sunday Schools, practised choir singing and taught in schools. A doctor from Malaita working there had established a fund to assist their ministry, and especially to pay the costs of visiting more isolated islands in the diocese. This meant that they did not have to rely on the Bishop alone to take them with him when he toured on a Church ship. The Section Father was the Bishop of Temotu, Amos Waiaru, originally from Santa Ana in Makira Region.

At Brother C E Fox Household on Makira, Fr Caspar Harara became Chaplain and the number of Brothers increased in 1984 from five to eight. This was the Section Headquarters for Makira Section, serving the islands of Makira (San Cristoval), Santa Ana, Santa Catalina, Ugi and Ulawa. This area later became the new Diocese of Hanuato'o, with its headquarters at Kirakira on Makira. On his retirement, Archbishop Norman Palmer took up residence on Makira and taught in the Training Centre for the Diocese. The Elder Brother wrote in 1983: "The main purpose.... is to go out in the areas of the Makira Region to carry out the revival work among the Christian people who have fallen away from the Church, to strengthen the Companions of the Brotherhood in their work and also to demonstrate the work of the Melanesian Brotherhood to the young people so that more young people may join us." On weekdays from Wednesdays to Saturdays they went out to nearby villages to take Bible study and services. He wrote: "The main aim of the Bible studies is to renew the Christian faith and lives of all the Christians who are weak, to believe and trust in God that only He is the benefit of our lives. We should love Him by obeying His commandments, so that we may respond to Him in everything He has given us in our daily lives."[15] The name of the Household was chosen to honour Charles Fox, who had spent many years in the area, both on Makira and Ugi before he first joined the Brotherhood.

The Isabel Section Headquarters had been established at Isaruwe and Fr Hudson Lagusu had been appointed Chaplain. Head Brother Patteson Ihomana, an Isabel man, had been released from his vows after years of service as aspirant, Novice, Brother, Assistant Head Brother and Head Brother. He was still a young man. His relative Ellison Vahi had been a Head Brother earlier. After so many men from the area covered by the

Isabel Diocese had served in the Brotherhood, it was fitting that at last a household should be based on Santa Ysabel itself, with the opportunity for Brothers to go out into different parts of the diocese. The new Bishop of Isabel was Ellison Pogolimana (or Pogo), who had been elected as Bishop while he was still serving as a curate in Dunedin Diocese in New Zealand, having completed his studies at St John's College, Auckland. This was much to the amazement of some people in New Zealand! He thus became Father of the Isabel Section and began his long association with the Brotherhood.[16]

By 1984, the Southern Regional Headquarters at Tumsisiro had acquired its own Chaplain and Tutor, Fr Jairus Karabani from Maewo, later to become Vicar General of the Diocese of Banks and Torres. There were four other households in Vanuatu: Wosak, Pentecost; Big Bay, Santo; Luganville, Santo; and Biam on Gaua in the Banks Islands. Five Brothers were serving in Fiji, and their Chaplain was a Fijian, Fr Apimeleki Qilio, whereas previously Indian and Tongan priests had held that position.

By now, thirty three Brothers were at work in Papua New Guinea, serving in four out of the five dioceses.The largest number were in the Diocese of the New Guinea Islands, as the Regional Headquarters was still at Pomete, New Britain. Fr George Kope taught the Novices, and was assisted by Mr Joseph R Wagela as Tutor. Fr George was also Regional Chaplain. A new development in the diocese was the Household on Nukumanu, which formed another Section with four Brothers. In the Highlands there was only the Section Headquarters in Aipo Rongo Diocese, based at Aiome, with Bishop Jeremy Ashton as Section Father.[17] Eight Brothers were based there. In Popondota Diocese, the Archbishop, George Ambo, was Section Father, and the Elder Brother of Dopomo Section, based at Kawowok, was Lawrence Ambeke from Papua. His assistant as Elder Brother of the Household, was Caulton Weris from Vanuatu, a future Head Brother (elected 1995), who had joined the Brotherhood as a professed Brother in 1977. The other Section in Papua was in Dogura Diocese, where the Section Father was Bishop Rhynhold Sanana. Each of these Sections had six Brothers.

The total membership of the Brotherhood had risen to 116 Brothers and 46 Novices, including Jonathan Gagae from Carpentaria Diocese. There were now Companions in the Solomons, Vanuatu, New Caledonia, Papua New Guinea, Fiji, Tonga, Australia, New Zealand, the United States of America, Canada and Great Britain.

The last Great Conference chaired by Archbishop Palmer, who had done so much over twelve years as the first Melanesian Archbishop of Melanesia to encourage and guide the Brotherhood and the Sisters of Melanesia, was in 1987. His successor as Archbishop was Amos Stanley Waiaru, Bishop of Temotu, who was succeeded as Bishop in that Diocese by Lazarus Munamua, a Polynesian from Tikopia. Archbishop Waiaru was installed as Archbishop and enthroned as Bishop of the Diocese of Central Melanesia on April 17, 1988, in St Barnabas's Cathedral, Honiara, in two ceremonies, held in the morning and evening of that day. Archbishop Amos was first enthroned as Primate by the Bishops of the Province led by the Senior Bishop, Bishop Harry Tevi of Vanuatu, and the retired Archbishop, who, appropriately, also blessed the new Archbishop as he was taking over the responsibilities of the office from him. In the evening the Archbishop was enthroned as Bishop of the Diocese of Central Melanesia by the Dean of the Provincial Cathedral of St Barnabas, which was also the Cathedral of the Diocese of Central Melanesia. The Dean, James Mason, was also Vicar-General of the Diocese, and later he became the first Bishop of the Diocese of Hanuato'o and Section Father of the Brothers there in the former Makira Region. An important chapter in the life of the Province of Melanesia was ending, and another was beginning. However, the episcopate as Archbishop of Amos Waiaru lasted only till August 31, 1993, when he resigned and retired. The Brothers were most grateful for his concern for them, "spiritually, physically and financially."[18]

In his place, the Bishop of Isabel, Ellison Pogo, was elected, and another important era in the life of the Brotherhood began. He was succeeded in Isabel Diocese by Bishop Walter Siba, from Vanuatu, who had been serving as Bishop of Popondota[19] in Papua New Guinea. The Diocese of Central Melanesia was later divided, so that a largely urban diocese for the Archbishop, based on Honiara, retained the name of Central Melanesia (covering the area of north Guadalcanal from around Maravovo to the Guadalcanal Plains), while rural Guadalcanal, Gela and Savo became a separate Diocese of the Central Solomons, with Charles Koete of Gela as its Bishop, and its headquarters at Tulagi on Gela, the capital of the country before the Second World War.

NOTES

1 A service of thanksgiving had been held on St Simon and St Jude's Day, 1979 to give thanks for the twenty years spent in the Brotherhood under vows by Brother Christian Ofamana and Brother William Tedi. This had been led by the Father of the Brotherhood, the Archbishop of Melanesia.

2 Minutes of the Melanesian Brotherhood and Companions Central Solomons Section meeting, April 23, 1980.

3 See Companions' Handbook, 1983, pp. 10-11.

4 Minutes of the Melanesian Brotherhood, Companions and Sisters of Melanesia Regional Conference, April 23, 24 and 26, 1981.

5 Named Fox Household, after Brother Charles Fox.

6 The United Church in the Solomons eventually gained autonomy and cooperated with the Anglicans in theological training at the Bishop Patteson Theological College, Kohimarama, in the 1990s.

7 By *October* 1983, however, there were 11 Sisters, 8 Novices and 1 aspirant, as well as two underage girls, according to the *Melanesian Brotherhood and Companions Newsletter,* October 1983.

8 Minutes of the Great Conference of the Melanesian Brotherhood and Companions, held at Tabalia, April 20-22, 1983

9 These islands would later become the Diocese of Banks and Torres.

10 The Committee included officers of the Brotherhood and others drawn from the Solomon Islands Region.

11 Minutes of the Melanesian Brotherhood Committee held at Tabalia Library on May 9, 1983, with observers from the Community of the Sisters of Melanesia.

12 See the letter from Sister Lily Tetehu in the *Melanesian Brotherhood and Companions Newsletter* of October 1983.

13 The *Newsletter* is undated, but appears to be from 1984.

14 *Melanesian Brotherhood and Companions Newslewtter*, October 1983.

15 *Melanesian Brotherhood and Companions Newsletter*, October 1983.

16 *Melanesian Brotherhood Daily Intercession Scheme*, 1984.

17 He was later succeeded by Bishop Paul Richardson, who also became a Companion.

18 *Spearhead Toktok*, No 5, April 1994.

19 Based in Popondetta, the spelling used by the Government. The Church decided to use a more phonetic spelling – Popondota.

CHAPTER EIGHTEEN

Head Brother John Coleridge Kuvi (from Gela, Solomon Islands) and Brother Nelson Leinga in England in 1993.

Brothers being sent out for Mission by Senior Bishop Lazarus –
St. Simon and St. Jude's Day, 1995.

Papua New Guinea Church Partnership

Registered Charity No. 249446 - Supporting the Anglican Church of PNG

St. Mary Abbots Hall
Vicarage Gate
London, W8 4HN

ANGLICANS
(percentage of population)

Source : National Census - 1990

THE BISHOPS AND THEIR DIOCESES - ACPNG

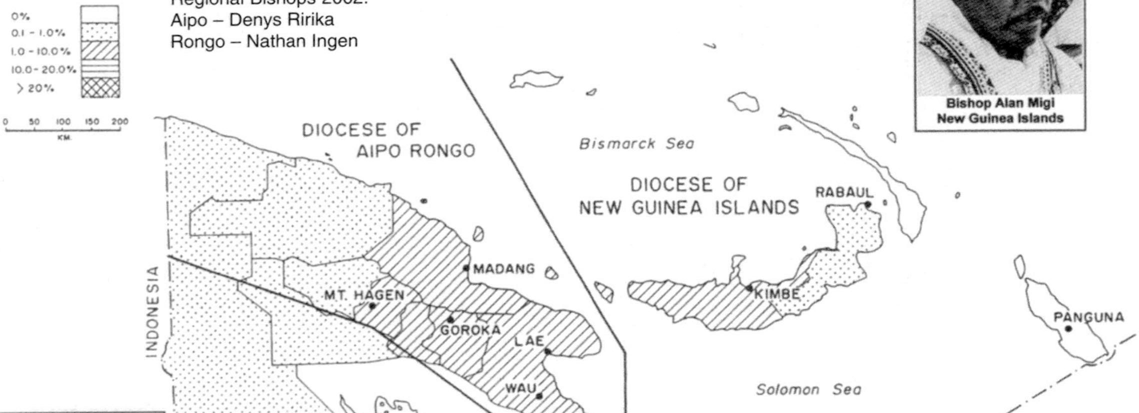

0%
0.1 - 1.0%
1.0 - 10.0%
10.0 - 20.0%
> 20%

0 50 100 150 200 KM.

Regional Bishops 2002:
Aipo – Denys Ririka
Rongo – Nathan Ingen

DIOCESE OF AIPO RONGO

DIOCESE OF NEW GUINEA ISLANDS

DIOCESE OF POPONDOTA

DIOCESE OF DOGURA

DIOCESE OF PORT MORESBY

Bismarck Sea

Solomon Sea

Coral Sea

Torres Strait

INDONESIA

SOLOMON ISLANDS

MADANG
MT. HAGEN
GOROKA
LAE
WAU
RABAUL
KIMBE
PANGUNA
POPONDETTA
PORT MORESBY
DARU
ALOTAU

Bishop Alan Migi
New Guinea Islands

Bp. Reuben Tariambari
Popondota

Retired 2002

Bishop Tevita Talanoa
Dogura

(from Tonga)

Archbishop James Ayong
(Primate) Bp. Aipo Rongo

2002
Bishop Peter Fox
from UK

CHAPTER EIGHTEEN

WIDER STILL AND WIDER

The Society of St Francis had been working since 1972 in Tanzania and had decided to withdraw after fourteen years, but found themselves with over half a dozen aspirants who had been waiting to join the Society, some of them for up to two years. Five were in Masasi Diocese and three in Rovuma Diocese nearby. The United Society for the Propagation of the Gospel passed Fr Brian's name to Brother James Anthony SSF, who had been charged with the task of examining the possibility of setting up an indigenous Brotherhood in Tanzania, with the backing of the Archbishop of Tanzania, John Ramadhani, and the Bishop of Masasi, Richard Norgate. The Archbishop felt that it would be good to start an indigenous community in Masasi Diocese as most of the aspirants came from there. Bishop Norgate, who had known the SSF from the beginning of its work in Dares-Salaam, offered Brother Amos SSF an appointment at the Cathedral and a house for him and Brother James Anthony to live in, as well as some houses for the use of the new Brotherhood and some land for members to cultivate. They began living together as a Brotherhood in May 1986. The aspirants wanted to have a Franciscan spirituality.

However, it was not intended to follow the Constitution of the SSF, and Brother James Anthony sought information about how the Melanesian Brotherhood was organised, and this Fr Brian supplied. Brother James Anthony wrote to him:"I had increasingly felt that our approach was wrong. Now we have the opportunity to try a different way, one which I hope is more attuned to African ways and open to African initiatives."[1] Three miles away from the new house was the African Sisterhood of St Mary, Chama cha Maria Mtakatifu,[2] which it was hoped would be able to encourage the Brotherhood. The SSF supported the new community financially for a year. In an explanatory paper written after initial plans were made, Brother James Anthony wrote: "Various people have suggested that the idea of vows should be reexamined and that the example of the Melanesian Brothers might be followed. There may emerge, of course, some vocations to a life commitment, but this would not be seen as the normal goal of the preparation period. Perhaps there might be a yearly renewal of commitment under the conditions of sharing goods, celibacy and obedience."[3] The idea was that the Bishop of Masasi would be their ultimate superior, and Brother James Anthony only an adviser, visiting them regularly. The aspirants wanted to learn about the word of God and spread the word of God, as they themselves put it. Brother James Anthony commented: "This points to a community with heavy emphasis on the scriptures and on evangelism and teaching." This would require "not only Bible knowledge but a converted heart open to the word itself and the ability to convey that word to others." They planned to build houses and a chapel eventually at Kwitouje. Fr Brian was able to answer Brother James Anthony's questions, and what was planned seemed very close in spirit to the Melanesian Brotherhood. The group was called Chama cha Fransisi Mtakatiku (Community of St Francis). However, a permanent community did not emerge, and the project in Tanzania came to an end.

Brother Geoffrey SSF, as Minister General, had visited Tabalia and had admitted Fr Brian, when Chaplain there, as the first Tertiary Brother of the Third Order SSF in the Solomon Islands. Brother Geoffrey was later given leave to establish, if possible, an African community in Zambia or Zimbabwe, when he had completed his term of office. The intention was to establish a community along the lines of the SSF, but with a specifically African ethos. It was decided to try and establish a community in Zimbabwe. At the time, there seemed to be more of a possibility of white and black Brothers working together in that country than there had been in Tanzania; also financial help from contacts in Hong Kong, Britain – the base of the charity run by the Third Order SSF, Franciscan Aid – and other places could be received and used to help with its establishment. In Tanzania, the emphasis in such a poor country had been to try and be largely self-supporting, and to identify with the poverty of the surrounding population, but this had not proved to be a strong enough foundation for a new community. By 2000, the new African community was established at St Augustine's Mission, Penhalonga, in the Diocese of Manicaland, with five Brothers, three from Zimbabwe and two from Zambia, with the possibility of others joining them.[4] Although, unlike the former community in Tanzania, it did not have 'Franciscan' in its name, it had adopted the title 'Community of the Divine Compassion', a reminder of the Society of the Divine Compassion in East London, England. This English community had come together with other Franciscan groups to form the Society of St Francis in the 1930s. It was only in 1931 that the members of the Society of the Divine Compassion had taken the traditional vows, which included life vows for those elected to them.

After the 1999 Great Conference of the Melanesian Brotherhood, it was planned in the future to establish, if possible, a Household in Canada to help native Canadians establish their own Brotherhood. Developments in the Church of Canada led to severe financial problems and other difficulties, so that the plans for Canada had to be postponed.

In 1989 Fr Brian was approached by the Anglican Consultative Council for an article on the Melanesian Brotherhood for the November 1989 issue of *Anglican Information.*[5] In it he wrote: "Various indigenous communities in other parts of the Anglican Communion have been interested in its Constitution and methods..... The Brotherhood carries on an important tradition, that of evangelists under vows, willing to be sent wherever the need is greatest, and proclaiming the Gospel 'not only with their lips but in their lives.' Could such brotherhoods of evangelists be formed in other parts of the Anglican Communion? Is there also a need for communities of Sisters who take vows for just a period of their lives? I believe these are questions which Church leaders and young people in many parts of the world should be addressing as we enter 1990 and are called by the Bishops to make the next ten years a real Decade of Evangelism, recovering the primacy of evangelism in the life of the Church."

Contacts with the Philippines led to the appointment of Fr Terry Revollido, a priest from the Philippine Independent Church[6] – a body that had broken away from the Roman Catholic Church in 1902 – to the staff at the Bishop Patteson Theological College, Kohimarama. When he returned to the Philippines, links were sustained by an invitation to the Brothers to come to work in that Church's Missionary Diocese of Palawan. Their work there, begun in 1997, led to the opening of a Christian Community Centre, supported by gifts from Melanesia, Canada, Australia, the United Kingdom (including some of the Brotherhood's Companions there) and the charity of the Third Order SSF, Franciscan Aid. Both the Brotherhood itself and the Church of Melanesia contributed, and this was seen as 'partnership in mission' between the Church of Melanesia, the Brotherhood and the Philippine Independent Church (Iglesia Filipina Independiente). The first Filipino Novice was admitted in February, 1999, and it was hoped that the Philippine Independent Church would be able to develop its own religious order, the IFI Christian Missionary Brotherhood, with the help of the Melanesian Brotherhood. In October 1999, Bishop Leon Estrella, Missionary Bishop of Palawan, was admitted as a Companion. However, Mrs Genoveva Torres, Principal of North Palawan Christian Institute had already been admitted as the first Companion there in December 1998.

The Community Centre was opened by the Obispo Maximo (Supreme Bishop) of the Philippine Independent Church, the Most Reverend Tomas Millamena, on August 15, 2000. It was to be a base for a variety of community and church activities initiated or supported by the Brothers, and from it they could go out into the parishes to pursue their wider ministries, including a special healing ministry conducted by Brother Zephaniah.[7] The work was all coordinated by Brother Andrew Letade, in charge of the 'Partnership Mission'. It represented the fulfilment of Brother Ini's belief that one day the Brothers would extend their work beyond the islands of the Pacific to those of South East Asia.

What, however, he had not forseen was the Missions which would be held by the Brothers and Chaplain in New Zealand and England in the 'Millennium Year', 2000. In England they were joined by Sister Doreen CSC, a Melanesian Religious Sister. Chester Diocese, England, had given money for the building of Chester House in Honiara, opened by the Reverend John Bull in 1997. This was one result of the fruitful link with the Province of Melanesia established in 1988 and strongly promoted by Canon Desmond Probets, then Vicar of Timperley, who had been the last European Dean of St Barnabas's Cathedral in Honiara. Chester House is run as a guest house by the Brothers, raising income for the work of the Brotherhood and providing a base for them in Honiara. Their Missions in Chester Diocese in 1993 and in mid-2000 led to the establishment of a strong group of Companions there. So the Brothers' work of evangelism and renewal after seventy five years had circled the world and touched the country where Bishop Steward and Brother Charles Fox had been born, as well as spearheading evangelism in Melanesia. The mission to Chester in 1993, conducted by Head Brother John Coleridge Kuvi and Brother Nelson Leinga, had prepared the way.

The 1990s saw another development which underlined the increasingly international character of the Brotherhood. The former Principal of the Bishop Patteson Theological College, a Canadian priest, Fr John Blyth, after working as an Associate, had decided to join the Brotherhood, and after profession in 1999 went to be the Chaplain and one of the tutors at Tumsisiro on Ambae in Vanuatu for a year, before becoming 'mobile tutor'. Before coming to Melanesia, he had been Dean of Calgary in Canada and then Chaplain of Vancouver School of Theology. He had also worked among Native Canadians.

The Reverend Richard Carter, a teacher who had himself studied and taught at the Theological College at Kohimarama and helped the Brothers and Novices, especially with the development of drama, was invited to become their Chaplain, based at Tabalia, in 1994. He held this office till 2000, and in that year became a Brother himself. He then went to England for the 'Mission' and to study for a further degree during 2000 and 2001, completing his thesis in 2002, while staying at the College of the Resurrection at Mirfield, attached to the Mother House of the Community of the Resurrection. He received his MA from Leeds University in 2002. This was the only theological college left in England run by a Religious Order, as the Society of the Sacred Mission had closed their college at Kelham near Nottingham many years before. Although English by birth, Brother Richard had taken his first degree at the University of Wales at its Aberystwyth campus, where he read English and Drama, and had decided to offer himself for ordination only after teaching at Selwyn College in the Solomon Islands. He was ordained priest at Tabalia in 1992. His father had been a parish priest in England before his retirement. Brother Richard brought great gifts of communication to Melanesia, especially through drama, which the Brothers used effectively in their missions to New Zealand and England in 2000. The Brothers also performed in the Philippines on their way back to the Solomon Islands, from which country all the indigenous Brothers involved in the mission in England had originated. At Mirfield, Brother Richard had joined Brother George Elo from Ysabel, who had come a year earlier to do further study. On his return to the islands in 2002, Brother Richard became the Brotherhood's Coordinator of Mission and Training for all three Regions. In the *Anglican Religious Communities Year Book 2000-2001*[8] he wrote about 'The Meaning of the Vow of Poverty in the Developing World'. The Archbishop of Melanesia had previously described him as "a gift to the Church of Melanesia," a great tribute to a European[9]. Meanwhile at Tabalia, Fr Johnson Bana and a team of Tutors, mostly trained Brothers, were teaching the many Novices. One Tutor, ex-Brother Barnabas Deva from Santa Cruz, had died in 1994, and had been greatly mourned.

By the year 2000 the number of Brothers had risen to about 350 and the number of Novices to 150, making the Brotherhood the largest religious order for men under vows in the Anglican Communion, and the only one almost wholly dedicated to evangelism and revival work. Brothers now took their first vows for four years, but these could be renewed for an indefinite period until a Brother felt called to do other work, or to fulfil duties to his family or home community, or wished to seek marriage or a job – or died while still professed. The average age of a Brother continued to be younger than that in any other religious order for men. The dress had been adapted to working in different situations and different climates, but black was retained as the basic colour for ordinary wear and white for the Eucharist, but always the Medal would be worn with 'uniform' and the appropriate sash usually worn around the waist. Long trousers, socks and shoes were sometimes used in colder climates, but a singlet and shorts or long loincloth would still be used in the bush.

The Solomon Islands had by now become the focus for the nurturing of vocations for four Anglican religious orders.[10] There were similar developments in Papua New Guinea, although the only Anglican religious order for women there was the indigenous Congregation of the Sisters of the Visitation of Our Lady, with eleven professed Sisters in 2000.[11] The Society of the Sacred Mission had returned to theological education by involvement in Newton Theological College, Popondetta. The Brotherhood by 2000 was concentrating its work in the Dioceses of Popondota, Aipo Rongo and Port Moresby,[12] having left its New Guinea Islands headquarters,[13] while the Society of St Francis had work at Popondetta, Dogura, Goroka, Haruro and Lae.[14]

In a paper prepared by the Australian Board of Mission in 2001 it was stated that the Brotherhood was well placed to meet the needs of the changing society in Papua New Guinea and the growing Church. The Brothers were working in some urban areas where there were squatter settlements and much deprivation, unlike the villages where most were subsistence farmers and could be self-sufficient in normal weather conditions. As in Melanesia, it was recognised that one of their greatest gifts was the ministry of music. Their singing drew people to worship! Evangelistic efforts were aimed at people who had let go of active faith, or who had never heard the Gospel. The Brothers wanted to see the development of spiritual vitality in the Church and hoped to take every opportunity to minister the word of God as the Church faced constantly both changes and challenges. Peter Fox, formerly General Secretary of the Melanesian Mission UK, stated that the Brothers "have a particular gift for working in the settlements with those on the 'margins'."[15] He looked forward to working with them when he became Bishop of Port Moresby in 2002, and not just in the capital. A rural mission had been begun at Pivo, three days' walk from Kerema in that diocese, and 83 people were baptised in 1999.[16]

In Vanuatu, by 2001 there were four Brothers at the Regional Headquarters and Novitiate on Ambae, with 76 Novices and aspirants, and an urban household was at work at Luganville on Santo island, with five Brothers, known as 'Canal Household'. A household named after Fr George Sarawia, first Melanesian priest, had been opened in the Diocese of Banks and Torres in the far north of the country.

At the 75th anniversary celebrations in the Solomons at Tabalia, about 6,000 people were present, including four woman Companions from Chester Diocese, representing the fifty or so Companions in Europe. The celebrations were held around the Feast of St Simon and St Jude in 2001, and flags of all the countries where the Brothers were working were flown from a specially constructed flagpost. The Solomon Islands Regional Conference and a traditional land ceremony, to establish the right of the Brotherhood to continue using the land at Tabalia with the agreement of the original landowners, were also conducted.

The influence of the Head Brother and other leaders in the recent period of great development has been very significant. Brother John Kuvi from Gela, Solomon Islands, was Head Brother from 1991 to 1995 and was full of imaginative ideas and plans for progress. He was a roving ambassador for the Brotherhood, who impressed people with his enthusiasm and spiritual joy. He visited the Philippines with Brother Caulton Weris, then Regional Head Brother for the Papua New Guinea Region, and prepared the way for the Brothers' work there. His visit to Chester Diocese with Brother Nelson in 1993 made a deep impression on him and he grew in confidence. He was particularly concerned with encouraging youth groups and youth events, but was also responsible for the ideas of having a new Office Book for the Brotherhood (published in 1997), of building Chester Rest House in Honiara, and of sending Brothers to the College of Higher Education in Honiara to train as teachers. He toured a great deal, and the day to day running of the Brotherhood and the maintaining of its discipline was often left to Brother Robin Lindsay from Papua New Guinea, his Assistant Head Brother, based at Tabalia. A mature, courteous and deeply committed Brother, Robin Lindsay was elected as Regional Head Brother for the Papua New Guinea Region in 1995. In that year Brother John Kuvi became Mission Coordinator and was put in charge of the Brotherhood's Office of Evangelism and Renewal, which operated for a few years.

Many of the wonderful ideas of John Kuvi's time were implemented under the partnership of Head Brother Caulton Weris from Vanuatu and

Assistant Head Brother George Siosi from Makira, Solomon Islands, who were elected in 1995.Brother Caulton was then the longest serving member of the Brotherhood, having served for 25 years. He brought stability and maturity to the work he did, and was honest, humble and wise. He was also methodical and careful about improving the self-sufficiency of the Brotherhood.

During his time as Head Brother, the farm was developed at Tabalia and Chester Rest House was built and equipped to take paying guests and to be a centre for the Brotherhood's mission in Honiara. Money raised was used to assist the Brothers' work in the dioceses of Solomon Islands, where missions were also planned and conducted by Fr Richard Carter and Brother George Elo. Some Brothers studied at the Bishop Patteson Theological College for ordination or as future Brotherhood tutors, and the first to be ordained after studying there was Brother George Elo. The finances and administration of the Brotherhood were run by the Brothers themselves, much of the responsibility being in the competent hands of Brother Leonard Dawea.

Brother George Siosi was an able Assistant Head Brother, and there was real team work as Head Brother Caulton and he worked closely with the Chaplain, Fr Richard, and the Tutor, Fr Johnson Bana from Isabel. The standard of the three-year Novice training rose, and at its heart was a disciplined prayer life. Brother George Siosi went to work in the Philippines in 2000. He and Caulton earned the respect, not only of their fellow Brothers, but of the Bishops and the Church at large, because of the quality and trustworthiness of their leadership and their awareness of the needs of others and their humble approach to their work.

With the election of Harry Gereniu from Malaita in 1999, the Brotherhood had for the first time a Melanesian Head Brother who had completed a sixth form education. He was a graduate of Selwyn College, the Church of Melanesia's secondary school on Guadalcanal. He was only in his second year of vows when elected and was the youngest Head Brother the Brotherhood had ever had. He has had to face the second most difficult period in the history of the Brotherhood, as serious troubles developed on Guadalcanal the very year he was elected. He led the missions with the Chaplain to New Zealand and England in 2000, and expressed the disappointment of people in Melanesia at the cancellation of the Archbishop of Canterbury's visit to Melanesia – presumably because of the 'ethnic tension' there – when the Brothers called on him at Lambeth Palace before returning to Melanesia. He proved to be a good speaker, writer, communicator and administrator. From 1999 to 2001 he was ably assisted by Brother George Basile from Maravovo village, Guadalcanal, as Assistant Head Brother, who was elected after serving three years in the Philippines. In recent years many more men who have had some secondary education have become professed Brothers.

In 2001 Brother George Da'agi from the Reef Islands in the Outer Eastern Solomons was ordained and remained for a while at Tabalia, while Brother Wilson Boe from Maewo, Vanuatu, prepared after his ordination to go to Papua New Guinea to be Chaplain to the Brothers there. Fr Fox Mark had become the Chaplain of the Brotherhood, based at Tabalia, and by 2002 there were 105 Novices at the Mother House.

In Papua New Guinea, the Brothers began new projects. In the Diocese of Popondota, St Christopher's Workshop was being developed and managed by Brother Nelson Kowari, as both the Manager and Instructor. At Lae, an important town on the north east coast, the Brothers were developing a resthouse. Both projects were planned to provide opportunities for Brothers to develop new means of self-sufficiency and to learn and improve skills which would be useful to them and also to the young people who would become involved. The Rest House also provided contacts with people travelling and needing a place to stay, as with Chester House in Honiara. The Brothers also decided to raise chickens and sell them, and to catch and sell fish where that was possible. They also built dinghies in coastal areas and rented them out, and established a new house on the coast at Deboin. All these were signs of life, growth and initiative.

NOTES

1 Letter to the author from Brother James Anthony SSF, April 18, 1986, written from Leicester.

2 Community of St Mary of Nazareth and Calvary.

3 Printed paper prepared by Brother James Anthony SSF for the SSF European Provincial Chapter and for others concerned, April 1986.

4 The Community of the Divine Compassion began at Kambazuma just outside Harare, the capital of Zimbabwe (formerly Rhodesia), with Brother Geoffrey SSF and another priest-brother taking responsibility also for three local churches. However, as the Bishop later had another use for the premises they were occupying, they all moved to Manicaland Diocese, where the Bishop, Elijah Masuko, was an SSF Tertiary (member of the Third Order). The Community of the Divine Compassion was established with a covenant relationship with SSF, but was financially independent. (Information provided by Brother Damian SSF in a letter dated October 13, 2001, when he was Provincial Minister of the First Order European Province, which also included SSF Brothers in Africa. Other information was provided by him in May 2001.)

5 *Anglican Information*, No 57, ACC, London. Fr John Cecil, a Roman Catholic priest on Ambae, Vanuatu, had been inspired in the 1970s by the Melanesian Brotherhood to establish a small Brotherhood there on similar lines. What specially appealed to him was the provision for the renewal of vows every few years, so that Brothers could serve for a number of years and then leave the Brotherhood.

6 Anglicans (Episcopalians) established full communion with the Philippine Independent Church in 1961.

The Philippine Episcopal Church is the Anglican Church there.

7 *Melanesian Brotherhood Partnership Mission,* paper No 1, Vol.1 (IFI, Puerto Princesa City, Palawan, Philippines). Fr Revollido became a Companion on a return visit to Tabalia for the Great Conference in October 1999.

8 Canterbury Press, Norwich, England.

9 Minutes of the Ninth Great Conference of the Melanesian Brotherhood, beginning on October 25, 1999.

10 The Community of the Sisters of the Church made the Solomon Islands a fourth Province of their Community, as it had a larger number of Sisters and Novices than any of its other three Provinces in England, Canada and Australia. Sister Doreen, who had been to work in England, helped in the Brothers' Mission there in the year 2000. She was from the island of Makira in the Solomon Islands. On her return to the Solomons, she was elected as the first Provincial of the new Province in 2001. The CSC planned to continue their social welfare work in Honiara by opening a Christian Care Centre, with the encouragement of the other religious orders. The women seemed to be more willing than the men to take life vows, probably because it gave them security from pressures to marry, and enabled them to serve the Church and people in ways which otherwise might not have been accepted.

11 This had been established by the Community of the Holy Name from Australia as part of their work when in Papua New Guinea, but it did not grow like the CSC or CSM.

12 In 2001, the Reverend Peter Fox, General Secretary of the Melanesian Mission, UK, who had at one time worked in the parish of Gerehu, Port Moresby, was elected Bishop of the Diocese of Port Moresby in the Anglican Church of Papua New Guinea. He had been admitted as a Companion of the Brotherhood at the Melanesian Mission Festival in London in 2000 by the Coordinator of the Companions in the United Kingdom, Fr Brian, and looked forward to working with the Brothers in his Diocese after his consecration on February 24, 2002. He was accompanied to Port Moresby by his wife, Angie, and two younger sons. The Brothers were working in the urban parish of the Holy Trinity, Hohola, Port Moresby.

13 Bishop Walter Siba had offered part of the Christian Training Centre at Popondetta to the Brothers in 1993 as a new Regional Headquarters, according to *Spearhead Toktok*, No 5, April 1994. It did not prove very suitable, being situated in a busy town, and a more rural location at Aiome in the Highlands was identified as the site of a new Regional Headquarters by 2001. By 2002 there were 83 professed Brothers in eighteen households in all five dioceses, four Brothers at Newton College and one assisting at Martyrs Memorial School.

14 Bishop Walter Siba had been consecrated Bishop of Popondota on May 4, 1990, and was a ni-Vanuatu from Pentecost island. His wife Nellie was from Solomon Islands. He had earlier been sent from the Church of Melanesia to be Principal of Newton Theological College and was already known in Papua New Guinea. On leaving Popondota Diocese on his election as Bishop of Ysabel, Solomon Islands, he was returning to the country where he had started his ministry. A Papua New Guinean, Reuben Tariambari, had become Bishop of Popondota by the year 2000. Bishop Tevita Talanoa from Tonga was Bishop of Dogura, having first come to Papua New Guinea as a Franciscan Brother. Archbishop James Ayong from West New Britain was Bishop of Aipo Rongo, and on 11 December 2001 two Assistant Bishops were chosen for that Diocese, Fr Nathan Ingen from Ainong in the Simbai District of Madang Province (the first Highlander to become an Anglican Bishop) and Fr Denys Ririka from Gona in the Oro Province of Papua. Bishop Siba had returned to Vanuatu in 1999 and joined the Faculty of Taloa College, where Anglican as well as Presbyterian clergy had begun to be trained. He left there in October 2001 and died of cancer in North Pentecost on March 1, 2002.

15 Personal communication to the author.

16 A paper produced by Papua New Guinea Church Partnership in England about 2000 also included other news of the Brothers from Papua New Guinea, notably the graduation of two Brothers with qualifications from the Bishop Patteson Theological College in the Solomons. Two other Brothers were completing their training at Newton Theological College and being joined there by others. They were being sponsored there by the Society of the Sacred Mission. A priest-Brother, Alphaeus Tubiara, was serving with the Brothers in the Diocese of Palawan in the Philippines.

CHAPTER NINETEEN

Fr. Richard Carter (Chaplain 1994-2000) & Brother Caulton Weris (Head Brother 1995-1999) at Chester House, Honiara, Solomon Islands.

Brother Caulton being installed as Head Brother by Senior Bishop Lazarus Muna.

Assistant Head Brother George Siosi (on left) being installed with other leaders, 1995, in the Chapel at Tabalia, Solomon Islands.

Brothers and Novices at Tabalia, Solomon Islands, providing a traditional welcome for visitors!

Brothers and Novices playing panpipes and guitar, Tabalia, Solomon Islands.

At work with a tractor!

Kopuria Household, Kolina, Guadalcanal, Solomon Islands with the Brotherhood Chaplain, Fr. Richard Carter, 1998.

On the steps of the Norman Palmer Household near All Saints' Church, Honiara, Solomon Islands.
At the front are (former) Brother Jonathan from the Torres Strait Islands, Australia, and Brother George Pasa from Savo Island, Solomon Islands.

Regional Head Brother, Robert Lindsay Umbude (whose visit to UK with John Septimus was sponsored by the Norwich PNG Link) brings greetings from the Malanesian Brotherhood to the 1996 Day Conference held in Norwich Cathedral in its 900th Anniversary year. Previously Assistant Head Brother, re-appointed again in 2002.

Photo: Luxton

PEOPLE OF PAPUA NEW GUINEA

With acknowledgements to the German Pacific Society, especially the late Dr. F. Steinbauer

Station Cross at Aum – 2 hours walk from Tsendiap.

Altar in the Melanesian Brothers' Chapel at Aum in the Highlands of Papua New Guinea.

Photos: PNGCP Luxton

WELKAM HOME!
The Bishop Elect of Port Moresby, and his family – Fr. Peter, Angie, John & Daniel are greeted at Jacksons Airport by dancers in traditional dress – 7th February 2002.
Also pictured: Vicar General, Fr. Denny Bray Guka and his wife.
Background (left) first Archbishop, David Hand.

Papua New Guinea Church Partnership (UK)

Papua New Guinea Regional Head Brother till 2002 Luke Ikoro at the Strategic Planning Meeting of the Anglican Church in Port Moresby November 1999.

Photo: Mrs. Chris Luxton PNG Church Partnership (UK).

The Franciscan Friary at Hautambu, as well as being a place of peace and prayer, is a thriving farming project, with crops, chickens and cows. The brothers also run a small store, which provides goods for the local people.

Photo: Melanesian Mission UK

The Brotherhood Section Headquarters in the New Guinea Highlands.

A Papua New Guinea Brother 1999.

Photos: Mrs. Chris Luxton PNG Church Partnership (UK).

Head Brother Harry Gereniu with Brother John Blyth, Priest-Brother from Canada working in the Philippines from 2003.

"THE PEOPLE OF MELANESIA ARE IN MY HEART" – Her Majesty The Queen. Archbishop Ellison Pogo received his knighthood at the hands of the Queen herself at Buckingham Palace on March 27th 2001. Lady Roslyn and Bishop Willie Pwaisiho and his wife, Kate, were able to accompany him. Afterwards at a small reception in his honour, Sir Ellison told those friends attending that he felt he was receiving this honour, not just for himself, but on behalf of all those who had struggled for a peaceful solution to the recent conflict on Guadalcanal. He said that the Queen had spoken to him of her real concern for the people whom he represented. "The people of Melanesia are in my heart", she said.

Photo: Melanesian Mission UK

The Reverend Brother George Elo, M.B.H., and others on the beach near Tabalia, Guadalcanal, with Savo Island on the horizon.

Brother George Elo, graduating at Leeds University, England, in 2001

Photos: Barbara Molyneux

Members of the First Order of the Society of St. Francis in 2001, in London at Partnership House, Headquarters of Church Mission Society (CMS) and the United Society for the Propagation of the Gospel (USPG). Brothers Godfrey James, SSF (from Ongtong Java, Solomon Islands) and Brother Gilson Kira SSF (from Papua New Guinea) were in England for a First Order meeting to discuss ministry to the poor.

Photo: PNGCP - C Luxton

The Brothers visiting England in 2000, with Bishop William (Willie) Alaha Pwaisiho, Rector of Gawsworth and Assistant Bishop of Chester, formerly the second Bishop of Malaita, Solomon Islands.

Photo: Barbara Molyneux

Brothers visiting the Roundabout Centre for young people in Birkenhead in the diocese of Chester, England.

Head Brother Harry Gereniu at Lindisfarne (Holy Island), in the north east of England, from whose former monastery Christianity first spread to many areas of England.

Photos: Barbara Molyneux

The Brothers visiting England in 2000 dressed for dancing and singing in the Bishop of Chester's garden, with their panpipes and 'Bamboo Band'.

The Brothers' play being performed in Christchurch, Birkenhead, one of the churches which the Brothers visited during their mission in Chester Diocese in 2000.

Photos: Barbara Molyneux

Flags of the nations with which the Melanesian Brotherhood and its Companions are associated, flying on a special flagpole erected at Tabalia for the 75th Anniversary Celebrations in 2001. *Photos: Barbara Molyneux*

People wearing the Brotherhood Diamond Jubilee T-Shirts standing in front of the 75th Anniversary Board at the Central Headquarters, Tabalia, Solomon Islands.

Customary ceremony with exchange of gifts recognizing the right of the Brotherhood to remain at Tabalia, on Guadalcanal 2001.

The Meditation Chapel near Tabalia.

Photos: Barbara Molyneux

The Brotherhood Flag – borne aloft while Brothers are touring or peace-making.

Photos: Barbara Molyneux

Sister Doreen, C.S.C. Provincial of the new Province of the Community of the Sisters of the Church in Solomon Islands.

THE
ANGLICAN CHURCH
IN THE
PACIFIC
Map prepared for The Australian Board of Missions
by H.E.C. Robinson Pty. Ltd. Sydney — Copyright.
KOREA
JAPAN
Sea of
Japan
East
China
Sea
RIOKIU
IS.
INDIA
CHINA
FORMOSA (TAIWAN)
Tropic
of
BURMA
LAOS
KAINAN
LUZON
THAILAND
PHILIPPINE
ISLANDS
CAMBODIA
VIETNAM
PALAWAN
South
China
Sea
MINDANAO
PALAU
IS.
SABAH
MALAYA
SARAWAK
Celebes
Sea
SUMATRA
Singapore
KALIMANTAN
Halmaher
CELEBES
Buru
Cera
Id.
NEW
GUINEA
INDONESIA
Djakarta
JAVA
TIMOR
Arafura Sea
Sumba
Id.
Christmas
Id.
Cocos Is.
Timor Sea
Darwin
INDIAN
OCEAN
NORTHERN
TERRITORY
WESTERN
Alice
Springs
QUEENSLAND
AUSTRALIA
AUSTRALIA
100°
120°
140°
40°
20°

Melanesian Brotherhood Partnership Mission

Winigit Kiddie School posing with Brothers Andrew, Headbrother Harry and Mrs. Castro – the teacher. Palawan Island, Philippines.

Building starts on the site of the new Christian Missionary Brotherhood of the Philippine Independent Church, supported by the Melanesian Brotherhood.

CHAPTER NINETEEN

DARKNESS AND LIGHT

As the Brothers prepared to celebrate their 75th anniversary, they had unexpectedly to go through a great test. For many years there had been a civil war in the western islands of the Solomons archipelago, the North Solomons Province of Papua New Guinea. At the independence of that country in 1975, Bougainville and Buka the main islands of that Province, had reluctantly agreed to remain as part of the nation, although a movement had arisen seeking secession. A large copper mine had been opened at Panguna on Bougainville island by Conzinc Riotinto, and compensation had been paid to local landowners. The new government was eager to benefit from the mining operation, but increasingly the population of the island turned against it. The tailings were poisoning rivers and fishing grounds, and it was felt that the wealth of the island was being siphoned off for the benefit of others. A 'Bougainville Revolutionary Army' was formed by some inhabitants, and the mine was sabotaged and had to be closed. The Central Government imposed a state of emergency from June 1989 and sent in its army, with Australian backing, and a long campaign ensued, ending with a ceasefire in 1998. People in south-east Bougainville had long connections with people in the Shortland Islands, the most western of the country called Solomon Islands. There were incursions from Bougainville, and goods and arms crossed the border. A Bougainville office was set up in Honiara. Eventually a peace agreement was brokered in 2001 with the help of New Zealanders, giving Bougainville limited autonomy and the opportunity eventually to choose whether to remain in Papua New Guinea or not.

In the Solomon Islands, the happenings in Bougainville affected people in various ways. They showed that armed resistance could work, that local militia could be effective, that increased power in an island province over its own affairs could be achieved, and that 'European' commercial enterprises could be closed down! A large number of Bougainville refugees arrived in Honiara, many of whom were Roman Catholics, and they were looked after by the Roman Catholic Church there; some made contact with Guadalcanal people. Their 'liaison person' was Martin Miriori. As if to mirror these developments in Bougainville, similar things began to happen on the main island of the country across the border, Guadalcanal.[1] On that island there had been for a long time a reaction to all the developments which had taken place on the north coast, to which the capital had been moved from Gela after the Second World War. The airfield liberated from the Japanese and used by the Americans had been developed as the international airport for the country and named 'Henderson Field' after one of the Americans who had fought there. The town of Honiara had grown rapidly, and there had been much development on the Guadalcanal Plains, the most significant area of fertile flat land in the country. On the other side of the island, the Weather Coast, which was difficult of access by land or sea, no such developments were possible, but there was nevertheless resentment that the people there were gaining little benefit from what was happening on their island. Some of them turned to a local leader, Moro, who had started a 'custom' movement in the 1960s. He urged them to go back to following traditional ways. A custom house was built as the physical centre of the movement, and people were urged to discard their 'European' clothing and return to traditional style dress. Moro even offered money to the administration, asking that he and his followers be released from following 'Solomon Islands' law and be allowed to follow their own 'custom' law. The request was refused, and so resentment at the development of their island for others remained.

This feeling began to spread among the general Guadalcanal population after independence in 1978 as more and more people from other islands began to pour into Honiara, the capital. Prominent among these were people from the most populous island, Malaita (Mala). They were often enterprising and resourceful and forceful in character. They provided much of the labour for the development of the oil palm plantations on the Plains, run by SIPL (Solomon Islands Plantations Limited) with the backing of the CDC (Commonwealth Development Corporation), and also for logging companies, small industries, factories, shops, hotels and taxi companies, as well as working in their own businesses. They established settlements in an area about twenty miles east and west of Honiara and beyond. Negotiations with landowners were haphazard, and there was no generally accepted policy about the settlement of people on indigenously-owned land. At independence, there had also been no legislation setting up a capital territory, as had happened in Papua New Guinea. Nor did the Solomon Islands Independence Constitution provide for the return of all alienated customary land to its original indigenous owners, as happened later in Vanuatu at that country's independence. Some Malaitans developed agricultural projects and thus appeared to be competing with local people who wanted to sell their market produce in Honiara. There was also pressure for places in schools, and many Guadalcanal people felt that those and other resources were being unfairly utilised by Malaitan and other 'immigrants' to their island. Early in 1999, Gold Ridge Mine on Guadalcanal was opened to extract the gold deposits which the 16th century Spanish explorers had suspected must be in the mountains of the country, and which may have led to them naming it 'Solomon Islands'. Profits from this gold mine were going to the Australian company responsible for the mining and the Solomon Islands Government, rather than to the development of Guadalcanal – at least, that is how things were perceived.

The simmering resentment was not obvious for years because of apparently good relationships between Guadalcanal and Malaitan people, particularly in the Churches and the central Church institutions, many of which were based on Guadalcanal, either in the capital or along the north coast. There were also many marriages between Malaitans and local people. However, late in 1998 a militant group emerged on Guadalcanal, known unofficially as the 'Guadalcanal Revolutionary Army'. In 1999 they began to call themselves the Island Freedom Fighters, then later changed this to the Isatabu Freedom Movement (IFM). The group demanded compensation of two and a half million Solomon Island dollars for the deaths of 25 people whom they claimed had been murdered over the years by people from Malaita, and also that all the settlers from that island return there. The group used various weapons, including traditional ones, and trained at camps in the bush. They dressed in bits of khaki military uniform or traditional loin cloths made of bark. Many young men joined them, and villagers feared to oppose them. Some of Moro's ideas reappeared: village women were ordered to wear grass skirts and men loin cloths (except on Sundays!). Three key secondary schools in different parts of Guadalcanal soon closed because of intimidation of Malaitan students and staff. Some men began to join the 'movement' and use it as a cover for criminal activities. When the 'army' was strong enough, it moved on the capital, telling all Malaitans around Honiara in a wide area east and west to move and return to their own island or support the IFM. Thus began the great exodus, leading to a situation where, proportionate to its population of 400,000, the Solomon Islands then had more displaced persons than any other country! It is estimated that 20,000 fled. There were as many as eleven Malaitan settlements and villages just around Tabalia, and in three weeks all had been vacated. Some people had to be evacuated by helicopter because they lingered too long. In the midst of all this, respect was shown to the Church of Melanesia institutions – the Melanesian Brotherhood Headquarters, the Theological College next door and Selwyn College at Maravovo, although the two Colleges did close for a while.

At first, there was little resistance by Malaitans, but two workers were killed at SIPL after employees there burned some Guadalcanal houses in retaliation for intimidation suffered. The well-armed police Field Force managed to keep the IFM out of Honiara and also insisted that road-blocks erected by Malaitans on roads into Honiara be removed. Some IFM militants were killed in 1999 in clashes with the police. Some Guadalcanal people in Honiara were targetted and intimidated by Malaitans and, effectively, the capital was closed to all people from the island. A state of emergency was declared. The Commonwealth brought in Mr Sitiveni Rabuka – who had earlier in 1987 led two coups in one year in Fiji! – to act as a mediator. He had gained more power by being elected as Fiji's Prime Minister for a time, and was an ex-general in the Fiji Military Forces. His initiatives, such as they were, were not successful in finding a way to peace. There were demands for compensation from the Guadalcanal people and also from Malaitans, who accused the Isatabu Freedom Movement of swearing at them and calling them 'dog sperm'. Compensations were paid and were associated with a cease-fire.

In all this, the religious orders were respected by both sides, and although road-blocks were erected by the police and Church trucks searched on entering or leaving Honiara, the Brothers and Sisters in 'uniform' were allowed to come and go freely, unlike others. Melanesian Brothers were placed at Selwyn College, and Brothers from Malaita and Guadalcanal continued to live together at Tabalia. Sanctuary was offered there to people fleeing, and the Brothers helped to escort people to safety with whatever belongings they managed to get together.

The economy came to a standstill, tourism ceased, and some of the institutions of other Christian denominations were targetted in various ways. The Prime Minister, Bart Ulufa'alu from Malaita, called it 'Solomon Islands' darkest hour'. His request to Australia for a small task force to defuse the situation was not responded to, partly because the situation in Fiji, where another coup had occurred, overshadowed the situation in Solomon Islands. A General Election in Fiji Islands in 1999 under the rules of the widely approved new Constitution of 1997 had led again to the dominance of the Labour Party. In 1987 it had been led by a Fijian, but in 1999 it was led by an Indo-Fijian, Mahendra Chaudhry. On May 19, 2000, this government was overthrown in a coup led by George Speight, a Fijian of mixed race. Parliament was stormed and its members held hostage for 56 days. On May 29, the army took over and declared martial law. An interim government was established after the hostages were released on July 13. All this was given wide coverage in the international media. The same could not be said of happenings in Solomon Islands.[2]

The displaced Malaitans had by now formed their own military unit, the Malaita Eagle Force (MEF) supported by some Malaitan members of the Royal Solomon Islands Police Force (RSIP) – especially the Police Field Force (PFF). Early in the morning of June 5 there was an MEF operation with the assistance of some Malaitan police, forming the so-called 'Joint operation'. They raided the Central Police Armoury at Rove, Honiara, and with the stolen weapons took over the police stations in Honiara and occupied the capital. Later that day, Andrew Nori, a spokesman for the MEF, demanded the resignation of the Prime Minister and the election of another by Parliament as the conditions for a return to normalcy. The MEF feared that Prime Minister Bart Ulufa'alu was in collusion with the IFM and would not be able to defend Malaitans and others in Honiara from an IFM attack. Ulufa'alu resigned a few days later. Although he himself was from Malaita, some other Malaitans were not satisfied with the actions he had taken.

Under the influence of the MEF, a Western Solomon Islander, Manasseh Sogavere, leader of the Opposition, was elected as Prime Minister by the Parliament, and he formed a new Government. There were discussions both within and outside the Solomons as to whether a coup had taken place or not – but the government had clearly been overthrown by force and the MEF had taken control of the capital. The police were divided in their loyalties. The MEF generally kept Honiara quiet, controlling Malaitan criminal elements where the police had not been able to do so. However, they did demand to be paid by the storekeepers for 'protecting' them. The coup resulted in a mass exodus of expatriates from the country led by Australia, although the British High Commissioner did not agree with his Australian diplomatic colleagues about the need for this and stayed. This exodus caused the conflict on Guadalcanal to affect the whole country, as volunteer teachers, medical workers and other staff suddenly left.

Fighting on the edges of Honiara led to wounding and deaths. Some wounded militants were brought by the Sisters of the Church (whose noviciate was on the Guadalcanal Plains) to the Central Hospital, but there they were attacked and killed. Melanesian Brothers at different times were being asked to act as guards at various places in Honiara, including the house of the Governor-General, the Reverend Sir John Ini Lapli, an Anglican priest and former Premier of Temotu Province. Others continued to be stationed at Selwyn College. The Archbishop of Melanesia, with the agreement of the Bishop of the Central Solomons, whose diocese included much of rural Guadalcanal as well as Gela and Savo, went out into the bush to contact warring parties and try to make peace.

The Head Brother (from Malaita) and Assistant Head Brother (from Guadalcanal) were involved with other Brothers in keeping warring militants apart by coming between them at the risk of their lives. A special section of Brothers had their own Chaplain, Fr Jack Aitorea, a former Franciscan Brother, as they went about their peacemaking and peacekeeping work. Two front lines were set up by the IFM and the MEF in different areas around Honiara, and they faced each other from bunkers at Alligator Creek and White River. The Brothers moved freely back and forth among the combatants, giving pastoral care to the militants, some of whom had been forced to take part against their will. The IFM Command, for example, had kidnapped some men for this very purpose. In some cases, the Brothers urged the militants to go home, and encouraged them not to get involved in rape, torture, the burning of houses, or other acts of violence and destruction. The Brothers were in a very difficult situation, sometimes being accused of siding with one side or the other as they strove to remain neutral, but they continued to minister through their prayers, counselling, use of holy water, and powers of persuasion and example. Harold Keke, leader of militants on the Weather Coast, the southern part of Guadalcanal, captured a Solomon Islands plane at Mbambanakira airstrip in that area. Fortunately the Brothers were able to secure the safe release of the pilot, who was from the Western Province of the country, an area not directly involved in the conflict.

Although over 100 people were known to have been killed in the fighting, the Head Brother believed the number of deaths could easily have been nearer 1,000 overall, as many people could not get to hospital for treatment, or to give birth, and may have died as a result. Killings and deaths in the bush may also have gone unreported. The Franciscan Brothers, with their noviciate in West Guadalcanal, assisted wherever and whenever they could. The return of so many Malaitans to their own island created problems there, especially concerning the use of firearms, but many brought with them skills which had up till then been employed in other parts of the country.

A cease-fire agreed by the warring parties on Guadalcanal on August 2, 2000, was not observed, but negotiations continued under pressure from Australia and New Zealand. The parties met in Townsville, Queensland, with the Archbishop of Melanesia present by special invitation, and the Townsville Peace Agreement was signed on October 15.[3] Although this covered many issues, it was done too quickly and proved difficult to implement in many respects.

The Melanesian Brothers helped organise the two-day peace and reconciliation celebrations in Honiara and its environs about a week after the signing of the Agreement. Both the MEF and the IFM, as well as civilians from Honiara and from other parts of Guadalcanal came together to shake hands and celebrate the peace. This event went largely unrecognised in the international press. Since this act of reconciliation, there has been no major conflict between the Malaita and Guadalcanal militants. Members of the Melanesian Brotherhood were seconded to join teams from the Peace Monitoring Council (PMC) on Guadalcanal and Malaita. Brothers visited villages with PMC workers to try and calm down violent situations in the absence of the police, and to see if they could find any illegal weapons. This co-option by the PMC was not an entirely positive experience for the Brotherhood. The Brothers were taken away from their community life and drawn into the cash-based lifestyle of the PMC. Eventually the Head Brother and the Archbishop of Melanesia, Father of the Brotherhood, withdrew the Brothers from working with the PMC. They decided that any future peacemaking efforts by the Brothers would be through the Church, and that they would not be co-opted by others. Very many Brothers had been used for this operation on Guadalcanal island, including the capital, so that the number of Brothers available for work in other provinces of the country, including Malaita, dropped greatly. Sadly, many of the Brothers involved in the events caused by the 'ethnic tension' were very exhausted by the experience and were released from their vows, and so ceased to be Brothers. However, Bishop Brown of Malaita considered that without the work of the religious communities, the situation could have developed into a Malaita against Guadalcanal ethnic slaughter.

The Townsville Peace Agreement led to new elections[4] and a government led by Sir Allan Kemakeza, a former police officer who had become leader of the People's Alliance Party and Deputy Prime Minister in the Sogavere Government until he was sacked.[5] He was installed by December 2001 as the new Prime Minister – an Anglican and a native of Savo, an island off the coast of Guadalcanal, but culturally and linguistically different from it. For his efforts the Archbishop was subsequently granted a knighthood (KBE), which he received from the Head of State, Her Majesty Queen Elizabeth II, Queen of Solomon Islands, at Buckingham Palace, London, on March 27, 2001.[6] Nineteen Melanesian Brothers and their 'peace' Chaplain, Fr Jack Aitorea, were awarded Solomon Islands medals, which were conferred by the Governor-General on the Brothers on October 28, 2001, at Tabalia during the 75th anniversary celebrations. The citation said that the Melanesian Brothers (*tasiu*) were "very instrumental in restoring peace back on Guadalcanal and had risked their lives.... on the front lines." Two Franciscan Brothers were also honoured.

Dr Terry Brown, the Bishop of Malaita, a Canadian and the only one of the six diocesan bishops of the Anglican Church in the Solomons not a Solomon Islander, wrote on August 29, 2001: "It seems to me the basic problems are not ethnic. The Solomons were a forgotten and neglected corner of the British Empire. Whatever happened, happened with little forethought or planning. Movement of labour, resettlement and 'development' took place with little thought of what might happen 50 years down the road. Unequal development, globalisation, corruption, competing world views (custom, western law, church), isolation, outside influence (Papua New Guinea and Bougainville), Asian economic exploitation (logging and mining) and the rise of local elites all had a part to play. Yet Solomon Islanders remain as honest, loving, intelligent people. However, it has also been an end of naiveté [which is] a blessing."

Helen Newton, a former teacher at Selwyn College, wrote on September 6, 2001: "These very special people [the Anglican Religious Orders] were in the forefront during the ethnic tension, as peace-makers and supporters of the innocent victims.... The Melanesian Brothers, unarmed, passed between the enemy lines and prevented untold bloodshed. Many people have a healthy respect for the Brothers' spiritual power, and fear to cross them[7] .... The Melanesian Sisters [CSM] live at Veranaaso, right in the middle of the Guadalcanal militants' territory. Like the other religious orders, they helped keep the peace during the tension. Now the Townsville Peace Agreement has been signed, they are helping many village women who have been left with nothing – not even clothing for themselves and their children."

The Archbishop of Melanesia made a report[8] to the Primates' Meeting of March 2001, one of the regular meetings of the spiritual heads of the thirty-eight autonomous member Churches of the Anglican Communion. In it, he wrote: "I must pay tribute to the Religious Orders, and particularly to the Melanesian Brotherhood, for their role. They were simply outstanding – the male Orders fearlessly moving from battle line to battle line, placing themselves between the lines, calming your Rambo-style militants, showing no favour except to the Gospel. The female Orders, equally as fearless, gathering the dead, tending the wounded, caring for the women and children. They command the greatest respect of both sides of the struggle – and the nation as a whole."[9] In 2002, he commissioned the Melanesian Brothers to work directly to collect weapons from around the islands from the two opposing rebel groups. The hundreds of weapons collected by the Brothers on both Guadalcanal and Malaita were dumped into the sea.

The Brothers' response to all the disruptions and challenges was to make a significant decision in the Brotherhood Council in 2000. At Tabahao, about a kilometre away from Tabalia up in the bush was the beautiful Church of St Peter, built by a Malaitan. It had been consecrated only in 1996, but in 2000 the place was deserted. The Brothers decided to use it for retreats, away from the bustle of Tabalia and the noise of Kohimarama. It would have its own routine, different from Tabalia. A few Brothers would care for it and keep the place clean, maintaining its spiritual atmosphere and taking care of retreatants. In this way, the Brothers felt they were recovering something of the spiritual life to which they had been called, and to which they wished to recall the Christians of the Solomon Islands and Melanesia as a whole. Those returning from Tabahao village on Guadalcanal established New Tabahao village in North Malaita, which became the centre of a new parish in the Diocese of Malaita.

Bishop Chisholm's idea that the SSF would be mostly involved in urban work and the Melanesian Brotherhood in rural work had not worked out in practice in either Papua New Guinea, Solomon Islands or Vanuatu. The two 'Brotherhoods' were eventually working in both urban and rural situations, although the Melanesian Brotherhood's main emphasis was more evangelistic and rural. They could both be seen as expressions of a basically Franciscan type of Religious Life. The SSF, however, had developed a strong presence in Europe, in all three of its Orders. This made for a rather different ethos, particularly as the SSF included the Community of St Clare as its Second Order of contemplative Sisters. The Melanesian Brotherhood has no equivalent of the Third Order (which can, unlike the other two Orders in SSF, include married people), but many of the Companions of the Melanesian Brotherhood are deeply committed and involved in the Conferences, meetings and support of the Brotherhood in a way which the Companions of SSF are not invited or expected to be. The two 'Brotherhoods' have been able to learn from each other how to be truly international, and also how to be identified with the people and the cultures of the places where they have been called to work. With its *three* Orders, the SSF is the largest of the religious communities in the Anglican Communion and the most widely spread, but by 2000 there were more *Brothers* under the traditional vows (as well as more Novices) in the Melanesian Brotherhood. Both religious communities since their foundation have made significant contributions to living the religious life in community and deepening the Christian lives of those who have joined them, or been influenced by them.

What then are their respective strengths and weaknesses? The Franciscans have had a strong core of priests and lay Brothers under life vows, giving the Society stability. However, taking life vows in the twentieth century became less and less attractive to many, and the number of professed Brothers in Europe began to fall and the average age rose. On the other hand, in the Pacific the Friars tended to be younger. However, the age and background of some of the novices has meant that they have sometimes been immature and not able to adapt to the more European ethos of the SSF. Some have joined in the hope of more education, but have not really wanted to take life vows. Celibacy for life has not attracted many male Melanesians, as the small number of Solomon Islander Roman Catholic clergy shows – in spite of the numbers who have gone for seminary training. A novice needs to have a strong vocation to the Religious Life or he is likely to become passive or stressed, and this can lead to unfortunate results for him and his community. Because of the high number of school leavers in Solomon Islands, there is a tendency for the religious communities to be used as a substitute for missed secondary school or even as a preparation for theological college, rather than as a special form of Christian service with its own way of life. In Papua New Guinea the SSF was involved in urban and rural evangelism and the training of evangelists in St Francis Evangelists Training College from 1963. But the Society of St Francis has had a more academically-based noviciate than that of the Melanesian Brotherhood, and there is a tendency towards following the traditional European monastic forms of prayer, work and study as found in various other religious Orders in its training of new members. These elements of training are also found in the Melanesian Brotherhood, but balanced usually by a stronger emphasis on evangelism and serving the poor, both in urban and rural areas. This has led some people in Solomon Islands to consider the Melanesian Brotherhood sometimes to be more Franciscan in practice than the SSF! It is hard for some of the Franciscan Brothers to face the prospect of a life vow, and many leave before they take it. On the other hand, there has tended to be a small core of Melanesian Brothers who have remained in the Brotherhood for 15 or 20 years or even more, and who have not been under pressure to take a life vow after a certain period as in the First Order of the Society of St Francis. The Melanesian Brotherhood provides literacy training for illiterate Novices from new Christian areas, and has a simpler life style, but the SSF sends some of its Brothers to work in other parts of the world, and has to prepare them for different ways of living. However, the same is beginning to apply increasingly to the Melanesian Brotherhood as well, and a higher standard of education and training is becoming necessary, at least for some. Provision has therefore been made in recent years for further education at the Solomon Islands College of Higher Education (SICHE), especially for Brothers who will work as primary school teachers, and at the University of the South Pacific (USP) Centre in Honiara and the Provincial Theological College at Kohimarama, while opportunities for higher education have also been provided for some Brothers in Papua New Guinea. The result has been more Brothers equipped to teach, both in the Brotherhood and beyond it. Meanwhile the SSF has established more firmly the Third Order which provides both married and single islanders with a special rule of life, and complements the work of the First Order Brothers with their traditional vows.

The Melanesian Brotherhood has sometimes lacked a core of really experienced Brothers, as taking a life vow has been considered a special calling, although some have considered it. There has always been, therefore, the problem of inexperience and sometimes immaturity, and the need for a vigilant discipline in the observance of the vows. However, all this has been largely compensated for by the youthful energy and vitality which has marked the community and enabled the Brothers willingly to undertake tasks which might have been daunting for older men. Above all, young people have been attracted to live part of their lives under the vows of poverty, celibacy and obedience, committed to spreading the Gospel in word and deed, and doing it in a way which respected the cultures of the people among whom they were working. These cultures were often related in some ways to the cultures of the Brothers themselves. Their youth and cultural sensitivity, as well as their overall commitment to the Gospel were – and are – their great strengths. Many ex-Brothers have trained for ordination, especially in the Church of Melanesia. The discipline they learned in the Brotherhood has helped them to cope with the hard work and isolation that parish clergy face in rural Melanesia.

In a new Millennium the Brothers are seeking God's will for the way ahead, rejoicing in his blessing and guidance throughout the Brotherhood's seventy-five years of joyful service and courageous witness to the One True God, Father, Son and Holy Spirit. They are working not only in the South Pacific but have now reached south-east Asia,[10] and in 2001 the Bishop of Exeter[11] invited Brother George Elo to work as a priest for a time in the parish of Tavistock in his diocese in Devon, from which diocese Bishop John Coleridge Patteson had gone to serve in Melanesia. He established a small household there with Brother Leonard Dawea, the first in England, or indeed anywhere outside the Pacific area. In the Brotherhood's 1997 book of *Offices and Prayers* there is a quotation from Bishop Patteson, which the Brothers have chosen to guide them: "The secret of these islands is to live together as equals. Let the people know that you are not divided from them but united in Christ's love." In that spirit, they continue in 'the true way of service'.

NOTES

1 Information on developments in Solomon Islands from 1999 onwards has been taken from personal newsletters, letters to the author and other written and verbal communications. The author is thereby indebted to: Fr Norman Arkwright SM, Solomon Islands; Mr Eddie Nielsen, former Consul for Solomon Islands in the United Kingdom; the Rt Reverend Dr Terry Brown, Bishop of Malaita; the Reverend Brother Richard Carter MBH; Canon Desmond Probets, Companion, Vice-Chairman of the United Kingdom Committee of the Melanesian Mission and Commissary for the Archbishop of Melanesia; the Rt Reverend Peter Fox, Bishop of Port Moresby, Secretary of the Melanesian Mission UK before his consecration and MBH Companion; Mrs Chris Luxton, General Secretary of Papua New Guinea Church Partnership; Brother Harry Gereniu, Head Brother of the Melanesian Brotherhood; the Most Reverend Sir Ellison Pogo, Archbishop of Melanesia; Miss Helen Newton, from Australia, former teacher (for four years) at Selwyn College, where Harry Gereniu, now the Head Brother, was one of her pupils; Mr Alan Waters, British High Commissioner in Solomon Islands for a period up to late 2000; Dr Ruth Savaona-Spriggs from Bougainville, who was involved in the Bougainville peace negotiations, the wife of Professor Matthew Spriggs of the Australian National University, Canberra; and Dr Christian Clerk, former Chairman of the Council of the Pacific Islands Society in the United Kingdom and Ireland. References in printed publications include articles in the *Church Times*, England, in the issues of October 27, 2000, on *Where religious orders are maintaining*

order, by the Reverend Canon John Pinder, MBH Companion, and July 20, 2001, on the Religious Life, by Janet Watts; also in *The Outrigger*, journal of the Pacific Islands Society of the United Kingdom and Ireland, issues No 40, Summer 2000, No 41, Winter 2000/ 2001, and No 42, Summer 2001; *Melanesia News*, No 50, May 2001, Melanesian Mission, England; *Church of Melanesia Newsletter*, No 1, December 2001, Honiara, Solomon Islands; *Anglican World*, 2001, the official magazine of the Anglican Communion, No 104, p.44, London, England, with photograph of the Sisters of the Church in Solomon Islands; *Melanesian Mission Newsletter*, Easter 2002, England.

2 For an account of tensions in Fiji Islands, Solomon Islands, Bougainville and West Papua, see *The Contemporary Pacific, a Journal of Island Affairs*, Vol 13, No 2, Fall 2001, Center for Pacific Islands Studies and University of Hawaii Press.

3 Although praising the Government for the Peace Agreement, many in the 'Civil Society' movement of concerned people, including the Solomon Islands Christian Association (SICA, the National Christian Council) were deeply alarmed when the Government attempted to put off a General Election by changing the country's Constitution. SICA was active in criticising this move and was accused by Prime Minister Sogavere of being 'immoral' and 'unchristian', although himself being a member of the Seventh Day Adventist Church, which had associated itself with SICA since its establishment in the mid-1960s. Some local SDA churches had indeed joined the 'civil society' opposition to the Government. The Anglican Bishops in the Solomons were so scandalised by Mr Sogavere's and others' criticisms of SICA that they issued the 'Church of Melanesia Council of Bishops' Statement on the Present Government's Criticism of the Solomon Islands Christian Association (SICA)', in which they in turn criticised that Government's corrupt economic practices, favouritism, desire for an army, slowness in implementing the agreement, and also the shelling of the Weather Coast of Guadalcanal, risking "the renewal of ethnic conflict" They stated: "Christianity that speaks only to the 'spiritual world' and not to the material world of government and politics is a false and heretical Christianity. SICA is to be commended, not criticised." It was signed by all six Anglican diocesan Bishops from Solomon Islands, and the Bishop of Vanuatu.

4 The elections were not without difficulties. Ezekiel Alabua, a former Prime Minister and a leader on Guadalcanal, had become very autocratic and had not learned the lesson of an attempted assassination by members of his own extended family! He created difficulties in the peace process because of his 'spirituality of martyrdom'. Another militant leader asked for one and a half million Solomon Island dollars to gain his permission for voting to take place in Tommy Chan's Honiara Hotel. Many *tinoni loki* on Guadalcanal ('big men') considered that they should make the decisions and that the people should obey. Many were making money for themselves, trying to get profit out of those they claimed to 'serve'. On Malaita there was an incident at Fourau in the north of the island when armed exmilitants attacked the polling station and threatened to burn it, because the polling officers refused to allow the unauthorised polling agent of the ex-militants' candidate into the voting area. The Bishop of Malaita reported: "Only the presence of a Melanesian Brother saved the day." Although in this case the ex-militants' candidate won by a small margin – and these happenings may have affected the result – polling was mainly peaceful and the international election monitors were generally positive. Mr Sogavere and some other former MPs were re-elected, but there were 31 new MPs elected as well – although a number of them were ex-militants or their supporters.

5 Sir Allan's election as Prime Minister was not greeted with enthusiasm, as his reputation had already been affected by rumours that he had benefitted financially during the troubles, and been involved in questionable dealings concerning compensation. Many people on both sides of the conflict were demanding money, both to reimburse them for losses and to settle disputes, claiming that it was the customary way in Melanesia. 24 million Solomon Island dollars were provided by Taiwan, and the distribution of this was widely seen as having been mismanaged, with some people receiving money to which they were not entitled (including members of the Government and their associates) and some legitimate claimants remaining unpaid. The Bishops' Statement said: "Favouritism in providing funds for lost and damaged properties and various compensations will be quite clear if the government provides a complete public list of all its payouts."

6 The Archbishop stated at a reception held in a hotel in London in his honour after the investiture that "he felt he was receiving this honour not just for himself, but on behalf of all those who had struggled for a peaceful solution to the recent conflict on Guadalcanal." He said that the Queen had spoken to him of her real concern for the people whom he represented. "The people of Melanesia are in my heart," she said.

(*Melanesia News*, No 50)

7 Helen Newton added, significantly: "There is a story told of a militant who died of 'unknown causes' after breaking one of the Brothers' walking sticks."

8 Reprinted in *Melanesia News*, No 50, in full.

9 Difficulties in implementing the Peace Agreement continued after the Archbishop's report. The Solomon Islands College of Higher Education closed temporarily and the students from Selwyn College were taken there to sit their examinations, so that they would not be interrupted or disturbed at Maravovo. On March 8, 2002, a Peace Walk organised by the International Peace Monitoring Team in Honiara attracted so much attention that the Government declared the day a public holiday. It was also the International Women's Day of Prayer, and women were prominent among the ten thousand or so participating. (A much smaller Walk took place in Auki, Malaita.) The Honiara Walk was led by the Sisters of the Church and the Mothers' Union. Tragically, on March 17 New Zealand's Deputy High Commissioner in Solomon Islands, Bridget Nichols, died in her garage in Honiara. She had previously once worked as a very popular volunteer legal adviser to the Western Province, based at Gizo, and was glad when called back to Solomon Islands. A Solomon Island Government enquiry deemed her death an accident, while the New Zealand enquiry declared the cause of her death could not be determined. However, killings continued as rival groups on Guadalcanal turned on each other, and similar events occurred on Malaita. Heinz Schurmann-Zeggel, spokesman on Pacific affairs for Amnesty International, said that the decision to grant amnesties to members of the militias, included in the Townsville Peace Agreement, had left some people thinking they could get away with further violence and murder. There were for a while no-go areas for the Police on the Weather Coast of Guadalcanal and in part of North Malaita. The Guadalcanal Liberation Front led by Harold Keke was not a party to the Agreement, and in August 2002 Keke decided that Fr Augustine Geve, a Roman Catholic Melanesian priest who was MP for South Guadalcanal, should be killed, accusing him of misusing funds intended for the Weather Coast people. Soon after, it was claimed that a deacon of the Seventh Day Adventist Church had been beheaded on the Weather Coast. The Prime Minister's office and the Treasury were surrounded with barbed wire and constantly guarded against armed intruders, and economic activity in many areas ceased or was severely restricted, while the Solomon Islands dollar suffered repeated devaluation. Government teachers, hospital cooks and other workers were not paid, or paid after long delays, and there were strikes. Students wishing to continue their studies for the University of the South Pacific were unable to do so. However, the Melanesian Brothers were able to arrange in 2002 for a reconciliation service for the Police, much to the amazement of advisers from overseas. Different members of the Police were able to apologise to one another for actions which had divided the Force. During 2002 the Brothers continued to collect and dispose of weapons, including those taken or distributed illegally by the Police.

10 The Brothers in the Philippines had admitted their first Novice, Alijandro Garcia Jnr, in February 1999 and were preparing some aspirants for admission to the new IFI Christian Missionary Brotherhood, the building of whose new Noviciate house had begun in early 2001 on land donated by a Filipino supporter. Brother Andrew Letade said it would be named 'Macdonald-Milne House', as Fr Brian was the trustee of the Third Order 'Franciscan Aid' charity responsible for projects supported in East Asia and the Pacific, and he had also been Chaplain of the Melanesian Brotherhood. In this way the Brothers graciously wanted to associate him with the new Brotherhood as well.

11 Bishop Michael Langrish and his wife Esther became Companions, so did a large number in Tavistock Parish. He also succeeded Barry Rogerson, Bishop of Bristol, as Chairman of Melanesian Mission UK.

CHAPTER TWENTY

TRANSFORMING MISSIONARIES

Reflections on the Missionary Calling of the Brotherhood by Brother Richard Carter MBH, Chaplain of the Brotherhood.

In the centre of the City of Chester in June 2000, a member of the Melanesian Brotherhood, in his black uniform and white sash, was asked by a passerby: "What are you doing in the UK? Are you a sports club or a music group?"

"No," he replied, "I am a missionary."

There was an awkward silence, for the word 'missionary' for many people carries a lot of negative associations: indoctrination, exploitation, moral condemnation, the destruction of indigenous cultures, the forceful sale of European civilisations, men and women who crossed continents in the name of God but who left behind the very conditions in which material interest would flourish. And today, new associations of door to door evangelists disturbing us with what seem like fanatical or miserable creeds preying on the vulnerable. Where did this young black Melanesian fit into this whole picture? And yet for the Melanesian Brother there was a wholly different perception of the word 'missionary'. For him the word 'missionary' linked him with that wonderful heritage and story of which this book has shown us a part: men like Bishops Selwyn and Patteson, Ini Kopuria and the Brothers, of whom he had heard stories since he was a child, men who had been empowered by the Gospel and who in bold humility had tried to live out that Gospel in the way of Jesus Christ, "to make God's loving plan for all people come true." This was a heritage of which he felt justly proud, for just as his own life had been inspired and formed by that vision of Christ-like service, so his own ministry and outreach witnessed to the working of the same Spirit.

The man in Chester High Street laughed. "You're a missionary? I suppose we need missionaries too these days in England!" he said, as if nothing could be more absurd. Yet is it absurd? Or is it possible that never before has the Church needed missionaries so much? If this is the case, we need to discover not only how mission can transform, but how mission must transform the missionary. Can these Melanesian Brothers help us to see again what it means to be a follower of Christ?

L111

I first came across the Melanesian Brotherhood in 1987. It was September 20th and the Feast Day of Bishop John Coleridge Patteson held at Kohimarama, the Theological College on Guadalcanal. It was the neighbouring community – the Melanesian Brotherhood – who led the singing. I can remember my first impression of them vividly: the vibrancy and energy of their voices, the *tete* seed rattles and bamboo drum keeping the urgent rhythm, and the tune and roaring harmonies which rose and twisted and swooped like a frigate bird. It is a quality of singing that remains quite unique and is very much an expression of this community. They sat together dressed in the white uniforms they wear for the Eucharist, white shirt and *lavalava* (a long loincloth), the black and white sash for the Brothers and the red sash for the Novices, clean, prepared, shining.[1] My impression then of this community's solidarity, joy, commitment and faith, has never left me, although I have now been working with the Brotherhood for a number of years and have had ample opportunity to see the struggles and difficulties the community also faces.

After the service was over, I went down to the Melanesian Brotherhood's Headquarters at Tabalia, for it is situated literally side by side with Bishop Patteson Theological College, and in fact provided the land on which the College is built. I remember that the Brothers who showed me round told me the story of their Mother House with great respect and reverence. To me, a newcomer, it was a simple set of buildings positioned around a grass square, some of them leaf roofed, some of them using corrugated iron.

Poverty of Spirit

In countries where there is often very little chance of formal education above primary school, many of those attracted to the religious life may initially be so because it provides opportunity and a way out of the village. The Brothers are seen to live a radical and exciting life style, and becoming a Brother provides a young man with the chance of three years of training, the chance to travel to different islands (and perhaps even to carry out mission overseas) and also to win a deal of respect from the local community. Less than one third of those joining the Brotherhood at this time have had any secondary education. The waiting lists to join the community are full: each year there is only space enough to select 30 to 40 Novices; many more that that apply each year.[2] Yet those joining the community know that it will not be an easy lifestyle; those who join simply for self-advancement, and do not grow beyond that stage, do not stay long.

Within the Melanesian Brotherhood there is a simplicity of life style.

They have few possessions or luxuries. They are not seen by the outside world to be working for profit. Within their own community resources are limited. More than forty Novices, for example, share each humid dormitory, sleeping on mats. They have no shoes, no watches. Most can fit their possessions into one bag. The community eats twice a day, root crops and some vegetables. Sometimes there is a little fish. In the bush areas they can usually find fruit, and always there are coconuts. At times there will be feast days when pigs will be killed and major fishing expeditions will go out, and then there will be plenty; at other times, when the floods and the rain come, there may be only sweet potatoes or even nothing. The Brotherhood aims to take special care of any guest who arrives at the community; the Brothers will therefore hold back to make sure all are properly fed before them. Portions are divided and divided again as guests arrive; often you will notice those who quietly go without, and this is done with no obvious complaint. The community are not advocating deprivation, neither are they glorying in a spirit of fasting. When there is plenty, they will eat as if there were no tomorrow. Yet the Brothers will tell you there is freedom in this way of life, this lack of grasping, a freedom to accept what the day provides, and to embrace both the feast and the famine. The Head Brother said to me: "It is good that sometimes I learn to go without; we cannot always have what we want, and this way I learn to appreciate what I do have." It can also lead to a greater awareness of the needs of others.[3]

There is a very real dependence upon God at the heart of this Brotherhood life style. It is connected in a very holistic way to God and to the community. The vow brings deep awareness of God in all things. There is an awareness of dependence on God in the storms, floods and cyclones which can so easily destroy the people's livelihood and homes. There is a deep awareness of God as Brothers set off by canoe for other islands or to fish in rough seas. There are prayers at times of planting and harvesting, for in a very direct way God is connected with the food that they will eat, for when the harvest fails they know what it means to go without. In this context the phrase in the Lord's Prayer, translated in Melanesia as, "Give us this day our food for today", becomes a radical expression of the need for God's providential care. There is faith too as a Brother with little formal education gets up to preach in a church, or teach in a school, or kneel down at the bed of the sick to pray for healing. The very work of the Brothers as missionaries enables and gives confidence, so that shared gifts and talents can grow. This cannot be described simply in terms of individual development: the Brothers and Sisters believe that they are doing the work of God, and put their trust in their belief that what God has commanded he will also empower.[4]

This vow of poverty, which all Brothers take, can lead to a new way of seeing and living, a new scale of values. In a youth culture which is increasingly drawing young people away from traditional life styles in search of work, cash and the new values of fashion, alcohol, freer sexual relationships, money and life centred around the townships and the capital, taking vows of poverty, chastity and obedience is a commitment to a very different set of values. Becoming part of a community, which is a mix of tribal groups, also challenges the prejudice and '*wantok* system'[5] which has led to division and mistrust between the different island groups. The decision to become a Brother affects the whole orientation of a person's life. It is a vocation which, although one may embark on it lightly, will ultimately involve personal struggle and the need for personal conversion, if one is to remain true to the spirit of this calling. This decision involves the whole person, the centre of his life. Archbishop Romero of El Salvador captures the meaning of this spiritual poverty and the change it brings:

> Blessed are the poor, for yours is the kingdom of God. You are the most able to understand what those do not understand who are on their knees before the false idols and who trust in them. You that do not have idols and do not trust in them because you have no money or power, you that are deprived of everything, the poorer you are the more you possess the kingdom of heaven, provided that you truly live that spirituality. The poverty that Jesus Christ dignifies is not simply a material poverty – not simply having nothing; that is bad. It is a poverty that awakens consciousness, a poverty that accepts the cross and sacrifice, not out of conformity, but because it knows that it is the will of God.[6]

Poverty of the spirit does not justify the poverty of real deprivation and must be distinguished from what Gutiérrez calls this 'poverty of death'.[7] Such poverty in Melanesia may mean landlessness, precarious housing, lack (or contamination) of water supply, disease, malaria and sickness, little access to education, hunger at times of crop failure, and vulnerability to natural disasters like flood and cyclone. Such poverty is poverty without choice; it is trapped existence from which there seems no escape or hope of transformation. It is a situation wholly contrary to the will of God. Within the Brotherhood itself, the Brothers will experience at times the darkness of that deprivation; they will share the struggles of the local community. They will know the fear of sickness and poor nutrition in the remote areas they are called to serve. They will also live the frustrations of poverty: no access to transportation; lack of resources to get things changed; requests for repairs, building and community projects ignored and turned down; land and new gardens destroyed by flooding after weeks of work. They will at times feel powerlessness, having no cash to implement solutions or alleviate need.

Poverty of the spirit stands both in opposition to such poverty, but also in solidarity with those who suffer: "It assumes voluntarily and out of love the condition of the needy of the world in order to bear witness to the evil it represents and to spiritual freedom before possessions."[8] The Brother has no material advantage over those he has been sent to serve, no layer of financial protection; the work he will do or not do in the towns and villages will depend in a very direct way on his faith and his ability to help and inspire the cooperation of the people. It is a mission not of handouts but of being present. His life in the general community will involve commitment to neighbour, a commitment that acknowledges that the Christian stands where Christ stands and is found where Christ was found, among those in greatest need. Hans-Rüdi Weber wrote:

> We must go beyond human justice to something even deeper, something for which it is difficult to find the right word. One may call it 'divine justice', 'the victory of the cause of God', 'shalom', or simply 'love'.... It does not cancel out either compassionate service or the struggle for justice even when the sources of human compassion have dried up, and to stay involved in the struggle for justice even when our human hopes for success have been shattered. This spirituality.... usually means self-sacrifice.[9]

The Message of the Gospel is Inculturated

In earlier missionary models it was the Western (white) missionary who either initiated and organised, or benevolently supervised, the way in which the encounter between the Christian faith and the local community was to take place.[10] This process may have accomodated or adapted to the local situation, but it was still one-sided and it was the Western missionary who set the agenda. The structure of the Church, even when it became 'independent', meant that within the Church itself, it was usually seen as the task of the Bishops and Church leadership to set the agenda.

The inculturation of the Christian message within the life of the Melanesian Brotherhood and other local religious communities has meant that the agenda and methods for achieving them could come from Melanesians themselves. Such a shift has freed talents and skills which are possessed by the community, and which have often remained dormant if the agenda or a programme is imposed from above. When organisation is couched in Western terms and involves unfamiliar administrative processes, the local community often fails to engage. There is a failure to realise that the community skills that many people possess as a natural part of their cultural heritage, may be the very skills required for Christian mission. When the indigenous missionary is able to inculturate the mission, people begin to realise that "the Word of God belongs to them."[11]

Another problem which prevents inculturation is that the culture often sees its own forms and expression as inauthentic or unworthy.[12] They believe that the Western forms of worship they have adopted have more power. There has been great difficulty, for example, in encouraging the local community to adopt the Pidgin Bible as opposed to the English translation, the argument being that the Word in a language they could understand had lost its dignity and mystery. The Melanesian Brotherhood and other religious orders have been very instrumental in encouraging the process of inculturation to take place. Inculturation is often the by-product of an involvement with the people rather than a conscious target of a programme of action. The Melanesian missionary orders have been able to break through this cultural prejudice by revealing for all to see, hear and witness, that the local culture has a great power and beauty to express the nature of God in its own forms. Within the church itself drums and conch shells can replace bells as a call to prayer; processions can be led by panpipes; local custom tunes, rhythms and chants can bring new life to liturgy. Custom dancing has entered the church as an expression of thanksgiving. God begins to speak the language of the people. Once the power and vitality of indigenous culture has been released, few would question its authenticity.

Yet this inculturation also extends far beyond the church building, so that the boundaries of the Christian faith can become inclusive of the lives people actually live. This is a 'double process'. "There is at once inculturation of Christianity and Christianisation of culture."[13] The process of the Christianisation of the culture is often problematic. Sometimes this process is achieved without conflict; in Melanesia, Christianity can enter deeply into any of the rites of passage of the community, so that childbirth, planting, fishing, hunting, celebrating, choosing leaders, sickness and death, can all become Christian occasions for prayer and blessing. If the missionary does not make the move to inculturate, then the Gospel can easily become confined to the mission station. If, on the other hand, the Christian message merges so completely into a culture that it loses its own identity, then the Gospel does not reach the people either, or the Gospel becomes simply a superstitious or cult practice. David Bosch in *Transforming Mission* wrote:

> Inculturation does not mean that culture is to be destroyed and something new built up on its ruins; neither, however, does it suggest that a particular culture is merely to be endorsed in its present form.... The philosophy that 'anything goes' as long as it seems to make sense to people can be catastrophic.... In a very real sense the Gospel is foreign to every culture.[14]

The Gospel will then, at times, come into conflict with the culture and must seek to maintain its prophetic voice. While the indigenous catechist or priest may have an empathy and understanding of the culture with which he is involved, he may find it far more difficult to act with impartiality, or be able to disentangle his own Christian response from his cultural loyalties. In a community, the priest or catechist will deeply fear offending that community and being rejected or alienated by it. This problem is very common. There are many issues in Melanesia, for example, where the Christian faith stands in stark contrast to culture: the whole concept of 'pay back', in which the victim takes revenge for a wrong done; violence towards women as a form of punishment; aspects of the tradition of paying 'bride price'; belief in magic; the use of curses and ancestral places of worship; the destruction of the environment; ethnic prejudice. These and many other issues may all lead a missionary into direct conflict with his community. Often the priest or missionary will simply remain silent rather than risk alienation from the community. The advantage of the indigenous missionary being part of a religious community, a Brotherhood or Sisterhood, is that he or she will have their own community to help them discern the Christian response, and to offer solidarity and support if there should be conflict in maintaining that response. The community will also represent a wide cross section of the islands, and not be confined to one ethnic perspective. This has been very obvious in a number of important social issues; it is the religious communities and the Mothers' Union who have consistently spoken out against domestic violence, for example. They have confronted very directly the use of magic or poison which still creates fear within the islands, a process the Brotherhood calls 'clearance'. It was also the religious communities who were brave enough to continue to speak out against inter-island ethnic tension and to oppose ethnic violence in a very tangible way.... They have also helped bring the issues of AIDS and Street Children on to the Church agenda.

It is Mission for Community by Community

Western evangelistic missionary approaches have often focused on the conversion of the individual in their preaching; they have constantly stressed the need for a 'personal relationship' with Christ. Gutiérrez warns against what he claims can become 'the privatisation of spirituality'.[15] This approach, he claims, has cultivated individualistic values as a way to personal perfection and isolated this exclusive group from the needs and struggles of the whole community. The new Churches which have been formed in the last ten years in Solomon Islands – Rhema Family Church, The Church of the Nazarene, the Church of the Living Word – have followed this approach.[16] The result has been to divide villages, parishes and communities throughout the islands. They have stressed a holiness code in which the individual convert is rebaptised, separates himself or herself from the rest of the community, claiming that they have now entered into a true relationship with Christ. Such a missionary approach has naturally given rise to great animosity. The missionary method of the Melanesian Brotherhood has always been aimed at the whole community. The chief of Surapau village describes this process:

> Luluwai, the chief of Surapau village, is complaining. He has heard that some people want the Brotherhood's household on his land to move to a different place. "If they want to move the Brothers, they'll have to cut my neck first," he says. "I'll go back to my heathen ways and so will the whole village," he threatens. When the South Sea Evangelical Missionaries came, they came only once and then went away. "I don't want to join a Church which comes and runs away," says Luluwai. "When the Brothers came they stayed with us, they cast out the devils and ancestral spirits and built their household. We helped them. I gave them the land to build their house." Luluwai says that before the Brothers brought the Church there used to be much fear. "If there was a problem, like you broke a custom, if you didn't sacrifice a pig, the devils would take revenge and kill one of

his children and bring sickness. Now problems can be settled in the Church. We have forgiveness. This time we are not frightened to welcome strangers. Those devils and spirits from before have no power now."[17]

The approach is to respect and include the existing community structures. In a village which already has a church, then that church and its leaders must be respected. Mission is carried out in a spirit of ecumenism. If the missionary concentrates on the individual and manages to convert him or her, he makes that person an outcast from the rest of the community, outside the structures of that community, but mission to the whole community means that the missionary is able to respect the whole group, dialogue and share with the whole group, not aiming to break that unity but to use it and transform it in the knowledge of Christ.[18]

Not only does the Melanesian Brotherhood aim to go *to* the whole community, but to go *as* community. In this the missionary acknowledges his or her own need for solidarity and dependence upon the combined gifts of the group. An often repeated Solomon Islands proverb is that one piece of firewood cannot make a fire; many pieces are needed to make the fire burn. A community acknowledges that talents are not in competition with one another, but are there to be shared. A community is full of diverse talents. Once these are offered to the whole group without the need to compete, there is so much more to offer to and appreciate in others: some may have gifts of preaching, others of music, of teaching, of planting, of fishing, of building, of organising, etc. A community evangelised by a community frees very exciting reciprocal possibilities. The mission witnesses to unity, not just in word but by its very being; it witnesses to the sharing of gifts, it can become a work force, a performing group, a worshipping community. The Brotherhood's missions have in the last ten years grown to include as many as fifty Brothers and Novices, especially during the Christmas period. The host community must request and invite the mission, and this activates a whole process of preparation which is in itself community building. Gardens will be prepared to feed the missionary influx, accomodation arranged, also transport and welcome. In a large scale mission such as this the Brothers would usually aim to stay about three days in each village before moving on to the next one. In the time spent with each community, there would be community prayer, there would be entertainment with reciprocal dancing and singing by the missionary group and the host community. There would also be shared meals and shared work sessions on a community project. The Brothers would share in all aspects of preparation with their hosts, fishing, gardening, food preparation. Eating together with the host community would also be a vital part of this process of growing intimacy and sharing. Often at the end of a mission then whole village will sit down together to share food and speeches.

During their time in the village they would also aim to divide up in order to visit every home, especially concentrating on the elderly, the sick and those who had special needs or asked for help with family or marriage problems. Such visits would always be focused around listening and prayer. The Brothers are much requested by the people because so many people are not looking for judgement or even advice; they are looking for someone simply to accept them in love and to intercede on their behalf to God. The Brothers' work is to vocalise simply and in faith the prayer of those most in need. This may sound a simple method, but even in the West it is acceptance, presence and prayer for which many people are longing, and this can bring deep hope and healing.

The Missionary Expresses His Love in Giving

Erich Fromm in *The Art of Loving* wrote: "The most important sphere of giving is not of material things but lies in the specifically human realm…. he gives that which is alive in him: he gives his joy, his interest, his understanding, he gives of his knowledge, of his humour, of his sadness – of all expressions and manifestations of that which is alive in him…. he enhances his own sense of aliveness. He does not give in order to receive, but giving itself is an exquisite joy."[19] There are many forms of giving. One of these is welcoming others. The following describes a typical feast day:

> Tabalia is preparing for the Brotherhood feast day of St Simon and St Jude. For two weeks people have been arriving from every part of the Solomons to join the celebration. The Brothers and Novices have vacated their rooms and dormitories; these will be for their visitors, and they themselves will sleep anywhere they can find – verandahs, sheds, even down at the piggery. More than 5,000 people will arrive in time for the weekend of the feast day. The taps dry up. No one complains. Water is carried half a mile from the river. No one is bossing, no one is shouting; there is an atmosphere of joy and celebration. The community is working together with a harmony that remains a mystery to the overseas guests. No

one pays, no one is quite sure where it has all come from, or who is feeding whom, but like the feeding of the 5,000, again and again there is enough for everybody. It is the miracle of reciprocity.[20]

Another form of giving is a generosity of time. A missionary approach which focuses obsessively on the organisation of every moment of time, and fails to respond to the needs of people, alienates the people. A mark of a transformed missionary approach is that it depends upon people, and making time for their needs rather than assuming that people must make time for them.

The Western world has sadly lost the meaning of this, where often every moment, including leisure time, must be planned and made accountable. In the developing world, people and relationships are nearly always more important than one's own plans and programmes. Part of the life of poverty will be being open and ready for others when they come, however inconvenient, and being willing to respond to others' needs.

> An old woman arrives at our community claiming that someone has harvested her garden and stolen her produce; she asks that the Brothers pray that the thief will be caught. Instead a group of Brothers go with her to make a new garden. Wherever you walk or work or pray, there are people willing to walk, work or pray with you. Is not this a need everywhere in the world?[21]

Giving is also reciprocal. The missionary is supported by the local community. All these religious communities have local supporters, associates or 'companions' who promise to support the communities financially, in prayer and in kind. If this support is not forthcoming, they know that the community will go without and suffer. It has encouraged local people to take a very real interest in their support. To deprive someone of the ability to share and be generous is one of the greatest forms of deprivation in our modern society. When Jesus said that it was better to give than to receive, he was not expressing a moral code but a simple truth. By realising that the missionary needs the support of the people, the poorest of villages themselves can become the hosts. The greatest generosity and joy is often found at the homes of those who have least, for all need an opportunity to give, and one of the greatest deprivations is surely to feel ashamed to offer, for fear that it will not be fit. Families will talk with joy about the way the Brothers or Sisters came and visited them or stayed with them, and often there is a real sense that this visiting, this sharing, has brought a touch of Christ.[22]

There is Creativity

The missionary approach, while living out its tradition, must always be responsive to all forms of creativity – drama, art, music, dance, building, gardening, carpentry, carving, comedy, the beauty of place and environment. It must encourage the full release of the potential of all involved. It should in this way encourage experimentation with no fear of failure, and yet, at the same time, aim to express with quality and with truthfulness the themes with which it is involved. Creativity is one of the most essential paths to conversion. Within the Melanesian Brotherhood dance and drama and music have become a vital part of the liturgy, and thus liturgy can be expressed, not in the voice of another culture, but with one's own voice and the instruments of one's own people. In drama, parable, story, dance and music, the story of Christ can become the people's own story and the hero become one of them. In creative mission the players are pulled into the event. A time past can become their own and the response to that story can become a decision for the present. To give two examples:

> Nifololi is one of the chain of islands which includes Nukapu, where Bishop Patteson died 125 years ago…. That night we performed the Bishop Patteson Drama on the sand in the middle of the village, set against a background of stars, coconut trees and sea, with the islands in the distance. It was lit by Tilley lamps, and the final scene by flaming torches of coconut husk with the wind blowing clouds of red burning ash into the air. It was real drama for this was their history that we were acting out, and their story that we were performing. Afterwards the chief of the village spoke. "We have heard this story many times before, but tonight for the first time we have seen it with our own eyes."[23]
>
> A new Bishop is being consecrated at Tulagi. The Brothers are leading the worship. The Gloria becomes a hymn of Melanesian praise. The Brothers are wearing custom dress, and as they sing, they dance, and the liturgy lives within the culture. As they weave backwards and forwards in this powerful dance, with the carved frigate birds in their hands, circling and diving, the whole chapel echoes with drums, rattles and the roaring harmony of their voices, and it seems that even the stones on the ground will start to dance and sing.[24]

In the Melanesian Brotherhood's missions, drama has also played a vital part, for it crosses barriers and expresses truths in many-sided ways which teaching finds hard to encompass. Drama as a method for mission can lead people to a new stance towards their lives, requiring that they question what they see; at its best it can cut across stereotypes and prejudice and constantly require that the spectator respond. In good drama the audience are not given a message, but they can discover new meaning for themselves. It has particular relevance in a culture where there is not high adult literacy and where the Christian teaching may sometimes seem too abstract and obscure. Drama has great power to lead people to deep questioning and transformation.

A dramatisation of *The Good Samaritan*, for example was performed around Guadalcanal at the end of the 20th century during the period of ethnic violence on that island. As it was played in the villages, with the militants standing around with guns, the parable confronted them with a Malaitan, their enemy, beaten up by militants and left dying on the road; they witnessed the priest walking by and refusing to get involved, and then the Government military in pursuit of the militants but refusing to stop, and then an old man from their own tribe, speaking the home language of the audience, hearing cries in a different language, the language of his enemy, stopping, bending down, gently cleaning away the blood and binding the wounds, then picking up the Malaitan and carrying him to safety. There was total silence, a deathly silence, when you know a whole huge crowd is listening to every sound, a tension so great that one feared the audience might suddenly attack the actors, and one no longer knew whether they saw the Good Samaritan as saviour or traitor. "Which of these was a true neighbour?" Some of the audience began to sob. The militants who were watching stayed until the end and then quietly disappeared into the night, perhaps carrying this parable with them. It touched the wound of ethnic hatred and cried out for a similar healing, and it was only the audience who could make that possible. It was a time when moralistic teaching would never have been heard, but the parable, as story and action, slipped past their defences.

How much the Church needs to restore drama and true creativity to its worship in this way, to challenge with sight and sound, to bring new energy and life, not dragging behind culture in a hopeless attempt to keep up with fashion, but challenging its congregations to see with new eyes the world in which its people live and move and have their being! I remember clearly the first day that the Brotherhood brought dancing into the church. We had been preparing a Passion drama and were rehearsing Christ's triumphant entry into Jerusalem using Passion, the Brotherhood donkey. The procession was full of joy; children had joined the Brothers waving huge palm branches and running at the side of the Christ figure on the donkey. The donkey was followed by Brothers dancing with drums beating. Then Bishop Willie Pwa'isiho who was watching our rehearsal called out for us to bring this procession all the way into the church. Everyone stopped. "No, don't stop," he commanded, "let the dancing continue all the way up the aisle." This was then to become part of the Palm Sunday liturgy, and later, dancing and drama were to find a place in the church for the Melanesian Brotherhood at the major celebrations, especially Christmas, Holy Week and Easter. The most famous of these dramatisations is perhaps the *Passion of Our Lord* which we have performed every four years at St Barnabas Cathedral and at Tabalia, attracting crowds as large as 5,000. The drama moves from a location to the place of crucifixion on top of a hill, persuaded by this huge crowd, who are both spectators and participants in this death of Christ. At Christmas a Nativity, which includes the donkey, goats and always a real baby, chosen from each village visited, has been played by the Brothers, with the Sisters, in every part of the Solomons. We have even created the stable in the sanctuary of the Cathedral itself, complete with the donkey. It is a chance for people to see with their own eyes that Christ came into all of our lives in this way, and that the stable is really no different from their own sago-palm custom kitchens and outhouses.

Drama has become an integral part of the Holy Week and Easter Liturgy. The Easter Vigil itself has become very special. A Brother rubs sticks to light the new fire. This small ember of fire is placed in a ball of tinder, held up by a Brother between coconut husks and blown into a globe of fire in the darkness; like God creating the world in the palm of his hand. The Paschal Candle is lit, and then the candles of all who have come to celebrate the resurrection. The procession leads up the hill to Tabalia, and as it goes, flaming torches are lit by the wayside so that the road becomes a flaming pathway as the Brothers sing, 'Thine be the glory'. It is a moment of wonderful celebration, in which all witness that 'Christ the Light of the World' is 'risen indeed'! The Church in the West needs to rediscover the miraculous. How can the missionary make the Church fundamentally necessary to people, not a dull diversion from life, not a collection of dusty rituals, not an institution simply perpetuating its own processes, but a living

Church, living as these Melanesian Brothers make the Church live? The Church needs to be an organic necessity, a hallowed place, a place which will confront us with the mysteries of the beauty and the tragedy of human life, life in God's image. Creativity is essential to the life of the Church. If the congregation cannot find the Spirit of the Creator God within the Church, they will go elsewhere, searching for beauty and the eternal in open spaces where God's Spirit is still free to move and dance and sing, and where creation has never ceased to let the seed fall upon the ground and die, so that it can yield a hundredfold.

It is a Message of Unity and Peace

The fact that the religious communities are open to all tribes, islands and nations has meant that they have been able to be inclusive in a way that many local communities are not. The Brotherhood sets out rules to prevent island or tribal divisions emerging within the community. All twenty seven of the Brotherhood households within the Solomon Islands, for example, are mixed according to language group and island origin. When they are together it is the rule that all Brothers speak the common language, Pidgin. Sharing everything, it is hoped the bond of their Christian community will bind them together even when there is prejudice and division in the wider society.

The strength of this approach was witnessed during ethnic tensions which took place from 1998 to 2000 between the people of Guadalcanal and Malaita. In this ethnic conflict, 20,000 Malaitans were forced to leave Guadalcanal by the armed Isatabu Freedom Movement who believed their land had for too long been exploited by the Malaitan migrants. The Malaitans proceeded to form their own militant group which took control of the capital Honiara in revenge for what had happened, receiving guns and, later, support from the largely Malaitan-dominated police force. In the following two years, all schools and clinics on Guadalcanal were closed. There were road blocks and constant murders, gun battles and revenge killings. It was only the religious communities who, though situated in the middle of the tension, refused to disband, but continued to live, Malaitan side by side with Guadalcanal person in the same community. As a symbol of that unity, in the midst of the conflict, in October 1999, the Melanesian Brotherhood elected a Malaitan as their Head Brother and a Guadalcanal man as his assistant. The religious communities remained the only ones trusted by both sides. Their communities became a place of safety for Malaitan refugees and later, when Malaitans controlled Honiara, the capital, were the only groups who had freedom of movement to provide essential supplies for all those suffering in Guadalcanal. Brothers were constantly called upon to help provide safe passage for those in danger or threatened by militant groups, and it was the Brothers too who were able to negotiate impartially with militants to try to stop the fighting and save lives. In May 2000, the Brotherhood sent out four groups of Brothers who camped in the no man's land between enemy lines for the next five months.

This is a copy of part of a letter they took to the militants on both sides in May 2000, in which they defined the essence of their mission:

> We come to you without weapons, guns or politics. We have no money to offer or compensation for the suffering you have been through. We come to you simply as your Christian Brothers to speak to you in the name of Jesus Christ.
>
> We live in a country created by God, a land full of many blessings, a country of many islands and tribes, but a land which many have always called 'The Happy Isles'. But today, on Guadalcanal and Malaita we hear a different story. This beautiful island, this rich and diverse people is being torn apart by fear, hatred, violence and division. If you travel through Guadalcanal today, from Honiara to the Weather Coast to the Guadalcanal Plains, you will witness a land created by God and a people created by God, but a land living in pain and sorrow and fear. We have lost the openness, the trust and the laughter we have always enjoyed. As Brothers we have seen the funerals, the tears and the cries of people both from Malaita and Guadalcanal. And now we all know the results of this tension, no transport, fear to travel, no schools or education, no medical supplies and clinics, homelessness, hunger, no markets, difficulty finding money, shame, suspicion and unhappiness. Honiara has become a place of stealing, violence and even murder in our streets. Is this what we want for our children? We are not here to blame anyone or to judge. The problems are obviously difficult to understand, and they need careful negotiation. Both sides and the Government must be fully represented in these discussions. There needs to be justice. There needs to be respect and there needs to be understanding. That can only take place if there is a readiness to forgive. There will never be happiness on this island unless those involved in this tension lay down their weapons and make peace. History shows us again and again that the way of violence and war and hatred leads to destruction.

> No happiness can be achieved through murder and death. In the name of Jesus Christ, we appeal to you: stop the killing, stop the hatred, stop the pay back.[25]

The religious communities fearlessly believed that God would provide protection from the extreme danger they put themselves in. Throughout the conflict the Melanesian Brotherhood were able to negotiate and secure the release of hostages taken during the struggle, and together with the other religious communities, the Franciscan Brothers, the Sisters of the Church and the Sisters of Melanesia, to ferry supplies to those in need, to help the wounded and to find the whereabouts of the bodies of the dead. The role the religious communities played obviously imposed great internal tensions upon those communities: Malaitan Brothers continued to work in Guadalcanal – controlled areas and Guadalcanal Brothers in Honiara and Malaita. This was nothing short of a miraculous grace, for it was a time when the whole island was bitterly divided by tribal and island divisions, and Brothers and Sisters from both sides of the ethnic divide were hearing news of how their own *wantoks* and people were suffering and even being killed in this conflict.

The Head Brother Harry Gereniu spoke of the need for the religious communities to show their own community solidarity as a sign of Christian hope and reconciliation, which it was their mission to extend from their households to the whole nation. And this indeed was the unity and Christian hope that religious communities, supported by the prayers of many throughout the nation, were able to continue to witness to. When a peace settlement was signed in Townsville, Australia, those involved in the conflict acknowledged the role of the indigenous religious communities as peacemakers. The Brothers also became members of the Peace Monitoring Council. Fr John Pinder, former General Secretary of the Melanesian Mission in England, visited the Solomon Islands in 2000 and wrote in the *Church Times*:

> They [the religious communities, both Brothers and Sisters] have shown amazing courage, literally putting themselves in the crossfire and going backwards and forwards across the lines to try to reduce tension and bring comfort and support to villagers in the battle zone. Wherever there is an incident they are quickly on the scene.[26]

The wounds of the ethnic conflict on Guadalcanal will still take many years to heal. The economy of the nation has been destroyed with all major income generating businesses and industries closed down. For those who have been directly involved in the conflict and bloodshed, particularly those young people who have been empowered and corrupted by guns and violence, and those who have seen and suffered brutality, it is going to be impossible to return unaffected to their former village life. The religious communities themselves have been under such tension. Never before called upon or needed so much, they have had a terrible strain imposed on their own community life by this experience. They have already led missions of healing and prayer all round Guadalcanal, but each religious community needs time to regroup, reestablish its prayerful centre and the routines of its day-to-day life, and recover from the impossible strain that the last few years have placed upon them. Yet they emerge from this conflict as an example to all of how the Christian Gospel is indeed the Gospel of peace, not just preached but lived out, and that this Gospel of peace and reconciliation is the only hope for the nation's future. This brief account of a period of history which has had, and continues to have, such a huge impact on the future of the Solomon Islands needs much greater coverage than can be recorded here. In fact the role of the religious communities themselves and their stories during this time of conflict could be a book in its own right. As the nation comes to terms with what has happened on this peaceful island, it is surely the religious communities that must emerge as a beacon of hope, a light which is still burning and a sign that evil can never put out the light of Christ.

Emerging Difficulties

There are of course difficulties which this religious community faces as it goes forward into this twenty-first century. In 1962 Charles Fox described how the Melanesian Brotherhood was sometimes looked upon by the priests as 'cheap labour'.[27] If there was any job to do which no one else could be found to do, then the Brotherhood would be asked: rebuilding churches, moving schools, transporting, acting as caretakers and security, taking messages, etc. In the recent ethnic tension many private businesses and church properties relied on the Brotherhood as night security to prevent break-ins and looting. While this may seem a legitimate act of service, it has meant that the community was often too widely stretched and fragmented, simply trying to fulfil requests, rather than discerning a more pro-active approach. During the ethnic tension, and since it too, it is the Brotherhood who are trusted to carry out the roles that no one else wants to or can fulfil, but this often means they are being pulled away from their community life of prayer and household postings.

There is also always the danger that the Brotherhood itself, respected for its spiritual *mana* or power, can be tempted away from a Christ-centred approach into cultic practices which reinforce superstition and fear rather than liberating people from them. A mythology has developed in which the people start trusting in the use of Brothers' collects and 'holy objects' – stones, walking sticks, holy oil and water, and prayers for binding devils, etc. While this faith has undoubtedly been used to bring healing and peace, at the same time people can also misinterpret, and death and sickness and injury can be used as evidence that someone has 'disobeyed' a Brother's prayer. Prayer in this context thus becomes a curse. The Brothers thus find themselves not only called upon to defend and heal, but also to use their prayers to attack and to punish. There are constant requests for Brothers to use their prayers to find and punish thieves, adulterers, perceived sinners and sorcerers. Individual Brothers may be tempted, or get caught up in the misuse of their perceived spiritual power, which can lead to greater fear and division within communities. It can also lead to authority and power being invested in individual Brothers, rather than in the saving love of Christ. There is always a danger of pride when a group is seen to possess miraculous powers, and such power can be used for evil. The test is always whether ministry leads to the fruit of the Holy Spirit or to division and greater fear and hatred.

Another of the difficulties to emerge is that the popularity of the religious communities with the wider community can cause feelings of rivalry and jealousy among others involved in church leadership, especially the priesthood, and in certain places this leads to a lack of cooperation which hampers the mission of the whole Church. Within the Brotherhood itself poor leadership can affect the morale and the mission of different households. Many of those elected to take leadership positions may have little leadership experience, and this can cause great frustration among the Brothers who are required to live under a vow of obedience.

The individual Brothers themselves can easily go astray from the disciplined rule. Moral failure, or failure to fulfil one's role within the community, breaks down the religious life not just of the individual but of the whole community. As Melanesian society develops materially with the rise of a cash economy and much larger urban culture and cultural freedom, there is also increased temptation for Brothers to abandon their vows of poverty, chastity and obedience. When one Brother transgresses the rule, it is often the whole Brotherhood which is blamed. This obviously has advantages and disadvantages. It is perhaps one of the hidden strengths of religious life that it must witness not only in times of achievement and success, but also witness to Christ when facing up to the weaknesses and errors of its own members.

Perhaps the greatest question of all facing the Brotherhood is, like religious communities before it, how to cope with its own growth, success and development, without losing touch with its spiritual roots which are its greatest strength. Increasingly the Brotherhood is being called upon to lead missions further afield and to organise itself in a way that will enable mission on a much wider level. Such missions in the modern world have needed organisation, administrative and financial skills, and the need for more training. They also require more resources for that training and more expenditure. As mission has increased and gone further afield, the Brothers have needed to consider more income-generating projects to support that outreach, and more outside financial support from supporters and overseas Churches. The future of the Brotherhood will depend on how well they will be able to balance that need for resource and manpower development with that 'poverty of spirit' which is so essential to their missionary calling.

A Melanesian Mission for the Wider Church

Bishop George Augustus Selwyn wrote in 1854:

> ...... as running water purifies itself, so Christian work is seen to correct its own mistakes. Is it then a hope too unreasonable to be entertained, that the power which will heal the divisions of the Church at home may come from her distant mission fields?[28]

There has been much talk in recent mission circles of the need to encourage reverse mission, not simply one-way mission from the North to the South, but from the South to the North, from the 'Third World' to the 'First World'. If partnership in mission is going to do more than simply alleviate a guilty conscience for past missionary failures, then, argues Andrew Kirk, it is vital that "the communities in the South share in person with communities in the North their gifts and understanding of mission in the way of Christ."[29] But is this process really possible, or is it once again a question of the West imposing the conditions and terms of the missionary approach, albeit using a different language? If it is to work, then the initiative, project and method must be owned by the missionary who comes from the South.

For the millennium year 2000 such a mission approach was carried out by the Melanesian Brotherhood in three different new cultural contexts:

thirty Brothers were invited to lead a mission in New Zealand, and fourteen Brothers were invited to lead a two-month mission in Chester and Exeter Dioceses in the United Kingdom, and then a mission in the Philippines. As the Melanesian Brotherhood set out to plan these missions, an implicit danger was that the Brotherhood would be treated as a cultural entertainment group, rather than as missionaries who had something real and vital to offer the Western Church. In planning, it was decided that as far as possible the Brotherhood would maintain the essence of its own missionary approach. What was it that this missionary approach was able to offer?

1. The missionaries were young. It was a fact often expressed by the host community that those leading the mission, 18 to 30 year old men, were the age group most lacking in the Anglican Church in the United Kingdom.
2. The missionaries did not belong to any one faction within the Church. The fact that they were all missionaries from the other side of the world allowed them to break through prejudices and boundaries that often divide the Church. Freed from the stereotype categorisation of 'evangelical' or 'liberal' or 'catholic', they were free to visit all churches and bring groups together. This had the effect of freeing host churches from the patterns that often confine them, and enabling them to discover beneath rituals and processes the reality of a shared faith.
3. There was a confidence in faith in marked contrast to a Western Church which has lost that confidence. They believed that God was at the centre of their lives and that prayer was an essential part of their day. This faith was expressed naturally without fanaticism, without shame, apologetics or academic explanation. Faith was simply the reality of their lives.
4. There was no pretence or affectation, and no inhibitions about sharing with people from all backgrounds: the homeless, those in the prisons, young people and teenagers. Constantly people opened up to the Brothers about their own belief and faith in a way they would have been embarrassed to do to someone of their own culture. The cultural differences protected them and enabled a greater honesty and intimacy, without fear of judgement.
5. The Brothers were able to express their faith in the vitality of worship. Frequently they were able to break through the rigidity and formalism of English Church tradition, while not appearing to threaten those who valued those traditions. It allowed the host community to relax and to participate

at a deep level. It transformed people's perspectives.

6. It was both teaching and learning, giving and taking. It was a mission which entered into dialogue with the host community. Both those on mission and those welcoming mission were interacting, learning about one another and learning about God.

7. It was a missionary group not seeking to compete; it acknowledged, and yet was unashamed of, its own inexperience and dependence on the gifts of others. It did not try to impose its own view or way of doing things, but simply offered in humility the faith gifts of its community.

8. It was a new voice, a voice and an expression which had not been seen or heard before in the UK. It was the first time many congregations had heard an eighteen year old preach, for example, or had heard Pacific panpipes, or witnessed Melanesian worship and celebration or a Melanesian type of drama. The mission was able to break through the confines of culture to see with new eyes a faith in God, not on the peripheries of life but at its centre.

An English couple wrote:

> The music was so pure, at once melodic, beautiful; it evoked among us a sense of a simpler other life, another world actually, and the Brothers danced and moved with the music in a way that was so at-one with the evening, with the spirit of brotherhood, with a sense of joy and wonder simply at being alive..... The next morning we went to Exeter's magnificent 12th century Cathedral where the Brothers were singing as part of the Sunday Communion Service. It was really quite amazing; within that immense and solid Gothic stone space that had stood for so many centuries, the Brothers danced proudly and unselfconsciously through the west door to a packed and amazed congregation. They were dressed in their native costumes, wearing white *lavalava*, bare-chested and barefooted, their bodies painted with white ash decorations and with sprigs of pine in their headbands. They wove and danced their way down the aisle towards the altar, beating time with bare feet, as they blew their magnificent panpipes and beat the ends of their large bamboos. Apparently a clergyman from Exeter, Bishop Patteson, in the 19th century had gone to Melanesia as a missionary and was martyred there..... The Brothers returning to Exeter brought that event full circle. It was very moving to see them. It made us all aware of what a tiny and amazing world we live in, that indeed time and space can be contiguous, and that,

as the Brothers sang and chanted, “We are all one family”.[30]

Today there is much talk of ‘partnership in mission’ and stress on the Gospel concept of *koinonia* (fellowship).[31] Real partnership in mission opens up exciting possibilities. The word ‘missionary’ can be uncoupled from geographical boundaries and become redefined to include the calling of Christians in all countries and cultures. The Mexico City Conference of the World Council of Churches in 1963 stated:

> The missionary frontier runs around the world. It is the line which separates belief from unbelief, the unseen frontier which cuts across all other frontiers and presents the universal Church with its primary mission challenge.[32]

In the Church of Melanesia, the Melanesian Brotherhood has been able to witness to the possibilities of such a mission. It is a mission which at its heart aims at exchange and relationship. It is a mission which does not begin from above but from below, and which can empower both the missionary and the one to whom the missionary is sent. This mission at its best can create a new sense of belonging and sharing with one another, a new sense of community. This mission spirituality is well summed up by David Bosch as mission in ‘bold humility’:

> We regard our involvement in dialogue and mission as an adventure, are prepared to take risks and are anticipating surprises as the Spirit guides us into fuller understanding. This is opting for.... a bold humility – or a humble boldness. We know only in part, but we do know. And we believe that the faith we profess is both true and just and should be proclaimed. We do this, however, not as judges or lawyers, but as witnesses; not as soldiers, but as envoys of peace; not as high pressured sales-persons, but as **servants of the servant Lord**.[33]

NOTES

1 For their pattern of daily worship, see Richard Carter (ed): *Offices and Prayers of the Melanesian Brotherhood*, 1997, Honiara, Provincial Press, p. 133. The prayer at the end of the Afterword is from this book.

2 The community has resisted setting academic entrance requirements; some of those selected may have had no formal education at all. Novices will be selected from each diocese and this selection will be based on signs of their calling and faith, experience and skills in all areas of life, church involvement and references, and also will try to make sure that each tribe, district, language group and island have Brothers in the community.

3 Richard Carter: *The Vow of Poverty in the Third World* from *Anglican Religious Communities Year Book, 1999-2000*, Canterbury Press.

4 “The Trinitarian nature of God’s mission is indispensable if one is to understand why God acts in the

world. Over and over again in the most significant literature on the subject, the *missio Dei* is said to spring from God's boundless and matchless love for the universe he has created, and paricularly for the beings within that bear his image…. The mission of God flows directly from who God is. It is impossible to be more basic than that. God's intention for the world is that in every respect it should show forth the way he is – love, community, equality, diversity, mercy, compassion and justice."
(J Andrew Kirk: *What is Mission?* p. 28)

5 *Wantok* means literally 'one talk' and is a term used to describe those of the same tribe who speak the same language. In many of the islands there may be as many as three, four or more different languages spoken. The '*wantok* system' is a term used to describe the way those of the same language group are seen to favour one another and feel an obligation to help one another. It is a system which is seen to lead to prejudice and nepotism.

6 From a sermon preached by Archbishop Oscar Romero, First Sunday in Lent, 1980. Found in James R Brockman: *Oscar Romero: Bishop and Martyr*, London, Sheed and Ward, 1982, p. 208.

7 G Gutiérrez *The Truth Shall Make You Free*, Maryknoll, Orbis Books, 1980.

8 Archbishop Oscar Romero in James R Brockman: *Oscar Romero: Bishop and Martyr*, p. 72.

9 Hans Rüdi Weber: *God and the Powerless, Experiments in Bible Study*, Geneva: World Council of Churches, 1983, p. 108.

10 See Roland Allen: *Missionary Methods: St Paul's or Ours?* London: World Dominion Press.

11 Bosch: *Transforming Mission*, Maryknoll, Orbis Books, 1991, p. 453.

12 Paolo Freire argues that "cultural invasion leads to such inauthenticity. In this phenomenon, the invaders penetrate the cultural context of another group, and, ignoring the potential of the latter, they impose their own view of the world upon those they invade and inhibit the creativity of the invaded by curbing their expression." *Pedagogy of the Oppressed*, London: Penguin Books, 1972.

13 Claude Geffre: *Theological Reflections on a New Age of Mission*, International Review of Mission, 1982, p. 482.

14 Bosch: *Transforming Missiom*, 1991, p. 455.

15 Gustavo Gutiérrez: *We Drink from Our Own Wells*, SCM, 1984, p. 15.

16 Manfred Ernst: *Winds of Change: Rapidly Growing Religious Groups in the South Pacific*, Suva, Pacific Conference of Churches, 1994.

17 *Anglicanism: a Global Communion* (Edited by Andrew Wingate, Robin Ward, Carrie Pemberton & Wilson Sitshebo), London, Mowbray, 1998, p.50.

18 Vincent Donovan describes the same importance of community conversion in his work with the Masai. See Vincent J Donovan: *Christianity Rediscovered*, Orbis Books, 1978, pp. 84-87.

19 Erich Fromm: *The Art of Loving*, HarperCollins, 1957, p. 19

20 Richard Carter: *The Vow of Poverty in the Third World*, Anglican Religious Communities Year Book, 1999-2000, Canterbury Press.

21 Carter: *The Vow of Poverty in the Third World.*

22 As above.

23 *Spearhead Toktok*, July 1996, Provincial Press.

24 Carter: *Religious Orders and the Development of the Anglican Church in the South Pacific*, in *Anglicanism, a Global Communion*, Mowbray, London, 1998, pp. 45-51

25 Unpublished letter signed by the Head Brother Harry Gereniu and Assistant Head Brother Wilson Basile, May 2000.

26 John Pinder: *Where Religious Orders are Maintaining Order*, Church Times, London, 27 October, 2000.

27 Charles Fox: *Kakamora*, Hodder & Stoughton, 1962, p. 76.

28 G H Curteis: *Bishop Selwyn of New Zealand and Lichfield*, London, 1889, p. 152.

29 Andrew Kirk: *What is Mission?* p. 204

30 Marc and Kim Millon: *Notes from a Devon Kitchen*, 27 July, 2000. www. quaypress.com.

31 Kirk: *What is Mission*? p. 184.

32 From Mexico City Conference of WCC, 1963, quoted by Kirk: *What is Mission?* p. 24.

33 Bosch: *Transforming Mission*, 1991.

AFTERWORD

By Brother Richard Carter MBH

The grass square outside the chapel at Tabalia has a large white cross and white altar. This is St. Simon and St. Jude's Square, the place where Brothers take their vows and are admitted as full member of the community. It is the place where Ini Kopuria made his promises in 1925. It is considered very much a sacred place and entered only with bare feet by the Brothers themselves.

The Brothers' Chapel of St. Mark is simple too: a rectangular building which focuses on a heavy wooden altar raised on polished cement floor. The altar is made from a local hardwood, *tubi*, and maintains something of the shape of the tree from which it was cut; it is solid, simple and strong. Behind it is a standing cross inlaid with mother of pearl shell; it is a joyful cross with a design which looks like the sun rising. On the walls behind it are spears and shields, symbols of the Brotherhood's mission to evangelise 'the heathen' who often confronted the Brothers with similar weapons. Above, there is a stained glass window portraying Ini Kopuria in front of a cross, a heathen man on his right, a Christian convert, who is a Companion, on his left, praying. It is here that the Brothers pray their seven daily offices and receive the Eucharist which is the heartbeat of their active ministry. There is nearby the coconut tree planted by Charles Fox, around which the coconuts still remain untouched as a sign of the fruitfulness of the life and the number of vocations coming into the Brotherhood. Behind the crowded novice dormitories is the ditch or drain which was dug by Charles Fox as a discipline for missing prayer; it is still a tradition of the community, for those who fail to keep the rule of prayer may still be asked to dig or clear this drain as a penance.

It is indeed a beautiful station which grows on you as you enter into its life and rhythm. It is full of birds, frangipani, hibiscus, mango trees, the bright light during the day of the burning tropical sun, and at night bright stars, and all the shapes of the moon – or at times, a deep velvety darkness when the generator is turned off at night and there is silence until morning. All the Brotherhood households throughout the Pacific have to some extent modelled themselves on this Mother House, to capture this same spirit of simplicity and prayer. Many who come to this community feel at home, as I did, from the very first time they attend its prayer and offices. The first office is at 5.40 a.m. The community gathers in the dark and greets the day; as the sun rises, it streams in refracted rainbows of colour through the stained glass window and dances on the altar and the celebrant's head; the song birds and parrots arrive outside and bounce on the flowering trees. At night the household slips into silence with the final roar of prayer. There is very much a sense of God's presence here, as if the doors and windows are all open and God is still walking in the garden. There is an openness to God which is hard to express in words. And there is among those who have been given the privilege of this vocation a naturalness of faith which is without sacrifice or pretence, but is as essential as the whole of creation, which also depends on Christ for its life and joins the Melanesian Brotherhood in its song of praise. This community preaches a direct Gospel, for God is as much part of their lives as the air they breathe or the water they wash in. At the heart of all that is good and life-giving within this vocation is the image of Jesus Christ calling: "Go, sell all you have, give your money to the poor, come and follow". And it is only when the community becomes separated from or forgetful of that call that it stumbles and falls. It is not a narrow call to take on something extraneous or imported, neither is it a conversion experience where someone is forced to change from one person into another; it is much more adequately described as a call which opens up a life which had been glimpsed but never fully explored, its potential, its goodness, its miraculous nature never before realised. Like a blind man who had lived in the shadows discovering his sight, Christ seems to be offered life, life in all its fulness.

A MELANESIAN BROTHERHOOD PRAYER FOR COMMUNITY LIFE

O Lord Jesus Christ,
when we wake each day to the sound of the bell,
when we kneel in silence and speak to you in prayer,
when we come to the altar and receive your body in our hands,
when we study your Word and try to understand,
when we wash our clothes with our hands in a bucket of water,
when we stir up a fire and blow it into flames,
when we ride on the truck with dust in our eyes,
when we are burnt by the sun as two by two we walk the roads,
when we stand in the mud of our garden,
when we brush the plantation and the sweat runs down,
when we cook food in the smoke of the kitchen,
when we are hungry and share together the food you provide,
when we are tired and dirty and swim in the river,
when night comes and the oil lamps are lit:
O let us be filled in all these things with love for you,
let us never forget that you are always with us
and all our lives belong to you. **Amen.**

BIBLIOGRAPHY

MELANESIAN BROTHERHOOD

Published Sources

Where no other publisher is given, the publisher is: The Melanesian Brotherhood, Tabalia, Guadalcanal, Solomon Islands.

Aerts, Theo (ed). *The Martyrs of Papua New Guinea: 333 Missionary Lives Lost During World War II.* Port Moresby: University of Papua New Guinea, 1994.

Anderson, Gerald H. (ed). *Biographical Dictionary of Christian Missions* (entry for Charles Elliot Fox). New York: Simon and Schuster Macmillan, 1997.

Anglican Information (periodical). November, 1989 issue, article by Brian Macdonald-Milne on the Melanesian Brotherhood. London: Anglican Consultative Council.

Anglican Religious Communities Year Book, 2000-2001 and *2002-2003.* Norwich: Canterbury Press.

Artless, S.W. (ed). *The Church in Melanesia* (ch.5, 'The Native Evangelistic Brotherhood', Rt. Revd. J.M.Steward). Melanesian Mission, n.d.

Atwell, Robert (ed). *Celebrating the Saints.* Norwich: SCM, Canterbury Press, 1998. (Entries include Ini Kopuria, Bishop John Coleridge Patteson and his Companions, George Augustus Selwyn.)

Bull, G.S. *Ebony Exiles.* About the Solomons community at Wailoku, Fiji. Privately printed. No date.

Burt, Ben. *Tradition and Christianity: The Colonial Transformation of a Solomon Islands Society.* Reading: Harwood Academic Publishers; Paris, Berlin, Tokyo, Amsterdam,Camberwell (Victoria, Australia), Langhorne (Pennsylvania, USA), 1994.

Carter, Richard. *Where God Still Walks in the Garden: Religious Orders and the Development of the Anglican Church in the South Pacific*, in *Anglicanism: A Global Communion*, Wingate, Ward, Pemberton & Sitshebo (eds). London: Mowbray, 1998. Also includes an article by Una Kroll on *A Vision for the Religious Orders in the Anglican Communion in the Next Century.*

Carter, Bro. Richard MBH. *From Creation to Salvation: A Drama for the New Millennium by the Melanesian Brotherhood, 2000.*

Carter, Bro. Richard MBH. *A Resource Book for the Training and Mission of the Melanesian Brotherhood.* 2000.

Church of Melanesia Newsletter. A quarterly publication of the Church of Melanesia. Issue No.1, December 2001. (Includes articles on missions by the Melanesian Brothers in New Zealand and UK, Chester Diocese Companions' visit to Solomon Islands, the 75th anniversary celebrations of the Melanesian Brotherhood and new leaders for the Sisters of Melanesia and the Sisters of the Church in Solomon Islands.)

Church Times. London, October 27, 2000. (Includes article by Canon John Pinder on Religious Orders in Solomon Islands.)

Church Times. London, July 20, 2001. (Includes article by Janet Watts on the Religious Life in religious communities in the Anglican Communion.)

The Constitution of the Melanesian Brotherhood as revised at the 8th Great Conference, 1995.

Elo, Brother George, MBH. *Aims, Methods and Achievements of the Melanesian Brotherhood.* A project submitted to the Faculty of the Bishop Patteson Theological College, (in partial fulfilment of the requirements for the Diploma in Theology). Kohimarama, Guadalcanal, Solomon Islands: BPTC, 1996.

Fox, C.E. *Lord of the Southern Isles: Being the Story of the Anglican Mission in Melanesia, 1849-1949.* London: Mowbray, 1958.

Fox, C.E. *Kakamora.* London: Hodder & Stoughton, 1962.

Fox, C.E. *The Melanesian Brotherhood.* London & Auckland: The Melanesian Mission, n.d.

Fox, C.E. *The Melanesian Brotherhood* (revised by B.J.Macdonald-Milne). London: The Melanesian Mission, n.d.

Fox, C.E. *My Solomon Islands.* Church of Melanesia, 1985.

Garland, Christopher. *Romney Gill, Missionary 'Genius' and Craftsman.* Leicester: Christians Aware, 2000.

Hand, Bishop David. *Modawa: Papua New Guinea and Me, 1946-2000.* Port Moresby, Papua New Guinea: published privately, 2002.

Hilliard, David. *God's Gentlemen: A History of the Melanesian Mission, 1849-1942.* University of Queensland Press, 1978.

Hilliard, David. *Protestant Missions in the Solomon Islands, 1849-1942.* PhD dissertation. Canberra: Australian National University, 1966.

Holy Cross News: *Newsletter of the Anglican Church on Bougainville and Tasman Islands*, No.22, 1986.

Hopkins, A.I. *In the Isles of King Solomon: An Account of Twenty Five Years Spent Among the Primitive Solomon Islanders.* Sydney: Seeley, 1928.

Hopkins, A.I. *From Heathen Boy to Christian Priest.* London: SPCK (St Christopher Books, No.33), 1st edition 1930, republished 1948. (Biography of Jack Talofuila of Malaita, Solomon Islands).

Introducing the Diocese of Carpentaria: Information Handbook. Adelaide: Adelaide Diocesan Board of education, 1976.

Jones, Kathleen. *The Saints of the Anglican Calendar.* Norwich: Canterbury Press, 2000.

Jones, Muriel. *Married to Melanesia.* London: George Allen & Unwin, 1974.

Kinahan, Timothy, 1983, updated by others 1990. *A Church is Born: The Anglican Church in Papua New Guinea, 1891-1991.* The Anglican Church in Papua New Guinea.

Lycett, Margaret. *Brothers: The Story of the Native Brotherhood of Melanesia.* London: SPCK, 1935.

Macdonald-Milne, Brian. *Spearhead: The Story of the Melanesian Brotherhood.* Watford: The Melanesian Mission, 1981.

Macdonald-Milne, Brian. *The Melanesian Brotherhood and the Tradition of Indigenous Evangelism in the Anglican Church in the Pacific Islands.* North Atlantic Missiology Project, University of Cambridge, Position Paper No.90. Currents in World Christianity, Westminster College, Cambridge, 1999. (Prepared for the 150th anniversary of the foundation of the Melanesian Mission.)

Melanesia News. No.50, May 2001. Melanesian Mission, England. (Includes a report by the Archbishop of Melanesia to the meeting of the Anglican Primates in March 2001 on events in Solomon Islands and religious orders.)

Melanesian Brotherhood Companions' Handbook. Various editions.

Melanesian Brotherhood Partnership Mission: Gospel of Hope to the Poor, Vol. 1, Nos. 1 & 2. Iglesia Filipina Independiente, de los Reyes Road 2, San Pedro, Puerto Princesa City, 5300 Palawan, Philippines, 2001.

Melanesian Mission Newsletter, Easter 2002. Melanesian Mission, England. (Includes information about Religious Orders and Mothers Union in Solomon Islands and Vanuatu, exmilitants on Guadalcanal, and the consecration of the Reverend Peter Fox as the Bishop of Port Moresby, Papua New Guinea.)

Morning and Evening Prayer (Simplified) of the Retatasiu (Melanesian Brotherhood). Taroaniara, Solomon Islands: Melanesian Mission Press, 16th (New) Edition, 1959 (completing 42,000 copies).

Newbolt, M.R. (ed). *John Steward's Memories.* Chester: Phillipson & Golder, 1939.

Offices of the Melanesian Brotherhood, (put into modern English and revised by the Great Conference, 1970). Duplicated.

Offices and Other Services of the Melanesian Brotherhood, 1975 (and subsequent editions).

Offices and Prayers of the Melanesian Brotherhood: Ira Retatasiu ta Melanesia. Tabalia, Solomon Islands: Melanesian Brotherhood, 1997.

O Sala Ususur, former magazine in the Mota language for the Diocese of Melanesia.

Prayers at Evensong. Duplicated. Used by the Melanesian Brotherhood.

The Outrigger. Newsletter of the Pacific Islands Society of the UK and Ireland: No.40, Summer 2000, includes article on the Melanesian Brotherhood Mission in Chester Diocese in 2000.

Rowell, Bishop Geoffrey, Stevenson, Bishop Kenneth & Williams, Archbishop Rowan (compilers). *Love's Redeeming Work: The Anglican Quest for Holiness.* Oxford University Press, 2001. (Includes contributions from the writings of Father Algy SSF, Bishop Philip Strong and Ini Kopuria).

Spearhead Toktok (periodical). Solomon Islands: Melanesian Brotherhood.

The Principles and Rules of the Melanesian Brotherhood. n.d.

The Southern Cross Log. Melanesian Mission, New Zealand & England. No longer published.
Tippett, A.R. *Solomon Islands Christianity: A Study in Growth and Obstruction.* World Studies of Churches in Mission. London: Lutterworth, 1967 (on behalf of the Commission on World Mission and Evangelism of the WCC).
Tristam, Bro. SSF (ed). *Exciting Holiness: Collects and Readings for the Festivals and Lesser Festivals of the Church of England.* Norwich:Canterbury Press, 1997. (included are George Augustus Selwyn, April 11; Peter Chanel, Roman Catholic Martyr in the South Pacific, April 28; Ini Kopuria, June 6; the Martyrs of Papua New Guinea, September 2; John Coleridge Patteson and his Companions, Martyrs, September 20; Day of Intercession and Thanksgiving for the Missionary Work of the Church, November 29.)
The Vocation of a Brother. Melanesian Brotherhood. Duplicated, no date (c.1960).
Voice from the Melanesian Brotherhood – 'Whom Shall I Send? Send Me'. Melanesian Brotherhood, Papua New Guinea Region, PO Box 29, Popondetta, Papua New Guinea and Papua New Guinea Church Partnership, London, c.1999.
Wetherell, David. *Reluctant Mission: the Anglican Church in Papua New Guinea, 1891-1942.* St Lucia: University of Queensland Press, 1977.
Wetherell, David.*The New Guinea Diaries of Philip Strong, 1936-45.* Melbourne, Australia: Macmillan, 1981.
Whiteman, Darrell. *Melanesians and Missionaries: An Ethno-historical Study of Socio-Religious Change in the S.W.Pacific* (PhD thesis). Department of Anthropology in the Graduate School, Southern Illinois University, March 1980.
Whiteman, Darrell. *Melanesians and Missionaries: An Ethno-historical Study of Social and Religious Change in the South West Pacific.* Pasadena: W.Carey Library, 1983.
Whonsbon-Aston, C.W. *Polynesia Patchwork: The Tale of a Pacific Diocese.* London: SPG, 1948.

Unpublished Sources

Ayong, James (later Archbishop of Papua New Guinea). *A Study in Apparent Failure.* Unpublished BTh thesis. Martin Luther Seminary, Lae, Papua New Guinea, c.1984.
Ball, Fr Ernest, SSM. Paper on *The Melanesian Brotherhood – A Religious Community.* Undated article in the author's possession.
Church of Melanesia Council of Bishops' Statement on the Solomon Islands Government's Criticism of the Solomon Islands Christian Association (SICA), May 6, 2001.
A Letter to all those involved in the Present Ethnic Tension, from the Head Brother, the Assistant Head Brother and All Members of the Melanesian Brotherhood. April, 2000.
Letters and reports by Brothers, Ex-Brothers, former Chaplains, former Missionaries in Melanesia, Melanesian Clergy and Laity.

Macdonald-Milne, Brian. Paper as presentation of research on the Melanesian Brotherhood, Queen's College, Birmingham, June 15, 1983.
Minutes of Great Conferences, Regional Conferences and Section Meetings of Melanesian Brotherhood and Companions; and of the Community of the Sisters of Melanesia.
Newsletters, letters and reports from: the Bishop of Malaita (the Rt Revd Terry Brown), Helen Newton, the Revd Brother Richard Carter MBH, Sister Catherine CSC, Mrs Chris Luxton (Papua New Guinea Church Partnership), Head Brother Harry Gereniu, the Revd John Ewington (on reestablishment of the Anglican Church on Nukumanu, Tasman Islands, in the mid-1980s).
Notes of interview with Laisa Loe, the widow of Ini Kopuria, written by the author while Chaplain of the Brotherhood, and with Mrs Jessie Sade, the widow of Fr Daniel Sade, written at Maravovo village, October 1995.
Notes of interviews conducted by the Reverend Richard Carter, August 1998, recorded as written or spoken by the interviewees.
Tape recordings of interviews of ex-Brothers in Vanuatu, recorded by Brother (now Father) Shadrack Vulum, translated from Bislama and written out in English by the author.

RELIGIOUS ORDERS

Community of the Cross

Community of the Cross, The (booklet). London: Melanesian Mission, c.1946

Community of the Sisters of Melanesia

Bore, Sister Emily. *The Historical Aspects of the Community of the Sisters of Melanesia (CSM): How and Why it is valuable to form the Melanesian Sisterhood in the Church of Melanesia and Visions for its Future.* Diploma dissertation, Bishop Patteson Theological College, Kohimarama, Solomon Islands. October 1993.
Community of the Sisters of Melanesia Rule, 1980.
Constitution of the Community of the Sisters of Melanesia, 1993.
Offices & Other Services of the Community of the Sisters of Melanesia, adopted from the Melanesian Brotherhood Office Book. Solomon Islands: Sisters of Melanesia, n.d.

Community of the Sisters of the Church

Sister, A, CSC. *A Life of Mother Emily, Foundress of the Anglican Community of the Sisters of the Church.* Solomon Islands: Community of the Sisters of the Church, n.d.

Community of the Sacred Name

Newsletters of St Christopher's Home. Naulu, Fiji.

St Christopher's Home: A Celebration of 25 Years of Love, Hope and Dedication, 1968-1993. Fiji: Community of the Sacred Name.

St Christopher's Home, 1968-1988; 1989 New Challenges and Hope for the Future. Fiji: Community of the Sacred Name.

Society of St Francis

Dunstan, Petà. *This Poor Sort: A History of the European Province of the Society of St Francis.* London: Darton, Longman & Todd, 1997.

SPAN (Newsletter of the Anglican Franciscans in the South Pacific), superseded by *Franciscan Angles* (Newsletter of Anglican Franciscans in Aotearoa/ New Zealand and Australia).

Society of the Sacred Mission

Mason, Alistair SSM. *History of the Society of the Sacred Mission.* Norwich, England: Canterbury Press, 1993.

MELANESIAN MISSION AND CHURCH OF MELANESIA

Anglican World: The Official Magazine of the Anglican Communion. Issue No. 104, Christmas 2001. (Includes account of the formation of the Solomon Islands Province of the Community of the Sisters of the Church, and the consecration of James Leftwich as National Aboriginal Bishop in Australia.)

Burt, Ben. *Tradition and Christianity. The Colonial Transformation of a Solomon Islands Society.* Harwood Academic Publishers: Chur (Switzerland), Camberwell (Victoria, Australia), Reading (Berkshire, England), etc. 1993. (Includes a study of missions on Malaita, Solomon Islands).

Cross, Gwen (Sister Gwen of the Cross). *Aloha Solomons.* Institute of Pacific Studies, University of the South Pacific, with the Solomon Islands Extension Centre, n.d.

Davidson, Allan K. *Mana and the Man: Robert Codrington, Missionary Scholar.* Unpublished paper.

Davidson, Allan K. *Useful Industry and Muscular Christianity: George Augustus Selwyn and His Early Years as Bishop of New Zealand*, in *The Use and Abuse of Time in Christian History*, Vol. 37 of *Studies in Church History* (edited by R.N.Swanson for the Ecclesiastical History Society). Woodbridge, Suffolk, England: The Boydell Press, 2002.

The East and the West, No.24, 1926 (includes article by A.I.Hopkins on *The Call from the South Seas*).

Fox, C.E. (ed). *The Melanesian Messenger.* Taroaniara, Solomon Islands. No longer published.

Gutch, Sir John. *Martyr of the Islands: The Life and Death of John Coleridge Patteson.* London: Hodder & Stoughton, 1971.

Hilliard, David. *The Making of an Anglican Martyr: Bishop John Coleridge Patteson*, in *Martyrs and Martyrologies*, Vol.30 of *Studies in Church History* (edited by Diana Wood for the Ecclesiastical History Society). Oxford: Blackwell, 1993

Laracy, Hugh (ed). *Pacific Protest: The Maasinga Rule Movement, Solomon Islands, 1944-1952.* Suva, Fiji: Institute of Pacific Studies, University of the South Pacific, 1983.

Melanesia Today: A Study Guide Book. London: SPCK, for Melanesian Mission, 1927.

Nobbs, Raymond. *George Hunn Nobbs, 1799-1884: Chaplain on Pitcairn and Norfolk Island.* Norfolk Island: The Pitcairn Descendants Society, 1984.

O'Connor, Daniel & others. *Three Centuries of Mission: The United Society for the Propagation of the Gospel, 1701-2000.* London & New York: Continuum. It includes a chapter by Sara Sohmer, *Anglican Tradition and Mission: Sources for Mission Methodology in the Nineteenth Century Pacific*, portions of which originally appeared in the Journal of Religious History, December 1994.

The Outrigger. Newsletter of the Pacific Islands Society of the UK and Ireland: No.42, Summer, 2001 includes short article on the investiture of the Archbishop of Melanesia with a knighthood.

The Response of Melanesia to the Holy Spirit. London: Melanesian Mission. No date (early 1930s).

Steward, Bishop John Manwaring. The Primary Charge delivered by the Right Reverend John Manwaring Steward, Bishop of the Diocese of Melanesia, in his Cathedral Church of St Barnabas, Norfolk Island, on Monday, 6th October, 1919. *Norfolk Island: Melanesian Mission Press, 1919.*

Veronica, Sister, of the Cross. *The School Island.* London: SPCK for the Melanesian Mission, 1949.

Wilson, Timothy (ed). *All One Body: Bishops of the Anglican Church Speak of Christian Faith and Action in Different Parts of the World Today.* London: Darton, Longman & Todd, 1969. (Includes article by John Chisholm, Bishop of Melanesia, entitled *Diocese of a Thousand Islands.*)

Yonge, Charlotte Mary. *Life of John Coleridge Patteson*, 2 Vols. London: Macmillan, 1874.

CHRISTIANITY IN THE PACIFIC

Arrowsmith, H.M. (ed). *The Cradle Church of Australia: The History of St John's, Parramatta (Part I to the year 1910).* Sydney: Pilgrim International Ltd., 1975.

Australasian Methodist Missionary Review (no longer published).

Breward, Ian. *A History of the Churches in Australasia.* Oxford History of the Christian Church. Oxford University Press, 2001.

Church Gazette. Diocese of Polynesia (no longer published).

Davidson, Allan K. *Selwyn's Legacy: The College of St John the Evangelist, Te Waimate and Auckland, 1843-1992. A History.* Auckland: The College of St John the Evangelist, 202 St John's Road, Auckland 1105, New Zealand, 1993.

Davidson, Allan K. *Semisi Nau: The Story of My Life. A Tongan Missionary at Ongtong Java.* Suva, Fiji: Institute of Pacific Studies, University of the South Pacific, 1996.

Dewey, Margaret. *The Messengers: A Concise History of the United Society for the Propagation of the Gospel.* London & Oxford: Mowbrays, 1975.

Ernst, Manfred. *Winds of Change: Rapidly Growing Religious Groups in the South Pacific.* Suva: Pacific Conference of Churches, 1994.

Forman, C.W. *The Island Churches of the South Pacific: Emergence in the Twentieth Century.* American Society of Missiology Series, No.5. Maryknoll: Orbis Books, 1982.

Frappell, R.M. *Anglican Ministry in the Unsettled Rural Districts of Australia, c.1890-1940.* PhD thesis, Sydney, 1991.

Frappell, R.M. *The Australian Bush Brotherhoods and their English Origins.* Article in *The Journal of Ecclesiastical History,* No. 47, pp.82-97. 1996.

Garrett, John. *To Live Among the Stars: Christian Origins in Oceania.* Suva & Geneva: WCC in association with the Institute of Pacific Studies, University of the South Pacific in association with WCC, 1982.

Garrett, John. *Footsteps in the Sea: Christianity in Oceania to World War II.* Suva & Geneva: Institute of Pacific Studies, University of the South Pacific in association with WCC, 1992

Goodall, Norman. *A History of the London Missionary Society, 1895-1945.* Oxford University Press, 1954.

Laracy, Hugh. *Marists and Melanesians: A History of Catholic Missions in the Solomon Islands.* Canberra: Australian National University Press, 1976.

Latourette, K.S. *A History of the Expansion of Christianity (1800-1914), Vol. V, The Great Century: The Americas, Australasia and Africa.* London: Eyre & Spotiswoode, 1943.

Macdonald-Milne, Brian. *The Experience of New Churches.* Preparatory paper for the Conference of European Churches in Goslar, West Germany, November 1982.

Macintosh, N.K. *The Reverend Richard Johnson.* Sydney: Seeley, 1975 (about the first Anglican Chaplain in Australia).

Moriarty, Rachel. *Vivian Redlich, 1905-1942.* In *Martyrs and Martyrologies*, Vol.30 of *Studies in Church History* (edited by Diana Wood for the Ecclesiastical History Society). Oxford: Blackwell, 1993

Morrell, W.P. *The Anglican Church in New Zealand: A History.* Dunedin: Anglican Church of the Province of New Zealand, 1973.

Russell, The Rt Revd M., LLD, DCL, of St John's College, Oxford. *Polynesia: or, An Historical Account of the Principal Islands of the South Sea, including New Zealand; the Introduction of Christianity; and the Actual Condition of the Inhabitants in regard to Civilisation, Commerce, and the Arts of Social Life.* Edinburgh: Oliver & Boyd. London: Simpken, Marshall & Co., 1842.

The English Carpentarian (subsequently known as *The Carpentarian* or *Carpentaria Link*). No longer published.

The International Review of Mission, No.17, 1928 (includes article by A.I.Hopkins and Johann Flierl on *Native Life in the S.W. Pacific from Two Points of View*).

Thompson, H.P. *Into All Lands: The History of the Society for the Propagation of the Gospel in Foreign Parts, 1701-1950. London: SPCK, 1951.*

Tomkins, Dorothea & Hughes, Brian. *The Road to Gona* Sydney: Angus & Robertson, 1969 (about the history of the Anglican Church in Papua New Guinea).

Ward, Kevin & Stanley, Brian (edd). *The Church Mission Society and World Christianity, 1799-1999: Studies in the History of Christian Missions* (including a chapter on the CMS and New Zealand by Allan K.Davidson). Grand Rapids, Michigan & Cambridge, UK: William B.Eerdmans; and Richmond, Surrey: The Curzon Press.

Whonsbon-Aston, C.W. *Levuka Days, or A Parson in Polynesia.* SPCK & SPG, 1936.

PACIFIC HISTORY AND CURRENT AFFAIRS

Carl, Andy & Garasu, Sr Lorraine, CSN (edd). *Accord: An International Review of Peace Resources*, Issue No.12, 2002. *Weaving Consensus: The Papua New Guinea Bougainville Peace Process.* London: Conciliation Resources in collaboration with Bougainville Inter-Church Women's Forum, 2002.

The Contemporary Pacific: A Journal of Island Affairs*, Vol.13, No.2, Fall 2001.* Article on *Melanesia in Review: Issues and Events, 2000.* Center for Pacific Islands Studies & University of Hawaii Press.

Derrick, R.A. *A History of Fiji.* Suva, Fiji: Government Press, 1963 (Vol.1 up to 1874).

Harcombe, David. *Solomon Islands: A Travel Survival Kit.* Victoria, Australia & Berkeley, California: Lonely Planet Publications, 1988 (1st edition). Guide to Solomon Islands.

Harcombe, David. *Vanuatu, A Travel Survival Kit.* Hawthorn, Victoria, Australia: Lonely Planet Publications, , 1991 (1st edition). Guide to Vanuatu.

Horton, D.C. *New Georgia: Pattern for Victory.* London: Pan/Ballantine Illustrated History of World War II, 1972.

Kuva, Aduru. *The Solomons Community in Fiji.* South Pacific Social Sciences Association. No date (1970s).

The Outrigger. Newsletter of the Pacific Islands Society of the UK and Ireland: No.41, Winter 2000/2001. (Includes article on the follow-up to the peace agreement between warring factions in Solomon Islands.)

Welchman, David and Watson-Gegeyo, Karen Ann. *Whose Knowledge? Epistemological Collision in Solomon Islands Community Development*, in *The Contemporary Pacific: A Journal of Island Affairs*, Vol.14, No.2, Fall 2002 (A study by a Malaita man and his wife, both academics, of development issues related to recent troubles in Solomon Islands.)

Wheeler, Tony. *Papua New Guinea: A Travel Survival Kit.* Victoria, Australia: Lonely Planet Publications, 1979 (various revised editions followed). Guide to Papua New Guinea.

PACIFIC ANTHROPOLOGY

Clifford, James. *Person and Myth: Maurice Leenhardt in the Melanesian World.* Berkeley: University of California Press, 1982.

Codrington, R.H. *The Melanesians: Studies in their Anthropology and FolkLore.* Oxford: Clarendon Press, 1891.

Cowan, J. *Elements of Aboriginal Tradition.* Glasgow: Harper Collins, 1997.

Firth, Raymond. *We, The Tikopia.* London: George Allen & Unwin, 1936.

Firth, Raymond. *History and Traditions of Tikopia.* Wellington, New Zealand: The Polynesian Society (Incorporated), 1961

Fox, Charles E. *The Threshold of the Pacific: An Account of the Social Organisation, Magic and Religion of the People of San Cristoval in the Solomon Islands.* London: Kegan Paul, Trench, Trubner & Co.Ltd, 1924.

Hogbin, H.Ian. Article on Ongtong Java in *The Australian Geographer*, Vol.1, No.2, 1929. Summary of lecture by the author, Science Research Fellow in Anthropology in the University of Sydney.

Keesing, Roger M. *Kwaio Religion.* Cultural Association of the Solomon Islands, 1977.

Swain, T. *Religions of Oceania.* England: Routledge, 1994.

Trompf, G. *Melanesian Religion.* Cambridge University Press, 1991.

MISSIOLOGY AND CHRISTIAN MISSIONS

Boff, Leonardo. *Ecclesiogenesis: The Base Communities Reinvent the Church.* Maryknoll: Orbis Books, 1986.

Boff, Leonardo. *New Evangelisation: Good News for the Poor.* Maryknoll: Orbis Books, 1991.

Bosch, David. *Transforming Mission: Paradigm Shifts in the Theology of Mission.* Maryknoll: Orbis Books, 1991.

Castro, Emilio (ed). *Melbourne Reports and Reflections*, in *International Review of Mission*, Vol. LXIX, Nos. 276-277, October 1980 – January 1981.

Donovan, Vincent J. *Christianity Rediscovered.* Maryknoll: Orbis Books, 1978.

Geffre, Claude. *Theological Reflections on a New Age of Mission*, in *International Review of Mission*, Vol. LXXI, No. 284, October 1982.

Gutierrez, Gustavo. *We Drink from our own Wells: The Spiritual Journey of a People.* Maryknoll: Orbis Books, 1984.

Gutierrez, Gustavo. *The Truth Shall Make You Free: Confrontations.* Maryknoll: Orbis Books, 1990.

Kirk, J.Andrew. *What is Mission?* London: Darton, Longman & Todd, 1999.

Macdonald-Milne, Brian. *The Eucharist as Witness to the Kingdom of God and Experience of God's reign.* In *International Review of Mission (Vol LXIX, No 274 April 1980) A quarterly journal published by the Commission on Mission and Evangelism of the World Council of Churches, Geneva, Switzerland.*

Moltmann, Jurgen. *The Way of Jesus Christ: Christology in Messianic Dimensions.* London: SCM Press, 1990.

Nacpil, Ermerito. *Mission but Not Missionaries*, in *International Review of Mission* Vol. LX, No. 239, July 1971.
Rowland, Christopher (ed). *The Cambridge Companion to Liberation Theology.* Cambridge: Cambridge University Press, 1999.
Saayman, W. & Kritzinger, K. (ed). *Mission in Bold Humility.* Maryknoll: Orbis Books, 1996.
Weber, Hans-Rüdi. *Experiments with Bible Study.* Geneva: WCC, 1983.

The Author of the History

Brian James Macdonald-Milne was born in 1935 in Surrey, England, of Scottish and English parentage, and was educated at Whitgift School, Croydon, Surrey, Corpus Christi College, Cambridge, and Cuddesdon Theological College, Oxford. He is a Master of Arts in Theology from Cambridge University and also a member of St Peter's College, Oxford. Ordained in the Anglican Diocese of Blackburn in 1960 as deacon and 1961 as priest, he served in the parish of Fleetwood, Lancashire, in charge of St David's Church, which now has its own parish. He sailed via Australia, Norfolk Island and the New Hebrides to the Solomon Islands in 1964 and served with the Anglican Church there for 14 years in various posts. He was then seconded to the staff of the Pacific Conference of Churches, and established the Pacific Churches Research Centre in the New Hebrides – now the Republic of Vanuatu – in 1978. (The Centre later closed.) On his return to England in 1980, he worked in Oxford University and in prisons in Oxfordshire before becoming Research Fellow for a year at Queen's College, the ecumenical theological college in Birmingham. Until his retirement in 1997 from fulltime parochial work, he served parishes in Cambridgeshire and North Essex, becoming also Rural Dean of Saffron Walden. He received Independence Medals from both the Solomon Islands and the Republic of Vanuatu. He is Coordinator for the Companions of the Melanesian Brotherhood in Europe, and a Brother of the Third Order of the Society of St Francis. He was Founding Secretary and later Chairman of the Pacific Islands Society of the UK and Ireland, and is currently Vice-Chairman. He is a member of the committee of the Melanesian Mission UK and belongs to the Papua New Guinea Church Partnership and the British Friends of Vanuatu. He edited *Reo Pasifika*, the journal of the Pacific Churches Research Centre, and co-edited *Yumi Stanap, Some People of Vanuatu: Leaders and Leadership in a New Nation* (Institute of Pacific Studies, University of the South Pacific and Lotu Pasifika Productions, 1981). He has also published booklets and articles for and about the Melanesian Brotherhood, of which he was Chaplain and Tutor from 1968 to 1973, and others for the Companions of the Brotherhood.

The Author of the Reflections

Richard Carter was born in England in 1959, the son of an Anglican priest, now deceased. His parents became members of the Third Order of the Society of St Francis. He read English and Drama at the Aberystwyth Campus of the University of Wales, and studied for a postgraduate certificate in Education at London University. He later became a Bachelor of Divinity of Melbourne College of Divinity. He worked for VSO (Voluntary Service Overseas) in teacher training in Yogyakarta, Java, Indonesia for four years, and then for the British Council. He did school teaching in Solomon Islands before studying and teaching at the Bishop Patteson Theological College, Guadalcanal, Solomon Islands. He was invited by the Melanesian Brotherhood to become its Chaplain in 1994 and was then ordained at the Mother House at Tabalia, Guadalcanal. In 2000 he was professed as a Brother and in 2002 completed an MA degree at Leeds University in England with a dissertation on 'Sensing Salvation: the Drama of Death and Resurrection within Liturgy.' He then became Coordinator of Mission and Training for the Brotherhood. He is one of only two white Brothers, and the only one from England. His mother and one of his brothers are Companions of the Melanesian Brotherhood. He became Chaplain to the Brotherhood again in 2003. He has contributed articles on the Religious Life, especially the Melanesian Brotherhood, to various publications, and has edited the most recent edition of the Office Book of the Brotherhood. He has also written training materials, and has written and directed dramas for the Brotherhood.

INDEX

Note: 'PNG' after an entry indicates a place in Papua New Guinea, the official name after Independence.
References to the 'New Hebrides' are usually to that country before Independence, when it became the Republic of Vanuatu.
'SI' indicates a place in Solomon Islands.
(n) indicates a reference or references in the Notes at the end of a chapter in the book.
Brothers or former Brothers of the Melanesian Brotherhood are usually shown with the title 'Bro' (Brother). Members of other communities may have letters after their names to indicate which Community or Order they belong to: SSF - Society of St Francis (First Order Brothers), CSM - Community of the Sisters of Melanesia, CC - Community of the Sisters of the Cross, CSC - Community of the Sisters of the Church, SSM - Society of the Sacred Mission.